MEXICO'S LEADERS

Their Education & Recruitment

MEXICO'S LEADERS

Their Education & Recruitment

Roderic A. Camp

The University of Arizona Press

Tucson, Arizona

About the author

Roderic A. Camp became Director of Latin American Studies at Central College, Pella, Iowa, in 1976. He holds a Ph.D. in Comparative Government from the University of Arizona and has carried out research on Mexico under fellowships from the American Philosophical Society, National Endowment for the Humanities, and Fulbright-Hays. He has written more than 20 articles on Mexico, published in American and Mexican journals, and continues his research interests in the area. He is author of *Mexican Political Biographies, 1935–1975, The Role of Economists in Policy Making: Mexico and the United States,* and of a revised version, in Spanish, of *Mexican Political Biographies.*

THE UNIVERSITY OF ARIZONA PRESS

Library of Congress Cataloging in Publication Data

Camp, Roderic A.
    Mexico's leaders.

    Bibliography: p.
    Includes index.
    1. Mexico—Officials and employees—Recruiting.
2. Mexico—Officials and employees. 3. Politicians—
Education—Mexico. I. Title.
JL1247.C35   301.44′92′0972   79-19836
ISBN 0-8165-0701-5
ISBN 0-8165-0660-4 pbk.

To the Memory of
John F. Morse
Whose generosity
made much of this
possible

Contents

Tables

[ix]

Acknowledgments

A book of this sort, based on extensive interviews and correspondence with so many men and women who are the subjects of this study, owes a great deal to many people. During the process of correspondence, initiated some years ago, I was helped in clarifying my questions in Spanish by Martha Chiarella and Martha Musi. Evelyn Loynachan and Reva Rydstrand have taken great pains in typing presentable letters to my Mexican correspondents.

While all of the Mexicans who have helped in researching this book are listed in Appendix B, several have gone beyond the limits of normal courtesy to bring me in contact with others and to make personal libraries and sources of information available. In particular, I owe a special thanks to Antonio Carrillo Flores, Victor Manuel Villaseñor, Hugo B. Margáin, Raúl Rángel Frias, Pedro Daniel Martínez, Sealtiel Alatriste, Manuel Hinojosa Ortiz, Eduardo Bustamante, Ernesto Enríquez Coyro, the late Julián Garza Tijerina, César Sepulveda, the late Manuel Ulloa Ortiz, and Alfonso Pulido Islas. Furthermore, I would like to thank the Central College Research Council and the American Philosophical Society for successive grants which made the correspondence and interviews with these and other distinguished Mexicans possible.

My research trips to Mexico were aided by the hospitality and help of old friends, who, in their own way, have contributed to the completion of this project. In this regard, I must thank Martha Musi, Leslie Adams Gogarty, and Terry Gogarty, whose interest and enthusiasm would be a stimulus to any researcher.

During the manuscript stages of the study, I received intellectual encouragement and constructive criticism from James W. Wilkie, Martin Needler, Peter H. Smith, John P. Harrison, William B. Julian, and Donald Racheter on individual chapters of this book. Peter Smith also shared biographical information used in this study. Howard Handelman and John Harrigan made useful suggestions concerning the third chapter. The University of Arizona Press is to be thanked for effecting publication. Lastly, Donald Mabry acted as a helpful critic throughout the entire writing process, both in a practical and intellectual sense. My wife Emily served this work in two capacities, as a reviewer and editor, and as my inter-library loan librarian, an essential ingredient at an under-graduate institution.

R.A.C.

Abbreviations

CEN	National Executive Committee
CFE	Federal Electric Commission
CNC	National Farmers' Confederation
CNOP	National Federation of Popular Organizations
CONASUPO	National Company of Public Commodities
CTM	Mexican Federation of Laborers
DDF	Department of the Federal District
ENP	National Preparatory School
FSTSE	Federation of Government Employees' Union
IEPES	Institute for Political, Economic and Social Studies
IMSS	Mexican Institute of Social Security
INFONAUIT	National Institute of Housing for Workers
IPN	National Polytechnic Institute
ISSSTE	Institute of Security and Social Service for Federal Employees
MPBP	Mexican Political Biography Project
PAN	National Action Party
PARM	Authentic Party of the Mexican Revolution
PEMEX	Petróleos Mexicanos
PNR	National Revolutionary Party (1929–1938)
PP	Popular Party (antecedent to PPS)
PPS	Popular Socialist Party
PRM	Party of the Mexican Revolution (1938–1946)
PRI	Institutional Revolutionary Party

PRUN	Revolutionary Party of National Unification (General Almazán's organization in the presidential campaign of 1940)
SNTE	National Union of Educational Workers
SUTDDF	Union of the Workers of the Federal District
SUTERM	United Electrical Workers' Union of Mexico
UNAM	National Autonomous University or National University of Mexico

1. Introduction: Recruitment and the Political System

Among scholars, there is considerable interest in the recruitment process in all political systems. Although many social scientists touch on this subject in broader works on political leadership, few define and describe the general characteristics of the process. This is unfortunate because while there is a general understanding of what political recruitment means, few scholars have attempted to set forth a framework from which we can analyze the implications of recruitment.

However, several scholars, most notably Robert D. Putnam, Lester Seligman, Kenneth Prewett, and David Schwartz, have suggested a definition of political recruitment and offered a descriptive framework of the issues most critical to that process.[1] Using their frameworks, I will attempt to describe the structural factors, and in chapter ii the cultural factors, that influence the process of political recruitment in Mexico, especially the relationship of that process to a single significant variable, education. The purpose of this work is to document and analyze the relationship between education and political recruitment during the critical years of Mexico's development from 1911 to the early 1950s, and to demonstrate its importance in understanding Mexican politics.

Data Sources for the Study

The data in this study come from four primary sources: a biographical data bank of men and women who have held public office in Mexico at a certain level from 1935 to 1976; an educational data bank of high-level political and

[1]

university leaders from 1935 to 1976 who graduated from the National University between 1911 and 1955; personal interviews and/or correspondence with more than one hundred living persons who have held such positions; unpublished and published literature describing and analyzing education and the political system in Mexico. The first two sources deserve some explanation because they are an integral part of the evidence for the conclusions in this study, and they have not previously been made available to the reader. The biographical data bank of political leaders that I have constructed, many of whom are described in my *Mexican Political Biographies, 1935–1975*, is a nearly complete population, rather than a sample, of all persons holding high-level offices between 1935 and 1976—a population 76 percent complete, including more than 900 political leaders. This data set will be referred to as the "Mexican Political Biography Project" (hereafter cited as MPBP; see Appendix A). No person who has been mentioned in the hundreds of secondary and primary sources as having been influential in Mexican decision making has been omitted. If a bias exists in this population, it is toward the highest office holders within this elite. All tables dealing with university graduating classes in the later chapters are based on a complete population of students from my "Educational Data Bank" (EDB) who became high-level officeholders after 1935. These data are from unpublished alumni records, official records of the National University, and information from former students and professors.

How Individuals Were Selected

There are several ways to obtain a sample or general population of a country's political elite. One of the more common approaches is known as the positional approach, which assumes that individuals holding formal political offices wield political power in that country. The weakness of this approach is that it might exclude more powerful individuals who have held no formal positions.[2] However, my selection of political leaders is also based on names obtained from dozens of standard works on Mexico or solicited from other political leaders I interviewed. Although some persons may have inadvertently been included who have not had much influence, I believe that no one known to have political influence was omitted. All individuals mentioned in standard works on Mexico as belonging to the Revolutionary Family or having had some definite political influence on the president have held one or more of the positions making up our population of elites. If I have excluded any individuals, they would most likely be leaders of the business sector and of the clergy. Since this study is concerned only with *political* leadership, their exclusion seems justified. Most military leaders with political influence have held one or more of the positions selected, so they are included in our population. Because these are the positions which, in the opinion of other scholars, have the most control over political decision making in Mexico, individuals holding these positions can be described as a political elite. Since completing the original data set of 999 political and academic leaders, I have completed biographical data cards on an additional 83 individuals. Although this data has not been used in most of the statistical tables, an examination of these individuals reveals the same patterns for all of the variables discussed in this volume.

The only other comprehensive data bank on Mexican political leaders is that compiled by Peter Smith. My data bank differs from that of Professor Smith's in several ways. First, it does not include political leaders who held office prior to 1935 (his covers 1900 to 1971). Further, although much of my original biographical data was incorporated into Smith's data set in 1974, my data base has been expanded qualitatively and now contains more detailed data on most individual biographees, particularly relating to education. Further, an individual biography was not included in the data set unless I had nearly complete information on the 59 variables I examined for each political leader. My goal in setting this standard was to increase the accuracy and completeness of my data. In doing all of the biographical research and coding myself, and updating this information on a continuous basis since 1972, I have developed something of a personal, mental data bank in the sense that I "personally" know each of the biographees in the data set. This has allowed me to use additional information I have about individuals that has not been coded for broad, statistical interpretations. I believe this knowledge has permitted me to make some qualitative assessments and interpretations of the statistical patterns that normally would not show up in such data. Lastly, as a result of intensive interviews and documentary research over a period of years, I have been able to provide considerable information concerning kinship ties, socioeconomic background, and personal political alliances, all previously undocumented and extremely important elements in understanding Mexican political careers.

Of the total population of political and educational leaders meeting the criteria in Appendix A, approximately 600 were known to be alive at the beginning of 1971, when correspondence began. Of these, I was able to find accurate, current addresses for approximately 300. Each person first received a letter asking for biographical information. On this first step there was a fifty percent response rate: 156 persons sent vitas or letters with such data. To this smaller group, a second letter was sent in 1972, asking concrete questions about educational experience and its relationship to political activity. During the years 1972 to 1975, 83 persons answered these letters, or follow-up letters. Some individuals provided me with as many as three different responses. These letters range in length from several paragraphs to eighteen pages of single-spaced, legal-size letter head. The average letter is approximately a two-page, single-spaced response. Using these correspondents as a basis, I conducted more than 75 interviews in Mexico City, Monterrey, and Washington, D.C. from 1974 to 1976. Of these 75, twenty had not originally been willing to correspond with me.

Of the 300 persons in the original target group, I have been able to correspond with and/or interview more than 100, or approximately 35 percent. Obviously, there are certain biases among a group of political leaders who respond to letters. However, there is a difference between those who respond to written materials and to interviews. The most reclusive are those persons who will only respond favorably to interviews. In my experience, only one person, a former governor of Yucatán, refused to be interviewed in Mexico.[3] It would seem, therefore, that there is little bias in my sample on the basis of those willing to be interviewed versus those unwilling to be interviewed. I do, however, have a larger proportion of those willing to give a written or oral answer versus those only willing to give an oral answer. A comparison of both interview sources revealed no differences in the sincerity of their answers or in the information they provided. If there is a bias in my sample of correspondents or interviewees, it is in their age. Because I had access to only living persons, fewer men were living who could respond to questions concerning the graduates from 1911 to 1920. Furthermore, because most of the graduates from the last 15 years of our study (1940–1955) were in the current administration, they were the most difficult to approach and gave the shortest interviews. (Interviews ranged from 45 minutes to three and a half hours in length, with the average interview lasting one and a half hours.) Therefore, I received more first-hand information from graduates of the 1920s, 1930s, and early 1940s, those men and women who dominated political life from 1940 until 1970. It should be remembered that throughout this work extensive written sources have been used to document experiences described in letters and interviews.

Recruitment in Mexico

Political recruitment has been defined in numerous ways. Putnam has defined it as referring to "the processes that select from among the several million socially favored and politically motivated citizens comprising the political stratum those several thousand who reach positions of significant national influence."[4] The processes most important to political recruitment appear to include the following:

1. Channels or routes to the top most commonly used by aspiring political leaders.
2. Sponsors or selectors of those who reach top political positions, and the means or certification they use to screen prospective leaders.
3. Credentials or qualifications of the aspirants.

The channels that future political leaders take to arrive at the top are not only of interest to the social scientist, but to the prospective political leader, who has limited alternatives in Mexico because of the structure of the political system. Recent evaluations of Mexico's political structure describe it as an authoritarian system, although having its own peculiarities.[5] Because it is an authoritarian system, it is assumed that political recruitment, socialization, decision making, and participation will not follow the same patterns as equivalent processes in a democratic political system.[6] Furthermore, although there is disagreement among scholars as to the role of the President in decision making and the importance of the official party or the Institutional Revolutionary Party (PRI) in the system, it is well established that to reach the top in the government bureaucracy or through electoral positions, one must have the sympathy of other political leaders, and at the very least, one must not be unsympathetic to the political philosophy of the President under which he serves. Structurally, Mexico operates under the environment of a modified one-party system, in which members of the only true opposition party (the National Action Party, PAN) never reach the highest positions of political power. This does not mean, however, that the only open channel to power in Mexico lies through the PRI. As I will argue in chapter iii, the official party provides only one of the channels through which political leaders reach top positions and, most importantly, despite its dominance over the political party system since 1929, it is *not* the most important channel for attaining administrative positions at the highest levels.

In analyzing paths of political recruitment, scholars normally look to political parties, bureaucracies, and local governments. It is my hypothesis that in Mexico, a social institution, the National University of Mexico (UNAM), has served as the most important institutional locus of political elite recruitment, clearly in numbers disproportionate to other educational institutions in Mexico. I further argue that the best chance of getting into Mexican politics and remaining at the top, especially since the 1950s, was to obtain a university education at the National University. In addition to the party, the bureaucracy and local government, labor unions and the army have played a crucial institutional role in the recruitment process, often providing a path for political leaders with different social and economic backgrounds and skill preparations. The unions most important in this process have been quasi-governmental unions that are part of the membership of the official party.[7] The importance of the army stemmed from the role of military leaders during and after the Revolution, particularly through the early 1940s. As will be demonstrated in both chapters ii and iii, this is a channel that has gradually closed.[8]

The institutional locus of political recruitment is not the only important factor. The openness or permeability of those institutions to future political leaders is equally important. In chapters iii and iv other biographical and career variables will be examined to indicate the permeability of the educational institutions, as well as other recruitment channels. This is what Lester Seligman describes as the certification process, whereby future political leaders are screened in some manner before becoming eligible for leadership positions.[9] According to most scholars, the nature and structure of the political system itself has an impact on who becomes eligible. For example, Mostafa Rejai hypothesized that the more advanced a political system, the more universalistic the recruitment base.[10] If Mexico's political system has advanced to some degree since the 1930s, it has not resulted in a significant expansion of those eligible to be recruited. I will argue, however, that despite an increase in permeability due to social changes resulting from the Mexican Revolution, there was only a brief respite in a pattern that has for social and economic reasons become increasingly closed to the average Mexican. I hypothesize that Mexican leadership, even with the recent influx of women and youth, has become more and more homogeneous, and the lack of permeability in the channels of recruitment are important causes.[11] Not only are the individuals themselves more homogeneous, but their recruitment experience, or the channel they follow, is taking on similarities to that of top British administrators during the earlier part of this century.[12]

It is also hypothesized that the university, as a social-political institution, has gradually formed an alliance with the bureaucracy to channel new political leaders into the Mexican political system, thus replacing other institutions of importance, particularly the labor unions and the military, and further restricting permeability. Putnam has concluded that, in many countries *educational institutions* play key roles in sifting and channeling aspirants, and that the educational and political recruitment systems are virtually merged.[13] We shall see this applied in detail to Mexico in further chapters.

Selection Characteristics

But recruitment channels are only one aspect of the broader subject of political recruitment, and while they contribute to a person's chances in the political system, they do not determine ultimate success. That falls to those who select the chosen few. Over the years, Mexico has evolved some selection characteristics, if not a selection system, which has become fairly consistent and has been influenced by some of the structural qualities described above and by some of the cultural traits identified in the following chapter.

How people are selected, and who does the selecting, is probably the subject least known and most debated among social scientists who have studied Mexico.[14] As I have argued in a recent article,[15] there is no single person or group of persons responsible for selection in every case, nor is the relationship between the person selected and the person doing the choosing always the same. Although some individuals are recruited directly into a position of political influence, without a political career, most follow one of a number of career patterns described in chapter iii. The institution of the Mexican presidency has evolved to dominate the political system, but the President does not personally select all of the important decision-makers. As illustrated in the selection of governors during the Luis Echeverría administration, there are many demands made on the President that contribute to the complexity of the selection process. Those elements coming to play in the selection of governors are: career experience, political friendships, and qualifications peculiarly suited to the political-economic situation of the state in question.[16] Even though some Mexicans have likened the Mexican system to that of an absolutist monarchy, the President delegates the selection power to many individual collaborators.[17]

If we accept the evidence that a variety of individuals serve as sponsors in the recruitment process in Mexico, we need to know who those individuals are and how they go about choosing one person over another. In a recent study of a single government agency, Merilee Grindle identified three patterns that were significant: recruitment through direct ties to individuals in the agency; recruitment mediated by another individual in the agency; and externally mediated recruitment.[18] For Mexican governmental agencies in general, it is hypothesized that university professors who are successful political leaders have been most important in the *initial* recruitment of individuals into public careers and in their ultimate success in high-level offices. This recruitment takes place in the prominent preparatory schools and the professional schools of several universities, most notably the National University. To a lesser extent, students who become active in political affairs are themselves recruiters if they achieve early success in politics. In some cases, their own political success is delayed for several decades, but once they reach a high-level position from which they do have the power to choose and recruit collaborators, they often reach back to contacts made during their student years, reinforcing the importance of the university as the central recruiter in Mexico. Even though it is not the scope of this book to discuss the political recruitment of persons prior to 1935, it is believed that both students and professors have played significant roles in the recruitment process well back into the late 19th century, again indicating the importance of adhering to tradition in Mexico's political culture. If this is so, then, despite certain structural and cultural changes since the Revolution, traditional structures, such as the National Preparatory School and the National Law School, continue to play significant political roles.[18]

The structure of the recruitment system in Mexico is one best described as closed rather than open. Ralph Turner has suggested the subtleties of a closed system in identifying differences between American and British elite recruitment. He sees the American system as characterized by an open contest in which the aspirant wins largely, though not exclusively, through achievement. On the other hand, he describes the British pattern, which has certain parallels with the Mexican recruitment system, as one consisting of "sponsored mobility," in which political recruits are chosen by the established elites or their representatives.[20] Although most political scientists analyzing the United States consider political recruitment through sponsorship to be the most common method of selection, they generally define sponsorship to mean that a politician is the candidate or representative of special interest groups or organizations.[21] In Mexico, however, top administrative officials are rarely the candidate of any interest group or organization; rather they are the candidate of a personal clique, led by an up-and-coming leader, a currently entrenched official, or a formerly influential political leader who wants to continue his influence or make a comeback.

THE SELECTORS

Why should we identify the people who do the selecting? First, as Schwartz has noted, prospective political leaders respond to the selectors because they control their ability to achieve an office and remain in it.[22] They may even make their behavior conform to their perceptions of what they believe the selectors want. But perhaps more important, although there is little hard evidence to support it, is that recruiters probably favor persons with attitudes, backgrounds, and character similar to their own. Whether or not the selectors do choose individuals who have similar ideas, there is little doubt that those persons who sponsor political careers control entry to such a career, particularly in a closed system where public popularity has little effect. Second, and perhaps most importantly, as Kenneth Prewitt suggests, those who do the selecting generally determine the criteria by which future leaders are chosen.[23] It will be shown that the most influential professors, in the eyes of political leaders, have themselves participated in public life. There will be an attempt to determine the homogeneity of the recruiters and those they recruit. Furthermore, I believe that the interchange between professors and students at the National Preparatory School and selected schools at the National University has contributed to the creation of a self-perpetuating elite of men and women who distinguish themselves in teaching and public careers. As professors/public men continue to increase their role as selectors in the recruitment process, we will see a change in the type of person in positions of political power in Mexico.

CREDENTIALS AND SKILLS

A third factor, identified by Putnam, and depending heavily on where recruitment takes place and who is responsible, is the credentials of the successful aspirants. As will be demonstrated in chapter iv, Mexico's political leadership, not surprisingly, is an elite by virtue of its level of education. Even as early as 1935, university education characterized political leadership, and has grown steadily to 1976. As Peter Smith argues, "university training is an almost absolute requirement for admission to the national elite, particularly the upper-level elite ..."[24] In addition to a general education, certain professional expertise is growing in importance as it has in many countries emerging from a post-revolutionary period. In the case of Mexicans, technical experts have become an ever expanding, self-perpetuating group within the political leadership. They too have become what Putnam calls "charter groups," replacing the older military men who received recognition because of their participation in the violent phases of the revolutionary period. Faculties or even small groups from regional universities form groups, or what will be called *camarillas,* and become prominent in certain administrations or even in individual ministries. For example, the Engineering School at the National University has developed a bailiwick in the Secretariat of Public Works and in Pemex, the government controlled petroleum agency. On the other hand, students from the National Medical School with political aspirations have largely confined their careers to the Secretariat of Public Health.

In the Echeverría administration, economists, while not predominant, took on the aura of technicians who could solve Mexico's complex economic-political problems. This trend, however, may be stemmed by the multiple failures of the *técnicos* to effectively resolve serious problems, and their responsibility for creating severe criticism of the regime during the last year. Decision-makers who lack the skills necessary to create public acceptance of their policies put severe restraints on the next regime and limit policy decisions.

In addition to intellectual skills, Mexico, like most other countries, requires certain inter-personal skills, those of persuasion and organization. However, there are two types of skills in this category: the ability to mobilize the masses, and the ability to maneuver effectively in small groups of colleagues. It is difficult to determine which skill is more important for political success in Mexico. It seems that Mexico is beginning to stress the latter skill more and more, even for the most influential position, that of president. While it may be that small group skills are more helpful in achieving political success in Mexico than mass mobilization skills, political stability and incremental change in Mexico may very well require mobilization skills. Many public figures have intimated to the author that this has been the cause of a number of failures in the most recent administration.[25] Such skills, then, may be of crucial significance to Mexico's future, and to her ability to solve her problems with or without the use of force.

Another type of credential particularly important in an authoritarian regime is loyalty or political reliability. Elite ideology in Mexico encompasses a wide range of political and economic beliefs, and therefore, ideology is not as homogeneous as one might expect it to be in an authoritarian regime. But ideological beliefs must come second to personal loyalty, especially loyalty to a superior and to the president under whom one serves. It has been assumed by most authors that loyalty in the Mexican case requires membership or affiliation with the official party. This is not the case. One only has to be sympathetic to the goals of political leaders; and PRI membership is only required of those individuals desiring to run for nominally elective offices. A number of high-level appointive office holders in the executive and judicial branches have never been members of any party, and some have been members of the opposition National Action Party.

Another category of credentials comes under the rubric of affiliations. For political recruitment in Mexico, the most important are family ties and *camarilla* affiliations, both of which predominate in social relationships at all levels. These will be demonstrated in considerable detail in the following chapter. Factional ties within the official party and government bureaucracy are also significant because of the heterogeneous ideological orientations of political leaders within the political hierarchy. Some top office-holders in each administration are selected because of their attachment to or identification with a political, economic, or personal clique. In Mexico, however, personal group representation is much more important than organizational representation, which is confined, for the most part, to lesser elective positions, although an occasional governor is strongly identified with labor and farmer unions. To a much lesser degree, geographic origin might be important in the selection process. Some scholars have speculated that Ángel Carvajal, the Secretary of Government in the 1952 to 1958 administration, was rejected as the final pre-candidate for President in favor of Adolfo López Mateos because he would have been the third consecutive president from Veracruz.[26] Carvajal himself believes his geographic origin was the most important reason for his losing the nomination.[27]

An issue that Putnam raises in his own descriptive framework is that of turnover and succession. I am not specifically concerned with this phenomenon, although I analyze its importance in the following chapter. This variable is dealt with in greater detail, and over longer periods of time, by Peter Smith.[28] I am, however, concerned with this element as it relates to the role of the university in the process of political recruitment. Some scholars have suggested that the higher the degree of elite turnover, the greater a system's policy innovativeness and flexibility. Mexico has had a substantial rate of elite turnover, especially since the Revolution, as is demonstrated in the following chapter, and as Peter Smith has shown for administrations since 1920.[29] It will argue, however, that because of the nature of the recruitment process, at least for those political leaders who have university educations, the recruiters and the recruits form a fairly homogeneous group, thus making significant policy differences from one administration to the next less likely.[30]

Elsewhere, I have suggested that certain agencies within the federal government have benefitted from a continuity in leadership extending beyond the limits of a six-year administration, giving them certain advantages over agencies having higher turnover rates.[31] In other agencies generally predominant on the Mexican scene, a number of retired public officials have argued that the lack of continuity in planning and policy implementation has plagued Mexican organization and development, and accounts in great part for its failure to deal with critical problems.[32] Lastly, because the Mexican system does not legally permit the reelection of a Mexican President, a tradition that has been adhered to since 1929, it has been suggested that the constant turnover rates have allowed greater access for youthful aspirants to positions of political power. While it is true that Mexican officials in top positions have become younger, particularly in the Echeverría administration, many insiders believe that youth has been seriously tainted by the failures of the Echeverría regime. Age, therefore, as a credential, may not be very important in the next administration, partly because university youth is less volatile today in Mexico than in the 1960s, and because the recruiters may revise the selection credentials to emphasize more experienced recruits.

We have identified a number of reasons why each element in the recruitment process is important in understanding the Mexican political system and its direction. There are several general conclusions that further explain the importance of this volume's focus. Because the recruitment process obviously determines who gets to the top by screening out those lacking certain credentials and promoting others, an understanding of this process contributes to our knowledge of what Mexico's governing political elite is like and why they act in certain ways. Furthermore, if prospective political leaders understand the recruitment process, and the role of the university and professors in that process, they will then follow career patterns designed to enhance their opportunities in the political system. The career patterns of the majority of Mexican political leaders are integrally related to their educational patterns.[33]

The majority of political leaders since 1935 have passed through university classes, and of those, the largest group has been educated at a single university. The impact of this experience on their behavior deserves serious examination, since, as in the British case, there is some evidence that beliefs of the political elite are influenced by their educational experience.[34] When questioned about the sources of their political, social, and economic beliefs, Mexican political leaders told the author that professors were the single most important source of these views. These were the same teachers who recruited them into public life.[35] Since 80 percent or more of Mexico's political leadership since 1935 has university or professional degrees, the focus of this study is on the recruitment of that group. The other 20 percent of the population who have held high-level offices in Mexico are dealt with only in chapters ii, iii, and iv, and not in those chapters that describe and analyze the preparatory schools and the university as a center for political recruitment. The size of this group of Mexican political leaders has been decreasing, and will have to be the focus of another study. For the majority, however, I attempt to provide a description of the environment in which most political leaders were educated during the ages of 13 to 22.

By combining oral interview sources with statistical data on the careers of Mexico's influential political leaders and educators, certain patterns or processes inherent in Mexico's political system emerge. For example, although it can be quantitatively demonstrated that there is a sizeable degree of turnover in leadership from one administration to another in Mexico, which might lead scholars to make certain assumptions on the basis of that turnover, those same assumptions might be significantly tempered or changed if it were argued that these office-holders, whether new or old, had been educated in the same institution, under the tutelage of the same professors who themselves were part of the political leadership. Thus, in using qualitative and quantitative sources, I hope to prove several original hypotheses about political leaders in Mexico—hypotheses that are essential for understanding the nature and the function of the Mexican political system. These hypotheses are that the university is the essential institutional locus for recruiting educated political leaders in Mexico, that professors and students who become political leaders use their contact with other students to recruit them into political life, and that an understanding of these two hypotheses explains, to a great degree, the unity of Mexico's political leadership and the resulting political stability unique to that country.

NOTES TO CHAPTER 1

[1]Robert D. Putnam, *The Comparative Study of Political Elites* (Englewood Cliffs: Prentice-Hall, 1976), pp. 46–70; Lester G. Seligman, *Recruiting Political Elites* (New York: General Learning Press, 1971), and David C. Schwartz, "Toward a Theory of Political Recruitment," *The Western Political Quarterly* 22 (September 1969): 552–71.

[2]For further rationale in support of the positional approach and the specific positions selected, see my *Mexican Political Biographies, 1935–1975* (Tucson: University of Arizona Press, 1976); Peter H. Smith, "Continuity and Turnover Within the Mexican Political Elite, 1900–1971," in James W. Wilkie, et al., eds, *Contemporary Mexico* (Berkeley: University of California Press, 1976), pp. 182–3; and Wilfried Gruber, "Career Patterns of Mexico's Political Elite," *Western Political Quarterly* 24 (September 1971): 467.

[3]For a discussion of some of the problems of interviewing in Mexico, and the value of interview material, see James W. Wilkie, *Elitelore* (Los Angeles: UCLA Latin American Center, 1973); and Richard E. Greenleaf and Michael C. Meyer, eds, *Research in Mexican History* (Lincoln: University of Nebraska Press, 1973). For support of my contention that anyone receiving an oral request to be interviewed in Mexico generally accepts, see

Susan Kaufman Purcell's statement that, "with one exception, I was able to obtain interviews with everyone whom I contacted" (*The Mexican Profit-Sharing Decision, Politics in an Authoritarian Regime* [Berkeley: University of California Press, 1975], p. 149).
[4]Putnam, *Comparative Study,* p. 46.
[5]See for example, Susan Kaufman Purcell, *The Mexican Profit-Sharing Decision*; Kenneth F. Johnson, *Mexican Democracy, A Critical View* (Boston: Allyn Bacon, 1971); Roger D. Hansen, *The Politics of Mexican Development* (Baltimore: John Hopkins University Press, 1971); Daniel Cosío Villegas, *El Estilo personal de gobernar* (Mexico: Joaquín Mortiz, 1974), *El Sistema político mexicano* (Mexico: Joaquín Mortiz, 1973), *La Sucesión: desenlace y perspectivas* (Mexico: Joaquín Mortiz, 1976), and *La Sucesión presidencial* (Mexico: Joaquín Mortiz, 1975); José Luis Reyna, "Redefining the Established Authoritarian Regime: Perspectives of the Mexican Polity" (paper prepared for the Center for Inter-American Relations, New York, 1975); William S. Tuohy, "Centralism and Political Elite Behavior in Mexico," in Clarence E. Thurber and Lawrence S. Graham, eds, *Development Administration in Latin America* (Durham: Duke University Press, 1973); and Peter H. Smith, "Continuity and Turnover Within the Mexican Political Elite."
[6]Susan Kaufman Purcell, *The Mexican Profit-Sharing Decision,* p. 8.
[7]For a good description of these unions see the second edition of Leon V. Padgett's *The Mexican Political System* (Boston: Houghton Mifflin, 1976).
[8]For a detailed analysis of this pattern, see my "Military and Political Military Officers in Mexico: A Comparative Study" (Paper presented before the North Central Council of Latin Americanists, Eau Claire, Wisconsin, 1977).
[9]Lester G. Seligman, "Political Recruitment and Party Structure: A Case Study," *American Political Science Review* **55** (1961): 77.
[10]Mostafa Rejai, "Toward the Comparative Study of Political Decision-Makers," *Comparative Political Studies* **2** (October 1969): 353.
[11]See for example my unpublished manuscript on "Women and Political Leadership in Mexico: A Comparative Study of Female and Male Political Elites;" for a comparision of official party and opposition party leaders, see Donald Mabry and Roderic A. Camp, "Mexican Political Elites 1935–1973; A Comparative Study," *The Americas: A Quarterly Journal of Inter-American Cultural History* **31** (April 1975): 452–69.
[12]Rupert Wilkinson, *Gentlemanly Power: British Leadership and the Public School Tradition* (New York: Oxford University Press, 1964).
[13]Putnam, *Comparative Study,* p. 51.
[14]See the excellent analysis of views among prominent Mexicanists during the 1960s in Carolyn and Martin Needleman, "Who Rules Mexico? A Critique of Some Current Views of the Mexican Political Process," *Journal of Politics* **31** (November 1969): 1011–34; for two more recent discussions, see Martin C. Needler, "Daniel Cosío Villegas and the Interpretation of Mexico's Political System," *Journal of Inter-American Studies and World Affairs* **18** (April 1976): 245–52; and Donald Mabry, "Changing Models of Mexican Politics, A Review Essay," in *The New Scholar* **V**, no. 1 (1975): 31–7.
[15]"Autobiography and Decision-Making in Mexico: A Review Essay," *Journal of Inter-American Studies and World Affairs* **19** (May 1977): 275–83.
[16]Roderic A. Camp, "Losers in Mexican Politics: A Comparative Study of Official Party Precandidates for Gubernatorial Elections, 1970–75," in James W. Wilkie and Kenneth Ruddle, eds., *Quantitative Latin American Studies: Methods and Findings,* Statistical Abstract of Latin America Supplement **6** (Los Angeles: UCLA Latin America Center Publications, University of California, 1977), pp. 23–34.
[17]See Alfonso Noriega's statement to the press that "we live in an institutional, hereditary and absolute monarchy," *Excelsior,* January 15, 1976.
[18]Merilee S. Grindle, "Patrons and Clients in the Bureaucracy: Career Networks in Mexico," *Latin American Research Review* **12** (Spring 1977): 44; and her book, *Bureaucrats, Politicians, and Peasants in Mexico: A Case Study in Public Policy* (Berkeley: University of California Press, 1977).

[19]For evidence of this earlier role, and the political leadership's recognition of the University's importance as a recruiter, see the lucid analysis by Alonso Portuondo, "The Universidad Nacional Autónomo de México in the Post-Independence Period: A Political and Structural Review," unpublished MA Thesis, University of Miami, Coral Gables, Florida, 1972.

[20]See his excellent article, "Sponsored and Contest Mobility and the School System," *American Sociological Review* **25** (December 1960): 855–6.

[21]Lester G. Seligman, "Political Parties and the Recruitment of Political Leaders," in Lewis J. Edinger, ed., *Political Leadership in Industrialized Societies* (New York: John Wiley & Sons, 1967), p. 312.

[22]David C. Schwartz, "Toward a Theory of Political Recruitment," p. 553.

[23]Kenneth Prewitt, *The Recruitment of Political Leaders: A Study of Citizen-Politicians* (Indianapolis: Bobbs-Merrill Co., 1970), p. 13.

[24]Peter H. Smith, "La movilidad política en el México contemporáneo," *Foro Internacional* **15,** no. 3 (1975): 407.

[25]Personal interviews in Mexico, October, 1976.

[26]Robert E. Scott, *Mexican Government in Transition* (Urbana: University of Illinois Press, 1964), p. 214.

[27]Personal interview with Angel Carvajal, Mexico City, October 25, 1976.

[28]*Labyrinths of Power: Political Recruitment in Twentieth-Century Mexico* (Princeton: Princeton University Press, 1979).

[29]Peter Smith, "Continuity and Turnover Within the Mexican Political Elite, 1900–1971."

[30]For a statistical analysis of changes in policy by administration, see James Wilkie, *The Mexican Revolution: Federal Expenditure and Social Change Since 1910,* 2nd edition (Berkeley: University of California Press, 1970).

[31]"The Cabinet and the Técnico in Mexico and the United States," *Journal of Comparative Administration* **3** (August 1971): 200–1.

[32]Personal interviews in Mexico, October, 1976.

[33]Some preliminary conclusions for state political leaders are presented in Roderic A. Camp, "Mexican Governors Since Cárdenas, Education and Career Contacts," *Journal of Inter-American Studies and World Affairs* **16** (November 1974): 454–81.

[34]Byron G. Massialas, *Education and the Political System* (Reading: Addison-Wesley, 1969), p. 88, for comments on the British experience; or for a general analysis of this impact, see Kenneth Prewitt, Heinz Eulau, and Betty H. Zisk, "Political Socialization and Political Roles." *Public Opinion Quarterly* **30** (Winter 1966–67): 574.

[35]I have fully documented the importance of professors in the socialization of Mexican political leaders and on their resultant political, social, and economic ideas in "The Making of a Government: The Socialization of Political Leaders in Post-Revolutionary Mexico" (unpublished manuscript).

2. Mexican Political Culture

In addition to an explanation of some of the structural characteristics of the Mexican political system, it is necessary to identify those factors or characteristics that are most salient in the political culture. However, any attempt to develop a sophisticated and predictable model of Mexican politics will flounder because of the very personalized nature of decision making in Mexico, regardless of whether we are dealing with policies or personnel. Recognizing such problems, I still believe it is worthwhile to discuss the following characteristics of the Mexican political culture: trust, personalism, bureaucratic families, and cooptation.[1]

Trust

Probably the most important cultural factor contributing to the Mexican style of politics is the nature of trust in Mexican society. Numerous students of the Mexican social system have commented on this quality and its prominence in political activity, suggesting that

> The most striking aspect of Mexican character, at first sight, is distrust. This attitude underlies all contact with men and things. It is present whether or not there is motivation for it.... It is rather a matter of irrational distrust that emanates from the depths of his being. It is almost his primordial sense of life. Whether or not circumstances justify it, there is nothing in the universe which the Mexican does not see and evaluate through his distrust. It is like an a priori form of his oversensitivity. The Mexican does not distrust any man or woman in particular; he distrusts all men and all women.[2]

Samuel Ramos wrote these words in the early 1930s, and they describe the generation of Mexicans who make up the majority of persons in our study. Although Ramos' assessment of trust in Mexican society is perhaps somewhat overdrawn, a high-level official in one public agency himself gave a comparable account: "When I took charge of this position, I found that although I had many friends, there were few I trusted enough to invite them to help me. There are three people I brought here whom I trust blindly . . . I trust them with my prestige, with my signature and with my honor . . . This is my *equipo*."[3] Trust is transferred to political activities in two important ways: the degree of confidence on the part of the masses in the honesty of all political leaders; and the nature of trust among Mexicans themselves, whether they are leaders or followers. While we are not concerned with the impact of the first characteristic, the second is an integral part of the most widely discussed characteristic of Mexican politics: personalism.

Personalism

This is a concept of politics that may be defined in several ways, including one which suggests that personalities predominate over ideologies.[4] When this is the case, political behavior within the system also follows certain characteristic patterns, most importantly the one described by William Tuohy in his interviews with state political leaders in Veracruz: " 'The only way to political success is through friends and contacts'; and 'politics here is men trying to gain the attention and favor of the governor. Some approach this by emphasizing good works; others rely more on maneuvering their qualifications in tangible works.' "[5]

What Tuohy's interviews suggest is that in order to be successful in Mexican politics, you need access to someone else who is already successful within the system. This aspect of personalism does not imply that all successful public men rely solely on friendship to carve a place for themselves within the party or administrative apparatus of Mexico, but that access to such persons through friendship gives them a much greater chance of being tapped for responsible positions. Peter McDonough, in his recent work on Brazil, has found friendship and kinship ties to be important to political and other elites. He concluded that "the chances of movement up into the system are conditioned by linkages established in the formative years of the elites."[6] If personal contact is so important, what, then, is the relation between trust and personal friendships in the Mexican political system? If Ramos and others are correct in their assessment of Mexican culture, then any Mexican, including public men, would find it difficult to place confidence in associates, particularly when sensitive questions were involved. Thus, Mexicans tend to place much greater reliance upon relatives, long-time friends, and *compadres* for filling positions of confidence.

While this is a general characteristic of the Mexican political system at all levels, it takes on added importance in a system which is reputed to be dominated by a single personality, the President of Mexico.[7] If, for the moment, we accept the suggestion that the President of Mexico controls and dominates personnel and policy decision making, then we can imagine a difficulty pointed out by a prominent Mexican public official: "One of the weaknesses of a Mexican President, and a restriction upon his ability to govern, is his inability to personally know enough capable men to fill the important positions in Mexican government."[8] Knowing individuals who are potential candidates for such positions is of considerable value in a political system where recruitment is limited. As Keith Legg has noted, "the ability to supply the name of the successful applicant for a position within your own organization not only reinforces personal links with the individual, but provides some control over the job specifications as well."[9] Lastly, there are certain structural characteristics which give added influence to the personalistic style of recruitment. William Touhy provides some insight into this aspect of the political system in his statement that "The political recruitment process is highly competitive, personalistic, often unpredictable, and forces constant shifting of jobs in the societal context of great economic scarcity. Thus, beside the possibility that Mexicans learn distrust early in life (basic socialization), there is the probability that it is a rationale response to the situations in which politicians commonly find themselves."[10] Given the emphasis on trust, the lack of job security, and the physical impossibility of knowing a sufficient number of men to fill responsible political offices, Mexican political leaders have had to develop a process for appointing persons in whom they would have personal confidence.

In order to solve the problems of appointing trustworthy associates to positions of leadership, Mexico has developed a peculiar system which is largely the product of personalism, familialism, and cooptation because personal loyalty, rather than political ideology, is still the overriding feature of the political culture. This system can be described realistically and symbolically as a political pyramid.[11] The corner-stone of that pyramid is loyalty to a process which benefits the participants, and, *from their point of view,* Mexico. The system, controlled informally by a durable group of men described loosely by some scholars as the "Revolutionary Family,"* demands the loyalty of subordinates, who in return receive the power to maintain their positions in the political hierarchy and to increase their influence within the Family.[12]

---

*For the purposes of this study, anyone holding four or more high-level offices (senator and above), has been a member of this group. There are, however, some family members who do not fit this description.

Without this loyalty the political structure would disintegrate and the mystery surrounding the selection process within the inner circle would disappear.* This loyalty is illustrated in one way by the fact that only a few men in the inner circle or on its fringes in the last 40 years have brought private disagreements into the public arena, and none, with the possible exception of Braulio Maldonando, former Governor of Baja California del Norte, has written a book about his political affairs which frankly and openly claims to illustrate the inner workings of the "Revolutionary Family."[13] The system demands political discipline and it receives it every year from numerous politicians. They may criticize the pyramid in private, but in public they maintain the silence of the often described Mexican mask. A clear example of this discipline, and how it contributes to the unpredictability of the political system, can be seen in the candidacy of Emilio Sánchez Piedras for Governor of Tlaxcala in 1974. He had been ostracized from active politics for the previous fourteen years, after making a speech in favor of Cuba in 1960 as leader of the Chamber of Deputies. He lost his leadership because of this speech, yet he made no attempt to criticize his superiors. His patience and self-discipline were rewarded when he became the official candidate for governor.[14]

The *Camarilla*†

Personalism is exemplified in the Mexican political process by the *camarilla* or political clique. Despite the key importance of this process in understanding the official political system, few North American scholars have analyzed this phenomenon. As Kenneth Johnson puts it, "the *camarilla* or political clique is central to understanding the creation, maintenance, and transfer of power within Mexico's PRI."[15] It is a term which denotes a personal clique, based largely on political loyalties between followers and leaders. A more formal definition, as one scholar defines it, is that a clique is a relatively constant collection of persons who see each other frequently for both emotional and pragmatic reasons.[16]

This personal clique, like the official system itself, tends to form a pyramidal structure within the larger pyramid of the official system. It should not be assumed, however, that *all* men in a particular *camarilla* are loyal to the man at the top; within the original *camarilla* there are many lesser *camarillas* headed by men who command their own loyalties. To give a

---

*One former governor of Yucatán refused to talk to me, because, as he told an intermediary, "there was someone else in the federal government who had disciplined him a number of years ago by telling him among other things not to make any further public statements about politics, and he was afraid of offending that individual."

†Portions of this section have been republished from the author's "Decisiones sobre el personal político," *Foro Internacional* 17 (Julio–Septiembre 1976): 51–83.

realistic explanation of this process, one needs to look at the political system to determine who is the leader of the Revolutionary Family, or for our purposes, the primary *camarilla* at a given time. Normally, except when a weak President succeeds a strong President, the head of the primary *camarilla* will be the President of Mexico. The secondary *camarillas* will often be headed by his closest associates, mostly in the cabinet or major decentralized agencies, the National Executive Committee (CEN) of the official party, and occasionally the unions or sectoral organizations. The tertiary *camarillas* are headed by men who are in turn loyal to the men closest to the leader of the Revolutionary Family. Other levels beyond this can be determined, although in the time period examined (1935–1975) no *camarillas* beyond the fifth level were identified. Symbolically, then, the *camarilla* becomes a small pyramidal group of men which in turn is engulfed by a larger and then still larger pyramidal structure, until the official system or pyramid itself emerges.

The *camarilla* has not been studied by scholars because it consists of a grouping of personalities, the extent of which can be determined only by identifying the personal loyalties and career connections among individuals. Despite the obvious difficulties of identifying such relationships, I have tried to do so for a sizeable number of men (437) by becoming familiar with their careers in some detail. The results of this effort have made it possible to identify primary level *camarilla* membership for 177 men, using the last seven presidents as primary *camarilla* leaders (Table 2.1). Even though this sample is by no means all-inclusive, the number of identifiable *camarilla* members is much greater for presidents who have been labelled by most scholars as "strong" (such as Lázaro Cárdenas and Miguel Alemán) than for those who are less influential. The durability and expansion of these *camarillas* seem to be determined by the continuing activity of the primary

Table 2.1

Membership in Primary Political Cliques of Mexican Presidents: 1935 to 1975

Presidential Camarilla Leader	Number of Members in each *Camarilla* Level					
	1st level	2nd level	3rd level	4th level	5th level	Total
Cárdenas	41[a]	65	31	14	—	151
Ávila Camacho	13	13	3	—	—	29
Alemán	43	41	22	2	—	108
Ruiz Cortines	15	10	9	4	6	44
López Mateos	24	6	—	—	—	30
Díaz Ordaz	16	9	8	2	—	35
Echeverría	25	13	2	—	—	40

[a]Membership in a particular clique is determined by one of three conditions: the *camarilla* leader personally appointed a person to a public post (excepting the general statement that the president is responsible for all appointments at high levels in his administration); the *camarilla* leader helped a person obtain a public position under someone else; or the leader and follower were relatives. This information is based on letters, interviews and published memoirs about 436 individuals in the MPBP.

camarilla leader in the political system. The Cárdenas and the Alemán *camarillas* should be especially noted. López Mateos' sudden death caused his *camarilla's* development to lose momentum, and out of necessity, members had to become part of another political clique. Ávila Camacho had a strong secondary *camarilla*, in large part due to the expansion of loyalties made possible by two brothers. In addition to these seven presidents, two men, José Vasconcelos and Plutarco Elías Calles fostered important groups who held positions from 1935 to 1975. Despite the decisive political break between Cárdenas and Calles in 1935, at least 46 officeholders from 1935 to 1975 were attached to political groups developed originally by Calles.

   Camarilla identifications, in addition to being inherently difficult to prove, are made more tenuous because they change as the fortunes of the *camarilla* leader changes. Richard Fagen and William Tuohy aptly describe the impact of fluctuating fortunes among Mexican political leaders: "Yet since careers are built out of a sequence of appointments largely dependent on personalistic loyalties and attachments, an aggressive and successful politician often assembles a coterie of followers *(brazos)* indebted to him as chief *(jefe* or *patrón)* and necessarily identified with him. Such groupings are commonly known as *camarillas*. At all levels there is thus substantial tension between the need to be identified with and protected by a patron, and the need to maintain sufficient independence of action, identification, and other contacts to rescue oneself should the patron's career and influence begin to decline."[17]

   Primary group loyalty has been more stable, since Mexican presidents have usually had consistent upward momentum inside the pyramid. However, when a president has had a very short political career, as in the case of José López Portillo, the relationships become more complex. This is best illustrated by the first-year appointments in his administration. Because López Portillo himself had such a meteoric rise to the presidency after a short, bureaucratic career, he brought very few persons with him who could be said to have been part of his original *camarilla*, or more important, to have been recruited by him. Instead, he recruited many prominent secondary *camarilla* leaders who had risen to the top under previous administrations. Further, those individuals who had been his superiors in his early career, such as Guillermo Rossell de la Lama, who was his boss in López Portillo's first public position, were recruited into cabinet positions. It must be remembered, as both Legg and Grindle suggest, that these personal alliances are reciprocal, similar to the patron-client relationship.[18] This reciprocity is particularly beneficial to the political mentor when his student surpasses the teacher, as in the case of López Portillo and his first employer, Rossell de la Lama. In practice, this relationship appears to result in individuals seemingly being pulled out of nowhere after terminating their public careers many years earlier. They emerge in the limelight, just as did Rossell de la Lama after leaving a high-level public office in 1964 and reemerging in 1976. Generally, however, secondary *camarilla* leaders tend to fluctuate more wildly in their career patterns, being with the "in group" in one administration and the "out group" in the next.[19]

The most powerful Family members can be identified in part through their ability to retain top-level positions regardless of the administration. This has been true of a very select group of Mexicans, numbering less than 50 in the last forty years. It is difficult to place a person in one *camarilla* throughout a career, because a man advances and sustains his position mainly due to his ability to see which superiors are also going to survive and advance within the system. The men who have been classified within a given *camarilla* in the following tables have been included because of their positive identification with that clique at some point in their careers, preferably at an early stage and before holding an office which would classify them as political influentials (Table 2.2).

In most cases of *camarilla* identification, the point at which a person is recruited into the group as well as into the system becomes apparent. Not surprisingly, the major sources of recruitment vary with the career experiences and training of the primary *camarilla* leader. These variations in the primary *camarilla* are carried over into the other levels because of the multiplying effect of the career associations of the original group. For example, revolutionary contacts are important in the primary groups of Cárdenas, Ávila Camacho, and to a lesser extent Ruiz Cortines, but they are nonexistent for all other presidents who were not personally involved in the Revolution and did not have military careers (Table 2.2). In terms of pre-career training, the presidents without formal university education (Cárdenas, Ávila Camacho, and Ruiz Cortines) do not have large numbers of school contacts in their *camarillas*, although all of them had significant contacts in grammar school, illustrating loyalties developed in childhood.[20] In contrast, the presidents with university education have an overwhelming number of contacts from this source (Alemán, López Mateos, Díaz Ordaz, and Echeverría).* Career emphasis is also revealed by the fact that Cárdenas, Alemán, and Ruiz Cortines had important roles in Michoacán and Veracruz politics in their early years, revealed in the data by the large number of state contacts, especially for the Cárdenas group. On the other hand, Díaz Ordaz and Echeverría never held important local elective positions (Echeverría being from the Federal District) and therefore, their *camarillas* reflect no such source of contact. The confidence or loyalty factor in the *camarilla* is revealed not only by long-term

---

*Díaz Ordaz's personal contacts as a student were reduced considerably by the fact that he went to the University of Puebla rather than the National University.

Table 2.2

Number of *Camarilla* Members and Their Recruitment,
From Cárdenas to Echeverría

Camarilla Leader and the Type or Location of Initial Recruitment	*Camarilla* Level					
	1st level	2nd level	3rd level	4th level	5th level	Total
Cárdenas						
Revolution	13	8	3	—	—	24
State	7	15	2	1	—	25
Private Sec'y[a]	5	9	4	2	—	20
School[b]	7	12	6	3	—	28
Relatives	1	4	6	2	—	13
Federal Bur.	5	7	5	4	—	21
Party	—	5	3	1	—	9
Union	—	1	2	1	—	4
Total[c]	38 (3)	61 (4)	31	14	—	144 (7)
Ávila Camacho						
Revolution	3	—	—	—	—	3
State	2	6	1	—	—	9
Private Sec'y	2	1	—	—	—	3
School	1	2	1	—	—	4
Relatives	2	3	—	—	—	5
Federal Bur.	1	1	—	—	—	2
Party	1	—	—	—	—	1
Union	—	—	1	—	—	1
Total	12 (1)	13	3	—	—	28 (1)
Alemán						
Revolution	—	—	—	—	—	—
State	4	3	6	—	—	13
Private Sec'y	—	6	3	1	—	10
School	33	22	5	1	—	61
Relatives	—	4	—	—	—	4
Federal Bur.	1	4	7	—	—	12
Party	1	—	1	—	—	2
Union	—	—	—	—	—	—
Total	39 (4)	39 (2)	22	2	—	102 (6)
Ruiz Cortines						
Revolution	3	1	2	—	—	6
State	6	4	1	2	—	13
Private Sec'y	—	2	—	—	—	2
School	1	2	1	2	6	12
Relatives	—	1	—	—	—	1
Federal Bur.	3	—	2	—	—	5
Party	—	—	1	—	—	1
Union	—	—	—	—	—	—
Total	13 (2)	10	7 (2)	4	6	40 (4)
López Mateos						
Revolution	—	—	—	—	—	—
State	1	1	—	—	—	2
Private Sec'y	—	1	—	—	—	1
School	19	3	—	—	—	22
Relatives	—	—	—	—	—	—
Federal Bur.	1	—	—	—	—	1
Party	—	—	—	—	—	—
Union	1	1	—	—	—	2
Total	22 (2)	6	—	—	—	28 (2)

Table 2.2

Number of *Camarilla* Members and Their Recruitment,
From Cárdenas to Echeverría

Camarilla Leader and the Type or Location of Initial Recruitment	Camarilla Level					
	1st level	2nd level	3rd level	4th level	5th level	Total
Díaz Ordaz						
Revolution	—	—	—	—	—	—
State	—	—	—	—	—	—
Private Sec'y	1	2	—	—	—	3
School	3	3	—	—	—	6
Relatives	1	1	—	—	—	2
Federal Bur.	1	—	—	—	—	1
Party	4	3	—	—	—	7
Union	—	—	—	—	—	
Total	10 (6)	9	— (8)	— (2)	—	19 (16)
Echeverría						
Revolution	—	—	—	—	—	—
State	—	—	—	—	—	—
Private Sec'y	2	2	—	—	—	4
School	13	5	—	—	—	18
Relatives	2	1	—	—	—	3
Federal Bur.	5	4	—	—	—	9
Party	2	—	—	—	—	2
Union	—	—	—	—	—	
Total	24 (1)	12 (1)	— (2)	—	—	36 (4)

Key: Revolution refers to those contacts made between individuals, usually in a subordinate-superior relationship, who became friends during the fighting from 1910 to 1920; State indicates relationships formed by persons serving together in the state bureaucracy; Private Sec'y (private secretary) includes those individuals who were personal assistants, secretaries, or physicians to political leaders at the national level; School refers to friendships made at primary school through the university; Relatives include both relationships by blood or by marriage; Federal Bur. (federal bureaucracy) indicates contacts made while working in the national bureaucracy; Party and Union covers those alliances developed while individuals were working for the official party or union bureaucracies attached to the party.

[a]One of the most interesting forms of political recruitment in Mexico has come about through the doctor-patient relationship. Six men in recent history have held high-level public offices after becoming the personal physician to a President or future President. These men have been included in the private secretary category.

[b]Seven men were recruited by Lázaro Cárdenas through the Colegio de San Nicolás (University of Michoacán) when he was Governor of Michoacán. While Cárdenas never attended this university, nor did he teach there, he did hold weekly reunions or seminars at his home in Morelia for professors and students.

[c]The numbers in parentheses include those men who could positively be identified as a member of a *camarilla* although their means of recruitment could not be determined.

friendships initiated early in a man's career, but also by the continued importance of the single most significant position for making contact, that of private secretary. This position, more than any other in the Mexican political system, requires a definite bond of loyalty and trust between the man holding the position and the individual employing him.

The trends in political leadership careers are also reflected in the recruitment trends of *camarillas*. Recruitment from state governmental positions have declined since Ruiz Cortines (the last president to serve as governor of his home state), amounting to one man in the last three primary groups.

The two prototype primary *camarillas* since 1935 are those of Cárdenas, recruited from revolutionary and state government sources, and of Alemán, recruited from educational and state government contacts.* A detailed examination of these two *camarillas* gives a more exact picture of how these relationships are developed, and what type of man is a *camarilla* member.

Cárdenas-Alemán *Camarillas*

Cárdenas, as a leader of one of the major primary *camarillas* in recent Mexican politics, was himself an example of revolutionary recruitment, first under Obregón, then under Calles. Cárdenas' group was made up of men recruited from six categories: Revolution or military, state positions, school, private secretary, federal bureaucracy, and relatives (Table 2.2). An example of a revolutionary contact was Eduardo Hay, who fought with Cárdenas under General Alvaro Obregón during the Revolution, and rose to prominence as Chief of Staff under Generals Iturbe and Villarreal. Cárdenas appointed him Secretary of Foreign Relations in 1935.[21] Private secretaries were also an important group in the *camarilla*, and three of them became quite prominent in politics. One in particular was Luis I. Rodríguez, who moved from being Cárdenas' private secretary in 1937 to Governor of Guanajuato from 1937–1938 and 1939–40, during the interim serving as President of the National Executive Committee (CEN) of the Party of the Mexican Revolution (forerunner of the official Party of the Institutional Revolution, PRI). Later he served as a Senator under Ruiz Cortines from 1952 to 1958.[22]

Even though Cárdenas did not attend a university, his personal contact with Efraín Buenrostro Ochoa in grammar school created the type of life-long personal loyalty and trust necessary to a man's career as a Mexican politician. Buenrostro went from Secretary General of Government under Cárdenas in Michoacán to Subsecretary of the Treasury and later became Secretary of

---

*Alemán's father was a Revolutionary general killed supporting the no-reelection movement against General Obregón in 1929. Alemán did have a godson in the Echeverria cabinet, and his son, Miguel Jr., was director of news for the federal television system.

Industry and Commerce during the presidential administration. During the Ávila Camacho administration he served as Director General of Pemex. The most successful among Cárdenas' Colegio de San Nicolás discussion groups was Gabino Vázquez, who became a judge in Morelia, Michoacán, and then served as Cárdenas' Secretary General of Government in Michoacán. In 1932, he represented the state of Michoacán in the Chamber of Deputies, and became Cárdenas' Director of the Department of Agrarian Affairs and Colonization in 1934. Cárdenas, who became prominent nationally because of his abilities as a governor of Michoacán, also brought many of his supporters into national politics, one of whom was Raúl Castellano Jiménez, Jr, who started his career under Cárdenas as a judge of the State Supreme Court of Michoacán. He served as Attorney General of the Federal District, and then became a Supreme Court Justice from 1963 to 1972. Although Cárdenas had many brothers and sisters, only one brother, Dámaso, became prominent, serving as Governor of Michoacán during the Alemán administration.

The continuation *(continuismo)* of the Cárdenas *camarilla* was brought about by many members of that primary group. An excellent example is the previously mentioned Luis I. Rodríguez, who helped his protégé, Carlos A. Madrazo, into politics after Madrazo served as his private secretary when Rodríguez was governor of Guanajuato and President of the CEN of the PRM. Madrazo went on to become a federal deputy in the Ávila Camacho administration, Governor of Tabasco in the López Mateos administration, and, like his mentor, President of the CEN of PRI in the Díaz Ordaz administration. He in turn formed a 3rd-level *camarilla*, which included his son Carlos, appointed *Oficial Mayor* of Public Works in the López Portillo administration, and Lauro Ortega, who along with Madrazo helped to found the National Federation of Popular Organizations in 1942. Lauro Ortega became Madrazo's Secretary General of the CEN of PRI, replacing Madrazo as interim President of the CEN when he resigned under pressure in 1965.[23]

The original Cárdenas *camarilla* had an identifiable total of 41 members, and contained 22 men who continued in high political-administrative positions beyond his administration. These 22 men held 43 high-level positions in succeeding administrations, most notably during the Ávila Camacho and Ruiz Cortines administrations (Table 2.3).

Alemán's *camarilla*, like that of Cárdenas, included a large group of men, but it was recruited from different sources: the grammar school, preparatory school, and university, and secondly, from state politics in Veracruz (Table 2.2). No members of the primary *camarilla* were revolutionaries or relatives, since Alemán himself was not a revolutionary, nor did he have any brothers active in politics. Alemán's group is the prototype of the new civilian-bureaucratic leadership characterizing Mexico since the mid 1940s.

The overwhelming number of men belonging to his *camarilla* came from school relationships made before Alemán was 23 years old. This is not only illustrative of the importance of the educational system for political recruitment in modern Mexico; it also indicates the importance of long-term friendships and trust required of the closest associates.

One of the most prominent of Alemán's original classmates at the National University of Mexico was Ernesto P. Uruchurtu, who held only minor judicial and administrative positions until 1946, when he became Alemán's Auxiliary Campaign Secretary in the presidential campaign. He then served a brief term as Secretary General of the National Executive Committee of PRI, leaving that office to become Subsecretary and later Secretary of Government. Ruiz Cortines appointed him Head of the Federal District Department in 1952, and at the end of the administration, he became a pre-candidate for President of Mexico. Despite the fact that he lost as a pre-candidate, he continued as Director of the Federal District Department under López Mateos and Díaz Ordaz, until he was forced to resign in the midst of an anti-corruption campaign in 1966.[24] Alemán did not make use of the position of private secretary for recruitment to his *camarilla*, because one man, Rogerio de la Selva, served continuously in this position from 1934 to 1946, beginning with Alemán's career as a State Supreme Court Justice in Veracruz. De la Selva also served as Confidential Secretary of the President under Alemán, and again became his private secretary when Alemán left the presidency and directed the National Tourism Council.

The secondary Alemán *camarillas* can be well illustrated by using the political group surrounding E. P. Uruchurtu. One of these men, Arturo González Cosío, served as his Auxiliary Secretary while Uruchurtu was Head of the Federal District Department. In 1970, he served in a middle-level position in the Secretariat of Industry and Commerce, and then became Secretary of Political Education for the CEN of PRI and a member of its new advisory council. Two years later, he ran against the ex-president of the National Action Party, Manuel González Hinojosa, in a race for federal deputy from the Federal District, winning the election.* Alemán's primary group, like that of Cárdenas, continued to influence politics in Mexico long after the Alemán administration ended in 1952. Twenty of the 38 primary group members served in 45 high-level positions in following administrations.

As Mexican presidents become younger, the primary group that creates itself around him will more likely continue to be influential in succeeding administrations. Personalism has not really been replaced by an in-

---

*Nomination by PRI to represent a legislative district is usually tantamount to election. However, this is not always the case, and in the 1973 elections the official party "sacrificed" several of their own candidates who were being disciplined for their behavior. I am using the phrase "winning the election" to indicate that the individual under discussion was not sacrificed to a strong opposition candidate.

stitutionalized office, but continues to function as a strong bond among political cliques built up through a web of loyalties culminating in the single *camarilla* leader. These *camarillas* compete with each other to take control of the Revolutionary Family, although complete control by one *camarilla* can never be absolute. Power struggles between various individuals within the official party are often conflicts between competing *camarillas*, rather than true ideological debates between the left and the right.

Collectively then, the high-level positions held by Mexicans at any one time are dominated by men from all the preceding *camarillas*, plus those men belonging to groups competing with the primary *camarilla* of the current president. The importance of *continuismo* in Mexican politics can be illustrated from an analysis of the career backgrounds of the 201 high-level officeholders in the Díaz Ordaz administration, a recently completed presidential term. Previous primary and secondary *camarillas* contributed the following numbers of men to the Díaz Ordaz administration: Cárdenas (6), Ávila

Table 2.3

Continuismo of the Primary Cárdenas *Camarilla* from 1940 to 1977

Position Held by *Camarilla* Member	Number of *Camarilla* members in Presidential Administration of:						
	Ávila Camacho	Alemán	Ruiz Cortines	López Mateos	Díaz Ordaz	Echeverría	López Portillo
Decentralized Agency	1	2	1	—	—	—	—
Cabinet	7	—	2	1	1	1	1
Governor	2	5	4	—	—	—	—
Ambassador	2	—	—	—	—	—	—
Senator	1	1	1	—	—	1	1
CEN/PRI	1	1	2	—	—	—	—
Union	1	—	—	—	—	—	—
Supreme Court	—	—	—	1	1	1	—
Total	15	9	10	2	2	3	2

Continuismo of the Primary Alemán *Camarilla* from 1952 to 1977

Position Held by *Camarilla* Member	Number of *Camarilla* members in Presidential Administration of:				
	Ruiz Cortines	López Mateos	Díaz Ordaz	Echeverría	López Portillo
Decentralized Agency	2	—	—	2	—
Cabinet	3	3	2	—	1
Governor	2	—	—	—	—
Senator	3	—	1	—	—
Supreme Court	3	6	6	6	1
Union	—	—	1	—	—
Pre-Candidate for President	2	—	1	—	—
Total	15	9	11	8	2

Camacho (3), López Mateos (5), Alemán (20), and Echeverría, as a competitive *camarilla,* contributed (10). Forty-four or 22 percent of the high-level officeholders in the Díaz Ordaz administration could be *positively identified* as being members of other primary cliques.

Continuismo is not just confined to identifiable primary and secondary *camarilla* members, but appears to be a characteristic of most high-level officeholders. The large majority of officeholders appointed to high-level positions in the Díaz Ordaz administration, for example, have held such positions in previous administrations. Specifically, 77 or 38 percent had previously held 1st-level positions in other administrations, 78 or 39 percent held 2nd-level positions, and 98 or 49 percent served in 3rd-level positions.* One-hundred and forty-nine persons served in one or more of these positions before taking office from 1964–70.[25]

Repetition in high-level positions was equally striking by members of the Díaz Ordaz administration. Of the original sample of 201 persons, 169 were eligible to hold office under President Echeverría (32 individuals were eliminated due to death, serious illness, or continuation in a position to which they were appointed by Díaz Ordaz). Of the 169 members of the Díaz Ordaz administration, 82 or nearly half, continued in high-level positions in the first half (1971 to 1974) of the Echeverría term.†

The Mexican political system is built on the continuation of a *camarilla* system that directly influences the president's ability to select persons for high political office. The president himself is a compromise choice made among competing groups. He has succeeded in achieving that office because he has been able to coalesce or at least not to offend the most important groups

---

*1st-level officeholders are those persons holding the following positions: Cabinet Secretary and Subsecretary, Director General of the major decentralized agencies, President of the Chamber of Deputies and the Senate, Secretary General of the major unions and PRI sector organizations; members of the National Executive Committee of PRI; Governors; the Chief Justice of the Supreme Court; and Ambassador to the United States, Great Britain, and the OAS. 2nd-level officeholders include: *Oficial Mayor* of the Federal Cabinet; Subdirectors of major decentralized agencies; Senators; Directors of secondary decentralized agencies; Secretary General of secondary national unions; Mayor of Guadalajara and Monterrey; President of PRI for the Federal District; President of the Federal Conciliation and Arbitration Board; and Vice-President of the Chamber of Deputies and of the Senate. 3rd-level officeholders include: Federal Deputies; Secretary General of Government (State); 3rd and 4th ranked cabinet positions; Justice of the Supreme Court and Subdirector of secondary decentralized agencies.

†Fifty-two individuals or 30.8 percent of Díaz Ordaz's appointees held 1st-level positions in the Echeverría administration, 18 or 10.7 percent held 2nd-level positions and 19 or 11.2 percent held 3rd-level positions. In 1971, the original 201 appointees had been reduced to 169 persons eligible for office because 18 had died, 13 were still in office through 1973, and one was seriously ill.

(qualitatively and quantitatively) as supporters of his own political power. His choice is not only limited increasingly by the political environment but also by rewards he must give to supporting *camarillas*. It is surmised that the President can sometimes defer making the choice to reward a *camarilla,* to which he is obligated, if the political environment has become unstable enough to demand the skills of a different person. In other cases, the reverse is true. While the final outcome in each case may seem inconsistent, it is only due to the fact that the secretiveness of the system makes it difficult to determine which of the two pressures (political obligation or political environment) is most important in keeping the whole system viable and satisfied.[26]

Bureaucratic Families

The strength of family ties in the Mexican system is of major significance because of the small number of persons who dominate high-level positions. One is tempted here to use the word nepotism, implying the appointment of ill-trained, uneducated, or less qualified relatives to bureaucratic sinecures. There are numerous cases of this in Mexico, particularly at the local and state level. For example, a notorious governor of Guerrero in the 1960s was alleged to have appointed 60 relatives to positions in his administration.[27] At the highest levels, family office holding is rarely outright nepotism; rather it is the result of a political culture that encourages dependence on the family for the degree of trust and confidence necessary to establish close political relationships. Personal relationships are equally important for the National Action Party (PAN) and the Popular Socialist Party (PPS), at least for candidates for federal deputies.[28]

Family ties are a passport, so to speak, allowing easy access into the highest political echelons. This access is easier to obtain because a relative has vouched politically for your loyalty through his own prior loyalties and commitments to the official system. More than 25 percent of all political leaders in Mexico (MPBP data) have had in-laws or blood relatives in important political offices (federal deputy or 4th ranked bureaucratic positions; see Table 2.4).

Other cultures, including our own, have been equally influenced by kinship relationships in determining access to high political office. For example, in administrations following the American Revolution, Sidney Aronson found that 40 percent of the high officeholders in John Adams' administration were related to each other or to previous high-level officeholders. Although this figure declined in Thomas Jefferson's administration to 34 percent, it remained at the same level during Andrew Jackson's presidency.[29] In a completely different cultural context, that of 20th-century Turkey, Joseph Szyliowicz concluded that elite kinship was an essential ingredient in the

Table 2.4

Political Leaders Who Had Relatives in Public Office in Mexico, 1935 to 1976[a]

Presidential Administration in which Position was Held	Number and Percentage of Leaders with Relatives by the Number of Times Each Elite Has Held Office				
	1st Time	2nd Time	3rd Time	4th Time	5th Time
1935 to 40					
No. of leaders	49	14	3	1	0
% of leaders	27.5	34.1	30.0	100.0	0
1940 to 46					
No. of leaders	35	19	10	3	0
% of leaders	31.5	29.7	35.7	42.9	0
1946 to 52					
No. of leaders	28	26	8	3	1
% of leaders	25.5	36.6	30.8	30.0	50.0
1952 to 58					
No. of leaders	21	13	12	4	3
% of leaders	25.0	24.1	32.4	30.8	37.5
1958 to 64					
No. of leaders	19	11	10	7	2
% of leaders	20.7	20.8	27.0	31.8	25.0
1964 to 70					
No. of leaders	27	21	7	8	7
% of leaders	26.7	29.2	20.0	30.8	36.8
1970 to 76					
No. of leaders	27	17	10	7	4
% of leaders	20.5	22.1	24.4	31.8	36.4
Sub-totals					
No. of leaders	206	121	60	33	17
% of leaders	25.4	28	28.4	32.7	34.0
Total sample	810	426	214	101	50

[a]This table excludes opposition party members and federal deputies. Data are taken from the MPBP. Percentages reflect the number of leaders with relatives in each category divided by the total number of leaders in that category.

career success of graduates from Mulkiye, an institution predominantly graduating public servants in that country.[30] Both of these studies suggest that regardless of the culture, kinship ties have played an important role in determining the level of achievement in political careers, particularly during the early stages of the introduction of a new elite political class.

Considering the small number of persons in the pool of political influentials, the number of *traceable* bureaucratic family relationships is sizeable. (I have also assumed that many family ties such as in-laws are not easily identifiable.) What is important is that the more times an elite has held high office, the more frequently he has had relatives in public office. The same pattern is present in the administration of José López Portillo, where 18 percent of the first-time, high-level officeholders in his regime had kinship relations, with that figure ascending to a level of 36 percent for fifth-time appointees* (Table 2.4). The types of relationships most common among political elites are: brothers (74); father/children (primarily sons) (88); uncles/ nephews (19); grandfathers and great grandfathers/grandsons and great grandsons (20); cousins (10); brother-in-law/sister-in-law (3); father-in-law/son-in-law (5); and husband/wife (2).

An example of two brothers who have recently held politically influential positions are Alfonso Martínez Domínguez, former President of the CEN of PRI and Head of the Federal District Department, and his brother Guillermo, past Director General of the Federal Electric Commission and Director General of *Nacional Financiera*, 1970–1974. A number of examples also existed in 1976 of the father/son relationship, including Mario Ramón Beteta, Secretary of the Treasury and son of Ignacio Beteta, former Chief of Staff to President Cárdenas. Presidents have not been immune to the tendency to have politically active families. This has been especially true of Cárdenas, Ávila Camacho, and Luis Echeverría. The relationship of uncle and nephew is best exemplified by President Echeverría and his nephew Rodolfo, who was *Oficial Mayor* of PRI and became Subsecretary of Government in José López Portillo's administration.

Family ties are not confined to one or even two generations, and some Mexican families, like the well-known Adams family in the United States, have continued in high public office for three or more generations. In recent years, the Riva Palacio, Sierra, and Rabasa families have contributed public men from multiple generations.

An example of a family that has devoted itself to public service in an exemplary manner is the Alatriste family. Sealtiel Alatriste, Jr, a past Subsecretary of National Patrimony and Director General of the Mexican Institute of Social Security, included in our sample of political elites, is the son of Sealtiel L. Alatriste, one of the young lawyers in the various liberal clubs founded during the first decade of the 19th century. He supported his more well-known cousins Aquiles and Maimo Serdan Alatriste. He was also involved in the political debates of the Revolution as a member of the Mexican Liberal Party, supporting Francisco Madero in 1910, and later serving President Obregón as an agent in New York. Sealtiel Alatriste, Jr's great-grandfather was General and Licenciado Miguel Cástulo de Alatriste, who became Governor of Puebla, and supported the liberals during the French invasion. He was captured and killed by the French in 1862. Sealtiel Alatriste's first cousin, Roberto Casas Alatriste, like his father, was an early revolutionary and supporter of Obregón. Twice a federal deputy, he later became one of the most noted

---

*This statement is based on an analysis of 82 members of the López Portillo administration made by the author in October, 1977.

independent public accountants in Mexico and Director of the School of Business at the National University.[31]

Frequently, families have several members holding the 1st-level positions, sometimes simultaneously. An examination of the highest level positions held by bureaucratic family members reveals the following distribution of positions:

Table 2.5

Highest Political Position Held by Two Members of a Single Family in Mexico, 1935–1975[a]

1st Family Member & Position Held	2nd Family Member & Position Held	No. of Families Having These Combined Positions
Cabinet-level .... Cabinet-level		64
Cabinet-level .... Governor		13
Cabinet-level .... Senator or Deputy		25
Cabinet-level .... Federal Bureaucracy		37
Governor .... Senator or Deputy		11
Governor .... Governor		04
Governor .... Federal Bureaucracy		10

[a]Each person was only counted once for the highest combination.

This form of political recruitment narrows the pool of high-level officeholders to a smaller number of familes and contributes to the continuism of family groups, if not individuals, in the political system.[32] For example, in the Díaz Ordaz administration, 37 officeholders were related to other individuals who either were in positions in his administration or had held positions in the 30 years prior to his term.*

In addition to the continuation of political and family groups, the system has always attempted to coopt receptive deviants who have left government and gone outside of the official system, thereby adding to the number of repeaters from the previous administrations and decreasing the number of positions available for new office seekers.

Cooptation

Cooptation has taken two forms in the Mexican system: bringing back the high-level member who has left the official family at a given time by forgiving his political sins and once again giving him access to high-level positions; or by allowing those who have opposed the system without ever really having

---

*Within the federal cabinet, there have only been five cases in the last 40 years of two brothers holding office simultaneously: the Merino Fernández's, the Ortiz Mena's, the González de la Vega's, the Campillo Sáenz's and the Bustamante's. *Hoy,* November 25, 1967, p. 25, erred in saying only one case of this had been true in Mexico. It should also be remembered that Ávila Camacho appointed his brother to a cabinet post during his administration.

a significant role within it to become part of the official family. Both types of cooptation have something in common: they illustrate the strength of personal loyalties in permitting this process to occur and also the importance that the system places on deferring to articulate and well-organized opposition.

From 1935 until 1975, 73 persons were coopted back into the official system, 13 of whom had participated in more than one opposition movement against the government. Historically, there have been three major military events producing a schism among the Revolutionary Family which has governed Mexico since President Carranza. The first event was the break between Carranza himself and Obregón; this accounted for eight men who remained loyal to Carranza and went into exile after his death, but later held high-level positions after 1935. An excellent example from this group is Francisco L. Urquizo, who rejoined the army in 1934, and became Subsecretary and Secretary of National Defense under Ávila Camacho. The second event was the De la Huerta rebellion in 1923, which accounted for eleven additional men leaving the official fold; most prominent among them were the Estrada brothers, who were coopted back into the system by Lázaro Cárdenas, and held positions in his and Ávila Camacho's administration.* The last major military uprising, the 1929 Escobar rebellion, was supported by at least eleven men who held high-level positions after 1935. Three of them became state governors.

All other individuals coopted into the system after 1935 have been participants in opposition party campaigns or candidates of other parties. The most important opposition political campaign, the 1929 Vasconcelos campaign, contained mostly political novices, but included an influential generation of Mexican public men.† Among them were a President, a precandidate for President, and a secretary of government. A large number of successful public men have participated in succeeding opposition campaigns, including the Almazán and Henríquez Guzmán campaigns of 1940 and 1952 respectively.

---

*A more obscure but extremely important event was the 1927 anti-reelection campaign of Generals Serrano and Gómez, who were killed by the government in 1927. Three well-known political figures of the 1940s were student orators in that campaign, the most prominent of whom was Miguel Alemán.

†When asked to list those events that had the most impact on their personal formation, 28 retired public men interviewed, who were students, professors, or young professionals in 1929, included this campaign. Dr Ignacio Chávez related to the author a personal account that is illustrative of the behavior of that generation. As a young doctor in 1929, he was an avid supporter of José Vasconcelos while serving as a personal physician to ex-president Calles. Calles, while knowing of Chávez's opposition to his own candidate in the presidential race never mentioned a word to Chávez about his feelings nor did he change physicians. Many years later, he told Chávez "that he had a great respect for him during the 1929 campaign because Chávez was not willing to trade his personal philosophy for a client."

A notable individual among those who participated in several of these campaigns was Efraín Brito Rosado, a long-time participant of out groups since his student days, who ran a tough campaign as Secretary General of the anti-government organization backing General Almazán against the official candidacy of General Ávila Camacho in 1940. Brito Rosado went into exile in Texas after his candidate lost in the official balloting.* He described to the author how President Ávila Camacho invited him back to Mexico and asked him in for a long interview. Brito Rosado had criticized him severely during the campaign, yet the President treated him with great respect and told him "that it would be a great pleasure to me personally if you would become a federal deputy during my regime." Perhaps because Ávila Camacho won a smaller margin than officially reported, he felt a real need to generously coopt opposition leaders back into the Mexican political system.[33] He exemplifies the process of conciliation, and several government officials told the author that Ávila Camacho lived up to his reputation as the "gentleman president."[34]

The most interesting aspect of the cooptation process in Mexico is that the majority of the elites studied here can be traced directly to a President or primary *camarilla* leader in whose term they held a high-level position. For example, all of the young participants in the Vasconcelos campaign personally knew two *camarilla* leaders: Adolfo López Mateos or Miguel Alemán. Personal friendship and loyalty are the ties that make it possible for a person in a politically influential position to bring a new person or return an old one into the system. Cooptation is a reflection that the political system as well as the leader of that system cannot function arbitrarily. While no one would

---

*General Emilio Madero, a sympathizer of General Almazán and brother of the martyred Mexican President, told one of the persons interviewed by the author that "I had not seen as popular a campaign for my brother as I saw for Almazán." Three cabinet secretaries in administrations since 1946 told the author that they believed Almazán won the 1940 election, and all remarked that had the author viewed the election himself, there would be no question in his own mind. This view goes beyond the more moderate statements by Albert Michaels, and from James Wilkie (quoting Marte R. Gómez and Emilio Portes Gil) that Almazán actually carried the Federal District and Ávila Camacho received only 75 percent of the total popular vote. See Michaels, "The Mexican Election of 1940," Special Studies No. 5, Council on International Studies (Buffalo: SUNY, 1971); and Wilkie, *The Mexican Revolution: Federal Expenditure and Social Change Since 1910,* 2nd edition (Berkeley: University of California Press, 1970), p. 180. However, in supporting this latter view, another former cabinet official who was a supporter of earlier opposition movements suggested that Almazán did quite well in the urban areas, especially among white-collar workers, students, and intellectuals. On the other hand, Ávila Camacho did better among the rural populations. He suggests that Almazán's support was more vociferous, came from a better-educated population, and made its opinions known to the press and to foreign correspondents. In reality, he believes Ávila Camacho garnered a much larger popular vote, and cautioned scholars to be careful to distinguish between the quality and quantity of support for various candidates in Mexico.

argue against the assertion that cooptation has involved methods ranging from a small bribe to threats of bodily harm, the need for carrying out this process reflects a perception by the leadership that this type of bargaining is necessary for the system as well as for the governing elite to survive. In effect, then, the need for cooptation forces a president to appoint men to political office because the stability of the entire system is threatened by the leadership of such men outside the system.

Camarillas, bureaucratic familes, and cooptation all have one thing in common—they strongly depend on personal loyalty and confidence in another individual. This chapter does not purport to say that personalism is a new and dominant trait of the Mexican political system, since it is one of the most often identified qualities of all Latin American political systems. Rather the attempt has been made to show that because personal trust and loyalty is such an overriding feature of the official system in Mexico, it accounts for the three types of activity described above, leads to a system that promotes the continuation of a small political elite, and explains some limitations on the recruitment process of the Mexican political system.

No administration since 1935, as illustrated by the Díaz Ordaz administration, is made-up entirely of one political group of completely new officeholders. In the last seven administrations, approximately 1800 positions have been available that meet the criterion established for our sample of the Díaz Ordaz administration. In actuality, however, only 900 persons have been drawn upon to fill those positions, indicating that over time the pool of officeholders is much smaller than the available openings. If the Díaz Ordaz regime provides a fair sample for other administrations since 1935 (and my research indicates that it does), the continuity of the ''Revolutionary Family'' itself is also apparent. While 26 members of his administration could be considered Revolutionary Family members (individuals having held four or more high-level positions, or identified by the impressionistic evidence of Brandenburg, Scott and others), half of them could be considered members of the Revolutionary Family in another administration. These are the men who provide the thread of personal continuity and leadership at the top, just as the same continuity is provided at the secondary and tertiary levels of administration. *Continuismo* has been a consistent part of the political leadership of Mexico. As long as personal loyalty remains a significantly strong value of the Mexican system, political groups, family groups, and cooptation, and the competing loyalties these engender, will remain a consistent characteristic of politics. As Cosío Villegas accurately concludes, the power of the presidency has grown since 1934, and the President of Mexico reigns over an expanding system which is increasingly difficult to manage.[35] ''In effect, the structure of political power consists of a hierarchy of interrelated groups and associations, the loyalties and relations of whose leaders culminate in the president, who in turn uses the mechanisms of the presidency to play one individual and interest against another in his attempt to assure political stability.''[36]

This, then, is a brief interpretation of a political culture that has been a product of Mexico's history and its institutions, and in turn, has affected institutional behavior and historical development. I have described some of the prominent cultural traits, which in the view of Mexican and North American scholars, have affected the political process and in particular, political recruitment. To some degree, these characteristics are true of all political systems, but in Mexico they appear to be much more typical of the culture in general, and the political culture in particular.[37]

Personalism, bureaucratic families, and cooptation all illustrate the importance of personal loyalty over other personal qualities such as ideological orientations. I will argue in the following chapters that trust in a collaborator, combined with favorable evaluations of his organizational, political, and intellectual skills are those qualities most highly valued in the recruitment of political leaders. These same qualities are important to a candidate in other political systems, but ideological beliefs are equally important in a list of candidate qualities. In Mexico, however, only a few political leaders are characterized by strong ideological beliefs, and they tend to be recruited through political party (or subsidiary organizational) channels and not through the bureaucratic channels. The lack of strongly held ideological beliefs among the more typical political elite in Mexico contributes to the emphasis on personal or small group loyalties within the political system.[38]

NOTES TO CHAPTER 2

[1]In her recent case study of CONASUPO, a major government decentralized agency, Merilee Grindle concluded that trust and the *camarilla* were among the major elements involved in upward mobility in the Mexican political system. *Bureaucrats, Politicians, and Peasants in Mexico: A Case Study in Public Policy* (Berkeley: University of California Press, 1977).
[2]Samuel Ramos, *Profile of Man and Culture in Mexico* (Austin: University of Texas Press, 1962), p. 64.
[3]Merilee Grindle, ''Patrons and Clients in the Bureaucracy: Career Networks in Mexico,'' *Latin American Research Review* **12**, no. 1 (1977): 49.
[4]These qualities can be seen at all levels of Mexican society in the writings of novelists, social scientists, and sociologists, whether they are Mexican or foreign. For examples see: Lola Romanucci-Ross, *Conflict, Violence, and Morality in a Mexican Village* (Palo Alto: National Press Books, 1973); Oscar Lewis, *Five Families* (New York: Basic Books, 1959); Cynthia Nelson, *The Waiting Village* (Boston: Little-Brown, 1971); Graham Greene, *The Power and the Glory* (New York: The Viking Press, 1940); José Ruben Romero, *The Futile Life of Pito Pérez* (Englewood Cliffs: Prentice-Hall, 1966); Juan Rulfo, *The Burning Plain* (Austin: University of Texas Press, 1971); Sidney Verba and Gabriel Almond, *The Civic Culture* (Boston: Little-Brown, 1965); Joseph A. Kahl, *The Measurement of Modernism* (Austin: University of Texas Press, 1968); Robert Scott, ''Mexico: The Established Revolution,'' in Lucian W. Pye and Sidney Verba, eds, *Political Culture and Political Development* (Princeton: Princeton University Press, 1965);

Louis K. Harris and Victor Alba, *The Political Culture and Behavior of Latin America* (Kent: Kent State University Press, 1974); Rogelio Díaz Guerrero, *Psychology of the Mexican* (Austin: University of Texas Press, 1975); and Evelyn P. Stevens, *Protest and Response in Mexico* (Cambridge: MIT Press, 1974).

[5]William S. Tuohy, "Centralism and Political Elite Behavior in Mexico," in Clarence E. Thurber and Lawrence S. Graham, eds, *Development Administration in Latin America* (Durham: Duke University Press, 1973), p. 271.

[6]Peter McDonough, "Cohesion and Mobility in a Technocratic Authoritarian System: Kinship, Friendship and Class Ties Among Brazilian Elites," paper presented at the 7th National Meeting of the Latin American Studies Association, November 2–5, 1977, p. 41.

[7]Carolyn and Martin Needleman, "Who Rules Mexico? A Critique of Some Current Views of the Mexican Political Process." *Journal of Politics* **31,** (November 1969): 1011–34.

[8]Personal interview with a former cabinet secretary, Mexico City, June, 1975.

[9]Keith R. Legg, "Interpersonal Relationships and Comparative Politics: Political Clientelism in Industrial Society," *Politics* **7,** (May 1972): 10.

[10]William Touhy, "Psychology in Political Analysis: The Case of Mexico," *Western Political Quarterly* **27** (June 1974): 296.

[11]See Octavio Paz for historical allusions to the symbolism of the pyramid in Mexico, in his *The Other Mexico: Critique of the Pyramid* (New York: Grove Press, 1972).

[12]Frank Brandenburg has the best description of who belongs in this group. See his *Making of Modern Mexico* (Englewood Cliffs: Prentice-Hall, 1964); and his "Mexico, An Experiment in One-Party Democracy" (unpublished Ph.D. dissertation, University of Pennsylvania, 1956), which has considerable information not in his book.

[13]Maldonado's book is entitled *Baja California: Comentarios políticos* (Mexico: Costa Amic, 1960). However, I believe the most revealing work is by Praxedis Balboa, *Apuntes de mi vida* (México, 1975), but because it is privately printed, it has not received scholarly attention. Other Mexicanists might include the recent work by Manuel Moreno Sánchez, *México: 1968–1972, Crisis y Perspectiva* (Austin: Institute of Latin American Studies, 1973), a critical evaluation of the system by a former pre-candidate for president and senate leader under Adolfo López Mateos. Given Moreno Sánchez's former role in the political system, this short work provides few revealing specifics about the process. For an evaluation of the value of recent autobiographical literature by public men in Mexico, see my "Autobiography and Decision-Making in Mexico: A Review Essay," *Journal of Inter-American Studies and World Affairs* **19** (May 1977).

[14]*Excelsior*, May 2, 1974.

[15]Kenneth F. Johnson, *Mexican Democracy: A Critical View* (Boston: Allyn and Bacon, 1971), p. 70.

[16]Jeremy Boissevain, *Friends of Friends: Networks, Manipulators, and Coalitions* (Oxford: Basil Blackwell, 1974), p. 174.

[17]Richard Fagen and William Tuohy, *Politics and Privilege in a Mexican City* (Stanford: Stanford University Press, 1972), pp. 25–6.

[18]Keith Legg, "Interpersonal Relationships," p. 9; Merilee Grindle, "Patrons and Clients," p. 38.

[19]Martin H. Greenberg, *Bureaucracy and Development: A Mexican Case Study* (Lexington: D.C. Heath, 1970), p. 68.

[20]Cárdenas went to grammar school with his Secretary of Industry and Commerce; Ávila Camacho went to school with Vicente Lombardo Toledano; and Ruiz Cortines' administrative career was dependent upon his contact with a school teacher who became a revolutionary leader. See my "Mexican Governors Since Cárdenas, Education and Career Contacts," *Journal of Inter-American & World Affairs* **16,** (November 1974).

[21]Roderic A. Camp, *Mexican Political Biographies, 1935–1975* (Tucson: University of Arizona Press, 1976), pp. 160–1; José López Escalera, *Diccionario biográfico y de historia de Mexico* (Mexico: Editorial del Magistrado, 1964), pp. 486–7; and *Enciclopedia de México* **6,** p. 368.

[22]*Polémica* **1,** no. 1 (1969): p. 69; *Hispano Americano* September 3, 1973, p. 29; and Camp, *Mexican Political Biographies,* pp. 277–8.

[23]*Hispano Americano,* January 26, 1945, p. 5; *¿Por Qúe?* September 25, 1969, p. 12ff.; *Enciclopedia de México* **5,** p. 220; and Daniel Cadena Z., *El candidato presidencial, 1976* (Mexico, 1975), p. 129.

[24]Carlos Morales Díaz, *¿Quién es quien en la nomenclatura de la ciudad de México?* (Mexico, 1971), p. 592; *Hispano Americano,* February 15, 1952, p. 3; and Arturo Gómez Castro, *¿Quién sera el futuro presidente de México?* (Mexico, 1963), pp. 136–7.

[25]For further evidence of these findings, see Peter H. Smith, ''Continuity and Turnover Within the Mexican Political Elite, 1900–1971,'' in James W. Wilkie, et al. eds.,*Contemporary Mexico* (Los Angeles: UCLA Latin American Center, 1976), pp. 167–86. Smith uses a larger sample for the Díaz Ordaz administration (610 incumbents). I am using a sample of 201 incumbents who are persons holding only those positions from *Oficial Mayor* on up. Therefore, my sample is more selective, because only the highest level officeholders are considered, whereas the Smith sample includes anyone holding a position in each of the three levels mentioned above.

[26]For some detailed examples of this at both the national and state level, see my ''El sistema mexicano y las decisiones sobre el personal político,'' *Foro Internacional* **XVII,** no. 1 (1976): 51–63; and ''Losers in Mexican Politics: A Comparative Study of Official Party Precandidates for Gubernatorial Elections, 1970–75,'' in James W. Wilkie and Kenneth Ruddle, eds, *Quantitative Latin American Studies: Methods and Findings,* Statistical Abstract of Latin America Supplement **6** (Los Angeles: UCLA Latin American Center Publications, University of Californa, 1977), pp. 23–34.

[27]*Hispano Americano,* February 14, 1972, p. 15.

[28]Karl M. Schmitt, ''Congressional Campaigning in Mexico: A View from the Provinces,'' *Journal of Inter-American Studies and World Affairs* **11** (January 1969): 98.

[29]Sidney H. Aronson, *Status and Kinship in the Higher Civil Service* (Cambridge: Harvard University Press, 1964), p. 142.

[30]Joseph Szyliowicz, ''Elite Recruitment in Turkey: The Role of the Mulkiye,'' *World Politics* **23** (April 1971): 396.

[31]Personal interviews with Sealtiel Alatriste, Jr, May, 1974 and June, 1975; and Miguel Alatriste de la Fuente, *Ensayo Biográfico del General C. De Alatriste, 1820–1862* (Mexico: Secretaria de Patrimonio Nacional, 1962).

[32]Robert Scott believes that strict nepotism in the federal bureaucracy is uncommon. See his ''The Government Bureaucrats and Political Change in Latin America,'' *Journal of International Affairs* (1966): 295, footnote 6.

[33]The director of Almazán's campaign, Pedro Martínez Tornel, served as Ávila Camacho's Subsecretary and Secretary of Public Works (Camp, *Mexican Political Biographies,* p. 207).

[34]Interestingly enough, he performed this conciliatory role for Cárdenas 15 years earlier. See Albert L. Michaels, ''The Mexican Election of 1940,'' Spec. Studies No. **5,** Council on International Studies (Buffalo: SUNY, 1971), p. 12. Jaime Torres Bodet, who served in his administration as Subsecretary of Foreign Relations and Secretary of Public Education, has several examples in his autobiographical *Años contra el tiempo* (México: Porrúa, 1969).

[35]Daniel Cosío Villegas, *La Sucesión presidencial* (Mexico: Editorial Joaquín Mortiz, 1975), p. 90.

[36]Robert Scott, *Mexican Government in Transition* (Urbana: University of Illinois Press, 1964), p. 259.

[37]For example, among a sample of ward committeemen, David Schwartz found that 68 percent considered the typical recruitment group to have been held together through the informal factor of friendship (''Toward a Theory of Political Recruitment,'' *Western Political Quarterly* **22** [September 1969]: 564).

[38]Seventy of the 78 individuals Merilee Grindle interviewed in CONASUPO used personal ties to get jobs in that agency, including the highly qualified technical advisers (p. 43).

3. Who Emerges
at the Top?

In a system characterized by personalism and numerous political cliques, what type of men and women eventually succeed in reaching the top? Using a nearly complete population of persons holding high-level public offices since 1935, some of the geographic, social, and career characteristics of Mexico's present and past governing elite* are surveyed in this chapter.

Urban-Rural Birthplaces

One of the most striking characteristics of the Mexican political elite is revealed by data on the place of birth of high-level officeholders. Mexico's political elite is urban in background, particularly in comparison to the total population.[1] While as late as 1940 only 27.4 percent of the Mexican population lived in communities over 5,000, 63.2 percent of the political elite were born in such communities. This pattern of representation can be found in other countries at comparable stages in their political development. For example, in Yugoslavia during the 1940s, only 19 percent of the population lived in communities of more than 5,000 persons, yet 31 percent of the communist political leadership in 1948 came from urban communities.[2] The

---

*Tables composed of data on individuals holding one or more *high-level* offices from the MPBP omit opposition party leaders, deputies, and persons who have held only federal deputyships. These tables are intended to reflect data on only the highest levels of political leadership, and those who are or have been sympathetic to members of the official party. Until 1976, no opposition party member achieved an elective position beyond that of federal deputy. In 1976, PRI supported the candidacy of a Popular Socialist Party leader for Senator from Oaxaca, who, of course, won the election.

urbanization of Mexico's leadership, however, does seem to have occurred more rapidly than in other societies.

If we break down our officeholders into groups by the positions they held, there are several interesting patterns. For example, only 45 percent of all state governors from this same period (1935–76) came from urban communities. While this figure is still greater than the population in general, it is substantially less than for the general political elite in Mexico. This difference is the result of several factors in the career patterns of governors.

As public men move up into national vs state and local political office, or into more influential positions, urban backgrounds tend to become more common. Peter Smith's figures show that among a sample of over 2000 political elites, 40.5 percent were born in a state capital, 45.8 percent were born in a city or capital, and 23.4 percent were born in a metropolis. Among a selected group of 159 upper-level political elites, 51.1 percent were born in a state capital, 45.8 percent were born in a city or capital and 31.9 percent were born in a metropolis.[3]

Those positions having the highest percentage of officeholders with urban backgrounds are: National Action Party (PAN) leaders, Private Secretaries, Supreme Court Justices, Popular Sector (CNOP) leaders, Justices of the Superior Court of the Federal District and Federal Territories, and Agent of the *Ministerio Público* of the Attorney General of Mexico. The figure for PAN is not surprising, since a comparative study of PRI-PAN revealed that one of the basic differences between the two political groups is that PAN elites have always been urban[4] (Table 3.1). Comparing my sample with that of Wilfried Gruber, who looked at a much smaller, selected sample of cabinet secretaries in Mexico, we find that 79.7 percent of his sample were born in cities over 10,000 in population compared to my figure of 63.2 percent for all political elites.[5]

The urban background of political elites, when put into the context of the *camarilla* system in Mexico, has some added significance. My data make it obvious that the majority of political elites come from urban birthplaces and backgrounds. People from rural backgrounds have less opportunity to make contacts with future political leaders since so few future elites come from the rural areas. A rural person's contacts would be restricted to educational institutions and later career activities. In contrast, it is remarkable how many political leaders who grew up during the first three decades of this century in the state capitals became early friends of other successful public men.[6] As suggested in chapter ii, the importance of trust has been characteristic of Mexican political culture, and therefore, childhood friendships provide very strong bonds among future political leaders. Such friendships have characterized most recent Mexican presidents and some of their closest collaborators. For example, Miguel Alemán and his Director of the Federal

District Department, Casas Alemán, were childhood friends in Córdoba, Veracruz; and Luis Echeverría and his Secretary of the Treasury José López Portillo, knew each other as children in the Federal District.

It is also important to know that Mexico's political leadership is increasingly urban, because (as two recent studies show) Mexicans from urban areas are increasingly voting for parties other than the PRI.[7] Although urbanites lead the official party, it is the rural population that provides the main source of party support. This fact suggests, therefore, that Mexico's leadership is coming from areas that do not support the official party and this pattern *may* increase the possibility for increased alienation between rank and file members and their leaders. On the other hand, although Mexico's leadership is disproportionately urban in origin, when party leadership is compared with that of PAN, twice as many PRI leaders come from rural backgrounds as do PAN party leaders. As many of its critics suggest, PAN is a much more narrowly based party, giving little representation at its highest leadership levels to men and women from rural backgrounds. PRI, however, draws its leadership from a more representative sample of Mexico's general population.

Socioeconomic Background

A large number of political elites come from urban areas because these areas have provided far greater access to educational opportunities than outlying rural communities. Secondary, preparatory, and university education have

Table 3.1

Urban and Rural Birthplaces of Mexican Political Leaders by Various Career Positions

| | Birthplace | | | | |
| | Urban | | Rural | | Totals |
Career Position Held	No.	Percent	No.	Percent	No.
PAN Party Position[a]	22[b]	78.6	6	21.4	28
Private Secretary	54	71.1	22	28.9	76
Justice of the Supreme Ct	43	70.5	18	29.5	61
Justice of the Superior Ct of the Federal District	22	66.7	11	33.3	33
Popular Sector Leader of PRI	16	66.7	8	33.3	24
Agent of the Federal Attorney General	43	65.2	23	34.8	66
PPS Party Position[a]	15	62.5	9	37.5	24
PRI Party Position[a]	154	61.1	98	38.9	252
Oficial Mayor (federal)	76	60.3	50	39.7	126
Federal Deputy	184	57.5	136	42.5	320
Senator	125	54.6	104	45.4	229
Local Judge	31	54.4	26	45.6	57
State Judge	23	51.1	22	48.9	45
Secretary General (state)	45	48.4	48	51.6	93

[a]These refer to all positions on the national executive committees of the three parties and to the top two positions at the state level.
[b]Based on data in the MPBP.

been essential to the successful careers of public officeholders and these levels of education were generally unavailable to Mexicans born in rural areas between 1890 and 1940. In addition, the socioeconomic background of parents is critical in determining the birthplace and access to such education.

This background has eluded researchers because Mexicans rarely give out information on it. The paucity of social, economic, and political biographical data on Mexican leaders for example, obliges Gruber to leave socioeconomic background out of his conclusions for lack of sufficient information. Using the largest available sample of such data (318 cases from the political elites in MPBP), it can be concluded that 64.2 percent of the Mexican political elite had parents who had professional or middle-class occupations in business or government. In contrast, only 35.8 percent had parents who were engaged in manual or unskilled farming, commercial, and industrial occupations.

The overrepresentation of middle-class backgrounds among political leaders is not confined to Mexico. In the United States, during the early years of our political development, Aronson found that even through the Jackson years, three-fourths of American leaders were professional people from high social class positions.[8] In a study of contemporary North American leadership, Thomas Dye concluded that 61 percent of these men and women were from middle-class backgrounds, 25 percent from upper-class backgrounds, and only 5 percent from lower-class families.[9] Although one might expect lower-class representation, especially from farm backgrounds, to increase in countries advertising themselves as peasant and worker's governments, this is not the case. A study of the USSR's Politburo leadership concluded that the peasant class was not represented.[10] Moreover, well-organized and effective Communist Parties in other countries have also been led predominantly by those from middle-class backgrounds.[11]

Alfonso Pulido Islas, who has served in several subcabinet positions since 1935, is representative of the political leaders born during the years 1900 to 1910 of middle-class parents. He is typical of his generation in place of birth, level, type and location of education, and in his public career. His father's background and achievements in reaching middle-class status typify the experience of many of the parents of future political leaders born during these years. A brief biography of Eugenio Pulido Islas, Alfonso's father, is illustrative as a prototype of the middle-class background of many Mexican public men.

Eugenio worked as an agricultural laborer in his native village of Guachinango, Jalisco from the age of 8 until he was 18. He learned to plow the land with a team of oxen and a wooden plow, helping his own father support four brothers and three sisters. He also assisted his father in the part-time trade of carpentry.

At age 18, on his own initiative, he began to visit other nearby villages, trying to encounter better opportunities or to learn new skills which would increase his earnings. At this time, even though he had not had the opportunity to attend primary school, he taught himself to read and to write. He moved to the small community of La Estancia de los López, Nayarit, northwest of Jalisco, where he learned how to make saddles and musical instruments. It was here that he met Pulido Islas' mother, Rebecca, who married Eugenio and had six children, four boys and two girls. After he was married for several years, Eugenio took up the trade of photography.

In 1906, he decided to move to Ixtlán del Río, Nayarit, an important political municipality and a center for trade by muleback and coach between Guadalajara and the western coast. He continued his photographic trade, and soon learned the art of printing and bookbinding. These three trades produced enough income to make him a lower middle-class member of the community; and much later, he started a successful soap factory. About this time, Eugenio became a promoter of free primary education, establishing a school in his own home with volunteer teachers. In 1913, he founded the first community association in Ixtlán, and supported ideas for improving the city. Progressively his own cultural education continued to grow and reach new levels until he eventually became a part of the "elite" of that provincial community. Eugenio, like many heads of middle-class families during the first decade of this century, wanted a change in political administration. He repudiated the Porfiriato because it denied the signficance of democracy and sustained the privileges of the rich, especially the large landholders.

He was an early reader of Francisco Madero's *The Presidential Succession,* and as a result, founded and served on the Political Committee of Ixtlán del Río in favor of the Madero candidacy in 1910. In his photography shop, he made quantities of pictures of Madero plus a number of Madero buttons to be distributed free to the local inhabitants. Eugenio, like Madero, was a political democrat, and an anti-reelectionist with a moderate social ideology; he wanted a change in the political system and a suppression of the abuse of economic power, but not a change in its basic structure. He fought against the *"Odiosa"* (Hateful) dictatorship, but not against the liberal capitalist system. His small economic successes and moderate political and social views characterized many parents of political leaders born during the first decades of this century.

In the data set, cross-tabulation of parental social-economic status and urban-rural birthplace demonstrates a noticeable relationship between professional and middle-class occupations on the one hand, and urban birthplace on the other. Of those elites with middle-class and professional parents, 75.8 percent were born in urban communities, whereas only 46 percent of those with parents with manual occupations came from urban environments.

The higher up the political ladder one goes, the stronger the concurrence between parents' occupation and urban-rural birthplaces. For example, 72 percent of the *oficiales mayores*, who are the third-ranked officials in cabinet level agencies, and who would have more important positions than senators or federal deputies (excepting legislative leaders) are of middle- or upper-class socioeconomic backgrounds, while only 63 percent of all political elites in Mexico are of middle- or upper-class backgrounds. For the federal deputies and senators in the data set, parents' background is almost evenly divided between humble and middle-class backgrounds for all political leaders. Certain positions, such as union leaders, will also be less likely to have elites with high socioeconomic backgrounds. Of the 53 union leaders for which I have such information, 68 percent came from parents in humble occupations. In contrast, an examination of some prestigious positions (which require a certain level of education), such as a seat on the Supreme Court, demonstrates a sharp increase in high socioeconomic backgrounds of the officeholders, in this case 82 percent. These and other data in this chapter show that the Mexican political elite has been an elite for some time and that it is becoming more of an elite.

It is valuable to examine parents' background by various generations to determine if there has been a consistent pattern in middle-class dominance, or if it has changed over the years. Interestingly, the data in Table 3.2 shows a trend through 1920 of an increase in middle- and upper-class backgrounds among political elites, reaching an apex of 71 percent among the 1910–1919 generation. This generation would have been children of parents who had grown up and begun their careers under the Porfiriato. There is a significant decline in middle-class background among the generation of 1920–29, accounted for because of the tremendous development of education facilities under the Obregón-Calles regimes.[12] Furthermore, if we assume that the Revolution opened up opportunities for political careers to the uneducated because of battlefield exploits and their economic results, then the 1920–29 generation is in part the children of the uneducated survivors of the Revolution. By 1930, the brief influx of political elites with humble backgrounds ended, and the middle- and upper-class family backgrounds again became increasingly prevalent. The Revolution, then, provided social mobility for only a few years to political leaders who ruled after 1935.

Birthplace, Age, and Education

Table 3.3 illustrates the educational pattern of Mexican elites born in rural and urban communities. Elites from rural areas are much more likely to have lower levels of educational achievement. For those public men who have only achieved primary, secondary, preparatory, or normal schooling, there is a high incidence of rural background. On the other hand, beginning with a university education, the relationship immediately changes, and urban-born elites have higher percentages at the university and professional educational levels. Only 12 percent of the urban-born elites never reached a university, while the same was true of 35.5 percent of the rural-born group.

Arthur Liebman found this to be true of Latin American countries in general. "One major determinant of whether a Latin American reaches the university is place of residence. Latin Americans who reside in rural zones are less likely to attend a university than their counterparts in the urban areas of the same country. In fact, urban youth are more likely to attend a school at

Table 3.2

Class Background of Mexican Political Leaders by Age (Generation)[a]

| Date of Birth | Class Background of Parents[b] | | |
	Middle and Upper Class	Lower Class	Totals
Before 1880			
No. of political leaders	2	0	2
% of political leaders	100.0	0	100.0
1880 to 89			
No. of political leaders	13	10	23
% of political leaders	56.5	43.5	100.0
1890 to 99			
No. of political leaders	37	33	70
% of political leaders	52.9	47.1	100.0
1900 to 09			
No. of political leaders	53	29	82
% of political leaders	64.4	35.4	100.0
1910 to 19			
No. of political leaders	36	15	51
% of political leaders	70.6	29.4	100.0
1920 to 29			
No. of political leaders	22	16	38
% of political leaders	57.9	42.1	100.0
1930 to 39			
No. of political leaders	22	8	30
% of political leaders	73.3	26.7	100.0
1940 to present			
No. of political leaders	4	0	4
% of political leaders	100.0	0	100.0
Sub-totals			
No. of political leaders	189	111	300
% of political leaders	63.0	37.0	100.0

[a]In this chapter we will use generation synonymously with date of birth. This table includes opposition party leaders and deputies.

[b]I have classified parents into two categories: lower- or middle- and upper-class. The rationale for this is that in Mexico, a person who is middle class is, relatively speaking, rich, particularly when we talk about a cultural environment which has made education available to that person's children. Therefore, in those cases where a professional person earned very little money, I have still classified the family as middle class. Lower denotes those persons who have earned a living through manual occupations or the performance of unskilled services, such as laborer, peasant, porter, mule driver, etc. I realize that the large number of missing observations from our socio-economic-status sample makes it susceptible to criticism. However, I believe that my interviews with Mexican public men and the Smith data confirm my conclusion that most public men come from middle-class backgrounds in Mexico.

any level. Thus, in Latin America, as of 1960, 25 percent of all rural children in the age group from 7 to 14 attended school, compared to 56 percent of urban youth in the same age group."[13] Evidence of this in Mexico can be seen in the data presented by Guy Benveniste, which shows that in the first grade slightly more rural students than urban students begin school in Mexico, but by the second grade, they are already attending school in smaller numbers than students in urban locations. On reaching the sixth grade, for each rural student attending classes, there were five urban students in 1965.[14]

Birthplace has not only had an impact on the level of education of public men in Mexico; it has also had an interesting impact on the type of degree completed by such persons. In only two areas, agricultural engineering and law, do rural-born political leaders exceed urban-born leaders on a percentage basis of those who had a professional degree. Agricultural engineering is the only field which rural-born leaders numerically dominate. With the exception of law, the other traditional fields (medicine and civil engineering)

Table 3.3

Birthplace and Level of Education of Mexican Political Leaders[a]

Level of Education Reached	Type of Birthplace		Totals
	Rural	Urban	
Primary			
No. of political leaders	27	11	38
% of political leaders	8.6	2.0	
Secondary			
No. of political leaders	36	19	55
% of political leaders	11.5	3.5	
Preparatory			
No. of political leaders	18	15	33
% of political leaders	5.8	2.8	
Normal			
No. of political leaders	30	20	50
% of political leaders	9.6	3.7	
University			
No. of political leaders	162	322	484
% of political leaders	51.8	59.9	
Post-professional			
No. of political leaders	11	33	44
% of political leaders	3.5	6.1	
M.A.			
No. of political leaders	5	23	28
% of political leaders	1.6	4.3	
Ph.D. or LL.D.			
No. of political leaders	11	49	60
% of political leaders	3.5	9.1	
M.D. or D.D.			
No. of political leaders	13	46	59
% of political leaders	4.2	8.6	
Sub-totals			
No. of political leaders	313 (36.8%)	538 (63.2%)	851 (100%)
% of political leaders	100.1[b]	100.0	

[a]This table includes opposition party leaders, and deputies. The data are from the MPBP.
[b]This figure does not total 100.0 due to rounding.

show no significant differences. The most striking differences show up in the urban-born leaders' domination over new professional fields, particularly accounting, architecture, and economics. In recent years, these fields have had an increased importance among political leaders in Mexico. The fact that only six individuals with rural backgrounds in the MPBP received degrees in these three professions suggests still another reason why urban-born leaders have an advantage over their rural-born counterparts.

Other variables have also affected the education of Mexico's political elite, including age, state, and region of birth. If we break down educational levels of political elites into nine categories—primary, secondary, preparatory, normal, university, post-professional, Masters, Ph.D. or LL.D., and M.D. or D.D.—we can see some specific as well as general trends in the education of various generations. Of the 88 elites born since 1930, all finished primary school and all but one finished secondary, and only 3 percent terminated their education at the preparatory school; thus, 91 percent obtained university educations.

Normal school has always provided an alternative for the Mexican who lacks sufficient funds or preparation to go through the college preparatory programs and then toward a professional degree. Not surprisingly, there was a sizeable increase of students receiving normal degrees after 1915 (Table 3.4). This trend continued among students attending school between 1925 and 1934, a time when great emphasis was placed on educational opportunities, and when many children whose parents had no formal education suddenly had access to such schools. Like other forms of pre-professional education, normal degrees then began to decline and by the generation of 1940, they too disappeared as part of the training of political elites.

An excellent example of a political leader from such a background is Carlos Hank González, who worked with his step-father as a shoemaker to continue his secondary education. Later, he attended the regional normal school at Toluca, México, becoming president of the student association. From that position, he was elected as Secretary General of the Youth Federation of the State of México at the age of seventeen, the first of many local party and administrative positions. He ultimately served as Governor of México from 1969 to 1975, and despite his German father, he was considered by some observers to have been a pre-candidate for President in 1975–1976. López Portillo appointed him as head of the Federal District Department, an important cabinet-level position, in 1976.

University education became more important as a prerequisite to reaching elite status after the Revolution. Whereas 63.5 percent of those elites born in the decade of the 1880s had university educations, 100 percent of those born after 1940 did (Table 3.4). However, there is one important age group paralleling the normal school generation, born between 1900 and 1909, whose

Table 3.4

Numbers of Political Leaders, by Generation, Completing Various Education Levels

Date of Birth (generation)	Primary	Secondary	Preparatory	Normal	University	Post Prof.	M.A.	Ph.D., LL.D.	M.D., D.D.	Totals[a]
Level of Education Reached										
Before 1880										
No. of political leaders	0	2	0	0	9	0	0	0	2	13
% of political leaders	0	15.4	0	0	69.2	0	0	0	15.4	100.0
1880 to 89										
No. of political leaders	9	7	5	2	30	1	0	2	7	63
% of political leaders	14.3	11.1	7.9	3.2	47.6	1.6	0	3.2	11.1	100.0
1890 to 99										
No. of political leaders	18	32	9	7	91	8	3	9	15	192
% of political leaders	9.4	16.7	4.7	3.6	47.4	4.2	1.6	4.7	7.8	100.1[b]
1900 to 09										
No. of political leaders	6	8	10	15	156	7	2	16	15	235
% of political leaders	2.6	3.4	4.3	6.4	66.4	3.0	0.9	6.8	6.4	100.2[b]
1910 to 19										
No. of political leaders	4	3	8	13	100	7	6	12	15	168
% of political leaders	2.4	1.8	4.8	7.7	59.5	4.2	3.6	7.1	8.9	100.0
1920 to 29										
No. of political leaders	2	4	1	6	63	10	4	11	3	104
% of political leaders	1.9	3.8	1.0	5.8	60.6	9.6	3.8	10.6	2.9	100.0
1930 to 39										
No. of political leaders	0	1	3	4	46	8	12	8	2	84
% of political leaders	0	1.2	3.6	4.8	54.8	9.5	14.3	9.5	2.4	100.1[b]
1940 to present										
No. of political leaders	0	0	0	0	2	2	0	0	0	4
% of political leaders	0	0	0	0	50.0	50.0	0	0	0	100.0
Subtotals										
No. of political leaders	39	57	36	47	497	43	27	58	59	863
% of political leaders	4.5	6.6	4.2	5.4	57.6	5.0	3.1	6.7	6.8	99.9[b]

[a]The numbers and percentages in each category under level of education will vary from table to table since all tables include data only from those cases where information is known for both variables.

[b]These figures do not total 100.0 due to rounding.

university education jumped 18 percent in a decade. Again, this seems due largely to the educational opportunities first made available by the Revolution to the generations of students attending classes from 1915 to 1925, the generation dominating Mexican public life from 1935 to the present. The data for the pre-1880 generation are interesting because they show a higher educational level which was unequaled until 1920 (Table 3.4). The percentage figure of 84.6 (eleven men with degrees) does not indicate a pre-Revolutionary generation that goes against the general trends described above; rather it is an exceptional generation of 13 men who survived the Porfiriato (they were between the ages of 31 and 41 in 1911) to serve in Revolutionary governments in old age. In effect, this indicates that these men had the formal educational skills (as well as political ones) needed to make the transition from a pre-Revolutionary to a post-Revolutionary government.

Age alone is an interesting variable among political elites. What is most remarkable about administrations from 1934 to 1964 is that each administration had a predominance of officeholders from the same or next youngest generation as that of the administration preceeding it (Table 3.5).

Table 3.5

First-Time High-Level Officeholders by Generation and Administration[a]

Administration in Which First Position Was Held[b]	Generation								
	Before 1880	1880– 1889	1890– 1899	1900– 1909	1910– 1919	1920– 1929	1930– 1939	1940– present	Totals
1935 to 40									
No. of officeholders	10	35	91	27	5	0	0	0	168
% of officeholders	6.0	**20.8**	**54.2**	16.1	3.0	0	0	0	100.1[c]
1940 to 46									
No. of officeholders	2	18	48	36	4	0	0	0	108
% of officeholders	1.9	16.7	**44.4**	**33.3**	3.7	0	0	0	100.0
1946 to 52									
No. of officeholders	0	8	25	48	22	2	0	0	105
% of officeholders	0	7.6	**23.8**	**45.7**	21.0	1.9	0	0	100.0
1952 to 58									
No. of officeholders	1	4	15	31	17	7	0	0	75
% of officeholders	1.3	5.3	20.0	**41.3**	**22.7**	9.3	0	0	99.9[c]
1958 to 64									
No. of officeholders	0	3	10	29	33	8	0	0	83
% of officeholders	0	3.6	12.0	**34.9**	**39.8**	9.6	0	0	99.9[c]
1964 to 70									
No. of officeholders	0	1	4	18	28	28	10	0	89
% of officeholders	0	1.1	4.5	20.2	**31.5**	**31.5**	11.2	0	100.0
1970 to 76									
No. of officeholders	0	1	1	9	22	32	50	11	126
% of officeholders	0	0.8	0.8	7.1	17.5	**25.4**	**39.7**	8.8	100.1[c]
Subtotals									
No. of officeholders	13	70	194	198	131	77	60	11	754
% of officeholders	1.7	9.3	25.7	26.3	17.4	10.2	8.0	1.5	100.1[c]

[a]The figures in this table exclude opposition party leaders and federal deputies.
[b]Data are from the MPBP.
[c]These figures do not total 100.0 due to rounding.

This is a consistent pattern; for example, Cárdenas drew most of his collaborators from the 1890 and the 1880 group, and Ávila Camacho from the 1900 and 1890 group. In effect, these data suggest that a single generation has dominated each two successive presidential administrations in Mexico since 1935. The 1890 generation controlled the Cárdenas and Ávila Camacho administrations, the 1900 generation the Alemán and Ruiz Cortines administrations, and the 1910 generation the López Mateos and Díaz Ordaz administrations. In 1970, however, this pattern was suddenly broken, and the impressionistic assumptions of most observers that President Echeverría was appointing young persons to high-level offices is borne out rather clearly in our data. Echeverría neglected his own generation (1920) for the younger 1930 generation, selecting 50 (or 40 percent) of his collaborators from this group. This is the first time since 1935 that a single generation did not dominate two successive administrations. However, López Portillo, who was from the same generation as Echeverría, went back to their generation (1920) for the majority of his collaborators, thus ignoring many of the younger leaders recruited by his predecessor, and reverting to the pattern of Presidents prior to Echeverría.

The state or region where an elite is born also has some effect on the level, type, and location of his education. Not surprisingly, the vast majority of political elites, 73.3 percent, went to public primary and secondary schools. This figure indicates that most middle- and upper-class parents were sending their children to public schools during the first third of the 20th century. If we break down primary and secondary public vs private education by region of birth, the only significant pattern appears in the data for the Federal District. The Federal District, which has been the most developed region in Mexico since 1900, had the greatest number of private schools available to parents of political elites.[15] In contrast to all other regions in Mexico, where at least 70 percent of the elites attended public schools, in the Federal District the figure was only 53.6 percent during the years 1880 to 1945.

If we examine each region in Mexico for the level of education reached by political elites, we find several interesting patterns. I would have hypothesized that the higher the level of economic development in each region, the higher the access to education; and therefore, educational achievement for political elites from those regions would also be higher. However, this pattern does not hold true. Instead, except for the Federal District, where 95 percent of the elites had at least a university education, the other wealthy regions in Mexico, the North and the West, had the lowest levels of educational achievement.

Why has this pattern occurred in Mexico? The variable which appears to be more important than economic development is the presence of a prestigious regional institution that has made preparatory and university education available without costly travel expenses and residence in an urban location. Except for universities in the Federal District, the most attractive preparatory schools in Mexico have been the Institute of Art and Sciences, Oaxaca; the Colegio de San Nicolás (the University of Michoacán), Morelia; the University of Guadalajara; the University of Veracruz, Jalapa; and the University of Puebla. The most attractive *regional* universities were Guadalajara, San Nicolás, Guanajuato, Yucatán, Campeche, Chihuahua, Veracruz, Puebla, and Oaxaca—in that order. These state universities, with the exception of the University of Guadalajara and the University of Chihuahua, are located in regions whose elites ranked high in levels of education (Table 3.6).

The North and West, which are the two regions next highest in economic development after the Federal District, have had the fewest public university programs from 1900 to 1930. Although the Colegio Civil of Monterrey was located in Nuevo León (today the University of Nuevo León), it

Table 3.6

Level of Education of Mexican Political Leaders by Their Region of Birth

| Region of Birth[a] | Level of Education | | | |
	Primary, Secondary & Normal	Preparatory	University and Post Professional	Totals
Federal District				
No. of leaders	5	1	133	139
% of leaders	3.6	.7	95.7	100.0
South				
No. of leaders	12	2	83	97
% of leaders	12.4	2.1	85.5	100.0
Gulf				
No. of leaders	18	5	94	117
% of leaders	15.3	4.3	80.4	100.0
East Central				
No. of leaders	23	6	101	130
% of leaders	17.7	4.6	77.7	100.0
West Central				
No. of leaders	28	6	108	142
% of leaders	19.6	4.2	76.2	100.0
North				
No. of leaders	34	9	104	147
% of leaders	23.2	6.1	70.7	100.0
West				
No. of leaders	31	7	88	126
% of leaders	24.6	5.6	69.8	100.0
Subtotals[b]				
No. of leaders	151	36	711	898
% of leaders	16.8	4.0	79.2	100.0

[a]Regional divisions are as follows: **North,** Baja California del Norte, Chihuahua, Coahuila, Nuevo León, Sonora and Tamaulipas; **West,** Aguascalientes, Baja California del Sur, Colima, Durango, Jalisco, Nayarit, and Sinaloa; **West Central,** Guanajuato, México, Michoacán, and Morelos; **East Central,** Hidalgo, Puebla, Querétaro, San Luis Potosí, Tlaxcala and Zacatecas; **South,** Chiapas, Guerrero and Oaxaca; **Gulf,** Campeche, Quintana Roo, Tabasco, Veracruz and Yucatán; **Federal District.**
[b]This table includes opposition party leaders and federal deputies from the MPBP.

did not graduate many students, particularly at the professional level, before 1930. Prior to 1930, most students who attended the University of Nuevo León completed their preparatory degrees and went on to national universities.[17] On the other hand, the University of Guadalajara is located in the West and has been very prominent in the education of political leaders in Mexico. However, the western region of Mexico includes seven states (Table 3.6), and only one, Jalisco, has had a major university. Furthermore, although both the University of Neuvo León and the University of Guadalajara have grown since the 1930s to become the largest state universities in Mexico, they are located in regions which have traditionally been the source of many opposition party leaders from the National Action Party. In the 1920s, for example, many of the Catholic Youth leaders, some of whom participated in the anti-government Cristero rebellion, were students at the University of Guadalajara.[18] Since the 1940s, these two public institutions have received competition from the two largest private universities in Mexico: the Institute of Technology and Higher Education of Monterrey (ITESM) and the Autonomous University of Guadalajara. Graduates from both of these institutions have not gone into politics.

The high educational level for the Gulf Region is explained by the predominance of three regional universities contributing to the education of political leaders from Campeche, Yucatán and Veracruz (see Table 3.7). The South, which has had only one university strongly represented among political leaders probably ranks second to the Federal District because of the attention given to that state in the field of education by Porfirio Díaz, a native of Oaxaca. In 1900, when primary school attendance was at a level of about 25 percent for most states in Mexico, Oaxaca had the single highest rate of primary school attendance at a level of 60 percent.[19] Therefore, many more Oaxacans were eligible to continue their education than elsewhere in Mexico. Today, however, Oaxaca ranks among the lowest of Mexican states in social and economic variables of development.

Unlike the United States, where university education is widely dispersed, Mexico's students are concentrated in a few institutions that are regionally or nationally important. This is true throughout Latin America. The Liebman study notes that ''as of 1966 higher education in Latin America was still a major city or capital city phenomenon. In 50 percent of the countries more than three-quarters of the students attended the principal university of that country, located in the capital. In over 85 percent of the countries, one-third or more of the students attended the country's major university located in the capital, while many of the remaining students attended other universities in the same city.''[20] In the United States, however, Thomas Dye found that 44 percent of the college-educated elites graduated from 12 prestigious universities, a figure equivalent to the percentage of educated Mexican leaders graduating just from the National University.[21]

If a region does not have a well-established institution of higher learning, students tend to go directly to the National University rather than to another nearby regional institution. Charles Myers notes the drawing power of Mexico City during the years of our study: "Between the end of the Revolution and 1940, the District maintained and probably increased its dominance of the manpower resources of the nation. Capacity in middle and higher education was even more heavily concentrated in the capital city in

Table 3.7

First-Time High-Level Officeholders by Administration and Region of Birth

Administration in Which 1st High-Level Office Was Held	Region of Birth							
	Fed. Dist.	East C.	West	North	South	Gulf	West C.	Totals
1935 to 40 Cárdenas								
No. of officeholders	13	34	30	24	17	21	38	177
% of officeholders	7.3	19.2	16.9	13.6	9.6	11.9	21.5	100.0
1940 to 46 Ávila Camacho								
No. of officeholders	13	21	14	19	11	13	20	111
% of officeholders	11.7	18.9	12.6	17.1	9.9	11.7	18.0	99.9c
1946 to 52 Alemán								
No. of officeholders	12	16	14	26	10	12	19	109
% of officeholders	11.0	14.7	12.8	23.9	9.2	11.0	17.4	100.0
1952 to 58 Ruiz Cortines								
No. of officeholders	6	11	10	12	13	19	10	81
% of officeholders	7.4	13.6	12.3	14.8	16.0	23.5	12.3	99.9c
1958 to 64 López Mateos								
No. of officeholders	9	15	8	16	12	13	12	85
% of officeholders	10.6	17.6	9.4	18.8	14.1	15.3	14.1	99.9c
1964 to 70 Díaz Ordaz								
No. of officeholders	20	12	16	15	5	14	14	96
% of officeholders	20.8	12.5	16.7	15.6	5.2	14.6	14.6	100.0
1970 to 76 Echeverría								
No. of officeholders	34	16	19	18	13	14	12	126
% of officeholders	27.0	12.7	15.1	14.3	10.3	11.1	9.5	100.0
Subtotals								
No. of officeholders	107	125	111	130	81	106	125	785d
% of officeholders	13.6	15.9	14.1	16.6	10.3	13.5	15.9	99.9c
Population 1950 Censusa								
% of officeholders	11.8	17.7	14.1	14.7	12.6	11.9	17.1	99.9c
Population 1910 Censusb								
% of officeholders	4.7	21.6	16.0	11.1	13.7	11.6	21.3	100.0

aThis census is representative of the years when most elites served in office.
bThis census is closest to the birthdate of 69 percent of the leaders in our sample.
cThese figures do not total 100.0 due to rounding.
dThis table excludes opposition party leaders and federal deputies. The data are taken from the MPBP.

these years than in later ones, and it is unlikely that a large percentage of the graduates settled elsewhere. There was, in addition, some migration to the District of people who had graduated from institutions in the states and territories.''[22] This general pattern is borne out by our data on political leaders. The National University in Mexico City, which is the most prestigious school in Mexico, attracts more students who become political leaders from all regions than any other school, and it attracts a higher percentage from within its own region than does any other school.

Three-quarters of all political leaders born in the Federal District in our data set attended the National University, and more than half of those born in other states left their home regions to attend the National University. Furthermore, other institutions in the Federal District, including the National Military Academy, the National Polytechnic Institute, and the Mexican Institute of Technology account for another five percent of regional students leaving their home states for an education. In fact, of the 127 political leaders in our study born in the Federal District who received a higher education, only three left the District to attend school elsewhere. Future political leaders seem to know the value of attending the National University for their political careers since while this same pattern exists for the general student population at the National University, their representation is more exaggerated. In 1925, when Mexico City had approximately 6 percent of the population, 25 percent of the National Law School graduates were born in the capital. In the 1960s, when Mexico City accounted for approximately 14 percent of the population, 59 percent of all students at the National University were natives of the capital.[23]

Can it be determined whether or not certain states or regions have been favored in the selection process of political elites in Mexico? If all political elites in our sample where regional background is known are examined, it can be seen that during the time our elites held office, they provided a very representative sample of the total population. In fact, the only area which might be described as having been well over-represented has been the Federal District, with 13.6 percent of the total but only 11.8 percent of the population as of 1950, and the North, with 16.6 percent of the elites but only 14.7 percent of the population (Table 3.7). In general, except for those regions, prospective elites have not benefited significantly by being born in one region versus another. However, if we look at first-time officeholders *by administration,* excluding federal deputies and opposition party leaders, we find several other patterns. During the last two administrations, there has been an overwhelming concentration of political leadership from the Federal District. This cannot be explained by the fact that Echeverría was born in the Federal District since President Díaz Ordaz started this trend and he was from Puebla. This overwhelming concentration from the Federal District has been continued and increased during the first year of the López Portillo administration. Furthermore, political elites from the North would have had a much better chance of obtaining office in the administration of Miguel Alemán, and to a lesser extent, under López Mateos. The only President other than Echeverría and López Portillo who excessively overrepresented his own region was Adolfo Ruiz Cortines, 1952–58, who favored the Gulf region with 23.5 percent of his appointees.

If we reduce our sample to a much more selective group of elites, that is, to those 212 persons who have held three or more political positions ranging from federal senator to president, we find only one region, the West Central, strongly overrepresented among the elites during the period 1935 to 1975. This dominant pattern continued to be true for the Revolutionary Family, of which 20 percent came from the West Central region.

An examination of birthplace patterns of elites by states rather than regions reveals an entirely different pattern. Seven states in Mexico have been favored by a margin of at least 25 percent in excess of their population in 1950. Those states were: Campeche, Tabasco, and Quintana Roo (Gulf); Colima and Baja California del Sur (West); and Coahuila and Sonora (North). Three states were underrepresented by at least the same margin: Jalisco (West), México (West Central), and Puebla (East Central).*

The overrepresentation of certain regions, particularly the capital city and the entity in which it is located, is true of many other countries, particularly when the political capital is also the dominant social and commercial center. For example, Joel Verner found that Guatemala City is the source of most high-level bureaucrats in Guatemala; and Paul Lewis, in his study of Spanish cabinet ministers, found both New Castile and Madrid to be overrepresented.[24]

Careers

To complete our composite picture of those who get to the top, we need to analyze the career background and the educational levels of all political elites or various subcategories of elites to determine any predominant patterns.

---

*It can be argued that by including all governors in our sample, we have overrepresented the smaller states. If we look only at political elites holding three or more offices, eliminating governors who have held only that position, we encounter the following distribution by state: Aguascalientes, Colima, BCS (West); Guanajuato (West Central); Campeche (Gulf) and Querétaro (East Central) were overrepresented. States which were underrepresented included: Tamaulipas and Baja California del Norte (North); Yucatán (Gulf); Oaxaca (South); Puebla (East Central), and the Federal District. The only states appearing consistently in both groups were Baja California del Sur as overrepresented and Puebla as underrepresented. Again, we do not perceive any apparent pattern. For a discussion of possible political and economic implications of regional and state birthplaces, see my "A Reexamination of Political Leadership and Allocation of Federal Revenues in Mexico, 1934–73," *Journal of Developing Areas* **10** (January 1976).

Of the various career patterns we might look at, one of particular interest to students of Mexico has been a military career. By and large, the men who fought the Revolution and became the first governors of the post-revolutionary period were military men. This career provided access to high political office for many persons in the 1930s, but as we shall see, elites with military careers began to decline rapidly by 1940. In fact, well over half of all elites having military careers served before 1940, when the last president with a military background held office (Table 3.8).

The clearest example of a successful officer in public life is Rodolfo Sánchez Taboada, who completed his second year of medical studies at the University of Puebla before joining the Revolution in 1915. As an army officer, he became known to Lázaro Cárdenas, and became his assistant. In 1935, Cárdenas appointed him Director of the important Presidential Complaints Department. After completing that job in 1937, he held first rank positions (Governor of Baja California del Sur, President of the National Executive Committee of PRI, Secretary of the Navy) until he died in office in

Table 3.8

Political Leaders Who Were Military Officers by Number of Times They Held Office and Administration[a]

Administration in Which Office Was Held	Number of Times in Office				
	1st Time	2nd Time	3rd Time	4th Time	5th Time
1935 to 1940					
No. of military officers[b]	46	10	3	0	0
% of military officers[c]	25.4	24.4	30.0	0	0
1940 to 1946					
No. of military officers	22	15	3	2	0
% of military officers	19.5	22.7	10.7	28.6	0
1946 to 1952					
No. of military officers	10	6	3	0	0
% of military officers	8.8	8.3	11.1	0	0
1952 to 1958					
No. of military officers	9	6	3	2	1
% of military officers	10.6	10.7	7.9	15.4	12.5
1958 to 1964					
No. of military officers	15	5	2	1	0
% of military officers	16.3	9.4	5.4	4.5	0
1964 to 1970					
No. of military officers	5	8	2	2	3
% of military officers	4.9	11.1	5.4	7.4	15.8
1970 to 1976					
No. of military officers	8	2	4	0	0
% of military officers	6.1	2.6	9.8	0	0
Totals					
No. of military officers	115	52	20	7	4
% of military officers	14.1	11.9	9.1	6.9	7.8

[a]This table excludes opposition party leaders and federal deputies. The data are taken from the MPBP.

[b]For the purposes of this study, a military officer is defined as an individual who made the military a full-time career and reached the rank of major or higher.

[c]Percentages reflect the number of leaders who were officers in each category divided by the total number of leaders in that category.

1955. All of these offices were appointive, and although he mixed party with administrative positions, he never held any local positions. As President of the National Executive Committee of PRI from 1946 to 1952, he started one of the most influential *camarillas* in contemporary Mexican politics.

Overall, there has been a general decline in the number of military officers becoming political elites from the Cárdenas to the Echeverría administration. Only seven (and two were Presidents) of the 129 men with military careers succeeded in reaching membership in the small group of the Revolutionary Family (102 elites holding four or more high-level positions between 1935 and 1975). In fact, of those elites (220) who have held three or more high-level positions in Mexico, only 20 or 9 percent were men with military backgrounds. In the last 40 years, only 14 percent of all political elites have had military careers.

Several conclusions can be reached from the decline in military officers holding high-level political offices. Perhaps most important, the military no longer serves as prime recruiter for men with political ambitions, nor does it provide an alternate route for those unlikely to pass through more typical careers. The decline in military officers contributes to the increased homogeneity of Mexico's political leadership. In a speculative vein, Mexico's political leadership, while professionalizing the military and pacifying its role in politics, has increasingly lost contact with its leadership and has made the military's political activities less visible. As Evelyn Stevens suggested, Cárdenas' purpose "in creating a special sector for the military men as a group, but most particularly for officers, had been to bring them into the open and force them to channel their political activities through the Party, where they could be controlled by the checks and balances provided by the other sectors."[25] In losing their visibility, both their actions and motives may become less known to political leaders, a situation which might permit the military to become more involved, rather than less involved, in public affairs.[26] As one student of military affairs concluded, the "key to non-intervention, then, based upon the Mexican experience, is to keep the Army involved in politics."[27] Its involvement, however, measured in political leadership, has diminished rapidly in recent years.

Excluding military careers, there are other career paths frequently followed by most political elites. They can be generally divided into two categories: state and local, and national. Within these two categories are two subcategories: 1) party, union, and elective and 2) administrative. Many political elites have followed a consistent pattern of a combination of a geographic plus an occupational category, for example, national-administrative. Among positions we would consider in the state and local category are, in order of their importance: governor, secretary general, state party president, state attorney general, mayor, state judge, state deputy, local judge, and councilman.

If we examine the most important local position, that of mayor, we find that only 50 or 6 percent of the more than 800 high officeholders held this position. Again, as was true of military men, only 4 or 4 percent of the members of the Revolutionary Family had been mayors. Local elective office has not been a very common experience for national political leadership. In contrast, 11 percent of all governors, the most important state political leader, have been mayors. This pattern is probably due both to the centralized nature of policy making in Mexico, where decision making resides in the hands of federal officeholders, and to the dominance of a single political group that controls the recruitment process. For example, in India, a country in which local leadership is much more competitive and has more prestige, over a third of the cabinet members have had this kind of experience before taking a cabinet post.[28]

Of the state and local positions mentioned above, the most important administrative as opposed to elective position is that of secretary general, appointed by the governor and serving as his second-in-command. Slightly over 10 percent of the government political leaders have held this position, although it has become much less important among those leaders born after 1920. In fact, there appears to be a decline in the percentage of most local positions held by national political leaders, since the same pattern is true for leaders who were state (4.8 percent) and local judges (6.4 percent) after 1920.

An excellent example of a political elite who reached the top through a state administrative career is Mario G. Rebolledo Fernández, who has served on the Supreme Court since 1955. A native of Jalapa, Veracruz, he completed his schooling and professional studies there, graduating with a degree in law in 1935. He became a state judicial agent in Veracruz and was promoted to Assistant to the State Attorney General before becoming an appeals court judge. The governor then appointed him as President of the State Board of Conciliation and Arbitration, in charge of settling labor-management disputes. He temporarily left his career in the judicial branch to become director of the most important state administrative agency, the Department of Government. After serving there, he became a state superior court justice and then Attorney General of Veracruz. Later he served as Secretary General of Government before moving to Mexico City to fill his first national position as Judge of the 15th Penal District in the Federal District. Before receiving an appointment as a Justice of the Supreme Court, he served on the Superior Court of the Federal District and Federal Territories. Of the four career patterns we suggested for national political elites, this pattern is the least common, although it is frequently followed by Superior and Supreme Court Justices.

A more common state and local pattern followed by national political elites before moving into positions in both categories at the national level is a combination of party-elective and administrative posts. Enrique Rodríguez

Cano, a close collaborator of President Ruiz Cortines, demonstrates this more typical pattern in his own career. He first served as a tax agent in Alamo, Veracruz, became active in local politics, and was elected mayor of the important town of Tuxpan from 1936 to 1938. In 1938, he moved to Jalapa, where he worked for the state legislature. Later, he became a state deputy and head of the state legislature under Ruiz Cortines, and then served as Secretary General of the League of Agrarian Communities for Veracruz in 1946. In 1948, he served as Subsecretary of Government for the state, and then was elected as a Federal Deputy. He did not complete his term before going to the Federal District as the *Oficial Mayor* of the Secretariat of Government in 1951. After Ruiz Cortines was elected President in 1952, Rodríguez Cano became his Secretary of the Presidency.

On the national level, the most important positions below the sub-cabinet level in order of importance have been: *oficial mayor,* senator, deputy, and agent of the *ministerio público* (under the Attorney General of Mexico or the Federal District). The latter is the most common *initial position* (7.6 percent) held by public men (Table 3.9). The position, which is not even mentioned in the standard works on Mexico, deserves considerable attention, since it has served as a proving ground for the talents of many distinguished men, and has served as a basis for the development of a *camarilla* of more than one attorney general.

Probably the most interesting group of agents under the Attorney General for the Federal District served during the administration of José Aguilar y

Table 3.9

Previous Positions Held by Political Leaders by the Number of Times They Held Office[a]

Previous Positions Held by Political Leaders	Number of Times in Office							
	1st Time		2nd Time		3rd Time		4th Time	
	No.	%	No.	%	No.	%	No.	%
Local								
District Judge	55	6.7[b]	37	8.4	27	12.4	13	12.9
Mayor	50	6.1	25	5.7	7	3.2	4	4.0
State								
Secretary General	93	11.4	62	14.2	36	16.5	22	21.8
State Party Leader	28	3.4	16	3.7	7	3.2	3	3.0
State Deputy	71	8.7	37	8.5	16	7.3	9	9.0
National								
Federal Deputy	323	45.0	164	37.4	86	39.4	40	39.6
Oficial Mayor	130	15.9	89	20.3	51	23.4	28	27.7
Agent of the Attorney General	61	7.5	41	9.4	26	11.9	17	16.8
Union Leader	96	11.7	61	13.9	30	13.8	22	21.8
Total sample	818 (100%)		438 (100%)		218 (100%)		101 (100%)	

[a]This table excludes opposition party leaders and federal deputies. The data are taken from the MPBP.

[b]Percentages reflect the number of leaders who held these offices in each category divided by the total number of leaders in that category.

Maya, from 1928 to 1930. Aguilar y Maya recruited the following young law graduates to his agency: Nicéforo Guerrero, José Hernández Delgado, Luis Garrido, Raúl Carrancá y Trujillo, Ángel Carvajal, and Andrés Serra Rojas. The first two followed him as Attornies General of the Federal District, in 1930 and 1931 respectively, and both became prominent national public figures during the 1940s and 1950s. Nicéforo Guerrero also became part of Aguilar y Maya's political clique, which controlled Guanajuato state politics for many years. The next two men distinguished themselves in the field of law and academics, Garrido becoming Rector of the National University and Carrancá y Trujillo his Secretary General. The last two, who were members of the 1925 (UNAM) generation, both became Assistant Attornies General of Mexico, and cabinet secretaries under Alemán. The position of *agente público* was particularly important for those generations born between 1900 and 1920, and has declined considerably in importance since 1920.

The other administrative position of importance, that of *oficial mayor,* has been held by 130 persons in our sample. However, since it is a position that is included as part of our sample, this is not a revealing figure. Instead, let us examine those persons who have held two or more positions to find out how important this position is in the career patterns of higher elites. Of the 438 elites in this category, 89 or 20 percent have been *oficiales mayores*. What is particularly important is that 28 or 28 percent of the Revolutionary Family and 18 or 44 percent of the 5th-time officeholders have held this position. This position, then, is increasingly present in the career patterns of those political leaders who are most successful.

Illustrative of the importance of this position to successful public men is its presence in the careers of most recent Presidents. Ávila Camacho was *Oficial Mayor* of the Secretariat of National Defense in 1933, his first national administrative position. Ruiz Cortines' first national position was also as *Oficial Mayor,* but of the Department of the Federal District. He also served in the same position in the Secretariat of Government in 1940. In 1958, Gustavo Díaz Ordaz used this same position as a stepping stone to the position of Secretary of Government. Luis Echeverría also held his first high-level office as *Oficial Mayor* of Public Education.

In general, the career paths followed most frequently by political elites in Mexico includes only national-administrative positions. Antonio Carrillo Flores, a well-known international statesman, who was a pre-candidate for President of Mexico, illustrates the career path of a successful, repeating officeholder. On the recommendation of his professors, he became a young agent of José Aguilar y Maya in 1930. He was then promoted, becoming Director of the Legal Department of the Office of the Attorney General of Mexico in 1931 and in 1934; he left that office in 1933 to serve as Secretary of the Supreme Court. In 1935, he became Director of the Department of Legal Affairs for the Secretariat of the Treasury, and in 1937 he became a founding

Justice of the Federal Tax Court. The following year, he served as an advisor to the Bank of Mexico, and then took over the important post of Director of Credit for the Secretariat of the Treasury (this position is now a subsecretary-ship), until he became Dean of the National School of Law in 1944. When he was appointed Director General of the National Finance Bank *(Nacional Financiera)* in 1945 at the age of 37, he was destined to serve in such top-rank positions until 1970.

If we look at our other subcategory, elective national positions, we find that the single most frequent position among all high-level political leaders is that of federal deputy, held by 323 or 45 percent of the MPBP. Not only is it the single most common position, but it remains a constant factor in the career experiences of all elites, whether they are two-, three-, or four-time officeholders. Thirty-nine percent of the Revolutionary Family have held this position.

Despite the fact that the position of federal deputy is prevalent in the career paths of many national elites—party, union, and elective career paths are not as common as administrative career paths for strictly national political elites. Elites following the elective, party, or union type of national career pattern tend to concentrate in certain agencies, or emerge as the top union and party leaders. However, national union and party leaders constitute less than 10 percent of our total elite group. Using another Revolutionary Family member, Alfonso Martínez Domínguez, we can trace an elective-union pat-tern on the national level. Martínez Domínguez was born in Monterrey, Nuevo León, but studied in Mexico City as a young boy. At age 14, he became a clerk in the Department of the Federal District in order to support his studies. Just five years later, in 1942, he had become the leader of a section of the Union of Federal District Employees. The following year he served as Chief Editor of the Public Relations Department of the Federal District Department, and then as Secretary General of the entire union. Using his union as a basis of support, he was elected as Federal Deputy from the 4th district of the Federal District. Remarkably, at the age of 27, he became Secretary General of the National Federation of Unions of Federal Employees. After serving for three years, he was again reelected as a federal deputy from Mexico City, and remained in high-level bureaucratic and party positions until he was selected as Secretary General of the Federation of Popular Organizations of PRI in 1961. He later served as Majority Leader of the Chamber of Deputies, President of the official party, and Head of the Federal District Department.

Conclusions

In summary, we can say that the typical Mexican political leader is geo-graphically representative of the Mexican population by region, but predomi-nantly comes from an urban background, although government appointees and official party officeholders still give stronger representation to those from rural backgrounds than do leaders of the most important opposition party, PAN. Furthermore, despite the presence of many persons from humble backgrounds, the more typical political leader has come from parents with middle-class or professional status in his respective community.

In terms of career patterns, the average elite has succeeded more regularly with a national administrative career, or an administrative-elective career on the state and local level that has carried him into the national level. The administrative-party career has been most common in those countries dominated by some type of authoritarian, one-party systems. In Spain, for example, this combination was quite common.[29] In the Soviet Union, long party experience and technical-managerial training was the most important career factor among contemporary Soviet leaders.[30] In the United States, with a competitive party system, most Presidents and Vice-Presidents in this century came from electoral positions, whereas most cabinet members came from within the federal bureaucracy.[31] In Mexico, however, both the President and his cabinet-level administrators have increasingly come from administrative careers.

Local political office has not played an important role in the career patterns of the majority of political elites, particularly the most successful. In general, only one region of Mexico has played a predominant political role in the background and career paths of successful political elites: the Federal District. Many persons with national political careers have never served elsewhere. Natives of the Federal District have come in greater numbers from middle-class families; have had much higher levels of education and better quality primary and secondary education; and have, particularly in recent years, been selected as political elites in much greater proportion than the population of the Federal District would warrant.

The conclusions from the background data on Mexican political leaders are important for understanding the process of who gets selected. A disproportionate number of leaders come from urban and higher socioeconomic backgrounds. Not surprisingly, these qualities become even more common in the upper levels of the political hierarchy. These background variables determine, to a great degree, the access of a future political leader to higher education. Since higher education is a prerequisite to top political positions in contemporary Mexico, then urban background and higher socioeconomic status are two characteristics that are increasingly important for gaining political office. They help to determine who follows the correct channels and who obtains the necessary credentials for admittance to the inner circles of political power.

Although the impact of the Mexican Revolution opened up educational channels to groups that historically had been underrepresented, this lasted for only a short time.[32] For the last 40 years, because a certain class background has remained dominant in higher education, the minority group from humble, rural backgrounds has been psychologically overwhelmed by its urban, higher status colleagues. Interviews with political elites of lower class backgrounds suggest that because of the strong class divisions traditional in Mexico, many of which remain to this day, students from humble backgrounds have been absorbed by their more numerous companions, and have been unable to provide the influx of ideas or experiences typical of their backgrounds which might have opened the system somewhat. A preparatory or university degree was a ticket that could change their family's condition, and they naturally conformed to the environment rather than attempting to change it.

The dominance of the National Preparatory School and the National University over the education of future political leaders has been equalled in few countries. Tradition and prestige continued to play an important role in explaining why only 3 of the 130 political leaders known to have been born in the Federal District or its environs left the immediate area to go to school elsewhere. In the United States, for example, we have no such parallel, either in the geographic domination of one or two cities, or in the ability of a single prestigious school in Washington, D.C., New York City, or along the eastern seaboard to educate such a disproportionate amount of the national political leadership. Not even in England, where there are numerous parallels with the educational-recruitment process in Mexico, has one institution had such an overwhelming impact on the education of political leaders.

Ninety-five percent of the political leaders with a university education received their training at public institutions, yet private institutions, while in the minority, account for far more than five percent of the total university graduates in Mexico. This fact explains another characteristic of Mexican recruitment—its emphasis on a traditional pattern, which started early in the cenutry. Because the selectors or gate-keepers came from and taught at the same institutions responsible for the education of new recruits, the process became self-perpetuating. It is difficult, if not impossible, for a graduate from a private institution to break this pattern. The reader who doubts the major thesis of this book—that the public universities are the location for most political recruitment in Mexico—need only ask why not one graduate from the prestigious Ibero-American University (an institution graduating many PAN leaders) or Monterrey Institute of Higher Studies (financed by the powerful Monterrey industrial group) has ever succeeded in reaching the top. This again reinforces the crucial variable of personal contact. Those few students who have come from such institutions as the Free Law School often succeeded because they were prominent student activists who had come in contact with National University student leaders, and because originally National University students split off from the Law School and formed this new institution. An examination of the Free Law School, the private school contributing more than half of the students with private university education to Mexico's political elite, reveals that the same recruitment practices occurred at that institution: the first university educated lawyer to become president after 1920 was Emilio Portes Gil, one of the student founders of the Free Law School, and he recruited several members of his administration from students and professors of that institution.[33]

The small role of the private school suggests an important characteristic about the Mexican political system that may have serious repercussions in the years to come. This is the lack of permeability to positions of political power in Mexico by a social and economic class that forms the powerful private sector. The simple fact is that the recruitment channels are closing off opportunities to recruits who have grown up in an environment sympathetic to the private sector. This is not true, for example, in the United States, where two-fifths of the American business elite have served in high government positions and where there is considerable interchange between the elites in the private and public sectors.[34] Specifically, 41 percent of recent United States cabinet members were business leaders before and after serving in that position, and 22 percent were business leaders prior to serving in the cabinet who did not continue their leadership roles in business after their government service.[35] In Mexico, such interchange is quite rare. Instead, political leaders who are prominent in business, become so *after* they have held high political office. In short, there is recruitment by the private sector from the public sector, but almost no recruitment by the public sector from the private sector.[36]

Political commentaries and editorials in Mexico have made it clear that there was little respect between the private sector (particularly the Monterrey group) and the Echeverría regime. This antagonism reached such a critical point in late 1976 that ex-President Alemán felt it necessary to praise private entrepreneurs and Mexican capitalists for their role in the country's growth.[37] The members of the Monterrey group, in reply to critical comments by President Echeverría, took the offensive by explaining their contributions to the Mexican people in a full-page advertisement in the major Mexican dailies.[38] Although these disagreements have been exacerbated by the personal statements of Echeverría, it would be fair to say that the leaders of both groups have little in common in their educational experiences and in their outlooks as well. After a year in office, despite his conciliatory attitude, López Portillo has done little to eliminate this tension with the Monterrey group, suggesting that the cause for such difficulties goes beyond the personality of a single President.[39]

NOTES TO CHAPTER 3

[1]My examination of biographical data indicates that nearly all political elites born in urban communities remain in those communities or move to other urban locations. Therefore, urban birthplace is used interchangeably with urban background.

[2]Leonard Cohen, "The Social Background and Recruitment of Yugoslav Political Elites, 1918–1948," in Allen H. Barton, et al., eds, *Opinion-Making Elites in Yugoslavia* (New York: Praeger, 1973), p. 55.

[3]Peter H. Smith, "Making it in Mexico: Aspects of Political Mobility Since 1946," paper presented at the American Political Science Association, August 29–September 2, 1974, p. 6.

[4]Donald J. Mabry and Roderic A. Camp, "Mexican Political Elites 1935 to 1973: A Comparative Study," *The Americas* **31** (April 1975): 466.

[5]See Gruber's "Career Patterns of Mexico's Political Elite," *Western Political Quarterly* **24** (September 1971): 474; also see James D. Cochrane, "Mexico's New Científicos: The Díaz Ordaz Cabinet," *Inter-American Economic Affairs* **21** (Summer 1967): 61–72, for examples from an individual cabinet.

[6]See Praxedis Balboa, *Apuntes de Mi Vida* (Mexico, 1975), for numerous examples in Cuidad Victoria, Tamaulipas, during the first decade of the 19th century; Alberto Bremauntz, *Setenta Años de Mi Vida* (Mexico: Ediciones Juridicos Sociales, 1968), for the same period in Morelia, Michoacán; and Jaime Torres Bodet, *Tiempo de Arena* (Mexico: Fondo de Cultura Económica, 1955), for Mexico City.

[7]José Luis Reyna, "An Empirical Analysis of Political Mobilization: The Case of Mexico" (unpublished Ph.D. dissertation, Cornell University, 1971); and Barry Ames, "Bases of Support for Mexico's Dominant Party," *American Political Science Review* **64** (March 1970): 153–67.

[8]Sidney H. Aronson, *Status and Kinship in the Higher Civil Service* (Cambridge: Harvard University Press, 1964), p. 99.

[9]Thomas R. Dye, *Who's Running America? Institutional Leadership in the United States* (Englewood Cliffs: Prentice-Hall, 1976), p. 152.

[10]George K. Schueller, "The Politburo," in Harold D. Lasswell and Daniel Lerner, *World Revolutionary Elites* (Cambridge MIT Press, 1966), p. 141.

[11]Sidney G. Tarrow, *Peasant Communism in Southern Italy* (New Haven: Yale University Press, 1967).

[12]Ricardo J. Zevada, *Calles el presidente* (Mexico: Editorial Nuestro Tiempo, 1971), p. 131ff.

[13]Arthur Liebman, *Latin American University Students: A Six Nation Study* (Cambridge: Harvard University Press, 1972), p. 37.

[14]Guy Benveniste, *Bureaucracy and National Planning, A Sociological Case Study in Mexico* (New York: Praeger, 1970), p. 127.

[15]See Roderic A. Camp, "A Reexamination of Political Leadership and Allocation of Federal Revenues in Mexico, 1934–73," *Journal of Developing Areas* **10** (January 1976); and Paul Drake, "Mexican Regionalism Reconsidered," *Journal of Inter-American Studies & World Affairs* **12** (July 1970): 401–15.

[16]For some interesting comparisons with Mexican presidents, see John G. Conklin, "Elite Studies: the Case of the Mexican Presidency," *Journal of Latin American Studies* **5**, no. 2 (1973): 247–69; for a larger sample including other elites, see Peter H. Smith, "Making it in Mexico;" and for an analysis of cabinet secretaries see David E. Stansfield, "The Mexican Cabinet: An Indicator of Political Change," *Occasional Paper No. 8* (University of Glasgow, 1973), p. 11.

[17]For a description of student life at the Colegio Civil during the decade 1910–1920, see Praxedis Balboa, *Apuntes de mi vida* (Mexico, 1975), p. 15ff.

[18]Donald Mabry, *Mexico's Acción Nacional: A Catholic Alternative to Revolution* (Syracuse: Syracuse University Press, 1973), p. 16ff; Franz A. Von Sauer, *The Alienated*

"Loyal" Opposition, Mexico's Partido Acción Nacional (Albuquerque: University of New Mexico Press, 1974), p. 19ff; and Jean A. Meyer, *The Cristero Rebellion: The Mexican People Between Church and State, 1926-1929* (Cambridge: Cambridge University Press, 1976).

[19]Daniel Cosío Villegas, ed., *Historia moderna de México. El Porfiriato, la vida social* (Mexico: El Colegio de México, 1957).

[20]Arthur Liebman, *Latin American University Students*, p. 40.

[21]Thomas Dye, *Who's Running America?*, p. 154.

[22]Charles Myers, *Education and National Development in Mexico* (Princeton: Princeton University Press, 1965), p. 112.

[23]See Mexico, UNAM, *Plan de estudios, 1924* (Mexico: UNAM, 1924), and Liebman, *Latin American University Students*, p. 40.

[24]Joel Verner, "Characteristics of Administrative Personnel: The Case of Guatemala," *Journal of Developing Areas* 5 (October 1970): 76-7; Paul H. Lewis, "The Spanish Ministerial Elite, 1938-1969," *Comparative Politics* 5 (October 1972): 103.

[25]Evelyn P. Stevens, "Mexico's PRI: The Institutionalization of Corporatism?," in James Malloy, ed., *Authoritarianism and Corporatism in Latin America* (Pittsburgh: University of Pittsburgh Press, 1977), p. 233.

[26]For a more detailed analysis of these points, see my "Military and Political-Military Officers in Mexico: A Comparative Study," (paper presented at the North Central Council of Latin Americanists, Eau Claire, Wisconsin, 1978).

[27]Franklin D. Margiotta, "The Mexican Military: A Case Study in Non-intervention" (unpublished M.A. thesis, Georgetown University, 1968), p. 165.

[28]Norman K. Nicholson, "Integrative Strategies of a National Elite: Career Patterns in the Indian Council of Ministers," *Comparative Politics* 7 (July 1975): 545.

[29]Paul H. Lewis, "The Spanish Ministerial Elite," p. 86.

[30]Zbigniew Brzezinzki and Samuel P. Huntington, *Political Power: USA/USSR* (New York: Viking Press, 1964), pp. 143-4.

[31]Joseph A. Schlesinger, *Ambition and Politics, Political Careers in the United States* (Chicago: Rand McNally, 1966), pp. 33-4.

[32]Peasants appear to be universally underrepresented in post-revolutionary societies, even those which are highly agrarian. See Leonard Cohen's data, which show that only 6 percent of the Yugoslav Central Committee are from peasant backgrounds in a society where 73 percent of the economically active population were peasants (p. 47).

[33]Personal letter to the author from Emilio Portes Gil, Mexico City, October 20, 1972; and personal interview, Mexico City, August 4, 1974.

[34]Richard E. Neustadt, "White House and Whitehall," *The Public Interest*, no. 2 (Winter 1966): pp. 55-69.

[35]Peter J. Freitag, "The Cabinet and Big Business: A Study of Interlocks," *Social Problems* 23 (December 1975), p. 148.

[36]Nora Hamilton, "The State and Class Formation in Post-Revolutionary Mexico," (paper presented at the 7th National Latin American Studies Association Meeting, Houston, November 2-5, 1977), p. 33.

[37]*El Heraldo de México*, October 19, 1976, p. 1.

[38]See for example *El Heraldo de México*, October 19, 1976, p. 5A.

[39]*Latin America Political Report*, November 4, 1977, p. 340.

4. The Educational Background of Political Leaders

Education in Mexico, as in most other countries in Latin America, is the privilege of a small minority. Various studies of Mexico's general population reveal that even the completion of secondary education is achieved by only a small percentage of the population. The educational level of the general population is low. Thus Mexico's political elite belongs to yet another elite—the educated minority.

Educational Levels

Historically, Mexico's political leadership has been well educated, a characteristic equally true of North American political leaders during the years following the Revolution.[1] Furthermore, compared with at least one other Mexican elite, top industrial leaders, Mexican political leaders have had much higher levels of education. Although recent statistics indicate that access to higher education is increasing among the general Mexican population, it should be remembered that the majority of the political leaders in our population (more than 90 percent) were educated prior to 1955.

In 1926, only 3,860 students were enrolled in basic secondary school in all Mexico. At least 114 or 3 percent of those students later became important political leaders in Mexico after 1935. Although this figure of 3,860 increased to over 65,000 by 1950, the vast majority of the population between the ages of 15 and 19 eligible to be in a secondary school were not enrolled. An even smaller percentage of the Mexican population enters preparatory school, the curriculum followed by students preparing to enter the university. In 1970, 233,000 students, or about 5 percent of the eligible population, were enrolled in a preparatory program.[2] Educational statistics in 1970 revealed the following profile for the general population: 56 percent over six years of age had a primary school education compared with 100 percent of the political elite; 6 percent had a secondary education compared with 99 percent of the political elite; and 1.5 percent had obtained a university degree compared with 92 percent of the political leadership. If we look at the educational levels in selected states (those having the highest and lowest levels), we find the mean educational attainment of the Mexican population 30 years of age and older to be the following:

State	Mean Years of Education in 1960
Federal District[3]	4.6 years
Baja California del Norte	3.4
Sonora	2.9
Chihuahua	2.9
Coahuila	3.0
Nuevo León	3.5
Tamaulipas	2.9
Zacatecas	1.6
Hidalgo	1.3
Tlaxcala	1.7
Guerrero	0.8
Oaxaca	1.0
Chiapas	1.1
Mexico (entire republic)	2.3

Since all the political leaders in our study are more than 30 years old, their educational achievements, given in a mean figure, is 15 years, in contrast to the 2.3 years for all Mexicans. In most regions of Mexico, persons with 15 years of education would form a very small group.[4]

Of the political leaders for whom I have complete educational data, 82 percent had a university or professional degree. What these figures do not indicate is that those persons who complete preparatory or degree programs are a much smaller percentage than those actually enrolled. Figures for general student attrition at the National Preparatory School and the National University in the 1940s indicate a completion rate ranging from only 23 percent to 70 percent, with the average figure well below 50 percent.[5] For state universities, the attrition rate is much higher, between 80 and 90 percent.[6] However, only 5 percent of Mexico's political leaders started a program and did not complete it, and many of those did so during the earlier, unstable decades from 1900 to 1930. This contrast in completion rates suggests that their financial backgrounds are more stable, allowing them to complete their degrees, or that as individuals, they have a stronger personal drive to succeed, whether it be in their education or career.

What is important is that even in the early years of Mexico's political development, a high percentage of its leaders had such an education. Of the 156 political officeholders who *first* held high office from 1934 to 1940 (and received an education prior to 1930), 66 percent had obtained university or progessional degrees in contrast to the 1.5 percent of the Mexican population in 1970. While political leaders have always been well-educated in Mexico, higher education was less important for members of earlier presidential administrations. Again, many individuals who earned their reputations as military leaders or civilian administrators during the violent years of the Revolution did so without university education. Larger numbers of these men served in the administrations of Lázaro Cárdenas and Manuel Ávila Camacho, both of whom typified men without higher educational backgrounds.

Lázaro Cárdenas' formal education ended with his primary studies in Michoacán. Manuel Ávila Camacho received some secondary education in the field of accounting before joining the army at the age of 18. However, unknown to most students of Mexico, as a young adult, he studied for a short while at the National Preparatory School, and was a student of Luis Cabrera.[7] Other developing countries that have undergone major revolutions have provided less opportunities for such individuals. In their study of the 1945 Chinese Politburo and Central Committee of the Communist Party, Robert North and Ithiel Sola Pool found that all except three individuals had a higher education. They concluded that, "despite the poverty of China and the very small proportion of families able to afford higher educations for their sons, leaders simply did not arise by making their own way through channels outside normal educational patterns."[8]

Access to political leadership positions for those persons without a university education can be seen in the career of Naxario S. Ortiz Garza. Ortiz Garza, a native of Saltillo, Coahuila, is typical of others of his age born in the decade of 1890 to 1900. His father was a small businessman, and he studied primary school at Public School No. 2 in Saltillo. He was able to complete his fourth year of preparatory studies at the famous regional school, Ateneo Fuente in Saltillo, before quitting for lack of funds. At the age of 14, he left school to work as a bookkeeper for a local business, and in 1913 he opened his own business. He joined the Revolution in 1915, and fought with General Francisco Murguía without any military rank. The Revolution took him to Chihuahua, where he became the purveyor for military trains running through the capital city. After the Revolution he returned to Torreón, Coahuila, where he became a businessman and entered politics, losing his first election as a councilman. In 1921, he won his first office as a councilman, and a year later became mayor. In 1923, he ran for federal deputy, and although he won the election, another candidate was given the office. His political fortunes changed in 1924 when he became campaign director for the successful gubernatorial race of General Manuel Pérez Treviño in Coahuila. In the ensuing years, he held office several times as mayor of Torreón and Saltillo, and he himself became governor of Coahuila from 1929 to 1934. Meanwhile, his mentor, Pérez Treviño, had become President of the National Revolutionary Party (PNR), and he and his supporters asked Ortiz Garza to run for the Senate in 1934. Later, Ortiz Garza started a large business, which was quite successful. Under Ávila Camacho, he was appointed as director of the decentralized agency which became CONASUPO, and in the following administration he served as Secretary of Agriculture, after having made a private fortune in growing grapes.[9] His political contacts and business-administrative skills were sufficient to make him successful without a university education.

There has been a gradual trend away from political leaders without higher education until they nearly ceased to exist in the Luis Echeverría administration. Almost 10 percent of the political leadership in the 1934–40 administration completed only primary education. While that figure did not decline noticeably in the following administration, it did taper off to less than 3 percent under President Miguel Alemán in 1946, and there was a general decline of political leaders with only primary and secondary educations from 1934 (23 percent) to 1976 (2 percent; see Table 4.1).

There has been a consistent increase in political leaders with higher levels of education. While 34 percent of the political leaders under Cárdenas had no university education, the same was true for only 8 percent of Luis Echeverría's collaborators. Furthermore, excluding medical degrees, and examining Ph.D.s, LL.D.s, M.A.s, and post professional work as indicative of greater emphasis placed on specialized educational skills, we find that a pattern begins with the 1946 administration, in which 9.3 percent did work beyond the basic university or professional degree. By 1970, 34 percent of Echeverría's appointees had availed themselves of this kind of education, a figure equal to the number of persons in the Cárdenas administration without any university education.

One of the questions raised by some researchers of political elites is whether or not higher education helps political leaders become more successful. If we look at members of the Revolutionary Family (again defined as having held four or more high-level offices), we do not find any remarkable differences in educational achievements over the years, although there is a gradual decline in the percentage of political leaders without university or higher levels of education (from 18 to 14 percent). Hugh Smythe and Peter H. Smith seem right in saying that while education does have some importance in the ability of a person to retain high political office, it plays a more significant role in giving a person access to political office rather than promoting him from one office to another.[10]

Table 4.1

Education of Political Leaders by Administration, 1935 to 1976

Time During Which 1st High-Level Office[a] was Held	Level of Education Achieved[b]									
	Primary	Secondary	Prepara-tory	Normal	Univer-sity	Post Prof.	M.A.	Ph.D., LL.D.	M.D.	Totals
1935–1940										
No. of political leaders	15	21	7	10	75	4	1	7	16	156
% of political leaders	9.6	13.5	4.5	6.4	48.1	2.6	0.6	4.5	10.3	100.1[d]
1940–1946										
No. of political leaders	8	7	5	4	65	3	0	5	6	103
% of political leaders	7.8	6.8	4.9	3.9	63.1	2.9	0.0	4.9	5.8	100.1[d]
1946–1952										
No. of political leaders	3	9	3	2	77	1	3	6	3	107
% of political leaders	2.8	8.4	2.8	1.9	72.0	0.9	2.8	5.6	2.8	100
1952–1958										
No. of political leaders	0	7	3	5	51	1	2	8	4	81
% of political leaders	0.0	8.6	3.7	6.2	63.0	1.2	2.5	9.9	4.9	100.0
1958–1964										
No. of political leaders	3	3	1	4	53	3	5	6	8	86
% of political leaders	3.5	3.5	1.2	4.7	61.6	3.5	5.8	7.0	9.3	100.1[d]
1964–1970										
No. of political leaders	1	0	3	3	63	8	2	9	10	99
% of political leaders	1.0	0.0	3.0	3.0	63.6	8.1	2.0	9.1	10.1	99.9[d]
1970–1976										
No. of political leaders	1	1	4	4	70	21	10	14	6	131
% of political leaders	0.8	0.8	3.1	3.1	53.4	16.0	7.6	10.7	4.6	100.1[d]
Subtotal[c]										
No. of political leaders	31	48	26	32	454	41	23	55	53	763
% of political leaders	4.1	6.3	3.4	4.2	59.5	5.4	3.0	7.2	7.0	100.1[d]

[a]The figures for each administration represent only those political leaders who first joined the political elite during the years specified.
[b]This sample includes only those persons for whom a definite level of education could be determined, obtained from the data in the MPBP.
[c]These figures exclude those individuals who were opposition party leaders or deputies.
[d]These percentages do not total 100.0 due to rounding.

Curriculum Choices

If higher education provides access to important political offices, perhaps specific educational degrees characterize most political leaders and have a favorable impact on careers. Of the political elites who held high-level offices in the last seven administrations, 82 percent actually completed a college or professional degree. Not surprisingly, 57 percent of college educated leaders received law degrees, making it the most important professional degree among Mexican politicians (Table 4.2). This was followed in order of importance by engineering (11 percent), medicine (9 percent) and economics (7 percent). However, if we compare the educational fields of political elites with that of the general population, we find major differences. Even in 1948, law degrees accounted for only 4 percent of the total degrees granted in Mexico. An examination of enrollment figures for the National University, where the majority of political elites received their degrees, shows that the largest schools since the 1950s, in order of enrollment, have been medicine, engineering, law, business administration, and architecture.[11]

It is not surprising that both law and medicine are well represented among elites educated in the first two decades of the 20th century, since the

Table 4.2

Type of Degrees Received by College-Educated Political Leaders

Time During Which 1st High-Level Office Was Held	Type of Degree Received								
	Law	Eco-nomics	M.D.	Archi-tecture	Engi-neering	Agri-culture	CPA	Other	Totals
1935–1940									
No. of officeholders	61	3	16	1	11	3	1	5	101
% of officeholders	60.4	3.0	15.8	1.0	11.0	3.0	1.0	5.0	100.2c
1940–1946									
No. of officeholders	50	1	6	0	4	2	0	12	75
% of officeholders	66.6	1.3	8.0	0	5.3	2.7	0	16.0	99.9c
1946–1952									
No. of officeholders	59	3	4	1	12	3	1	6	89
% of officeholders	66.3	3.4	4.5	1.1	13.5	3.4	1.1	6.7	100.0
1952–1958									
No. of officeholders	37	2	5	0	11	1	2	7	65
% of officeholders	57.0	3.1	7.7	0	16.9	1.5	3.1	10.8	100.1c
1958–1964									
No. of officeholders	39	4	8	0	7	1	1	11	71
% of officeholders	55.0	5.6	11.2	0	9.9	1.4	1.4	15.5	100.0
1964–1970									
No. of officeholders	42	9	11	3	11	5	3	8	92
% of officeholders	45.7	9.8	12.0	3.3	12.0	5.4	3.3	8.7	100.2c
1970–1976									
No. of officeholders	53	21	7	3	12	9	1	14	120
% of officeholders	44.2	17.5	5.8	2.5	10.0	7.5	0.8	11.7	100.0
Subtotala									
No. of officeholders	341	43	57	8	68	24	9	63	613b
% of officeholders	55.6	7.0	9.3	1.3	11.1	3.9	1.5	10.3	100.0

aThis table excludes opposition party leaders and federal deputies. Data are taken from the MPBP.
bThose leaders with degrees total only 613 since cases where the type of degree was unknown were omitted.
cThese percentages do not total 100.0 due to rounding.

other fields were not available in Mexico until the 1920s and 1930s.[2] However, a close examination of the data in Table 4.2 indicates that law has always been a significant field among professionally educated political elites, and that it has remained a fairly consistent proportion among those degrees sought by political leaders. Students with future political ambitions have typically chosen law on the assumption that this is the career followed by most political leaders in Mexico. That assumption has been correct, and law degrees seem to be perpetuated, in part, by a self-fulfilling prophecy. The newest field being chosen by an increasing number of successful politicians is economics. Since 1952, the number of economists has actually doubled in each succeeding administration, reaching 18 percent during 1970–76. Medicine, a traditional profession like law, has not followed a steady pattern, starting out as the choice of 16 percent of the college educated officeholders in the Cárdenas administration, declining in the Alemán period, and climbing back to 12 percent under Gustavo Díaz Ordaz. Recently, it has declined to pre-1952 levels. Engineering and architecture have both grown as educational choices among Mexico's political elite, leveling off at 10 and 3 percent respectively. In the initial year of the López Portillo administration, these same patterns continued to be prevalent, since 51 percent of his appointees have law degrees, 20 percent economics degrees, and 13 percent engineering degrees.

Earlier, we suggested that *level* of education has only a slight influence on the ability of political leaders to retain high public office in Mexico. However, if we instead examine the *type of education* of Mexico's Revolutionary Family, we find a very distinct increase in the prevalence of law degrees, although this was more substantial in administrations prior to 1970. Nearly 63 percent of the Revolutionary Family from 1934 to 1976 had law degrees, followed by medical degrees (6.8 percent) and engineering degrees (4.9 percent). Persons with no college education, as suggested earlier, are well-represented among the Revolutionary Family, particularly during the administrations from 1952 to 1970. The striking increase in law degrees among members of the Revolutionary Family remains important if we narrow down our group of elites to the 50 men who have held five or more positions. Law degrees predominated, being the professional field of everyone with degrees in the 1940–46, 1946–52, 1952–58, 1958–64 administrations, and accounting for 63 percent and 91 percent of the five-time officeholders in the 1964 and 1970 administrations respectively. The only other fields represented were economics and medicine.

The emphasis on certain types of education is important because it suggests characteristics about the recruitment process. As Lester Seligman argues, ''over a period of time we may deduce effective political opportunity from the characteristics of those nominated and/or elected. If one group, for example, lawyers, is underrepresented or overrepresented among the elites, it may be assumed that differential political opportunities have produced such results."[13] In addition to the fact that the availability of legal education preceded that of other fields and that the skills emphasized in the practice of law were integrated into the bureaucratic process and the practice of politics in Mexico, law graduates, particularly from the National University, have been the foremost recruiters and have formed the most successful *camarillas* in recent administrations. Since membership in a successful political *camarilla* is essential to repeating in high political office, it is only logical to expect that leaders of these *camarillas* surround themselves with men from the same professional backgrounds. No university educated President of Mexico, from Cárdenas to López Portillo, received a degree in a field other than law.[14]

Specialized education may also be related to career success if we attempt to distinguish between those political leaders with largely administrative careers and those who have confined much of their experience to party and electoral positions. The line dividing these two types of political leaders is a fine one. However, if on the basis of specialized education and previous experience, we distinguish between these two types of careers, it can be shown that political leaders with advanced education and specialized experience have directed certain government agencies more frequently than others.[15] Furthermore, some agencies, either because of legal statute or tradition, require that their directors have a particular type of degree (Public Health: medicine; Attorney General: law; Hydraulic Resources: engineering). In short, the type of education may well be a prerequisite for appointments to specific positions within the government. Variations of this pattern have occurred elsewhere in other political systems.[16] For example, in India, Nicholson concludes that the Congress Party recruits individuals who are recognized for non-political qualifications, but that these leaders generally end up in insignificant ministries.[17] This is not the case in Mexico, since many of the well-qualified technician-politicians have emerged as heads of the most important economic agencies.

Educational Institutions

Although I have implied in chapter ii that childhood friendships may be important to political careers in Mexico,[18] political recruitment generally does not take place until the average Mexican reaches his teens, and is attending normal or preparatory school.* Of those elites who attended pre-

---

*Students in Mexico, who want to further their education beyond the secondary school level, have two choices: normal and preparatory. Normal school is a teaching certification program generally followed by students who lack the funds to finish in other professional fields. Preparatory schools, in contrast, prepare the student for a regular university program in most professional fields, and are attended by those students planning to obtain a university degree. Unlike the United States, primary and secondary teachers in Mexico do not require a college degree.

paratory school, we have information on the location of specific institutions for 376 persons. Although our sample is smaller than usual, it illustrates the small number of preparatory schools which contributed to the education of Mexico's political elite. In fact, only three schools were each responsible for more than four percent of the first-time, high-level officeholders between 1935 and 1976: the National Preparatory School (Mexico City), the Instituto de Artes y Ciencias de Oaxaca (Oaxaca), and the Colegio de San Nicolás de Hidalgo (Morelia). The National Preparatory School has been responsible for the education of an overwhelming number of leaders: 52.6 percent. Its influence among preparatory schools, as far as political elites are concerned, has been more important since 1946 (Table 4.3). The preparatory education of public leaders has not been decentralized in recent administrations, despite the rapid increase of preparatory schools on the state level in Mexico. The Revolutionary Family is more illustrative of the centralization of education at

Table 4.3

Preparatory Institutions Attended by First-Time High-Level Officeholders

Time During Which 1st High-Level Office Was Held	Institutions Attended[b]								
	ENP[a]	Oaxaca	Guada-lajara	Pue-bla	Mexico	Vera-cruz	San Nicolás	Other	Totals
1935–1940									
No. of officeholders	20	2	5	5	3	5	9	22	71
% of officeholders	28.2								100.0
1940–1946									
No. of officeholders	23	3	1	1	0	1	5	13	47
% of officeholders	48.9								100.0
1946–1952									
No. of officeholders	37	5	0	2	1	0	1	10	56
% of officeholders	66.1								100.0
1952–1958									
No. of officeholders	25	0	2	0	1	3	2	13	46
% of officeholders	54.4								100.0
1958–1964									
No. of officeholders	30	2	0	0	1	0	3	12	48
% of officeholders	62.5								100.0
1964–1970									
No. of officeholders	27	0	4	1	0	2	0	9	43
% of officeholders	62.8								100.0
1970–1976									
No. of officeholders	36	4	0	1	0	3	0	21	65
% of officeholders	55.4								100.0
Subtotals									
No. of officeholders	198	16	12	10	6	14	20	100	376
% of officeholders	52.6	4.3	3.2	2.7	1.5	3.7	5.3	26.6	100.0

[a]More than 90 percent of our sample educated at the National Preparatory School received their education before it decentralized into numerous branches in Mexico City.

[b]Key: ENP = National Preparatory School; Oaxaca = Institute of Arts and Sciences of Oaxaca; Guadalajara = University of Guadalajara; Puebla = University of Puebla; Mexico = Scientific and Literary Institute of Mexico in Toluca; San Nicolás = Colegio de San Nicolás in Morelia; Other = Thirty-two other institutions at which no more than 4 political leaders attended any single school.

the National Preparatory School, since 19 out of 20 (95 percent) four-time officeholders with known preparatory institutions attended the National Preparatory School.

Upon completion of their preparatory education, future political leaders have generally followed one of three patterns: they have attended a university in Mexico City (75 percent), attended a state or regional university (24 percent), or dropped out after completing the preparatory degree. Only a few students who complete their preparatory studies in Mexico City go on to universities in the provinces. Ninety-nine percent of the college educated political leaders who started their preparatory studies at the National Preparatory School finished their university studies at the National University or National School of Agriculture. The few students who followed other patterns did so for political or economic reasons, like Salvador Azuela Rivera, who was involved in disruptive political activities at the University. Salvador, son of the distinguished Mexican Revolutionary novelist Mariano Azuela, received his primary education in Lagos de Moreno, Jalisco. His preparatory studies were initiated at the Colegio de San Nicolás, but were irregular due to his father's activities during the Revolutionary years from 1910 to 1920. He later enrolled at the National Preparatory School and became a prominent student leader. Because of his role as an important participant in a student strike, he was expelled from the National Preparatory School by José Vasconcelos in 1923. The following year he became Private Secretary to the Governor of Michoacán, and finished his preparatory studies in Morelia. He then became a law student at the Colegio de San Nicolás, where he became a collaborator of Lázaro Cárdenas, and at the same time he served as a professor of Mexican and World History. He reentered the National University in 1929, this time as a law student, and again became a prominent student leader, participating in the 1929 presidential campaign and in the university autonomy movement. Eventually, he completed his law degree.[19]

University education among Mexico's political leadership is more centralized than is their preparatory education. The National University is the single most important educational institution, responsible for educating nearly two-thirds of all elites with university or professional degrees* (see Table 4.4). If we add to that figure the number of graduates from the National Military College, the Naval Academy, the National School of Agriculture,

---

*Ironically, José Vasconcelos, the opposition candidate for president of Mexico in 1929, was responsible for federalizing the educational system in Mexico as Secretary of Education under President Alvaro Obregón. Although his goals were different, his efforts ultimately encouraged the concentration of university students in Mexico City and became just another aspect of the centralization of political control and economic and cultural power in the capital. See Josefina Vázquez de Knauth, *Nacionalismo y educación en México* (Mexico: Colegio de México, 1970), pp. 137–8.

and the National Polytechnic Institute, 77 percent graduated from national institutions. Like the National Preparatory School, the National University was not as well-represented in the Cárdenas and Ávila Camacho administrations. However, beginning with the Alemán administration, the National University has been strongly represented in the last five administrations with the exception of that of Ruiz Cortines. Not surprisingly, the Presidents who were alumni of the National University generally had the highest percentage of appointees with degrees from that institution: Alemán, López Mateos and Echeverría, although one non-alumni, Díaz Ordaz, had equally high numbers of UNAM graduates. José López Portillo, also a graduate of UNAM, chose a high proportion of his campaign aides from the University and over two-thirds of his administration's high-level officeholders were UNAM graduates. As a political leader's career advances, UNAM becomes more important.[20] The percentage of Revolutionary Family members who were UNAM graduates exceeded the percentage of first-time officeholders who came from that university. Other important universities, excluding national institutions, contributing to the education of political leaders in Mexico include the Free Law School, the University of Guadalajara, and the University of Guanajuato.

Education and Position

We have determined certain educational patterns for Mexico's general political elite and the Revolutionary Family. However, if we further break down the political elite by public office, there are distinct characteristics for specific positions held by the elite. Although the educated members of Mexico's prospective political leadership have a greater chance of succeeding, some positions offer increased opportunities to the uneducated.

Those elites with little formal education have been quite successful in obtaining high-level offices provided they emerged through the ranks of the semi-official and official unions in Mexico. Among the most important for future political leaders have been the Mexican Federation of Labor, the National Farmers Federation, the National Federation of Popular Organizations, the Federal Bureaucrats Union, the National Teachers Union, and the National Railroad Workers Union. Of the 121 elites who were state and national secretaries general, 50 (41.3 percent) did not have a university education. The figure for those without university degrees would be higher if we excluded the National Federation of Popular Organizations, which includes professional and bureaucratic unions, whose members (by virtue of their occupations) often have professional degrees.

Typical of such political success is the career of Alfredo Navarrete, who was born in the Valle de Acambay, Morelos in 1893. He worked as a peon as a young boy and did not have the opportunity to attend school beyond

Table 4.4

Universities Attended by Mexican Political Leaders by Administration[a]

Administration in Which 1st High-Level Office Was Held	UNAM	University Attended						
		National Military Academy	National Agriculture School	Free Law School	National Polytechnic Institute	University of Guadalajara	University of Guanajuato	National Naval Academy
1935–1940								
No. of political leaders	48	7	1	5	0	7	5	1
% of political leaders	48.5							
1940–1946								
No. of political leaders	45	8	3	4	2	2	0	0
% of political leaders	53.6							
1946–1952								
No. of political leaders	70	3	2	4	3	0	2	3
% of political leaders	74.5							
1952–1958								
No. of political leaders	37	4	3	1	3	2	1	2
% of political leaders	53.6							
1958–1964								
No. of political leaders	55	4	2	2	3	0	2	3
% of political leaders	72.4							
1964–1970								
No. of political leaders	62	1	2	2	2	4	2	3
% of political leaders	70.5							
1970–1976								
No. of political leaders	98	6	8	1	5	0	1	1
% of political leaders	68.1							
Subtotals								
No. of political leaders	415	33	21	19	18	15	13	13
% of political leaders	63.5	5.1	3.2	2.9	2.8	2.3	2.0	2.0

University Attended

Administration in Which 1st High-Level Office Was Held	University of Chihuahua	Colegio de San Nicolás	University of Veracruz	University of Campeche	University of Yucatán	University of Puebla	University of Oaxaca	Other Universities	Totals
1935–1940									
No. of political leaders	3	6	2	1	1	2	1	9	99
% of political leaders									100.0
1940–1946									
No. of political leaders	2	4	1	1	2	1	1	8	84
% of political leaders									100.0
1946–1952									
No. of political leaders	2	0	0	2	0	0	0	3	94
% of political leaders									100.0
1952–1958									
No. of political leaders	2	0	2	2	1	0	1	8	69
% of political leaders									100.0
1958–1964									
No. of political leaders	0	0	0	0	0	0	0	5	76
% of political leaders									100.0
1964–1970									
No. of political leaders	0	0	2	1	1	1	0	5	88
% of political leaders									100.0
1970–1976									
No. of political leaders	2	0	0	1	1	2	2	16	144
% of political leaders									100.0
Subtotals									
No. of political leaders	11	10	7	8	6	6	5	54[b]	654
% of political leaders	1.7	1.5	1.1	1.2	0.9	0.9	0.8	8.3	100.2[c]

[a]This table does not include opposition party leaders or federal deputies. Data are taken from the MPBP.
[b]No more than three individuals graduated from any single university in this group and a sizeable number of these graduated from institutions in the United States and Europe.
[c]Totals more than 100.0 due to rounding.

[79]

the primary grades. In 1904, he migrated to Mexico City, where he worked at several industrial jobs and finally became a laborer at the San Lázaro Railroad Station in Mexico City at the outbreak of the Revolution. Interested in politics, he first became a member of the Reyes Club, and later joined the Anti-Reelectionist Club. Through self-education and personal training, he became a train conductor during the Revolution, and a labor organizer and leader. Much later, in 1934, he served as Secretary General of the National Railroad Workers Union, an influential political position in Mexico.[21]

From the low percentage of union leaders with university educations, it is obvious that other skills, particularly those used in handling the conflicting interests of the union members with government and industry, have been nearly as important as formal education. Furthermore, skillful, uneducated leaders are more likely to stay tied to unions than to move up through other public positions generally held by university educated elites. The large number of teaching certificates held by union leaders indicates the number of individuals who have used teachers' unions as a channel for their political careers (see Table 4.5).

Table 4.5

Educational Levels of Political Leaders Who Were Union Officials[a]

Level of Education	Union Background		
	Union Leader	Non-Union Leadership	Totals
Primary			
No. of political leaders	10	31	41
% of political leaders	8.3	3.8	
Secondary			
No. of political leaders	10	50	60
% of political leaders	8.3	6.1	
Preparatory			
No. of political leaders	8	28	36
% of political leaders	6.6	3.4	
Normal			
No. of political leaders	22	30	52
% of political leaders	18.2	3.7	
University and/or Advanced Professional Degrees			
No. of political leaders	71	677	748
% of political leaders	58.7	82.9	
Subtotals			
No. of political leaders	121 (12.9%)	816 (87.1%)	937[b] (100%)
% of political leaders	100.1[c]	99.9[c]	

[a]Union officials refers to those individuals holding positions as secretaries general of national and state union organizations.
[b]Data are taken from the MPBP.
[c]These percentage figures total do not add up to 100.0 due to rounding.

It is interesting, however, that the younger generation of union leaders tends to be better educated, particularly if we are talking about bureaucratic unions. For example, the last six secretaries general of the Federal Bureaucrats Union were the following:

Aceves Alcocer, Gilberto	1970–1975	Completed preparatory with some business administration
Robledo Santiago, Edgar	1967–1970	Rural and Urban Teaching Certification
Bernal, Antonio	1965–1967	Law degree
Robles Martínez, Jesús	1964–1965	Engineering degree
Sánchez Mireles, Rómulo	1959–1964	Law degree
De la Torre Grajales, A.	1956–1959	Completed secondary

Other leaders of major unions in 1975 included the late Francisco Pérez Rios, Secretary General of the Unified Union of Electricians (SUTERM), who succeeded in completing four years at the National Polytechnic Institute; and Celestino Salcedo, Secretary General of the National Farmers Federation (CNC) until 1977, who completed his engineering degree in Saltillo, Coahuila.

While today the uneducated political leader would have the best opportunity to succeed through a union career, not surprisingly, historically, a greater percentage of uneducated persons have been successful politically by following military careers. Nearly half, or 47 percent, of the 101 political leaders who were professional military men did not attend military or civilian colleges (Table 4.6). Considering that this was the path followed most commonly by persons from rural backgrounds during the Revolution, it is remarkable that 54 percent had university or professional degrees. Most of these officers graduated from the National Military College in Mexico City, the Military Medical School, or the Naval Academy in Veracruz, although many hold professional degrees from civil institutions, primarily the National University. Most military politicians have been concentrated in governorships, deputy and senatorial positions, and party offices. However, increasingly, this path is being cut off for prospective political leaders, since so few military officers are now recruited to political positions, whether we are talking about governorships (one in 1976), federal deputyships (three or 1.3 percent in 1976), the official party (none in 1976) or the subcabinet and cabinet (one excluding the secretariats of defense and navy).[22]

Dr. Rafael Moreno Valle, a recent governor of Puebla, exemplifies the opportunities of this career for the immediate post-Revolutionary generation. Born into a humble family in Atlixco, Puebla in 1917, he attended primary school in his native village. Both of his brothers joined the army, and one became a Lt Colonel in the Revolution. Probably influenced by this family experience, he completed his preparatory studies at the National Preparatory School and then was accepted as a student at the Military Medical School, from which he graduated as a military surgeon with the rank of major in 1940. During World War II, he attended special military schools in the United States, and later completed studies at Tulane University in orthopedics. After the war, he joined the staff of the Central Military Hospital, becoming chief of medical services and later director. He became a professor at the Military Medical School and at the National University. In 1958, he held his first public office as a senator from Puebla, and four years later he was appointed to the National Executive Committee of PRI as Secretary of Political Action. In 1964, Díaz Ordaz selected him as his Secretary of Public Health, and Moreno Valle became the first Military Medical School graduate to hold that position.[23]

Another position that has provided access to national political positions of importance for men without university education is that of federal deputy. When compared with all political elites, persons who entered our elite sample through a federal deputyship had lower levels of education. Although federal deputies were better educated than union leaders, the percentage of federal deputies *without* university educations was higher than the percentage of all

Table 4.6

Educational Levels of Political Leaders Who Were Military Officers[a]

Level of Education	Military Background		
	Military Officer	Non-Military Leadership	Totals
Primary			
No. of political leaders	18	23	41
% of political leaders	17.8	2.8	
Secondary			
No. of political leaders	17	43	60
% of political leaders	16.8	5.1	
Preparatory			
No. of political leaders	7	29	36
% of political leaders	6.9	3.5	
Normal			
No. of political leaders	5	47	52
% of political leaders	5.0	5.6	
University and/or Advanced Professional Degrees			
No. of political leaders	54	694	748
% of political leaders	53.5	83.0	
Subtotals			
No. of political leaders	101 (10.8%)	836 (89.2%)	937[b] (100%)
% of political leaders	100.0	100.0	

[a]Military officers refers to only those individuals who were career officers and reached a rank of major or higher.
[b]Data are taken from the MPBP.

political elites who did not have such educations (Table 4.7). The federal deputies in this sample are persons who have repeated as federal deputies or held other high-level positions, and are therefore not representative of the educational achievements of all federal deputies, who would have lower educational levels. For example, in examining the educational levels of all federal deputies for the 1952–1955 legislature (the median legislature for the 14 included in this sample), we find that of the 143 deputies, six had normal certificates (4 percent), 49 had college or professional degrees in the fields of law, economics, accounting, or medicine (34 percent), and at least half a dozen were career military officers. Fully 60 percent of the 1952–1955 deputation did not have college educations, as contrasted to the 27 percent figure for the selected group of federal deputies.[24]

Federal deputyships, like all positions in Mexico, have become filled increasingly by the educated minority. Comparing figures for the 1952–1955 deputation with those for the 1973–1976 deputation, the situation is almost the reverse. One-hundred and thirty-three or 55 percent of the most recent legislature had professional or university degrees in fields more wide-ranging than the earlier group, and 21 or 9 percent had normal certificates. Only 3 out of 240 were career military officers.[25] Other Latin American countries have

Table 4.7

Educational Levels of Political Leaders Who Were Federal Deputies

| Level of Education | Legislative Background | | |
	Federal Deputy	Other Political Leaders	Totals
Primary			
No. of political leaders	22	19	41
% of political leaders	5.5	3.5	
Secondary			
No. of political leaders	33	27	60
% of political leaders	8.3	5.0	
Preparatory			
No. of political leaders	17	19	36
% of political leaders	4.3	3.5	
Normal			
No. of political leaders	36	16	52
% of political leaders	9.1	3.0	
University and/or Advanced Professional Degrees			
No. of political leaders	289	459	748
% of political leaders	72.8	85.0	
Subtotals			
No. of political leaders	397 (42.4%)	540 (57.6%)	937[a] (100%)
% of political leaders	100.0	100.0	

[a]Data are taken from the MPBP.

comparable levels of education among legislative members. For example, Joel Verner found that 44 percent of the 1966–1970 Guatemalan legislature had college degrees, of which three-fourths received their degrees from the University of San Carlos in Guatemala City. Ninety-four percent of all the legislators had completed a secondary education.[26] Despite the significant changes in the educational achievements of federal deputies in the last 20 years, at least a third still do not have a university degree, showing that Mexicans without high levels of education still may hold a national political position. The educational changes reflected among all federal deputies are true of our selected group of elites who have been federal deputies. Of all deputies from 1935–1976 who had reached *only primary and secondary school* levels in our sample, 68 percent with primary education and 82 percent with secondary education were deputies before 1955 (data from MPBP).

An excellent example of a Mexican politician who used his success as a federal deputy to improve his status educationally and politically is Manuel Orijel Salazar, who was born in the Federal District during the second decade of this century. He attended primary school in the Federal District from 1920 to 1927, and then began to work. After 14 years, he went back to school and completed his secondary training in 1943. He continued with his preparatory training, studying for one year in 1944–1945. Meanwhile, he had become quite active in the Federal Bureaucrats Union, and began holding positions in the official party organization in the Federal District. These political activities made it possible for him to be selected as a federal deputy in the 9th legislative district in Mexico City, and he served in that capacity from 1946 to 1949. He began holding more important positions within the official party, becoming Secretary of Bureaucratic Action for PRI. Then, in 1957, he returned to his preparatory studies, completing them at the National Preparatory School. He then entered the National Law School, and finished his degree in 1962. His degree allowed him to become chief of lawyers for the board of arbitration of the Federal Bureaucrats Union. He was then reelected as a federal deputy in 1964, and became a national secretary of the Federal Bureaucrats Union. After skipping only one term, he was elected for the third time as a federal deputy in 1970, becoming one of the few Mexicans in recent history to achieve this political feat.[27]

The other national elective position of importance, other than that of federal deputy, is senator. Our sample of senators can be considered representative since we include data on 229 senators holding that position since 1935, or slightly over half the total. Table 4.8 indicates that senators have a very high level of education: 70.7 percent have university or professional degrees, a figure below that of elites who were not senators (82 percent), but substantially higher than for federal deputies. As with federal deputies, university educations have become more prevalent among senators in recent terms, particularly during the 1964 administration.

Typical of many senators with university degrees has been the education and political career of Carlos Román Celis, a native of Coyuca de Catalán, a *municipio* in the tropical lowlands of Guerrero. He completed his primary studies in Catalán, and began his secondary education in Teloloapan, Guerrero in 1945, completing his studies in the Federal District where he attended night school. He won a prize in physics and chemistry as a night school student, and then continued his studies at night at the National Preparatory School, where he also distinguished himself as a student. In 1948, he became president of the student society at the National Preparatory School. After finishing his studies there, he continued at the National Law School and graduated in 1953. Meanwhile, he participated as an orator for Adolfo Ruiz Cortines in the 1952 presidential campaign, and covered that campaign as a reporter for *Mañana*. He was selected as an alternate federal deputy for Guerrero, and served as Director of the Press Office for the Mexican Institute of

Table 4.8

Educational Levels of Senators By Legislature

Legislature	Primary	Secondary	Prepara-tory	Normal	University and/or Advanced Professional Degrees	Totals
Pre-1935						
No. of senators	3	1	2	0	8	14
% of senators	21.4	7.1	14.3	0	57.1	99.9[a]
1935–1940						
No. of senators	3	6	3	1	27	40
% of senators	7.5	15.0	7.5	2.5	67.5	100.0
1940–1946						
No. of senators	3	6	1	1	12	23
% of senators	13.0	26.1	4.3	4.3	52.2	99.9[a]
1946–1952						
No. of senators	3	2	3	1	20	29
% of senators	10.3	6.9	10.3	3.4	70.0	99.9[a]
1952–1958						
No. of senators	0	5	3	1	25	34
% of senators	0	14.7	8.8	2.9	73.5	99.9[a]
1958–1964						
No. of senators	3	5	1	3	27	39
% of senators	7.7	12.8	2.6.	7.7	69.2	110.0
1964–1970						
No. of senators	0	0	0	1	30	31
% of senators	0	0	0	3.2	96.8	100.0
1970–1976						
No. of senators	0	1	2	3	13	19
% of senators	0	5.3	10.5	15.8	68.4	100.0
Subtotals						
No. of senators	15	26	15	11	162	229[b]
% of senators	6.6	11.4	6.6	4.8	70.7	100.1[a]

[a]These percentages do not total 100.0 due to rounding.
[b]Data are taken from the MPBP.

Social Security. In 1955, he ran as a federal deputy, winning a three-year term. In 1958, he became one of Guerrero's senators for the next six years.[28]

Most observers of the Mexican political system would rank senators as holding more prestigious and influential positions than federal deputies. If this is true, then it appears that as a person goes higher up the ladder of political influence, he is more likely to have a university education. Obviously, national union leadership positions are more important than that of the average federal deputy and senator, but these positions are in a category by themselves, since they generally require longtime activity within the union itself, stemming, at least initially, from a profession similar to that of other union members.

A third elective position, that of governor, is the highest state elective position, and one which I would rank above that of senator in political importance for larger states, and below senators but above deputies for smaller states. (In making reference to educational levels for federal deputies in general, I am referring to the figures from a total population of the 1955 legislature, and not to the data in Table 4.7 from the MPBP.) A previous study of governors shows that 62 percent of all governors from 1935 to 1973 had university or professional educations, putting governors between deputies and senators in terms of education.[29]

If we continue to examine the educational achievements of Mexico's political elite, but focus on administrative positions, we find the same pattern emerging among these officeholders as was true of elective officials. Figures for *oficiales mayores,* who are the third-ranked cabinet-level officials, and in my opinion, more significant in their political influence than federal senators or deputies, reveal that a remarkable number, 85 percent, received college or professional educations[30] (Table 4.9). In the 1970–76 administration, only two of the 28 key agency directors did not have university educations, indicating that higher education is almost a prerequisite for a subcabinet position in Mexico. In the top administrative levels, well over 90 percent of political leaders have attended a university, a figure above that of third-ranked officials. Educational levels are consistent with the political importance of the office. This characteristic appears to be true for other countries too. Quandt reached the conclusion that "of the variables for which sufficient data exist, university education is the characteristic most likely to increase in frequency in the upper ranges of power. In eighteen out of nineteen cases, the political unit with the greater authority contained the larger number of university-educated men."[31]

If we examine a third category of political offices, that of party leadership positions, we find other interesting patterns. For the official party, university education has been typical of party leaders in percentages equal to political elites in general. For high officials of the party, university education has not been as important as for administrative officeholders, since only 65

Table 4.9

Education Levels of *Oficiales Mayores*

Level of Education	Administrative Background		
	Oficial Mayor	Other Political Leaders	Totals
Primary			
No. of *oficiales mayores*	2	39	41
% of *oficiales mayores*	1.5	4.8	
Secondary			
No. of *oficiales mayores*	10	50	60
% of *oficiales mayores*	7.5	6.2	
Preparatory			
No. of *oficiales mayores*	2	34	36
% of *oficiales mayores*	1.5	4.2	
Normal			
No. of *oficiales mayores*	6	46	52
% of *oficiales mayores*	4.5	5.7	
University and/or Advanced Professional Degree			
No. of *oficiales mayores*	113	635	748
% of *oficiales mayores*	85.0	79.0	
Subtotals			
No. of *oficiales mayores*	133 (14.2%)	804 (85.8%)	937 (100%)
% of *oficiales mayores*	100.0	99.9[a]	

[a]This figure does not total 100.0 due to rounding.

Table 4.10

Education Levels of Regional and National PRI Party Leaders

Level of Education	Positions Held				
	President of CEN	Secretary or Sec'y Gen. of CEN	Regional President	Other Party Position	Totals
Primary					
No. of PRI party leaders	3	4	0	3	10
% of PRI party leaders	21.4	7.0	0	2.2	4.1
Secondary					
No. of PRI party leaders	1	3	5	6	15
% of PRI party leaders	7.1	5.3	13.9	4.4	6.1
Preparatory					
No. of PRI party leaders	1	3	1	4	9
% of PRI party leaders	7.1	5.3	2.8	2.9	3.7
Normal					
No. of PRI party leaders	0	5	4	10	19
% of PRI party leaders	0	8.8	11.1	7.3	7.8
University and/or Advanced Professional Degrees					
No. of PRI party leaders	9	42	26	114	191
% of PRI party leaders	64.3	73.7	72.2	83.2	78.3
Subtotals					
No. of PRI party leaders	14	57	36	137	244
% of PRI party leaders	99.9[a]	100.1[a]	100.0	100.0	100.0

[a]These figures do not total 100.0 due to rounding.

percent of the party presidents and 74 percent of the party secretaries had university degrees compared to over 80 percent for administrators. The official party (which likes to advertise itself as representative of a cross-section of the Mexican population) when measured in terms of educational achievements, has allowed to some extent for uneducated Mexicans to succeed to high office—a condition that is not true for PAN, the most important opposition party. All of PAN's presidents and secretaries general for whom we have complete information (8) have university degrees. Even members of their National Executive Committee (25 or 96 percent with college degrees) have been exceptionally well educated, better than any group within the government political elite. In a more detailed study of PRI and PAN leaders by Donald J. Mabry and me, we found this same pattern:[32]

Educational Degree	Number of Leaders		Percentage	
	PRI	PAN	PRI	PAN
Law	158	48	32.6	53.3
Medicine	35	11	7.2	12.2
Economics, CPA, Engineering, Science	110	13	22.7	14.4
Other college degrees	41	9	8.5	10.0
Sub-total	344	81	71.0	89.9
No degree	139	9	28.7	10.0
Unknown	2	0	0.4	0.0
Totals	485	90	100.1	99.9

The higher percentage of college-educated leaders was even true for federal deputies from PAN when compared to PRI. Again, citing the data from that study, we could conclude that PAN recruits from a different stratum of society, namely a more educated and urban group.

We have data on leaders of the other important party in Mexico, the Popular Socialist Party (PPS), which presents itself to the public as a party of the people, or more specifically, a working man's party. In reality, political leadership in Mexico, regardless of parties, has much in common in terms of education, since PPS presidents have all had university educations, and only two or 14 percent of its known secretaries and secretaries general have not had university educations. Among a very small sample of other PPS party leaders (eight individuals), the vast majority were teachers, a profession which is well organized in unions, where PPS is strong. Interestingly enough, no PPS leaders had only primary or secondary educations, despite the party's image as a blue collar party.

The importance of teachers in the PPS is illustrated by the career of Jesús Luján Gutiérrez, a party federal deputy for the PPS from 1970 to 1973. Luján Gutiérrez was born in a small village in 1934 in the border state of Chihuahua.

He attended Public School No. 192 in Ciudad Juárez, and then went to the rural normal school in Salaices, Chihuahua from 1948–1953. He received his teaching certificate and became a primary and secondary school teacher in his home state. In 1961, he went back to school, completing another certificate from the Higher Normal School of Chihuahua. During his long career as a teacher, he became a principal of several primary and secondary schools, and finally a government inspector for public and private primary schools.[33]

Conclusions

There are several noteworthy characteristics about the educational background of Mexico's political elite. First, all high-level Mexican political leaders are part of a small minority of Mexicans who have received any form of education beyond the primary school level, since 82 percent have received a university or professional degree. Second, higher education has become more prevalent among the political elite in recent administrations. Third, while educational fields have become more diverse among political leaders, law is still the first choice of an overwhelming majority of successful public figures, and even more so for members of the Revolutionary Family. Fourth, a significant number of officeholders have received their educations at both the preparatory and university levels at the National University of Mexico at a rate which is disproportionate to that of the general educated population. Fifth, prospective political leaders, without higher levels of formal education, will be more likely to achieve success if they follow careers in the national unions, as federal deputies, or even in the official party. Sixth, as we look at individual positions and rank them in order of influence or prestige, we generally find rising levels of education as we move up the political ladder. Last, in terms of education, major opposition parties in Mexico, the PPS and PAN, are more selective than is the official party. Education, then, serves as a prerequisite to a successful political career for most of Mexico's political leadership, and will become even more essential to the prospective leader in achieving admittance to this select group of men and women.

Gabriel Almond and G. Bingham Powell have argued that increased structural differentiation and role specialization takes place as development occurs.[34] In Mexico, role specialization is reflected in the *relative* educational levels of political elites over the years, in particular, the increase of graduate degrees, and the diversity in professional specializations among political leaders. Individuals who have developed special skills have done well in elite political positions. Those recognized largely for their technical and administrative talents have had more staying power. Paul H. Lewis, in his study of the Spanish cabinets since 1938, concluded that technicians stayed in office an average of more than two years more than the politicians in equivalent positions.[35] I also found this pattern to be true at the cabinet level in Mexico, where individuals with technical experience and education repeated in office more frequently than their strictly political counterparts.[36] Our educational data support the changes in degree specialization among Mexican political leaders, but at the same time they indicate the continuation of two traditional educational patterns—the dominance of lawyers and of graduates from the National University.

Why have law school graduates continued their influence, even in positions with responsibility over complex economic and technical problems? Tradition and recruitment both play important roles in explaining the continued domination of lawyers as a professional group in Mexico's political leadership. The importance of bureaucracy and an accompanying legal tradition has been a dual characteristic prominent in the history of Mexico since the time of the Spanish conquest. Law, like medicine, was the traditional degree earned by 19th-century and early 20th-century graduates. Since 19th-century politics was an arena enjoyed mainly by the middle and upper classes, college-educated participants came largely from these two professions. Therefore, both professional groups were strongly represented among the political elite during the initial decades of the 20th century.[37] But both did not remain well represented. A background in medicine declined among political elites because it provided neither a useful administrative skill nor professional training emphasizing interpersonal skills necessary to succeed politically. It had been initially well represented for only one major reason—it was among the largest professional programs in Mexico. It was logical to expect that a fair number of educated political leaders would come from that faculty. Proportionately, however, medicine was not well represented among the political leadership by the 1930s.

While medicine became less appropriate to public life, except in the public health field, law remained important, or perhaps grew in importance during the transitional years of the 1920s and 1930s. The Revolution, and the structural upheaval resulting from that movement, produced revisions in all of the major legal codes in Mexico as well as the creation of legislation in new areas, such as labor law. Rather than stagnating, the National Law School, under the innovative leadership of deans who themselves were public men and who created much of the new legislation, developed a curriculum corresponding to these changes. It is no accident, for example, that Miguel Alemán attributes his own interest in political activity as well as recognition of his skills to his successful legal career in the untested field of workman's compensation law during the early 1930s.[38] The study of law, unlike its companion professions, had a wide-ranging curriculum, involving courses in sociology, geography, and political economy, which provoked interest in and discussion about social, economic, and political issues. Furthermore, the Law School was the center of intellectual and political activities among students, which contributed to the development of interpersonal and communications skills.

The Law School remained dominant not solely because of the demand for its skills and its initial representation among political leaders, but because of the men who served as political recruiters in Mexico.[39] As I suggested earlier, recruiters tend to favor individuals modeled after themselves; and furthermore, they must come into contact with the prospective leader if they are to recruit him.[40] The bulk of the recruiters have been lawyers, who have recruited from their own alma mater, the National Law School. The President of Mexico, his secretaries of government and of treasury, who all would be in a position to appoint large numbers of individuals to important public and party offices, have been lawyers, if they were college educated (with one exception). Furthermore, it can be demonstrated how students, professors, and administrators were recruited by one generation of lawyers, and in turn became recruiters of later generations.[41] And it is not surprising that the newest profession to make itself felt among educated political leaders is that of economics, a school born from the Law School.

Another important implication of the data presented in this chapter is the continued domination of the National University among university-educated political leaders, although its share of college-educated Mexicans continues to decline.[42] Diversification in education is beginning to occur, particularly among state political leaders, who are more frequently coming from the state universities, although they often pursue careers in the national bureaucracy.[43] But this trend will be slow, because most of the individuals who are in a position to recruit for the federal bureaucracy, the single most important institution for successful national careers, are located at the National University. Although the National University provides training in all of the skills needed by political officeholders, no one would suggest that UNAM does this best, at least in many professional fields. But UNAM still carries the prestige of being the institution that educates Mexico's leaders, and it provides a political environment, unlike its more serious private counterparts, essential to a public man's training.[44] As long as it continues to maintain this image in the eyes of students with political ambitions, and as long as recruiters continue to teach there in large numbers, UNAM will wield influence in the education of Mexico's political leadership disproportionate to its educating role in society.

NOTES TO CHAPTER 4

[1]For evidence of earlier educational levels in Mexico, see Peter H. Smith, "La Política Dentro de la Revolución: El Congreso Constituyente de 1916–1917," *Historia Mexicana* **22,** no. 3 (1973): 383, and his *Labyrinths of Power: Political Recruitment in Twentieth-Century Mexico* (Princeton: Princeton University Press, 1979). For the high educational levels of early North American politicians, see Sidney H. Aronson, *Status and Kinship in the Higher Civil Service* (Cambridge: Harvard University Press, 1964), pp. 123–4.

[2]For educational statistics, see Clark Gil, *Education in a Changing Mexico* (Washington, D.C.: GPO, 1969); Arturo González Cosío, *Historia Estadística de la Universidad,*

1910–1967 (Mexico: UNAM, 1967); Inter-American Development Bank, *Economic and Social Progress in Latin America* (Washington, D.C.: IADB, 1974); Víctor L. Urquidi and Adrián Lajous Vargas, *La Educación Superior en México, 1966* (México: ANUIES, 1966).

³Charles N. Myers, *Education and National Development in Mexico* (Princeton: Princeton University Press, 1965), p. 24.

⁴*Ibid.*, p. 58.

⁵Lucio Mendieta y Núñez and José Gómez Robledo, *Problemas de la Universidad* (Mexico: UNAM, 1948), p. 240.

⁶Richard King, *The Provincial Universities of Mexico: An Analysis of Growth and Development* (New York: Praeger, 1971), p. 18.

⁷Francisco Javier Gaxiola, *Memorias* (Mexico: Editorial Porrúa, 1975), p. 254; Jorge Prieto Laurens, *Cincuenta Años de Política Mexicana, Memorias Políticas* (Mexico, 1968), p. 82.

⁸Robert North and Ithiel Sola Pool, "Kuomintang and Chinese Communist Elites," in Harold Lasswell and Daniel Lerner, eds, *World Revolutionary Elites (Cambridge:* MIT Press, 1966), p. 381.

⁹Letter to the author from Nazario S. Ortiz Garza, Mexico City, August 12, 1974.

¹⁰Hugh H. Smythe, "The Nigerian Elite: Role of Education," *Sociology and Social Research* **45** (October 1960): 71; Peter H. Smith, "Making it in Mexico: Aspects of Political Mobility Since 1946," paper presented to the American Political Science Association, Chicago, 1974, pp. 14–16; and William B. Quandt, "The Comparative Study of Political Elites," *Comparative Political Series* **I** (Beverly Hills: Sage, 1970), p. 189.

¹¹See González Cosío, *Historia estadística de la universidad*, p. 83ff., for the National University.

¹²Joel G. Verner found law and medicine to dominate among educated Guatemalan administrators, "Characteristics of Administrative Personnel: The Case of Guatemala," *Journal of Developing Areas* **5** (October 1970): 82.

¹³Lester Seligman, *Recruiting Political Elites* (New York: General Learning Press, 1971), p. 4.

¹⁴Lawyers dominate the political system in the United States. Thomas Dye found that 56 percent of the top leaders entered political careers as practicing lawyers and the number who had legal educations was even higher (*Who's Running America? Institutional Leadership in the United States* [Englewood Cliffs: Prentice-Hall, 1976], p. 160).

¹⁵Roderic A. Camp, "The Cabinet and the *Técnico* in Mexico and the United States," *Journal of Comparative Administration* **3** (August 1971): 189ff.

¹⁶For changes in professional training in Turkey from 1929 to 1950 see Frederick Frey, *The Turkish Political Elite* (Cambridge: MIT Press, 1965), pp. 282–3.

¹⁷Norman K. Nicholson, "Integrative Strategies of a National Elite: Career Patterns in the Indian Council of Ministers," *Comparative Politics* **7** (July 1975): 546.

¹⁸The primary school friends of López Portillo had places of honor at his inaguration. Of those who attended elementary school with the president, two (Jesús Reyes Heroles and Gabriel García Rojas) hold high-level positions in his administration. *Excélsior,* December 2, 1976, p. 12.

¹⁹Letter to the author from Salvador Azuela, Mexico City, July 14, 1974; and a personal interview, June 26, 1975, Mexico City.

²⁰The predominance of a single university on the education of a country's political elite is not confined to Latin America or other developing nations. In Japan, Tokyo University has produced the greatest number of graduates in cabinet positions in recent years (40 percent). See Peter Cheng, "The Japanese Cabinets, 1885–1973: An Elite Analysis," *Asian Survey* **14** (December 1974): 1063.

²¹Alfredo Navarrete, *Alto a la contrarevolución* (Mexico, 1971).

²²Robert North and Ithiel Sola Pool concluded that the rise of soldiers in the leadership of China after the communist revolution also broadened recruitment of the Chinese political elite ("Kuomintang," p. 390).

²³Roderic A. Camp, *Mexican Political Biographies, 1935–1975* (Tucson: University of Arizona Press, 1976), p. 226.

[24]México, *Congreso de la Cámara de Diputados del XLII Congreso de Los Estados Unidos Mexicanos* (Mexico, 1954).

[25]México, Cámara de Diputados, *Directorio XLIX Legislatura* (Mexico, 1973).

[26]Joel Verner, "The Guatemalan National Congress: An Elite Analysis," in Weston Agor, ed., *Latin American Legislatures: Their Role and Influence* (New York: Praeger, 1971), pp. 305–6.

[27]Roderic A. Camp, *Mexican Political Biographies*, pp. 238–9.

[28]Personal interview with Carlos Román Celis, June 9, 1974, Mexico City.

[29]Roderic A. Camp, "Mexican Governors Since Cárdenas, Education and Career Contacts," *Journal of Inter-American Studies and World Affairs* 16 (November 1974): 454–81.

[30]See Martin H. Greenberg, *Bureaucracy and Development: A Mexican Case Study* (Lexington, Mass.: D.C. Heath, 1970) for an enlightening description of this position.

[31]William B. Quandt, "Comparative Study," p. 189.

[32]Donald Mabry and Roderic A. Camp, "Mexican Political Elites 1935–1973: A Comparative Study," *The Americas* 31 (April 1975): 456. Adapted from Table I.

[33]Camp, *Mexican Political Biographies, 1935–1975*, p. 193.

[34]Gabriel Almond and G. Bingham Powell, Jr., *Comparative Politics: A Developmental Approach* (Boston: Little-Brown, 1966).

[35]Paul H. Lewis, "The Spanish Ministerial Elite, 1938–1969," *Comparative Politics* 5 (October 1972): 97.

[36]Roderic A. Camp, "The Cabinet and the *Técnico*," p. 200.

[37]See Peter H. Smith, *Labyrinths of Power*.

[38]Personal interview with Miguel Alemán, Mexico City, October 27, 1976.

[39]This pattern has been equally persistent in England, where conservative party ministers have had notable ties to each other through public school and through Oxford and Cambridge. This same pattern is being repeated among Labour party ministers. See Ted Tapper, *Political Education and Stability, Elite Responses to Political Conflict* (New York: John Wiley, 1976), p. 88; and Austin Ranney, *Pathways to Parliament: Candidate Selection in Britain* (Madison: University of Wisconsin Press, 1965), p. 100.

[40]Roderic A. Camp, "Education and Political Recruitment in Mexico: the Alemán Generation," *Journal of Inter-American Studies and World Affairs* 18 (August 1976): 295–321. Merilee Grindle, in her recent study of CONASUPO found that of the 59 officials she interviewed who had specialized technical training, all but one "were recruited on the basis of prior friendship or school ties" (*Bureaucrats, Politicians, and Peasants in Mexico: A Case Study in Public Policy* [Berkeley: University of California Press, 1977], p. 46).

[41]As John Price has argued, the scholastic system has long served as a testing institution for prospective recruits to the higher civil service in Europe, and serves as the sole agent of recruitment for the higher civil service in England ("Education and the Civil Service in Europe," *Western Political Quarterly* 10 [December 1957]: 832).

[42]Echeverría's government also attempted to reduce the influence of UNAM among public institutions in Mexico. See Yoram Shapira, "Mexico, the Impact of the 1968 Student Protest on Echeverría's Reformism," *Journal of Inter-American Studies and World Affairs* 19 (November 1977): 568.

[43]For evidence of this, see my "Mexican Governors," pp. 464–5.

[44]For some recent, insightful comments on the National University and its educational role, see Larissa Lomnitz, "Conflict and Mediation in a Latin American University," *Journal of Inter-American Studies and World Affairs* 19 (August 1977): 315–38.

5. Preparatory Schools: Career Mobility and Political Recruitment

Scholars have assumed that the typical institutions in Mexico, like the official party, the bureaucracy, the labor and agrarian unions, and the professional organizations have been largely responsible for the recruitment of political leaders. While these institutions have been instrumental in forming career contacts and in providing paths for upward mobility, they have not always served as the *initial point* of recruitment for those who ultimately serve in the highest public offices. Instead, recruitment often takes place in preparatory schools and universities before the prospective public figure is integrated into the official party or other government structures. It is essential to understand this process because those who have control over recruitment, how it takes place, and where, ultimately determine how much influence political leaders have on their own future, the political opportunities of other leaders, and the nature of decision making and public policy.[1]

Preparatory schools in Mexico have institutional characteristics that give them advantages over the above-mentioned organizations in serving as a locus for political recruitment. Although examples can be cited of politically active secondary students, most Mexicans who became politically active as students did not do so until they reached preparatory school. The preparatory schools, like the universities, have the chronological advantage of having a prospective political leader in their midst long before other political institutions. Mexican political leaders generally embark upon political careers at an earlier age than their European or United States counterparts. In more open political systems, scholars have found that few individuals seek public office before they are 30 years old because they lack the skills, contacts, and

[94]

reputation necessary for a political career.[2] In Mexico, however, it can be argued that preparatory schools and universities serve as communities for future political leaders to develop their skills in a politicized environment, to increase their contact with professors having political experience and students interested in public careers, and to demonstrate their competence as students in the classroom and in student political activities. In the United States, law schools appear to play a somewhat similar role for senators, who generally began their careers sooner than other types of political leaders because these schools provided them with more political skills and contacts.[3]

Preparatory schools are also in a naturally advantageous position because political organizations, which demand a high degree of allegiance, generally appear to recruit individuals at a young age. For example, in his study of Italian, French, and United States communist party leaders, Robert Holt found that over half had joined the party or participated in radical political activities before the age of 18.[4] These same individuals have been found to have improved their chances for top leadership positions because of their early recruitment.[5]

In Mexico, the importance of early recruitment and career mobility can be demonstrated by the success rate of political leaders who were student political leaders. Of the first-time officeholders in the MPBP, 22 percent were student leaders. However, of Revolutionary Family members, 38 percent were politically active as students. This figure suggests that student political activity increases an individual's political career opportunities in Mexico. The reasons for this are fairly obvious. The successful student activist demonstrates very openly and early his political abilities to fellow students and professors, while at the same time developing interpersonal skills essential to a successful political career. As David Schers suggests in his study of the National Confederation of Popular Organizations and how it recruits its leadership, a "group of friends" accepts the leadership of one of its members from the beginning, and the primary function of the group is helping its leaders to get political positions.[6] Personalistic cliques like these are often started at preparatory and university institutions. A person who takes a leadership role as a student develops a personal following, and rarely relinquishes it as his political career evolves.

Lastly, students who have political ambitions know that their career mobility within government and education structures can be improved through social contacts with professors and other students, particularly at the National Preparatory School and the National University.[7] In a political system that relies as much on personal contact as does Mexico's, the importance of sponsors, or "who you know" is essential to political success.[8] Students with political ambitions are therefore attracted to professors with political experience or contacts. Professors who are interested in building up their personal followings and increasing their chances in the future are interested in having their students in important public and academic posts.

In order to determine who is responsible for initial recruitment and how that recruitment takes place at preparatory schools, it is necessary to examine those institutions most frequented by the political leaders in our study and to identify and discuss the student activities of future political leaders that contributed to their recruitment. As demonstrated in Table 4.3, the three most important preparatory institutions in the education of Mexican political leaders have been the National Preparatory School, the Colegio de San Nicolás de Hidalgo (Morelia), and the Institute of Arts and Sciences of Oaxaca.

The National Preparatory School

EARLY DEVELOPMENT

In 1911, the National Preparatory School was confined to one location, the old Colegio de San Ildefonso in Mexico City, where the National Academy of History and Geography is now housed. During this decade, students wanting to go beyond the primary school level went directly into the general preparatory or normal school cycle, since a separate secondary program did not exist in Mexico until 1926. Because educational opportunities at the preparatory level were limited to a few regional *colegios*, the National Preparatory School took on the burden of providing preparatory education for many Mexicans.* The lack of educational opportunities at this level during the 1910s and early 1920s was significant for future political leaders because like the Turkish *Mulkiye*, a civil service school established in that country in 1859, the National Preparatory School served as a channel or funnel in the recruitment of individuals from rural areas who followed public careers.[9] Furthermore, it brought together a large majority of the future political and social leaders into a single location, much like the public schools in Great Britain, thereby increasing their contact with one another. However, unlike Great Britain, whose leaders in the early 20th century were often educated at a number of public schools, the vast majority of Mexican leaders attended only one institution, the National Preparatory School.

The purpose of the National Preparatory School, as seen by one student of its history, was twofold: first, to prepare students for specialization in various professional careers, particularly law and medicine; and second, to give students a general cultural education.[10] During this period, the cur-

---

*The word *colegio* is commonly used today for secondary schools in Mexico. However, in the past, it was used in the title of most state and regional universities. We will use it interchangeably with the word university in the context of state colleges.

riculum for most students lasted five years, and until 1914 was still very much influenced by the positivistic ideas of pre-Revolutionary generations. In 1911, there were 1345 students enrolled in the preparatory program, but only 85 of those graduated that year. By 1914, the figure had grown to over 1800 students, making the single building overcrowded and inadequate for teaching.[11] Although the quantitative effect was to bring future political leaders together, the education of future political leaders at the National Preparatory School seems to have had a qualitative effect on their beliefs and ideas through common socializing experiences. These have been attested to by these leaders in another study.[12] It is not the purpose of this book to demonstrate these common socializing experiences, but it is important to consider them briefly as they relate to political recruitment, personal allegiances, and to the functioning of the political system.

COMMON EXPERIENCE

Most of the political leaders who were educated at the National Preparatory School during the 1910s, and who were witnesses to many of the notable events of the Revolution, emerged with a strong commitment to peace and stability in contrast to the instability characterizing their formative years.[13] Furthermore, many of these young men developed a sense of unity not found in later, larger, and more diverse generations, and this unity helps to explain the continuity in leadership and political stability characterizing Mexico since 1946.[14] This belief in unity and political order became an ideological link or thread that tied personal alliances together even when some members held varying ideological views on other issues.

These common educational experiences are significant for political recruitment in two important ways. First, as Joseph Szyliowicz and Rupert Wilkinson suggest in their studies of the Mulkiye and British public schools, a certain relationship exists between the culture of the schools and the administration agencies that recruited their graduates.[15] In short, the pattern of behavior that often provided for success within the bureaucracy and cabinet in these two countries was inculcated in the educational institutions. If it is true, as many scholars of political recruitment suggest, that those in a position to do the recruiting tend to choose persons with like values and patterns of behavior to join them in the government, then an individual's place of education enhances his ability to move into and up the career ladder. In addition, as Lewis J. Edinger has concluded in his study of German leaders, scholars studying political leadership not only need to think in terms of the circulation of elite personnel, but need to consider the circulation of elite values.[16] For understanding the Mexican and other authoritarian political systems, it may be far more important to know if the ideas of political leaders are substantially different from one administration to the next rather than knowing what percent of the leadership itself is new. I believe it can be argued that the education of sponsors and their political recruits under the same professors and at the same institutions has a moderating effect on changes in political elite personnel.

The National Preparatory School, then, becomes the first institution to screen, train, and identify future political leaders. Of course, as the previous chapter makes clear, not all political leaders pass through this educational institution. However, not a single institution, with the exception of the professional schools at the National University, could claim to have had such a sizeable group (198 individuals) pass through its ranks during an equivalent period of time, including the army, labor unions, or any sectoral party organization.

RELATIONSHIP TO PUBLIC LIFE

Technically, public education in Mexico is part of the federal bureaucracy, from the primary public school teacher to the professor of graduate studies at the National University, since all are governed (despite university autonomy in 1929) by federal funds and federal regulations.[17] More important for the National Preparatory School and the University is the relationship of both to public life in Mexico.* University life cannot be separated from public life, since reputations made at the university are crucial to successful public careers and public men are equally crucial to the education of students who become future public leaders.† Although this has been much less true of the preparatory school than the university, it is difficult to separate the two. The majority of young professors who were appointed during the period of our study had been prominent students of the professors they replaced, students of professors who became deans, directors, or rectors, or friends of other students who ultimately held the previous two positions. Those preparatory and university administrators with political ambitions have used these positions as stepping stones to high-level political careers.[18] It is for this reason that examples of recruitment to these positions will also be examined to demonstrate the frequent interchange between high-level academic and public careers.

---

*The 1929 agreement between President Portes Gil and the National University included several important provisions that gave the government considerable influence over the university. In particular, the president was allowed to choose the rector from a slate of three candidates selected by the University Council, and furthermore, he could revise the use of financial resources by the university.

†I am not arguing that all university administrators are political appointees, but that public men have been influential in selecting the candidates who hold prominent university positions. See chapter vii for details about the selection of university administrators.

Even though the National Preparatory School was closed down on several occasions in the decade from 1910–1920, it became one of the few preparatory schools in Mexico to maintain at least some semblance of a continuing program on a year-by-year basis.* This attracted greater numbers of students from the provinces. As a result of its stability, the National Preparatory School became an intellectual and educational center for the majority of persons who went on to the university. The curriculum and size of the school during this period were conducive to student contact. Since the program generally ran over a five-year period, students were divided into five groups according to the year they began their studies. As is true of secondary schools in the United States, the higher the grade, the smaller the number of students. Therefore, those students who actually completed the fifth year of preparatory school graduated with 50 to 75 students as their companions, making it possible for them to know personally most or all of their classmates, as well as students from earlier or later years.[19]

I have interviewed or corresponded with 13 of the surviving members of those classes (1911–20) of the National Preparatory School who distinguished themselves in public careers *after* 1935 (Table 5.1). All of these persons recall in some detail the various members of their class, as well as friends in earlier or later classes. The National Preparatory School helped create lasting friendships among students who embarked on different professional careers. This accounts for friendships among students who followed careers in medicine, law, literature, and economics, and therefore studied at different professional schools at the National University.[20]

STUDENT RELATIONSHIPS

Student contacts were encouraged in a number of ways during the 1910s at the National Preparatory School. For example, because of the diversity of intellectual currents, students were prompted to become actively involved in a variety of student intellectual activities.[21] One notable literary figure and public man, Jaime Torres Bodet, described their youthful efforts as a veritable "Fountain of Youth."[22] Social groups also flourished. Luis Garrido and

---

*In 1922, the following schools with preparatory programs were represented at a conference in Mexico City: Colegio de San Nicolás, Colegio Civil de Monterrey, Colegio Civil de Querétaro, Instituto de Ciencias y Artes de Oaxaca, Instituto de Pachuca, Hidalgo, Instituto Juárez, Durango, Colegio de Guanajuato, Escuela Preparatoria de Aguascalientes, Escuela Regional Preparatoria de San Cristobal de las Casas, Universidad del Sureste de Mérida, Escuela Preparatoria Tapachula, Chiapas, Instituto Científico de Chihuahua, Instituto de Toluca, México, Escuela Preparatoria de Ciudad Victoria, Tamaulipas, Instituto Científico de San Luis Potosí, Escuela Preparatoria de Guadalajara, and the Instituto de Ciencias y Letras de Zacatecas. See Mexico City, Escuela Nacional Preparatoria, *Memorial del primer congreso de escuelas preparatorias de la república* (México: Editorial Cultura, 1922), p. 8.

Table 5.1

Graduates of the National Preparatory School From 1911 to 1920
Who Held High Public Office From 1935 to 1976

Name of Graduate	Year[a]	Highest Position in Public Life Since 1935[b]
Icaza y López, Xavier	1912	Justice of the Supreme Court
Ortiz Tirado, José María	1912	President of the Supreme Court
Baz, Gustavo	1913	Secretary of Public Health and Welfare
Bassols, Narciso	1915	Secretary of Government
Caso, Alfonso	1915	Secretary of National Properties
Castro Leal, Antonio	1915	Ambassador to UNESCO
Gómez Morín, Manuel	1915	President of the CEN of PAN
Lombardo Toledano, Vicente	1915	Secretary General of the CTM
Martínez Tornel, Pedro	1915	Secretary of Public Works
Mendieta y Núñez, Lucio	1915	*Oficial Mayor* of Agrarian Affairs
Olea y Leyva, Teófilo	1915	Justice of the Supreme Court
Beteta, Ignacio	1916	Chief of Staff of National Defense
Carreño Gómez, Franco	1916	Justice of the Supreme Court
Chávez, Eduardo	1916	Secretary of Hydraulic Resources
De la Colina, Rafael	1916	Ambassador to the United States
García, Trinidad	1916	Dean of the National Law School
Garrido Díaz, Luis	1916	Rector of the National University
Gaxiola y Z., Javier	1916	Secretary of Industry and Commerce
Rojo Gómez, Javier	1916	Head of the Department of the Federal District
Sandoval Vallarta, Manuel	1916	Subsecretary of Public Education
Zubirán, Salvador	1916	Rector of the National University
Zuckermann D., Conrado	1916	Subsecretary of Welfare
Brito Foucher, Rodulfo	1917	Rector of the National University
González de la Vega, Francisco	1917	Attorney General of Mexico
Gorostiza, José	1917	Subsecretary of Foreign Relations
Loyo, Gilberto	1917	Secretary of Industry and Commerce
Torres Bodet, Jaime	1917	Secretary of Public Education
Beteta, Ramón	1918	Secretary of the Treasury
Campos Ortiz, Pablo	1918	Subsecretary of Foreign Relations
Bustamante, Miguel E.	1919	Subsecretary of Health
Alatriste, Sealtiel	1920	Director General of IMSS
Beltrán, Enrique C.	1920	Subsecretary of Forest Resources
Gual Vidal, Manuel	1920	Secretary of Education
Martínez García, Pedro D.	1920	Subsecretary of Health
Perez Moreno, José	1920	*Oficial Mayor* of Hydraulic Resources
Sousa, Mario	1920[d]	Secretary of Industry and Commerce

[a]Indicates the year a person graduated if the student followed a normal five-year cycle. Some students, however, completed their studies in less time, while others extended their preparatory education by several years. Since we wish to indicate other classmates of individual graduates, we will use the normal graduation year, whether or not the person actually graduated earlier or later.

[b]For purposes of these tables, we will include high-level party positions, whether official or opposition party positions, and rectorships of UNAM and IPN as public offices.

[c]An italicized name indicates the person corresponded with and/or was interviewed by me. This format will be used throughout the book.

[d]Although we do not have complete figures available, approximately 600 students graduated during the years 1912 to 1920 at the National Preparatory School. At least 6 percent of these graduates were highly successful public men *after* 1935. Of these public men, at the time of the interviews, 14 were dead and one was in a coma, leaving 21 graduates still alive. Thirteen or 62 percent of those still living were interviewed.

Franco Carreño founded the Manuel Gutiérrez Nájera Society, whose members included, among others, Jaime Torres Bodet and Octavio Vejar Vázquez, both of whom became secretaries of Public Education. They met regularly to listen to and discuss the poetry and essays of the members, and they continued to meet after 1917 when they entered professional schools. Even though the classes at the National Preparatory School were larger than the professional schools at the National University, there was an equal amount of student contact. One means for circulating ideas and socializing with one another was the numerous student newspapers published by preparatory students during this period.[23] Francisco González de la Vega recalls that students from various states got together on that basis. For example, students from his native state of Durango held social gatherings that developed many early friendships.[24]

These activities helped to cement student friendships, and such friendships have been helpful to successful public careers. This has occurred in two ways: a student has been responsible for recommending or obtaining a public position for his companion in his early career, thereby recruiting him into national governmental positions; or, much later, after acquiring a position of some importance, he has recommended or appointed a student companion to an important position. Since few students are usually in a position to recommend a co-student for a position immediately after graduation from preparatory or professional school, student relationships are generally more significant for later career positions. This form of influence cannot legitimately be defined as political recruitment, unless a person has not held public office and is asked to serve in a top government position by a former classmate. While this has occurred with a number of officeholders, most men and women have entered public careers before or immediately upon graduation from professional school. Since we are concerned primarily with the role of the preparatory schools and the university as a recruiting agent in Mexico, and second with their influence on career mobility, let us first illustrate the first pattern.

Luis Garrido Díaz, who graduated from the National Preparatory School in 1916, was an intimate friend and co-student with Narciso Bassols, a member of the 1915 graduating class. Bassols, one of the most brilliant graduates of the National Preparatory School, was a political activist who continued his studies at the Law School and became president of the Student Association of that school. In 1919, he supported a gubernatorial campaign in Aguascalientes, and then completed his law degree in 1921, after which at the age of 23, Bassols became a professor of legal guarantees and *amparo* at the National School of Law, served as the Secretary of Government for the state of Mexico in 1925 under the important political figure, Carlos Riva Palacios, and a short time later wrote the Agrarian Law of 1927.[25] During this period he was appointed Dean of the National Law School, and in this position, he invited Garrido Díaz to become a professor of forensic law. Shortly thereafter, he recommended Garrido Díaz for his first national office as a Federal Agent under José Aguilar y Maya, the Attorney General of the Federal District.

It was at this point in his career that Garrido Díaz became close friends with José A. Ceniceros, a co-agent and member with Garrido Díaz on the Committee to Revise the National Penal Code. His early public career was affected by Ceniceros, who, like Bassols, held prominent positions as a young man. Garrido Díaz, without becoming a member of the official party, went on to become subdirector of the government paper, *El Nacional*, under Ceniceros, in 1936; Director of the Federal Insurance Agency in 1939; and in 1948, Rector of the National University.[26] As a multi-talented individual, he would have been a success without the assistance of Bassols, but he might never have followed a public career. Furthermore, his career path, determined in part by his friendship with Bassols as a young student, in turn affected the careers of other individuals. For example, because of his position as a federal agent, he also became friends with Raúl Carrancá y Trujillo, who later distinguished himself as a judge and law professor. In 1933, he and Garrido Díaz founded the journal *Criminalia*. Garrido Díaz's friendship with him and respect for Carrancá y Trujillo were the reasons why he asked him to serve as his Secretary General of the National University in 1952, the second most influential position at the university.*

Former co-students do have the opportunity of appointing each other to high-level positions when one of them arrives at a position of some responsibility. This is known to be true of four of our high-level officeholders graduating from 1911 to 1920 (Table 5.2). Jaime Torres Bodet, a graduate of the National Preparatory School in 1917, was a friend and co-student with José Gorostiza, who later went into the Mexican Foreign Service. Many years later, when Jaime Torres Bodet became the head of Mexico's delegation to the UNESCO conference in 1945, José Gorostiza accompanied him as an advisor. At the end of 1946, Torres Bodet became the Secretary of Foreign Relations, and he appointed Gorostiza Director General of the Diplomatic Service and asked him to represent Mexico at the Rio Conference in 1947. In 1948, Torres Bodet headed the delegation to the·Bogotá Conference, and again Gorostiza accompanied him as an advisor. In 1949, he became Secretary General of UNESCO, and another friend and co-student, Antonio Castro Leal, became Mexico's Ambassador to UNESCO, serving until Torres Bodet resigned in 1952.[27]

---

*These, and other examples, are duplicated throughout the text by many public men in this study.

STUDENT-PROFESSOR RELATIONSHIPS

However, at the preparatory school level, political recruitment has taken place most frequently as a result of the relationship between students and their professors (Table 5.2). There are two common patterns similar to those among students. First, professors are frequently responsible for introducing students into public life, either because of their own position in government, or their personal friendship with someone else in government. Second, successful students who reach responsible public positions often remember their professors as talented and responsible individuals, or want to repay them for assisting their careers, and try to recruit them to high-level public positions. Again, this can be considered recruitment only when the professor has not already made public life his second career. Occasionally, professors will reach high public offices, and they will recruit former students who were talented in the classroom who otherwise might not have gone into public service. As Daniel Cosío Villegas describes it, even though most professors were part-time and did not have offices in which to receive students at school, students still were able to cultivate close relationships, including friendships, with the professors of their choice.[28]

The most influential professor in this period, both intellectually and in terms of his impact on the careers of young students, was the eminent

Table 5.2

The Recruitment of the 1911–20 National Preparatory Classes

Name of Recruitee at ENP	Relationship to Recruiter[a]	Recruiter or Sponsor
Bassols, Narciso	Co-student	Antonio Castro Leal
Baz, Gustavo	Personal Physician	Lázaro Cárdenas
Beltrán C., Enrique	Former Professor	Guillermo Gándara
Beteta, Ignacio	Revolutionary Associate	Lázaro Cárdenas
Brito Foucher, Rodulfo	Former Professor	Roberto Medellín Ostos
Caso, Alfonso	Co-student	Alberto Vázquez del Mercado
Castro Leal, Antonio	Former Professor	José Vasconcelos
Chávez, Eduardo	Administrative Subordinate	Lázaro Cardenas
De la Colina, Rafael	Revolutionary Associate	Candido Aguilar
García, Trinidad	Co-student	Manuel Gómez Morín
Garrido Díaz, Luis	Former Professor	Narciso Bassols
Gaxiola, Javier	Relative	Francisco J. Gaxiola
Gómez Morín, Manuel	Former Professor	Alejandro Quijano
González de la Vega, Francisco	Former Professor	Antonio Caso
Gorostiza, José	Former Professor	Narciso Bassols
Gual Vidal, Manuel	Former Professor	Luis Chico Goerne
Lombardo Toledano, Vicente	Co-student	Alberto Vázquez del Mercado
Mendieta y Núñez, Lucio	Former Professor	Manuel Gamio
Pérez Moreno, José	Co-student	Eduardo Chávez
Rojo Gómez, Javier	Law Partner	Emilio Portes Gil
Sousa, Mario	Former Professor	Roberto Medellín Ostos
Zubirán, Salvador	Former Professor	Gastón Melo
Zuckermann Duarte, Conrado	Former Student	José Alvarez Amezquita

[a]Known forms of political recruitment to *national* positions only.

philosopher Antonio Caso. Caso served as a professor of philosophy at the National Preparatory School, and as a professor of sociology at the School of Law. In 1921, he became Rector of the University, selected by his co-student José Vasconcelos, his predecessor in the rectorship and the newly appointed Secretary of Public Education. He immediately began to expand the offerings of the university through night extension courses. He asked many of his former students, who were graduates of professional schools or students still completing their programs to serve as instructors for those courses.* Caso also asked his former student, 18-year-old Jaime Torres Bodet, to serve as a professor of general literature for the free preparatory courses in 1920. One year later, when Caso became Rector, Torres Bodet became Secretary of the National Preparatory School.[29] What is most remarkable about this period is that many young university students became professors of students just two or three years behind them. Qualified professors were scarce, adequate amounts of funds were erratic, and many former professors had abandoned their posts because of the changes in government. With few exceptions, nearly all of the individuals in Table 5.1 began teaching before they reached the age of 25.

STUDENT ACTIVITIES AND CONTACTS

In the early years of the National Preparatory School, it could be expected that students and professors, as well as students themselves, would have become more easily acquainted because of the small size of the student body and classes, as well as the low student-professor ratio.[30] As the National Preparatory School began to grow in size after 1920, we would expect this contact, and therefore recruitment, to decrease. Instead, we will see its importance increase as the result of several factors. First, as indicated in Table 5.3, most high-level officeholders came from the preparatory generations from 1910 to 1940; had we included public men holding office *prior to* 1935, many more persons would have been included in lists of graduates in tables 5.1 and 5.2. Second, the number of older students with successful careers had a multiplier effect, increasing the number of younger co-students who could be recruited into public activities. Third, in 1946 a member of the 1920–24 preparatory generation, Miguel Alemán, became the first president since 1920 to have graduated from the National Preparatory School.[31] Fourth, in 1926, numerous secondary schools were established, draining off large groups of students from the National Preparatory School and reducing its

---

*Among them, Vasconcelos appointed Luis Garrido (later Rector of the National University), Franco Carreño (later Justice of the Supreme Court), Agustín García López (later Secretary of Public Works), Xavier Villaurrutia (poet), Salvador Novo (later Director of Theater for Bellas Artes), Salvador Azuela (later Dean of the School of Philosophy and Secretary General of the National University), Samuel Ramos (philosopher and later *Oficial Mayor* of Public Education) and Mario Sousa (later Secretary of Industry and Commerce).

size.* Fifth, the 1929 presidential campaign and the university autonomy movement brought many students together both inside and outside of the preparatory school, giving them a unity they had not had previously.[32]

Many of these students during the 1920s were the first in their families to have an opportunity for this level of education. Because of their different social and economic backgrounds, students were more curious about each other and about the changes that had brought them together, and they actively discussed the many cultural, literary, and political trends of the decade.[33] Social groups proliferated, even more so than in the previous decade. Students from the provinces, like Andrés Iduarte of Tabasco, organized their companions from home and held many stormy meetings involving political issues of the day.[34] These provincial groups provided another form of contact between students. Some of the student houses in Mexico City became known for their social gatherings.[35] The Casa de la Troya, one of the more notable of such homes, was a gathering place for students, many of whom became prominent in public or university affairs.† At the same time, many of these

Table 5.3

Generations of Preparatory School Graduates Who Became Public Men[a]

	Institution[a]								
School Generation	Oaxaca	Pue-bla	Guada-lajara	Mexico	Vera-cruz	San Nicolás	Other	ENP	Totals
Pre 1910	1	1	1	2	0	2	5	3	15
1910 to 1920	3	4	2	1	3	7	18	22	60
1921 to 1925	3	1	3	2	1	3	18	26	57
1926 to 1930	4	0	3	0	1	4	10	44	66
1931 to 1935	1	0	3	1	4	3	14	28	54
1936 to 1940	2	1	2	0	1	1	11	23	41
1941 to 1945	1	0	2	0	4	0	9	21	37
1946 to 1950	1	2	1	0	0	1	11	17	33
1951 to 1955	1	0	1	0	1	0	6	12	21
1956 to 1960	0	0	0	0	0	0	7	12	19
1960 to present	0	0	0	0	0	1	5	5	11

[a]Includes all members of the *General Political Elite* from the MPBP.
[b]See Table 4.3 for a key to these institutions.

---

*During the early 1930s, the student to professor ratio was 10 to 1. In the late 1930s, the 1940s, and early 1950s, it remained at approximately 6 to 1. The enrollment at the National Preparatory School from 1924 to 1929 was the following: 1924, 2,328; 1925, 2,810; 1926, 1,703; 1927, 1,336; 1928, 1,315; and 1929, 1,388. The sudden drop in 1926 is due to the establishment of secondary schools throughout Mexico. Enrollment at the National Preparatory School did not reach pre-1926 levels until 1935.

†Some of those students included Antonio Armendáriz (Subsecretary of the Treasury, 1952–58); Daniel J. Bello (Subdirector General of the Bank of Mexico, 1970–76); Ernesto Escobar Muñoz (Governor of Morelos, 1946–52); Ricardo García Villalobos (Dean of the National Law School, 1958–62); Baltasar Dromundo (author and federal deputy); and Manuel González Ramírez (educator and historian).

social or intellectual groups founded student newspapers. Manuel González Ramírez suggests that the unrest of his generation "had in journalism a vehicle in which to manifest itself."[36] In 1923, seven student newspapers were being published,* all by students who later distinguished themselves in public affairs.[37]

Mexican students not only created their own newspapers for disseminating literary and political ideas; they were also greatly stimulated by a national oratory contest organized by *El Universal*. Efraín Brito Rosado, himself a former national champion from this decade, describes the cultural milieu in which these events were held.

At that time, the majority of the students had a love for culture, a love of culture for its own sake and independently of the fact that it was a part of the preparation for a professional education with an economic perspective. The oratory contest organized by the daily *El Universal* contributed to this cultural milieu. Today contests with diverse names have proliferated, some of which are quite mystifying. Then, we saw our university as an ineffable backwater of knowledge and spiritual liberation, which elevated us to the high-point of our routine battle for survival.[38]

Some of the preparatory students who later distinguished themselves in public life were active participants in these contests, held in the Hidalgo Theater.†

Students concerned with the lack of education and culture prevailing among the less fortunate of the Mexican population attempted to organize programs to help. One organization founded during this decade was the Vasco de Quiroga Society, which aimed at giving free instruction to workers and

---

*The names of these newspapers and the editors and collaborators were: *Policromias*, edited by Raúl Noriega, later *Oficial Mayor* of Treasury, 1951–58, and director of the major government daily, *El Nacional*, 1938–47; *Eureka*, edited by David Romero Castañeda, Federal Deputy; Antonio Ortiz Mena, later Secretary of the Treasury 1958–70; Gabriel Ramos Millán, Senator, 1946–47 and first Director of the National Maize Commission, 1947–49; Adolfo Zamora, Director General of the National Urban Mortgage Bank, 1947–53; Manuel R. Palacios, Director General of National Railroads, 1946–52; and financed by Miguel Alemán; *Cóndor*, edited by, among others, Ángel Carvajal, Secretary of Government, 1952–58 and pre-candidate for president, 1958; *Avalancha*, directed by Carlos Zapata Vela, Federal Deputy, 1940–43, 1960–63; *Bronces*, under the responsibility of Guillermo Tardiff; *Tribuna*, under the editorship of Manuel González Ramírez, who became Director of the National Preparatory School, and José Gómez Robleda, later Subsecretary of Education, 1952–58; *Agora*, edited by José Chema de los Reyes, founder and director of the Night School of the National Preparatory School and Andrés Iduarte, literary figure and Director of the National Institute of Fine Arts, 1952–54.

†Among the oratory participants were Alejandro Gómez Arias (Vice-President of the PPS, 1947); Donato Miranda Fonseca (Secretary of the Presidency, 1958–64 and pre-candidate for president of Mexico, 1964); Salvador Azuela (Mexican delegate to UNESCO, 1947); Luis I. Rodríguez (President of the National Executive Committee of the official party, 1938–39); Fernando López Arias (Attorney General of Mexico, 1958–62 and Governor of Veracruz, 1962–68); Antonio Rocha (Attorney General of Mexico, 1964–67 and Governor of San Luis Potosí, 1967–73), and Carlos Zapata Vela (Federal Deputy).

teaching them how to read.[39] The student members of this group used the classrooms of the National Preparatory School at night to provide instruction to workers invited by students on visits to various local factories.* The Society was imitated throughout the states, where similar organizations took on the names of other historical figures in Mexican culture.[40]

Lastly, former students suggested that political activities were fomented by the Federation of University Students, also responsible for social benefits to preparatory students. For example, the Federation established centers where students could receive free medical and dental assistance from students in the last years of their professional programs. Legal advice was made available to poorer students in need of a lawyer. All of these services were widely used. In addition, the Federation issued a credential that students presented to commercial establishments for a 10 percent discount on their purchases, and a 50 percent discount on fares for the National Railroads of Mexico and the city bus service.

Student life, then, provided many opportunities for contact among preparatory students. Again, as in the previous decade, the number of students was small enough to make it possible to "know practically all of the future professional people of the epoch, independently of the career they might follow."[41] These many forms of student contact served to promote lasting friendships and the development of early political alliances among various members of these generations. The extent of these alliances and their impact on recruitment and career mobility can be illustrated in some detail through an examination of student members of the 1920–24 generations of the National Preparatory School.

IMPACT ON RECRUITMENT

Of those student members with known career information, an overwhelming number, 45 percent, made public service their career (Table 5.4). Miguel Alemán, because of his rapid rise as a political figure, is a classic case of a student who was able to initially recruit some of his close friends into politics, promoting them as he moved up the ladder of political influence. Perhaps the best example of this initial recruitment through Alemán occurred with Gabriel Ramos Millán, a close friend who helped him edit the National Preparatory newspaper, *Eureka*. Alemán began his career as a practicing lawyer for labor interests in 1928, with Ramos Millán serving as his colleague in several of these litigations. When Alemán became Governor of Veracruz in 1936 at a very young age, he appointed Ramos Millán to his first government position.

---

*Some of the directors included Ángel Carvajal, Manuel Sánchez Cuen (Subsecretary of Industry and Commerce, 1948–52); Andrés Serra Rojas (Secretary of Labor, 1946–48); and Roberto Medellín Ostos (Secretary General of Public Health, 1935–37 and Rector of UNAM, 1932–33).

Table 5.4

**Political Careers of Members of the 1920–24
National Preparatory School Generation**[a]

Name of Student	Type of Career	Highest Public Office Held Since 1935
Aceves Parra, Salvador	government	Secretary of Health
Alarcón, Lamberto	government	Director of Customs in Acapulco
Alemán, Miguel	government	President of Mexico
Anaya Valdepeña, Gabriel	....	....
Aragón Echegaray, Enrique	architecture	....
Armendáriz, Antonio	government	Subsecretary of the Treasury
Armijo, Leoncio	letters	....
Azuela, Salvador	education	Director General of the Fondo de Cultura Económica
Briseño, Alfredo	government	Justice of the Superior Court of the Federal District
Brown, José	....	....
Burguete, Ezequiel	government	Justice of the Supreme Court
Bustamante G., Andrés	medicine	....
Bustillo Oro, Juan	letters	....
Carrillo Cárdenas, Marcos	law	Federal Deputy from Oaxaca
Carrillo Flores, Antonio	government	Secretary of the Treasury
Carrillo Flores, Nabor	education	Rector of UNAM
Carvajal, Angel	government	Secretary of Government
Cisneros, Carlos	engineering	....
De Lille, José	medicine	Sec'y of National Preparatory
De los Reyes, José María	education	Federal Deputy from Hidalgo
Domínguez, Augusto	law	....
Domínguez, Horacio	....	....
Domínguez, Virgilio	education	....
Dovalí Jaime, Antonio	government	Director General of PEMEX
Dromundo, Baltasar	letters	Federal Deputy from Federal District
Eguía Liz, Bernardo	....	....
Elorduy, Edmundo	government	Justice of the Superior Court of the Federal District
Fernández B., Manuel	....	....
Flores Zavala, Ernesto	law	Dean of the National Law School
Frías Solís, Alfredo	....	....
Galícia Sánchez, Anatolio	law	....
García Fomenti, Arturo	government	Director General of Social Action
García Maynes, Eduardo	education	Secretary General of UNAM
García Villalobos, Ricardo	government	Director General in the Treasury
Gómez Arias, Alejandro	law	Vice-President of the PPS
Gómez Esqueda, Rubén	government	Director General of Social Action
González Blanco, Alberto	government	Justice of the Supreme Court
González Cárdenas, Antonio	government	*Oficial Mayor* of the Federal District
González Mena, Antonio	....	....
González Ramírez, Manuel	government	*Oficial Mayor* of Quintana Roo
Hernández Bordes, Ernesto	....	....
Iduarte, Andrés	education	Director of Bellas Artes
Jiménez P., Federico	....	....
Larios, Oscar	....	....
Larroyo, Francisco	education	Ambassador
Leduc, Renato	letters	....
Lira, Miguel N.	government	District Court Judge

Table 5.4 (Continued)

**Political Careers of Members of the 1920–24
National Preparatory School Generation**[a]

Name of Student	Type of Career	Highest Public Office Held Since 1935
Martínez, José Guillermo	....	....
Mirlo, Josué	....	....
Moreno Galán, Pablo	letters	....
Múñoz Cota, José	letters	....
Noriega, Alfonso	education	Secretary General of UNAM
Noriega, Raul	government	*Oficial Mayor* of the Treasury
Novaro, Octavio	letters	....
Novo, Salvador	letters	Director of Theater for Bellas Artes
Ortiz Mena, Antonio	government	Secretary of the Treasury
Ortiz Mena, Rafael	government	Subsecretary of the Presidency
Pérez Martínez, Héctor	government	Secretary of Government
Pérez Verdia, Enrique	law	Director General of ENP No. 4
Ponce de León, Salvador	letters	....
Salas, Angel	music	....
Sánchez Cuen, Manuel	government	Subsecretary of Labor
Serra Rojas, Andrés	government	Secretary of Labor
Sierra, Santiago X.	law	Secretary General of Durango
Silva E., Leonardo	medicine	*Oficial Mayor* of National Properties
Solorzano, Roberto A.	law	Senator from Colima
Tardiff, Guillermo	letters	....
Torres Rincón, Julio	....	....
Villaurrutia, Xavier	letters	Director of Theater for Bellas Artes
Zamora, Adolfo	law	Director of the National Urban Bank

[a]Data for this table comes from personal interviews with teachers and students from the National Preparatory School during these years, from unpublished lists of an alumni organization known as the Grupo Preparatorianos 1920–24, A.C., and from publications of the National Preparatory School.

To help Alemán win the presidential nomination in 1945, Ramos Millán organized a middle-class association to support his candidacy. In turn, he was rewarded by Alemán through his nomination as one of the federal senators from México, and in 1946 Alemán appointed him as the first director of a new decentralized agency the president had established.

As the data in Table 5.2 indicate, only some students, with careers as fast paced and upward as Alemán's, were able to recruit co-students into politics. A far greater number, however, are extremely influential on the careers of fellow students once one of the individuals or a mutual friend has reached a position of such influence that he may have some control over appointments in his agency or be able to recommend appointments to someone who has the power. This means that a single individual, who appoints only several friends to office, has a multiplying effect if those friends in turn are able to bring their choices into power with them. In this way a dozen persons in Table 5.4, who became close friends at the National Preparatory School, ended up holding important positions in the Alemán administration.*

How this kind of contact can change a person's career, rather than be responsible for his initial recruitment into public life, is illustrated by two other preparatory students from Table 5.4—Antonio Carrillo Flores and Ezequiel Burguete. They both eventually completed their law degrees from the National University in 1929. Burguete, who was quite fond of his home state of Chiapas, returned to the capital city of Tuxtla Gutiérrez as a representative of the federal treasury office. Antonio Carrillo Flores, who was from the Federal District, was recommended by his law professor, Narciso Bassols, for a post as a federal agent to the Attorney General in Mexico City.[42] In 1931, Carrillo Flores became director of the legal department of the Attorney General's office. He then wrote Burguete, and asked him to return to Mexico City to work for him. He accepted, and held several positions under Carrillo Flores as a federal agent. In 1935, Carrillo Flores moved to the directorship of the legal affairs department of the Secretariat of the Treasury, and Burguete went with him as a lawyer. Burguete attributes his return to Mexico City specifically to Carrillo Flores.[43]

GROWTH AND CHANGE

Despite the fact that the preparatory school began to grow in size more rapidly than the professional schools, students, even during the decade of the 1930s, still found the same opportunities as their predecessors for initiating important friendships. Although large percentages of future political leaders continued to come from the National Preparatory School after 1940, the decade of the 1930s produced the largest group in the last 40 years.

Nevertheless, growth and change in curriculum from five years to two years made contact between professors and students more limited. The composition of the teaching staff began to change. Persons teaching at the National Preparatory School were less responsible for recruiting students into public life because they themselves were not active in such careers. The size of the faculty increased, making it impossible for students passing through the preparatory curriculum all to have the same professors. By 1940, at the end of

---

*These 12 officeholders during the Alemán years were Antonio Armendáriz, National Securities Commission; Antonio Carrillo Flores, Director General of the National Finance Bank; Ángel Carvajal, Secretary of National Patrimony; Adolfo Zamora, Director General of the National Urban Mortgage Bank; Antonio Ortiz Mena, Subdirector of the National Urban Mortgage Bank; Héctor Pérez Martínez, Secretary of Government; Andrés Serra Rojas, Secretary of Labor; Manuel Sánchez Cuen, Subsecretary of Industry and Commerce; Raúl Noriega, Ambassador to the United Nations; Leonard Silva E., *Oficial Mayor* of National Patrimony; Alfred Briseño and Edmundo Elorduy, justices of the Superior Tribunal of Justice; and Antonio González Cárdenas, *Oficial Mayor* of the Federal District Department.

the decade, the National Preparatory School employed 178 professors, of whom only eight could be described as public men.[44] This does not mean that the impact of professors on their students' careers did not continue to be felt, merely that professors at the professional schools assumed a proportionately more important role than the preparatory instructors.

Offsetting the increased size of the school to some extent was the division of the students into groups according to the curriculum they followed, such as law and social science, medicine, and architecture. Within the National Preparatory School, students were grouped together in similar classes. Most of the future public leaders followed the law and social science curriculum.

The activities of the early generations also typified this decade. Political activities were important in bringing together students from various groups as well as different schools. In particular, the strike of 1933 at the National

Table 5.5

**Graduates of the National Preparatory School From 1921 to 1930
Who Held High Public Offices from 1935 to 1976[a]**

Name of Graduate	Year	Highest Position in Public Life Since 1935
Azuela, Mariano	1922	Justice of the Supreme Court
González Blanco, Salomón	1922	Secretary of Labor
Torres Sánchez, Enrique	1922	Governor of Durango
Aranda Osorio, Efraín	1923	Governor of Chiapas
Magdaleno, Mauricio	1923	Subsecretary of Public Education
Rivera Pérez Campos, José	1925	Justice of the Supreme Court
Rivera Pérez Campos, Ricardo	1925	Director General of the National Preparatory School
Rojina Villegas, Rafael	1925	Justice of the Supreme Court
Serrano Castro, Julio	1925	Subsecretary of Labor
Galván Campos, Fausto	1926	Senator from Morelos
García González, Alfonso	1926	Head of the Department of Tourism
Moreno Sánchez, Manuel	1926	Majority Leader of the Senate
Pizarro Suárez, Nicolás	1926	Director General of ISSSTE
Aguilar Alvarez, Ernesto	1927	Justice of the Supreme Court
Aguirre Beltran, Gonzalo	1927	Subsecretary of Public Education
Beltrán Beltrán, Amando	1927	President of the Federal Arbitration Board
Canudas Orezza, Luis Felipe	1928	Secretary General of Agrarian Affairs
Sánchez Gavito, Vicente	1928	Ambassador to Great Britain
Alvarez Amezquita, José	1929	Secretary of Public Health
Brito Rosado, Efraín	1929	Senator from Yucatán
Carrillo, Alejandro	1929	Secretary General of the Federal District
Figueroa, Rubén	1929	Governor of Guerrero
López Mateos, Adolfo	1929	President of Mexico
Rangel Couto, Hugo	1929	Subsecretary of National Properties
Brena Torres, Rodolfo	1930	Governor of Oaxaca
Castillo Tiélemans, José	1930	Governor of Chiapas

[a]Excluding the 1924 graduates listed in Table 5.4.

University brought together students and professors at the National Preparatory School. The other important event was the 1940 presidential campaign, involving a number of students and professors.[45] Intramural games contributed to friendships among students from the National Preparatory School, the National University, and the Free Law School.[46] President Echeverría, like President Alemán, surrounded himself with several friends from the National Preparatory School, some of whom, like Carlos Gálvez Betancourt, were part of his group from the very beginning of their public careers; whereas others such as Jesús Reyes Heroles, who had followed a political career under different mentors, received his most important appointment from Echeverría as President of the National Executive Committee of PRI in 1972, and then, in 1976, was appointed Secretary of Government by his other friend and classmate, José López Portillo (Table 5.6). Few men have had the good fortune to be friends with and to attend school with two future Presidents of Mexico.

The National Preparatory School became an important location for developing close contacts among students and professors, particularly for those with political interests. In demonstrating how these contacts were encouraged, and how they frequently contributed to an individual student's

Table 5.6

**Graduates of the National Preparatory School From 1931 to 1940
Who Held High Public Office From 1935 to 1976**

Name of Graduate	Year	Highest Position in Public Life Since 1935
Cisneros Molina, Joaquín	1931	Governor of Tlaxcala
Flores Betancourt, Dagoberto	1931	Secretary General of the FSTSE
Jiménez Cantu, Jorge	1933	Secretary of Public Health
Barros Sierra, Javier	1934	Secretary of Public Works
Hiariat Balderrama, Fernando[a]	1934	Subdirector of the Federal Electric Commission
Lanz Duret, Fernando	1934	Senator from Campeche
Moreno Valle, Rafael	1934	Secretary of Public Health
Martínez de la Vega, Francisco	1936	Governor of San Luis Potosí
Espinosa Gutiérrez, Fernando	1937	Subsecretary of Public Works
Castellaños, Milton	1938	Governor of Baja California del Norte
López Portillo, José	1938	President of Mexico
Reyes Heroles, Jesús	1938	President of the CEN of PRI
Salvat Rodríguez, Agustín	1938	Head of the Tourism Department
Dzib Cardozo, José de Jesús	1939	Assistant Attorney General of the Federal District
Echeverría, Luis	1939	President of Mexico
Sepulveda, César	1939	Dean of the National School of Law
Velasco Curiel, Fernando F.	1939	Governor of Colima
Bracamontes, Luis Enrique	1940	Secretary of Public Works
Gálvez Betancourt, Carlos	1940	Secretary of Labor
Salmorán de T., María C.	1940	Justice of the Supreme Court

[a]Hiariat Balderrama became Subsecretary of Government Properties in 1977.

recruitment into political life, or more important, his career mobility at a middle or later stage in his public career, I am not suggesting that this was the sole means by which political friendships and alliances were initiated, or even that early friendship is the only consideration for political appointment. There were numerous companions of political leaders with interpersonal skills and superior intellectual talents who were not interested in political careers, and although they were offered positions, they refused them. Still others, while perhaps friends, showed no special skills or talents for public life, and were never approached about political offices. As I have demonstrated for state and national political positions of some importance, friendship alone is not the only requirement necessary for being recruited or appointed at midcareer to political office, even if the individual doing the appointing is president.[47] Despite his immense political power, the Mexican president is limited by a number of other variables. This discussion does demonstrate, however, that as far as the National Preparatory School is concerned, personal political alliances were started there which continued through law school, and often were essential to an individual's entire political career. At the same time, because of the initial friendship, the opportunity to see concretely a friend's skills, and the need for complete confidence in immediate subordinates emphasized by the political culture, political leaders often found it necessary to come back to friends when in need of important subordinates.

The Institute of Arts and Sciences of Oaxaca, 1911–40

Both the patterns and style of education at the regional schools were similar to those of the National Preparatory School. The Institute of Arts and Sciences of Oaxaca was typical of many state *colegios* established during the nineteenth century. Among the more prominent of such schools were the Institute of Science and Letters of México in Toluca, the Colegio Civil of Nuevo León, and the Colegio Civil of Puebla. As far as public men are concerned, regional universities were more important to the preparatory generations from 1910 to 1930 than to later generations.

Among the students who graduated from the Institute in Oaxaca was Francisco Alfonso Ramírez, a prominent deputy in the 1920s and later a supreme court justice. He went to school at the Institute during the heart of the Revolution, graduating in 1914. During these years, students had classes from 7:00 am to 6:00 pm. The majority of the students were from the middle class, if only in the sense that their parents appreciated the value of education; in a true economic sense, they were not middle class. Parents who were wealthy enough sent their children to Mexico City to study. There were some very poor students, but during these years, no scholarships were available. However, students were often helped by professors who provided them with employment in their various professions, such as law and medicine. Further-more, the state of Oaxaca made arrangements for employing students so that they could attend classes between working hours. A very few students re-ceived jobs as assistants at the Institute itself, and this served to subsidize their education.[48]

There were very few students attending the Institute during the Revolu-tion. A number of students came from neighboring states such as Chiapas, which did not have good institutions offering preparatory programs. Eduardo Bustamante, who received most of his pre-university education at the Insti-tute, recalls only about 25-30 in the entire general preparatory program, approximately half of whom came from little communities throughout Oaxaca. The small number of students was conducive to interchange and contact among students and professors. Because of the size of the school, students became well acquainted with most older and younger students of all generations.[49]

All of the surviving students interviewed by the author remember di-verse social and cultural activities at the Institute. Some of the professors and students joined together to form an intellectual club called the Bohemia of Oaxaca. They met regularly in various homes in Oaxaca to discuss literature, music, social questions and philosophies, and they published a literary and cultural magazine.[50]

The professors at the Institute during these years were all part-time, since the economic situation of the state government was precarious, and professors received no compensation. Among the more prominent professors were Dr Alberto Vargas, a federal deputy; Dr Ramón Pardo, also a federal deputy; Dr Aurelio Valdivieso, a senator; Francisco Modesto Ramírez, the father of Francisco Alfonso Ramírez and a federal deputy and presi-dent of the supreme court; and Jesús Acevedo, a lawyer and Interim Governor of Oaxaca.[51] Because they were unpaid, some professors did not feel an obligation to prepare for their classes, and a few actually missed them altogether. On the other hand, those who taught did so out of an interest in or prestige from teaching, and therefore most instructors were well prepared and interested in their students. In particular, Francisco A. Ramírez recalled that Professor Vargas, his literature teacher during his last term at the Insti-tute, always received his students in his office and outside of class in his own home.[52]

The general environment of the Institute during the Revolutionary period was thought to be "liberal." In fact, many persons considered it improper to send their children there because it was too liberal. In reality, the Institute had a very humanistic orientation, and politically speaking, only a few professors were vociferous in expressing their criticisms of the traditional government and some of those became supporters of Madero. Some profes-sors taught history with a religious slant to it, while others took the view that the role of the Catholic church was part of a process of retrogression in Mexico's historical development. The positivism of Comte was still quite influential at the Institute in the second decade of this century. Although none of the students I interviewed recalled the use of Catholic-oriented texts, they do remember that many of the books used were of foreign origin.

Despite the fact that most of the professors were politically neutral in their instruction, the majority of students were sympathetic to the Revolution, and most of these supported Madero. Later, several professors and many students became active participants in the Revolution.[53] Political awareness increased in 1915 when the students of the Institute affiliated with the National Federation of Students in Mexico City. They attended a series of national student congresses, cultivating relations with student organizations at the institutes in Puebla and Toluca, México.* Students did feel the effects of the Revolution in 1915, when Constitutional forces arrived in Oaxaca and temporarily closed the Institute. In 1916, students asked to have it reopened, and the request was granted, but professors had to teach without salaries again.

Although contact among students and between students and faculty was equal to or greater than that taking place at the National Preparatory School during this period, students who were recruited into national public life at this stage were rare, since they often remained in their own states, thereby not achieving national prominence. Students who remained at the local university for their professional education were more likely to be recruited into public positions at that point in their education, rather than during the preparatory years. At the preparatory school level, then, the Institute of Arts and Sciences of Oaxaca, while important to some extent for *state* political careers, was not important for national public careers. Students who left the Institute of Arts and Sciences of Oaxaca to complete their professional studies at the National University made more significant friendships there. For example, Eduardo Bustamante was recruited into public service in the Secretariat of the Treasury by his law professor, Manuel Gómez Morín.[54] Other students, such as future president Gustavo Díaz Ordaz, transferred first to the University of Guadalajara, then to another regional school, the University of Puebla. While still a law student, Díaz Ordaz started out as an office boy in the Department of Government for the state of Puebla, and upon graduation, embarked on a judicial career.[55]

The Colegio de San Nicolás de Hidalgo, 1911–40

Another state university important in the education of future public men was the Colegio de San Nicolás in Morelia, Michoacán, now known as the Uni-

---

*Francisco Alfonso Ramírez was President of the Student Congress of Oaxaca in 1916.

versity of Michoacán. This *colegio,* unlike the Institute of Arts and Sciences of Oaxaca, has a long history, that extends back into the colonial period.

The students at San Nicolás came from all parts of Michoacán, even though in some villages only the Tarascan language was spoken.[56] Generally, like those at the National Preparatory School, the vast majority of students came from lower-middle and middle-class backgrounds. The best student from each *município* in Michoacán received a scholarship to the *Colegio.* There were a number of students from poor families, and the students from wealthy families were few. Most of the students coming to Morelia from the rural areas received their first cultural education here. Eduardo Villaseñor, a scholarship student from the small community of Angamacutiro, attended the Colegio during the 1910s. He described his student life this way:

> In all respects my years at San Nicolás were unforgettable. I made friends with companions from my class, but above all with others from older groups or in their professional programs; those few of us on scholarships slept in a room high above the School of Arts . . . This type of brotherhood at San Nicolás extended to those who had gone before or after me.[57]

Another student during this period, Ignacio Chávez, began his studies in Morelia in 1908, and completed the full preparatory program at the *Colegio.* While only one year ahead of Villaseñor, he became his professor of history in the preparatory program. Again, as was true at the other preparatory schools, there was intimate contact among students at all levels at the *Colegio.*

Students at the *Colegio* during the first decade studied in a comparatively calm environment, except during a strike which took place in 1912, in which they attacked the government and the imposed reelection of the state governor, Aristeo Mercado.[58] After considerable student agitation in favor of the Maderista cause, the school authorities expelled students and repressed free speech. In retaliation, the students and the majority of the professors formed a substitute college known as San Nicolasito, and held classes from July to September, 1912. Once the state government changed, students resumed regular classes at the *Colegio.*

The instructional materials at the *Colegio* during these years, with the exception of classical languages, were similar to those in France, since the textbooks in physics, chemistry, botany, zoology, and mineralogy were in French. The transition taking place in the intellectual viewpoints being presented at the *Colegio,* similar to the cross-currents experienced by the students at the National Preparatory School, was more important than the formal curriculum. Ignacio Chávez describes the impact it had on him:

I believe I was very fortunate to have been able to study in the Díaz period since I was exposed to some dogmatic values, among them the necessity for peace and the need for self-discipline. When the Revolution occurred and came to Michoacán, and I shifted my education to Mexico City, I was able to see, in the middle of my youth, two different points of view regarding the social, economic, and political development of Mexico. In other words, I had the advantage of being educated in two distinct ethical systems. This resulted in three things. First, I learned how to be very disciplined, and I believe this experience put a stamp on most of the students who went through this type of education. Second, after 1910, changes occurred which encouraged young students to attempt to understand Mexico and to ask questions about why traditions were being destroyed. The old values were destroyed, but the new ones had not yet been created. Some professors were able to adapt, but others found it extremely difficult, and the revolutionary changes, combined with the effects of World War I, were just too great to face. Third, a demand was created for persons to hold positions in this rapidly changing environment, and many students of my generation were asked to take on tremendous responsibilities at a young age. For example, I was asked to become Rector of the Colegio de San Nicolás at the age of 23.[59]

Another student of this period, who attended the normal and preparatory program from 1910 to 1916, described the prevailing intellectual philosophy as "a new concept of the world and of man based on science, on experimentation and on reality; a new political-social revolutionary ideal, all of which came to transform my mind little by little and made me act with the liberal groups of students, with the new *antiporfirista* revolutionary sector and, in general, with the progressive sectors that were fighting with a program of changes for the masses of workers and peasants oppressed by dictatorial regimes."[60]

An important generation of preparatory students who became public men graduated from the *Colegio* during the beginning of the second decade of this century. Among this group were Dr Manuel Martínez Báez, whose father was a renowned professor and rector of the *Colegio*, and who himself became Secretary General and Rector of the *Colegio*, later serving as Subsecretary of Health in the 1940s; Antonio Martínez Báez, brother of Manuel, a distinguished professor of law, member of the Arbitration Tribunal of the Hague, and Secretary of Industry and Commerce in Mexico; Gabino Fraga, another well-known jurist, Justice of the Supreme Court and Subsecretary of Foreign Relations; Eduardo Villaseñor, Director General of the Bank of Mexico and Subsecretary of the Treasury; Rodolfo Chávez, penal lawyer and Justice of the Supreme Court; Ignacio Chávez, brother of Rodolfo, internationally known cardiologist and Rector of the National University; Samuel Ramos, whose father was a doctor and professor at the *Colegio, Oficial Mayor* of

Education and Dean of the School of Philosophy at the National University; Dr Salvador González de Rejón, professor and Dean of the National Medical School; Alberto Bremauntz, Justice of the Superior Tribunal of Justice and Rector of San Nicolás; and Alberto Coria, Federal Deputy and Justice of the Superior Tribunal of Justice. Given the small number of students, this was a remarkable group of preparatory graduates, exceeding in percentages those who became prominent in public life from most generational groups at the National Preparatory School. Their relationship, however, did not produce significant career or recruitment patterns, except that Ignacio Chávez went back to Mexico City at the request of Dr Martínez Báez, and ultimately became prominent in national medicine.[61] With those two exceptions, each of the others followed separate careers, although several had mutual friends who influenced their careers.

The Colegio de San Nicolás, like the Institute of Arts and Sciences of Oaxaca, initiated limited contacts among future *national* public leaders at the preparatory school level. Numerous graduates were recruited into state and local political activities in both institutions. In comparison, however, the National Preparatory School played a much more significant role in the recruitment of students into public life and in the development of friendships having an impact on career mobility in public office.

NOTES TO CHAPTER 5

[1]Lester Seligman, *Recruiting Political Elites* (New York: General Learning Press, 1971), p. 2.

[2]Herbert Jacob, "Initial Recruitment of Elected Officials in the United States: A Model," *Journal of Politics 24* (November 1962): 712.

[3]Donald Matthews, *U.S. Senators and Their World* (Chapel Hill: University of North Carolina Press, 1960), p. 50.

[4]Robert T. Holt, "Age as a Factor in the Recruitment of Communist Leadership," *American Political Science Review 48* (June 1954): 487.

[5]*Ibid.;* and Walter Oleszek, "Age and Political Careers," *Public Opionion Quarterly 33* (Spring 1969): 100–3.

[6]David Schers, "The Popular Sector of the Mexican PRI," (unpublished Ph.D. dissertation, University of New Mexico, 1972), p. 52.

[7]Larissa Lomnitz, "Conflict and Mediation in a Latin American University," *Journal of Inter-American Studies and World Affairs 19* (August 1977): 318.

[8]Dwaine Marvick, "Political Recruitment and Careers," *International Encyclopedia of the Social Sciences 12;* (New York: Crowell, Collier and Macmillan, 1968), p. 278.

[9]Joseph S. Szyliowicz, "Elite Recruitment in Turkey: The Role of the Mulkiye," *World Politics 23* (April 1971): 380.

[10]Octavio González Cárdenas, *Los cien años de la Escuela Nacional Preparatoria* (Mexico: Editorial Porrúa, 1972), p. 70.

[11]Valdemar Rodriguez, "National University of Mexico: Rebirth and Role of the *Universitarios,* 1910–1957," (unpublished Ph.D. dissertation, University of Texas, 1958), p . 35.

[12]Roderic A. Camp, "The Making of a Government: The Socialization of Political Leaders in Post-Revolutionary Mexico" (unpublished manuscript).

[13]Roderic A. Camp, "The Mexican Revolution as a Socializing Agent: Mexican Political Leaders and Their Parents," paper presented before the Rocky Mountain States Council of Latin American Studies, Tucson, 1977.

[14]Roderic A. Camp, "The Values and Ideological Beliefs of Mexican Political Leaders Since 1946," paper presented before the Mid-West Association of Latin Americanists, St Louis, 1977.

[15]Joseph Szyliowicz, "Elite Recruitment," pp. 389–90; and Rupert Wilkinson, "Political Leadership and the Late Victorian Public School," *British Journal of Sociology 13* (1962): 320–30, and *Gentlemanly Power: British Leadership and the Public School Tradition: A Comparative Study in the Making of Rulers* (New York: Oxford University Press, 1964).

[16]Lewis J. Edinger, "Post-Totalitarian Leadership: Elites in the German Federal Republic," *American Political Science Review 54* (March 1960): 81.

[17]For some comments on this, see Josefina Vázquez Knauth, *Nacionalismo y educación en México* (Mexico: Colegio de México, 1970), p. 149; and Jesús Silva Herzog, *Una historia de la Universidad de México y sus problemas* (Mexico: Siglo Veintiuno, 1974), p. 53ff.

[18]See Jesús Silva Herzog's comment that Octaviano Campos y Salas, who went from the Deanship of the School of Economics to a cabinet secretaryship, went to the School two or three times during his deanship because he was only interested in political office (*Mis ultimas andanzas, 1947–1972* [Mexico: Siglo Veintiuno, 1973], p. 168).

[19]Luis Garrido Díaz, *El tiempo de mi vida, memorias* (Mexico: Editorial Porrúa, 1974), p. 51.

[20]Personal interview with Francisco González de la Vega, Mexico City, July 23, 1974.

[21]Letter from Pedro Daniel Martínez, Mexico City, February 13, 1974.

[22]Letter from Jaime Torres Bodet, Mexico City, August 1, 1972.

[23]Personal interview with Lucio Mendieta y Núñez, Mexico City, July 27, 1974.

[24]Personal interview with Francisco González de la Vega, Mexico City, July 23, 1974.

[25]Roderic A. Camp, *Mexican Political Biographies, 1935–1975* (Tucson: University of Arizona Press, 1976), p. 30; *Biographical Encyclopedia of the World* (New York: Institute for Research in Biography, 1946), p. 212; *Diccionario Porrúa* (Mexico: Editorial Porrúa, 1970), p. 96; *Enciclopedia de México 1*, p. 533; and Ronald Hilton, ed., *Who's Who in Latin America: Mexico* (Stanford: Stanford University Press, 1946), p. 9.

[26]Camp, *Mexican Political Biographies*, p. 127–8; *Hispano Americano*, October 29, 1973, p. 13; *Diccionario Biográfico de México*, 1970, pp. 153–4; *Hispano Americano*, September 28, 1951; Personal letter from Luis Garrido Díaz, April 18, 1972; and Luis Garrido Díaz, *El tiempo de mi vida*.

[27]For an insightful account of his career, see his multi-volume memoirs, especially, *Años contra el tiempo* (Mexico: Porrúa, 1969), *Equinoccio* (Mexico: Porrúa, 1974), and *La tierra prometida* (Mexico: Porrúa, 1972).

[28]Letter from Daniel Cosío Villegas, Mexico City, May 14, 1974.

[29]Letter from Jaime Torres Bodet, Mexico City, August 1, 1972.

[30]Arturo González Cosio, *Historia estadística de la universidad, 1910–1967* (Mexico: UNAM, 1968), pp. 73, 100.

[31]Roderic A. Camp, "Education and Political Recruitment in Mexico: The Alemán Generation," *Journal of Inter-American Studies and World Affairs 18* (August 1976): 295–321.

[32]Roderic A. Camp, "La campaña presidencial de 1929 y el liderazgo político en México," *Historia Mexicana 27,* No. 2 (1977): 231–59.

[33]Letter from Clemente Bolio, Ciudad Juárez, Chihuahua, July 18, 1974; Manuel Rivera Silva, *Perspectivas de una vida, biografía de una generación* (México: Porrúa, 1974), p. 71; Letter from Amando Beltrán B., Mexico City, August 24, 1974.

[34]Andrés Iduarte, *Niño, Child of the Mexican Revolution* (New York: Praeger, 1971), p. 143.

[35]Baltasar Dromundo, *La Escuela Nacional Preparatoria Nocturna y José María de los Reyes* (Mexico: Porrúa, 1973), p. 33.

[36]Manuel González Ramírez, *Mexico, Litografía de la ciudad que se fue México* (Mexico, 1962), p. 69.

[37]Baltasar Dromundo, *La Escuela,* p. 33; letter from Manuel R. Palacios, Mexico City, February 1, 1973; letter from Adolfo Zamora, Mexico City, March 12, 1973; and Manuel González Ramirez, *México,* pp. 130–1.

[38]Letter from Efraín Brito Rosado, Mexico City, April 23, 1974.

[39]Personal interview with Manuel R. Palacios, Mexico City, July 1, 1975.

[40]Letter from the last director of this society, Antonio Fernández del Castillo, Mexico City, April 18, 1975; also see his "Palabras del Señor Lic. Antonio Fernández del Castillo," (México: Academia Nacional de Historia y Geografía, 1968), pp. 4–5.

[41]Letter from Alfonso Barnetche G., Mexico City, May 8, 1974.

[42]Personal interview with Antonio Carrillo Flores, Mexico City, June 26, 1975.

[43]Personal interview with Ezequiel Burguete F., Mexico City, June 19, 1975.

[44]Mexico City, Universidad Nacional Autónomo de México, *Anuario de la Escuela Nacional Preparatoria, 1940* (Mexico: UNAM, 1940).

[45]Personal interview with Mario Colín Sánchez, Mexico City, August 13, 1974.

[46]Octavio González Cárdenas, *Los cien años,* p. 91.

[47]Roderic A. Camp, "Autobiography and Decision-Making in Mexican Politics," *Journal of Inter-American Studies and World Affairs 19* (May 1977): 275–83; "Losers in Mexican Politics: A Comparative Study of Official Party Precandidates for Gubernatorial Elections, 1970–75," in James W. Wilkie and Kenneth Ruddle, eds, *Quantitative Latin American Studies: Methods and Findings 6,* Statistical Abstract of Latin America Supplement Series (Los Angeles: UCLA Latin American Center, 1977), pp. 23–34; and "El sistema mexicano y las decisiones sobre el personal político," *Foro Internacional 17* (July–September 1976): 51–82.

[48]Personal interview with Francisco Alfonso Ramírez, Mexico City, August 14, 1974.

[49]Personal interview with Eduardo Bustamante, Mexico City, July 24, 1974; Letter from Dr Miguel Bustamante, Mexico City, March 13, 1975.

[50]Personal interview with Francisco Alfonso Ramírez, Mexico City, August 14, 1974.

[51]Letter from Francisco Alfonso Ramírez, Mexico City, March 2, 1974.

[52]Personal interview with Francisco Alfonso Ramírez, August 14, 1974.

[53]To capture the flavor of the Revolution in Oaxaca, see Francisco Alfonso Ramírez, *La revolucion mexicana en Oaxaca* (Mexico: Instituto Nacional de Estudios Históricos de la Revolución Mexicana, 1970).

[54]Personal interview with Eduardo Bustamante, July 24, 1974.

[55]Camp, *Mexican Political Biographies, 1935–1975,* p. 95; *Enciclopedia de México 3,* pp. 237–8; *Justícia,* January, 1970; and *Hispano Americano,* April 11, 1977, p. 7.

[56]See comments by Eduardo Villaseñor, *Archivos del Instituto de Cardiología de México* (Julio–Agosto 1970), p. 547.

[57]Eduardo Villaseñor, *Memorias-Testimonio* (México: Fondo de Cultura Económica, 1974), p. 26.

[58]Alberto Bremauntz, *Setenta años de mi vida* (México: Ediciones Jurídico Sociales, 1968), pp. 44–5; letter from Eduardo Villaseñor, Mexico City, July 18, 1974.

[59]Personal interview with Dr Ignacio Chávez, Mexico City, August 15, 1974.

[60]Alberto Bremauntz, *Setenta años de mi vida,* p. 46.

[61]Ignacio Chávez, "Discurso," La Universidad de Michoacán, Morelia, Michoacán, November 11, 1972.

6. The National Professional Schools: Career Mobility and Political Recruitment

The preparatory schools have had an important role in the recruitment and career mobility of political leaders in Mexico, but in contrast to the professional schools at the National University, their influence is much less comprehensive. The reasons for this are several. Although political leaders in Mexico tend to commit themselves to public careers much sooner than their North American counterparts, many future political leaders have not yet made up their minds about their careers during their years at the preparatory school. However, once students graduate from preparatory school and decide to continue their education, they generally must make a commitment to a professional program and subsequently a career. Those who see little future for themselves as independent professionals or employees for private firms end up in public administration. If they are to excel in public life, the contacts they make and the activities they engage in at the professional schools often have a critical impact on their initial recruitment and later careers.

The time at which students usually make their career choices is not the only reason why professional schools are more important than the preparatory schools. Certain professional schools, particularly the law school and the economics school attract students in greater numbers who will become Mexico's future leaders. To be known and admired by these fellow students increases the likelihood of a successful public career if one is interested in politics. Furthermore, although a good number of professors who have taught at the National Preparatory School and even at the more important regional preparatory schools have had public careers, proportionately greater numbers of successful public men have taught at the National Schools of Law,

Economics, and to a lesser extent Engineering and Medicine. Since it is professors, more than students, who are responsible for initial recruitment and the placement of graduates in the public sector, a slow or rapid start in a public career may well depend on contact with such a professor.

The universities that are important to Mexican political leaders have been the National University, the National Military College, the National School of Agriculture, the National Polytechnic Institute, the University of Guadalajara and the Free Law School (Table 4.4), However, like the National Preparatory School, the National University has been responsible for educating an overwhelming number of high-level officeholders in Mexico (63.5 percent). Within the National University, the schools of law, economics, engineering, and medicine have been most important in the education of public men.

The National School of Law, 1911–20

The students at the National School of Law from 1911 to 1920, like their counterparts at the National Preparatory School, attended classes during a period of political turmoil in Mexico City. Alfonso Caso, who enrolled at the National School of Law in 1913, described this period:

> We studied in the midst of all the difficulties inherent in the armed fighting then in the country. Frequently we had to go by foot to our classes, since there were no street cars or buses, and on some occasions, a cart pulled by mules, which we suspected by its smell had been used to transport manure, served as our means of transportation.
>
> The city frequently had its light and water, and practically all municipal services, cut off. Sometimes the University had moved up the examination before the end of the course because it had been announced that the City was taken by a group of revolutionaries and it was likely that there would be a complete change of officials.[1]

The students at the law school, however, were a much smaller group than the student body at the preparatory school, and, in reality, they declined in number during this decade. The number of degrees granted during these years were as follows: 1910 (18); 1911 (21); 1912 (17); 1913 (11); 1914 (19); 1915 (2); 1916 (19); 1917 (37); 1918 (33); 1919 (35) and 1920 (44).[2] It was not until 1917 that conditions stabilized enough to allow for an increasing number of graduates to receive degrees from the law school.

Throughout the decade, the total number of students enrolled in the five-year program at the School of Law never exceeded 300 persons. Most of the law students were men since the first law degree was not granted to a woman until 1920. Francisco González de la Vega, who started law school in 1918, says that students had frequent contact with older as well as younger colleagues because of the small size of the school.[3] As Alfonso Caso has noted, the size of the student body permitted students in one class to know all students from the first through the fifth year.[4] The classes generally contained 8 to 10 students, and were usually held from 6:30 to 9:30 pm to allow students to hold jobs.

Most students did work, since they were from lower-middle and middle-class backgrounds. Many of them were quite poor. González de la Vega is a good example, despite the fact that his father was a judge, since he died while Francisco was quite young. In order to support himself in school, González de la Vega became a porter. Later, he was fortunate enough to receive a scholarship from the Secretariat of the Treasury after distinguishing himself as the outstanding first-year law student. For González de la Vega, the opportunity to become a law student was made possible by the Revolution, an opportunity he used to improve his social and economic position in life.

Student contact during this period promoted professor-student contact too. Many young professors had just graduated from the National School of Law, and therefore, had known some of their new students as companions from younger generations. This decade was unusual because the majority of professors who had taught at the law school identified intellectually with the pre-revolutionary regime.[5] Because of this, many severed their ties with the National Law School after 1911, making it necessary for administrators to recruit promising young graduates to teach.[6] Before 1915, few of the older professors worked for the government because they disagreed with its revolutionary philosophy. González de la Vega described the situation:

> We, as students and professors, had to improvise. This is the reason why such young men, including myself, became professors at the National Law School and the university in general. If you distinguished yourself at the Law School, you would be harvested and utilized by being named to professorships at the university as well as being given positions in government too. Many of my professors were only three or four years older than I.[7]

Young students promoted to professorships and government jobs were numerous: Lucio Mendieta y Núñez, who took a position under Manuel Gamio as chief of the Department of Population in 1921, gave a class in agrarian law at the law school at the invitation of his former co-student, Narciso Bassols; González de la Vega, nominated by his former professor, Antonio Caso, became a law school professor only one year after he graduated in 1920; Manuel Gómez Morín became a professor of public law when he graduated in 1918, and Subsecretary of the Treasury in 1919–21 followed by his appointment as Dean of the National Law School in 1922;

Narciso Bassols, already professor of guarantees when he graduated in 1920, became dean of the law school in 1929; Alfonso Caso served as a professor of law the year before he graduated; Vicente Lombardo Toledano became a professor at the National Preparatory School in 1918, secretary of the law school in 1919, and director of the National Preparatory School in 1922, holding all positions within three years of his graduation in 1919; and Antonio Castro Leal became secretary to the rector of UNAM in 1920.

The professors who taught at the law school were a mixture of old and new, very much like the preparatory school.[8] The students supported a mixture of ideas, but unlike their professors, the majority of them were revolutionaries. As Alfonso Caso remembers, they included:

> Zapatistas, Carranzistas, Villistas, Conventionists, and without lacking, of course, three or four representatives of the old porfirista aristocracy, who passed their life longing for the "Centenary Celebrations"; but, in general, the whole School vibrated with revolutionary unrest.[9]

These divisions among students produced a stimulating philosophical environment at the university. But the environment was not just a product of political dissension, since members of these generations also provided a renaissance of ideas about art forms, music, and Mexican culture.

Like several other periods in the history of the National Law School, the 1910–20 decade produced three outstanding generations, led by a famous group known as the "Seven Wise Men": Manuel Gómez Morín, Alberto Vázquez del Mercado, Teófilo Olea y Leyva, Vicente Lombardo Toledano, Alfonso Caso, Antonio Castro Leal, and Jesús Moreno Baca.[10] These were students who enrolled in the National Law School in 1914–15.* Attached to this first generation of students was a second important group of younger students, who enrolled in 1916–17. Among the most important members of this younger generation were Narciso Bassols, Daniel Cosío Villegas, and Miguel Palacios Macedo. Lastly, a third and younger group, known later as the *Contemporáneos,* was led by Jaime Torres Bodet and José Gorostiza who began law school in 1918.[11]

In 1916, the generation of 1915 founded the Society of Conferences and Concerts, whose membership included younger generations.[12] The purpose of these conferences and concerts was to encourage intellectual discussion and to support artistic and cultural activities. The active students of the post-1914

---

*There is much confusion in the literature concerning the exact membership of the original "Seven Wise Men." Because Jesús Moreno Baca died quite young, many authors have attempted to substitute another name for his. The other students who graduated with this group are more important than the exact composition of the original seven.

generations were influenced in their endeavors by the famous prerevolutionary lecture society, the Ateneo de la Juventud.* The intellectual leaders of this group were the young professors of the post-1915 generations, whose notable students were sometimes called the children of the Ateneo.[13] In 1912, José Vasconcelos was president of the Ateneo group, and they decided to create an extension university to make culture available to the Mexican people.[14] They established a Popular University administered by members of the Ateneo and staffed by professors who served without salaries. This university remained in existence from 1912 to 1922, and in addition to its cultural impact on Mexico, played a significant role in the university environment of the post-1915 generations. It served to promote friendships among the 1915 to 1920 generations, and between these generations and the older generations who graduated before 1910.[15] Many members of the post-1915 generations served in administrative capacities and taught at the Popular University.†

In 1912, another event took place which was to affect the composition and number of students attending the National Law School during the first half of this decade. The dean of the law school instituted several reforms that some students believed were arbitrary. Secondly, because of the rapid changes of government affecting the administration of the National Law School, many students felt a need to separate the university from the political environment. For these and other reasons, a group of law students from various years went on strike and approached President Madero asking his support for and recognition of a separate law school. Such a school, known as the Free Law School (ELD), was established in July, 1912, drawing off a number of students from the National Law School and hurting this institution severely. This explains, in part, why the number of law degrees granted by the latter school declined.[16] This event promoted student friendships among those who participated in the strike, like that between Emilio Portes Gil and Ezequiel Padilla,[17] which were important to later public careers.

Formal student political activity was also important in this period. In 1916, the first Federation of University Students of the Federal District was founded.[18] This became one of the foremost student organizations in Mexico. Its importance was felt in the national government by 1918, as illustrated by the fact that student attachés were appointed to various embassies. Two of these student attachés were recruited to notable diplomatic careers: Pablo Campos Ortiz, Ambassador to Great Britain, 1957–63, and Luis Padilla Nervo, Secretary of Foreign Relations, 1952–58. Others obtained political

---

*The members of the original society included José Vasconcelos, Pedro Henríquez Urena, Alfonso Reyes, Antonio Caso, and Martín Luis Guzmán.

†Among those were Vicente Lombardo Toledano, Narciso Bassols, Miguel Palacios Macedo, Jaime Torres Bodet, Teófilo Olea y Leyva, and many other artists, writers, and intellectuals.

experience through student elections. For example, in 1918, Manuel Gómez Morín ran for the presidency of the Student Society of the law school, which he won with the help of his campaign manager, Vicente Lombardo Toledano. Narciso Bassols, and his friend Miguel Palacios Macedo, also became president and secretary general respectively of the Student Society of the law school. These student campaigns and positions contributed to the political skills and reputation of the participants, from which some benefitted in later life.

Relationships between students and professors flourished outside of the classroom. For example, Manuel Gómez Morín remembers the opportunities for reading made available at the home of Professor Agustín Aragón, through his friendship with Aragón's nephew, Teófilo Olea y Leyva, which in turn produced friendships with other professors and intellectuals.[19] Antonio Caso was another professor who entertained in his home where students met other members of the Ateneo Generation.

Graduates of this decade also were active in student publications. Gómez Morín recalls his own career:

> We particpated in student publications. I worked as a proofreader in *El Demócrata*. During 1915, I briefly collaborated on a newspaper published by Dr Atl. Later, I worked regularly in the recently founded *El Universal* in order to produce, with Alberto [Vásquez del Mercado] a university page; and a short while later, he worked on *The Herald* of Mexico of General Alvarado, who initiated the first editorial page in which Vicente [Lombardo Toledano] and I worked alongside of Don Enrique González Martínez, Martín Luis Guzmán . . .[20]

While the prominent members of various generations, despite close friendships, often went their separate ways in terms of public and private careers, they frequently were responsible for initiating the public careers of others or influencing their later career positions. Vicente Lombardo Toledano, in an interview with James and Edna Wilkie, describes the supporters he recruited while he was the young governor of Puebla:

> It was an emergency situation. The people of Puebla saw us as strange animals. It was said that this was not a government, but a Greek Aeropagus, nothing more than intellectuals. The majority of us were not from Puebla and that was true. The only person born in Puebla was myself; but my collaborators were Alfonso Caso, consulting lawyer to the state government; Pedro Henríquez Ureña, one of the most important men of the Ateneo, director of public education of the state; Agustín Loera Chávez, another intellectual charged with the university extension, and many more, who because of their friendship, accompanied me on something more than a political adventure in the Puebla government, because we came to govern a very important state in a full,

armed revolution. As my helpers, while still students, were some of the most brilliant youths of that time, like Salvador Azuela and others, who had a salary of two pesos daily plus room and board.[21]

Other students of this generation also helped their companions obtain employment. Alberto Vázquez del Mercado, a co-student with Manuel Gómez Morín, helped Gómez Morín obtain a job with the law firm of Miguel Alessio Robles. Alessio Robles in turn introduced Gómez Morín to the famous revolutionary leader General Salvador Alvarado, and Gómez Morín served as his private secretary when Alvarado became Secretary of the Treasury under President Adolfo de la Huerta.[22] Alberto Vázquez del Mercado, while serving as Secretary of Government for the Federal District, asked two other co-students, Alfonso Caso and Vicente Lombardo Toledano, to work for the Federal District.[23] Gómez Morín had an impact on the later careers of several of his co-students. His best friend during his law school days was Teófilo Olea y Leva, who later helped Gómez Morín found the National Action Party in opposition to the government. Another co-student, Trinidad García, who served as Dean of the National School of Law from 1934 to 1935, also became a founding member of PAN and served on the national executive committee of that party.

José Vasconcelos, also a member of the Ateneo, used his position as rector of the university, and, more important, as Secretary of Public Education, to bring many of his brilliant students into government. For example, in 1921, he appointed his friend and co-member of the Ateneo, Antonio Caso, Rector of the National University. Later, to settle a dispute between himself and Caso, Vasconcelos appointed Vicente Lombardo Toledano, a student of Caso's, Director of the National Preparatory School. These examples are duplicated many times by other students and professors graduating during this decade.

The National School of Law, 1921–30

While the National University produced a brilliant generation of students during the decade from 1910 to 1920, the following decade was responsible for a much greater percentage of high-level officeholders. In fact, over 25 percent of the top officeholders between 1935 and 1976 graduated from the National University in the ten-year period from 1921 to 1930. It was also during this decade that many of the members of the Ateneo of 1910 and the younger generations attached to it (Table 6.1) became mentors and teachers of the prominent students of the following decade. The law school attracted the greatest number of professors who were public men and graduated the largest number of students who became public men. However, as we shall discover, formal student activities became increasingly important as a means of student contact, especially with students from other schools at the National University and students of provincial universities.

During the 1920s, two generations were particularly important to public life. These two generations were the law students graduating in 1925–26 and 1928–29. In large part, they became important political generations because one of their members, Miguel Alemán, had continued his studies beyond the National Preparatory School and would become president in 1946. While Miguel Alemán served to influence the careers of many of his co-students and professors, the resurgence of organized student congresses, the 1929 presidential campaign, and the university autonomy movement contributed greatly to politicizing students and professors and encouraging close friendships among many persons from different schools and geographic locations.

Table 6.1

**Graduates of the National School of Law From 1910 to 1920
Who Held High Public Office From 1935 to 1976**

Name of Graduate	Year	Highest Position in Public Life Since 1935
Islas Bravo, Antonio	1910	Justice of the Supreme Court
Castillo Nájera, Francisco	1912	Secretary of Foreign Relations
Serrano, Gustavo	1912	Secretary of Industry and Commerce
Vázquez, Genaro V.	1913	Secretary of Labor
Valenzuela, Gilberto	1914	Justice of the Supreme Court
Avila Breton, Rafael	1915	Governor of Tlaxcala
De la Fuente, Fernando	1915	Justice of the Supreme Court
Vázquez Vela, Gonzalo	1915	Secretary of Public Education
Villa Michel, Primo	1915	Secretary of Government
Araujo, Emilio	1917	President of the Senate
Icaza y Lopez, Xavier	1917	Justice of the Supreme Court
Ortiz Tirado, José María	1917	Justice of the Supreme Court
Suárez, Eduardo	1917	Secretary of the Treasury
Vasconcelos, Eduardo	1917	Governor of Oaxaca
Campos Ortiz, Pablo	1918	Subsecretary of Foreign Relations
Díaz Infante, Luis	1918	Governor of Guanajuato
Caso, Alfonso	1919	Secretary of National Properties
Castro Leal, Antonio	1919	Ambassador to UNESCO
Gómez Morín, Manuel	1919	President of the CEN of PAN
González de la Vega, Angel	1919	Subsecretary of the Treasury
Lombardo Toledano, Vicente	1919	Secretary General of the CTM
Olea y Leyva, Teófilo	1919	Justice of the Supreme Court
Aguilar y Maya, José	1920	Attorney General of Mexico
Bartlett, Manuel	1920	Governor of Tabasco
Bassols, Narciso	1920	Secretary of the Treasury
Eboli Paniagua, Abenamar	1920	Justice of the Supreme Court
Fraga, Gabino	1920	Subsecretary of Foreign Relations
García Rojas, Gabriel	1920	Justice of the Supreme Court
García Téllez, Ignacio	1920	Secretary of Government
González de la Vega, Francisco	1920	Attorney General of Mexico
Mendieta y Núñez, Lucio	1920	*Oficial Mayor* of Agrarian Affairs
Santos Guajardo, Vicente	1920	Subsecretary of Government

First, let us examine the relationship between Miguel Alemán and his professors and co-students—a relationship more important to his Law School contacts than his preparatory school associates. In stressing Alemán as an example, it should be clear that he is being discussed because he is the first President after 1935 to come from both schools, and, as chapter ii makes clear, his collaborators have had a continuous impact in Mexico, extending even to the López Portillo administrations.

Miguel Alemán was a member of the 1925 generation, or that group that normally would have graduated in 1929. Therefore, his contact with the 1928–29 graduating law classes occurred because of student friendships. On the other hand, his friendship with and respect for members of the 1925–26 graduating law classes was the result of a teacher-student relationship. At the end of this decade, 52 professors taught at the National School of Law[24] (Table 6.2). Of those professors, we have been able to obtain educational and career information on 36. Nine of these professors were members of the 1915–1917 generations, again illustrating the importance of those generations for future law students. Perhaps more remarkable is that ten members of the 1925–26 graduating class or 28 percent of the 1930 faculty whose background we identified were teaching within five years after they had graduated (see Table 6.2). The first generation of students these professors could have instructed was the 1925 generation. As young professors, recently graduated from the law school, they had little means to recruit members of the 1925 generation into public life. Instead, Miguel Alemán and other students who quickly rose to prominent public positions were able, by 1946, to affect the careers of many of their former young professors. Alemán himself selected his professors for the following positions: Manuel Gual Vidal, Secretary of Public Education; Ramón Beteta, Secretary of the Treasury; Mario Sousa, head of the Department of Agrarian Affairs & Colonization; Mario de la Cueva, President of the Federal Board of Conciliation and Arbitration; Antonio Taracena, Senator from Tabasco; Antonio Martínez Báez, secretary of Industry and Commerce; J. Jesús Castorena, governor of Guanajuato; Agustín García López, Secretary of Public Works; and Fernando Casas Alemán, head of the Federal District.

Although Miguel Alemán was influential in the public careers of some of his young professors, older professors were often responsible for the recruitment of their best students into public careers. José Aguilar y Maya, himself a graduate in 1920, was responsible for recruiting a number of students as federal agents when he served as attorney general for the Federal District and professor of Public Law. Among these were Antonio Carrillo Flores, Andrés Serra Rojas, and Ángel Carvajal—all graduates of the National Law School during the 1920s. Several members of the "Seven Wise Men" were extremely influential on the careers of their students. Manuel

Table 6.2

Professors Teaching at the National School of Law in 1930

Name of Professor	Field Taught	University and Year Graduated	Public Office Held
Aguilar y Maya, José	Public Law	1920 UNAM	Attorney General of Mexico
Alvarez del C., Juan Manuel	Public International Law	1912 NI	Federal Deputy
Azuela, Mariano	Guarantees	1929 UNAM	Justice of the Supreme Court
Bassols, Narciso	Guarantees	1920 UNAM	Secretary of Government
Beteta, Ramón	Political Economy	1926 UNAM	Secretary of the Treasury
Borja Soriano, Manuel	Contract Law	1898 UNAM	Notary Public
Brito Foucher, Rodulfo	Public Law	1923 UNAM	Rector of UNAM
Carreño, Franco	Introductory Law	1923 UNAM	Justice of the Supreme Court
Caso, Alfonso	General Theory	1919 UNAM	Secretary of National Properties
Caso, Angel	Civil Process	NI NI	NI
Caso, Antonio	Sociology	1904 UNAM	Rector of UNAM
Castorena, J. de Jesús	Industrial Law	1925 UNAM	Governor of Guanajuato
Chico Goerne, Luis	Sociology	1918 UNAM	Justice of the Supreme Court
Cortés, Ricardo	Civil Process	NI NI	NI
Cossío y Cossío, Roberto	Commercial Law	1929 UNAM	Secretary General of the CEN of PAN
De J. Tena, Felipe	Commercial Law	1899 Michoacán	Justice of the Supreme Court
De la Cueva, Mario	General Theory	1925 UNAM	President of Federal Arbitration Board
De P. Fernández, Francisco	Inheritance & Estate Law	NI NI	NI
De P. Herrasti, Francisco	History of Law	1903 UNAM	None
Echeverría, Carlos	Civil Law	NI NI	NI
Escalante, Angel	Penal Law	NI NI	NI
Esteva Ruiz, Robert A.	Commercial Law	1899 UNAM	Subsecretary of Foreign Relations
Fraga, Gabino	Administrative Law	1920 UNAM	Subsecretary of Foreign Relations
Gallardo, Everardo	Forensic Penal Law	NI NI	NI
García, Trinidad	Introductory Law	1919 UNAM	Dean of the National School of Law
García Rojas, Gabriel	Inheritance & Estate Law	1920 UNAM	Justice of the Supreme Court
Garza, Ernesto G.	Penal Law	NI NI	NI
Garza Galindo, Agustín	Inheritance & Estate Law	NI NI	NI
Gómez Morín, Manuel	Public Law	1919 UNAM	President of the CEN of PAN
González Aparicio, Enrique	Political Economy	1925 UNAM	Dean of the National School of Economics
Gual Vidal, Manuel	Contract Law	1926 UNAM	Secretary of Public Education
Lanz Duret, Miguel	Constitutional Law	1904 UNAM	Director of *El Universal*
Lombardo Toledano, Vicente	Industrial Law	1919 UNAM	Secretary General of the CTM
López Lira, José	Sociology	1914 Guanajuato	Secretary of National Properties
Luna y Parra, Pascual	Finance and Fiscal Law	NI NI	NI

Table 6.2 (*continued*)

Professors Teaching at the National School of Law in 1930

Name of Professor	Field Taught	University and Year Graduated	Public Office Held
Martínez Baez, Antonio	Constitutional Law	1925 UNAM	Secretary of Industry and Commerce
Medina, Hilario	Constitutional Law	1925 UNAM	Chief Justice of the Supreme Court
Mendieta y Núñez, Lucio	Administrative Law	1920 UNAM	*Oficial Mayor* of Agrarian Affairs
Monroy, Atenedoro	History of Law	1889 Puebla	*Oficial Mayor* of a state agency
Ortega, Rafael	Civil Law	NI NI	NI
Peniche López, Vicente	Guarantees	1920 Yucatán	Dean of the National School of Law
Rojo de la Vega, Rafael	Forensic Civil Law	NI NI	NI
Sánchez Pontón, Luis	Public Law	1910 Puebla	Secretary of Public Education
Sierra, Manuel J.	Public International Law	1906 UNAM	*Oficial Mayor* of the Treasury
Soto Obregón, Jesús	Introductory Law	NI NI	NI
Souza, Mario	Political Economy	1925 UNAM	Secretary of Agrarian Affairs
Suárez, Eduardo	Public International Law	1917 UNAM	Secretary of the Treasury
Taracena, Antonio	Penal Law	1926 UNAM	Senator from Tabasco
Teja Zabre, Alfonso	Penal Law	1909 UNAM	Justice of the Superior Court of the Federal District
Valles, Adolfo	Civil Process	NI NI	NI
Vázquez, Francisco M.	Civil Process	NI NI	NI
Zevada, Ricardo J.	Administrative Law	1925 UNAM	Director General of the National Foreign Trade Bank

Key: NI = No information

Gómez Morín, who was the founder and first director of the Bank of Mexico in 1925, and who served as an advisor to the secretary of the Treasury, began to recruit students and professors to study Mexico from an economist's viewpoint in a new Technical Tax Department. At this time, through the year 1929, economics was offered as a section of studies in the law school. Gómez Morín helped many students obtain their first public employment.[25] At least five of the students who worked for him in this new department distinguished themselves in public life.* He also recruited former students or co-students who became professors in the 1920s, and these included Antonio Martínez Baéz and Ramón Beteta. All of these law school graduates became distinguished public men and professors, and they too recruited their best students to public careers.[26] This relationship between professors and students, and

---

*Among the students in that office were Eduardo Bustamante, Mario Sousa, Emigdio Martínez Adame (secretary of the CEN of PRI), Eduardo Garduño (Subsecretary of the Treasury), and Enrique González Aparicio.

then students who themselves became professors, has continued generation after generation.

Of the 36 professors at the law school in 1930 with known educational backgrounds, 31 graduated from the National University (Table 6.2). Of those professors, only two, Francisco de P. Herrasti and Manuel Borja Soriano, could be described as full-time educators and had not held high-level positions in academia or government. Most of these 31 professors had studied under the older professors who were still teaching in 1930, and it was those same older professors, in many cases, who were responsible for their *teaching* careers as well as their public careers. For example, Antonio Martínez Baéz, who was an outstanding student member of the 1921 generation, served as Narciso Bassols' student assistant at the Institute of Social Research at the National University during his last year as a law student in 1925. In 1929, he substituted for Bassols as a professor of constitutional law when Bassols became Dean. Martínez Baéz remained in that position from 1929 to 1967, with leave to serve as a cabinet secretary from 1948 to 1953. In 1966 he became a professor emeritus of the National Law School.[27] Bassols was equally responsible for the teaching career of another fine student, Ricardo J. Zevada, who became a professor of administrative law immediately following his graduation in 1925. Luis Chico Goerne, professor of sociology, secured an appointment for Antonio Carrillo Flores as a professor in 1932.[28] Indirectly, the revolution contributed to student friendships, since educational backgrounds of students from the provinces, who made up the majority at the National Law School, followed erratic patterns, resulting in law students who were often the same age, but enrolled in different generations. Antonio Martínez Baéz believes this is one of the reasons there was considerable friendship among the members of the 1925–26 and 1928–29 groups. Other students, like Eduardo Bustamante and Miguel Alemán himself, graduated with generations different from the ones they began with, since they took an overload and graduated one to two years early, becoming friends with members of older generations.

As we suggested earlier, one of the most important activities which encouraged student friendships was the increase in student political activities in the 1920s. At the beginning of the decade, students in Mexico organized the first International (Latin American) Student Congress, which met in Mexico City in September, 1921. In part, the environment for this type of student congress, which attracted student activists and intellectuals mainly from Latin America, was made possible through the efforts of José Vasconcelos, who as Secretary of Education recruited students throughout Central and South America. Antonio Martínez Baéz, a member of the 1921–25 generation, estimated that 20 to 25 percent of his co-students were from Central

America. The National University sent a large delegation to the congress, the majority of whom were representatives of various schools to the Mexican Federation of University Students. Seven members* of the Mexican delegation became prominent figures in public life.[29] Although these meetings increased contact among student leaders, they did not serve as a stimulus to student friendships among the various state universities. However, also in 1921, Mexican university students held the 2nd National Student Congress, which met at Puebla. Students from provincial universities, and from different schools within those universities, were well represented.[30] A number of them became governors of their home states in the 1940s. Following this congress, others were held during the 1920s at Ciudad Victoria, Oaxaca, Culiacán, and Mérida, and the last or 7th congress took place in Monterrey in January, 1930.

The congresses held during the years 1927 and 1928 served to form a nucleus for the beginnings of a student movement in opposition to the government of President P. Elias Calles and to the reelection of General Alvaro Obregón to the presidency in 1928. As early as 1927, the students at the 4th National Student Congress, meeting in Oaxaca, "made it clear that they were determined to take positive action should Calles insist on going on with his plans to run Obregón as the official candidate. In that case, the student Congress declared, it would offer José Vasconcelos as the candidate of Mexican youth."[31] Two presidents of the Confederation of University Students, Ángel Carvajal, 1927–28, and Alejandro Gómez Arias, 1928–29, 1929–30, became prominent leaders in the campaign of José Vasconcelos, which took place not in 1928, but in 1929, during the special presidential election held after General Obregón had been assassinated as the president-elect of Mexico. Other student participants in the congresses who became active in the campaign included Salvador Azuela, Secretary of the Federation of University Students under Gómez Arias; José María de los Reyes, delegate to the 4th National Congress; and Herminio Ahumada, delegate to the 5th National Congress[32] (see Table 6.3).

José Vasconcelos' campaign in the summer and fall of 1929 attracted student leaders from other schools at the National University as well as from the National Preparatory School. In effect, law school students who were political activists came in contact with preparatory students who were also student activists. The single most important preparatory school participant, in terms of his future public career, was Adolfo López Mateos, who became

---

*These seven were Daniel Cosío Villegas, Miguel Palacios Macedo, Rodulfo Brito Foucher, Eduardo Villaseñor, Ramón Beteta, Vicente Lombardo Toledano, and Arturo Martínez Adame.

Table 6.3

Students and Professors Who Supported the Vasconcelos Campaign of 1929

Name of Supporter	Year	Degree and University		Highest Public Office Held
Aceves Parra, Salvador	1931	Medicine	UNAM	Secretary of Public Health
Ahumada, Herminio	1930	Law	UNAM	Director General, Federal District
Alvarado, José	1934	Law	UNAM[a]	Member of the CEN of the PP (PPS)
Armendáriz, Antonio	1932	Law	UNAM	Subsecretary of the Treasury
Azuela, Salvador	1931	Law	UNAM	Director General of the Fondo de Cultura Económica
Brito Rosado, Efraín	1936	Law	UNAM	Senator from Yucatán
Bustamante, Octavio N.	1930	Law	UNAM	District Court Judge
Bustillo Oro, Juan	1930	Law	UNAM	Film Director
Carpy Manzano, Ernesto	1927	Law	UNAM	Attorney General of Michoacán
Carrancá y Trujillo, Raúl	1920	Law	Madrid	Justice of the Superior Court of the Federal District
Carvajal, Angel	1928	Law	UNAM	Secretary of Government
Chávez, Ignacio	1920	Medicine	UNAM	Rector of UNAM
Cosío Villegas, Daniel	1923	Law	Michoacán	Director General of the Fondo de Cultura Económica
Del Campo, Germán	DNA	DNA	UNAM[c]	DNA
De la Selva, Salomón	NI	NI	UNAM	Diplomat and Poet
De los Reyes, José María	1932	Law	UNAM	Federal Deputy from Hidalgo
Dromundo, Baltasar	NI	Law	UNAM	Federal Deputy from Chihuahua
García Sela, Miguel	1927	Law	UNAM	Federal Deputy from Puebla
Garrido Díaz, Luis	1922	Law	UNAM	Rector of UNAM
Gómez Arias, Alejandro	1931	Law	UNAM	Vice President of the PPS
Gómez Morín, Manuel	1919	Law	UNAM	President of the CEN of PAN
González Aparicio, Enrique	1927	Law	UNAM	Dean of the National School of Economics
González de la Vega, Angel	1919	Law	UNAM	Subsecretary of the Treasury
González de la Vega, Francisco	1920	Law	UNAM	Attorney General of Mexico
Heliodoro Valle, Rafael	1911	Normal School[b]		Editor of *El Universal*
Henestrosa, Andrés	1924	ENP	DNA[a]	Federal Deputy from Oaxaca
Heuer, Federico	NI	Law	UNAM	Department Director, National Properties
López Arias, Fernando	1934	Law	UNAM	Attorney General of Mexico
López Mateos, Adolfo	1934	Law	UNAM	President of Mexico
Magdaleno, Mauricio	1933	Law	UNAM	Subsecretary of Public Education
Mantilla Molina, Roberto	1933	Law	UNAM	Dean of the National School of Law
Medellín Ostos, Octavio	1919	Law	UNAM	Secretary of Government of the Federal District
Medellín Ostos, Roberto	1908	Engineering	UNAM	Secretary General of Health
Novo, Salvador	NI	Literature	UNAM	Director of Theater, Bellas Artes
Moreno Sánchez, Manuel	1932	Law	UNAM	President of the Senate
Novoa Ochoa, Carlos	1926	Law	UNAM	Director General Bank of Mexico
Pacheco Calvo, Ciriaco	NI	Economics	UNAM	NI
Palacios, Manuel R.	1926	Law	UNAM	Director General of National Railroads
Palacios Macedo, Miguel	1920	Law	UNAM	Subsecretary of Industry
Pellicer Cámara, Carlos	NI	Law	UNAM	Senator from Tabasco
Pous Ortiz, Raúl	NI	Law	UNAM	Director of Preparatory Education
Ramírez y Ramírez, Enrique	1933	ENP	DNA[a]	Member of the CEN of PPS and PRI
Rangel Frías, Raúl	1938	Law	UNAM	Governor of Nuevo León
Salazar Mallén, Rubén	1932	Law	UNAM	Secretary of PRUN

Table 6.3 *(continued)*

Students and Professors Who Supported the Vasconcelos Campaign of 1929

Name of Supporter	Year	Degree and University		Highest Public Office Held
Vázquez del Mercado, Alberto	1919	Law	UNAM[d]	Justice of the Supreme Court
Vejar Vásquez, Octavio	1923	Law	UNAM	Secretary of Public Education
Yáñez, Agustín	1929	Law	Guadala-jara	Secretary of Public Education
Zapata Vela, Carlos	1931	Law	UNAM	Federal Deputy from the Federal District

Key: PRUN = Revolutionary Party of National Unification (General Almazán's organization in the presidential campaign of 1940); PP = Popular Party; NI = No information; ENP = National Preparatory School; and DNA = Does not apply.

[b]Andrés Henestrosa and Enrique Ramírez y Ramírez did not complete their studies at UNAM, probably because they became prominent writers and journalists as students, professions which did not require an advanced degree. José Alvarado completed his studies, but not his thesis at UNAM, and he too was a journalist.

[b]In Honduras.

[c]Prominent student orator killed during the campaign. Jorge Prieto Laurens says he died in the arms of Adolfo López Mateos and Angel Carvajal (*Cincuenta años de política mexicana, memorias* [Mexico, 1968], p. 285).

[d]Miguel Palacios Macedo held prominent governmental positions prior to 1929, but after 1935, he was influential only through his authorship of major economic legislation in Mexico. Alberto Vázquez del Mercado's position as Supreme Court justice was 1929–1931. He too held no position after 1935. Daniel Cosío Villegas held the directorship of the Fondo de Cultura Económica at a time when the President of Mexico did not exert direct control over appointments to this position. That was not to occur until Gustavo Díaz Ordaz was President.

acquainted with various members of the Alemán and other law school generations. Many of the student participants in the campaign later held positions during the López Mateos administrations (1958–64).* Because of the prominence of the 1929 campaign, student activity in the previous presidential campaign of 1927 is often overlooked.† For example, Manuel R. Palacios supported the candidacy of Gilberto Valenzuela for president in 1927, and

---

*Antonio Armendáriz, Ambassador to Great Britain; Raúl Carrancá y Trujillo, Justice of the Superior Court of the Federal District; Angel Carvajal, Justice of the Supreme Court; Ignacio Chávez, Rector of UNAM; Miguel García Sela, Federal Deputy from Puebla; Mauricio Magdaleno, Senator from Zacatecas; Manuel Moreno Sánchez, President of the Senate; and Enrique Ramírez y Ramírez, Federal Deputy from the Federal District.

†An even earlier precedent was set in 1923 by the campaign of Adolfo de la Huerta (a graduate of the National Preparatory School) in opposition to General Calles for president. As Praxedis Balboa notes in his book, the majority of students were in favor of the De la Huerta campaign. One of those students, Antonio García López, organized a legal aid office to assist students and professors who were being persecuted by the government for their support of De la Huerta. Despite widespread student support for De la Huerta, Balboa, who was a leader of the student faction for Calles, was able to get 200 student members from various schools within the university to participate in his party. See his *Apuntes de mi vida* (México, 1975), pp. 22ff for some fascinating details about student political activity in 1923.

Miguel Alemán supported General Arnulfo R. Gómez.[33] Many of the students who participated alongside of Alemán in this campaign[34] held positions during his administration.*

Another event that became intertwined with the Vasconcelos campaign was the student strike during the summer of 1929.[35] While there was not a cause and effect relationship between the strike and the campaign, both events drew from the same student leadership:

> All, or practically all of the leaders of the May movement had a solid student political experience and a complete conscience for the autonomist ideal, proved by the reports and documents of the student congresses of 1927 in Oaxaca, of 1928 in Culiacán, of January 1929 in Yucatán—which raised Gómez Arias to the presidency of the National Student Congress. They supported the thesis of orderly self-determination for higher preparatory and professional instruction. Even more: this was the fundamental banner of the National Youth Congress which met in March of 1926 in Mexico City . . .[36]

Students of the law school and of the preparatory school initiated the strike in response to an attempt by the Dean of the Law School, Narciso Bassols, to implement some reforms dealing with calendar, curriculum, and examinations. When the president of Mexico closed the National Law School on May 8, 1929, a number of professors came out in support of the student efforts to have a say in academic changes. Most important was the support of Aquiles Elorduy, a former Dean of the Law School and a professor of many of the students of the 1920s (Table 6.4).[37]

Once the president closed the law school, student leaders such as Salvador Azuela and Alejandro Gómez Arias also joined in with their personal support and with the sympathy of the National Student Congress. Two days later, on May 10, the law students met at the preparatory school, voted on several resolutions, and formed a strike committee. On the following day, they began circulating a pact in which the signatories promised not to attend classes. Within several days, and after clashes with the police, the law school students attracted the support of the School of Economics, followed by the National Preparatory School and then by other schools at the National University. From a vague beginning, student demands accelerated and the idea of autonomy of the university from the federal government was born.† Within

---

*These were Francisco J. Santamaría, Governor of Tabasco from 1947–52; Efraín Brito Rosado, federal deputy from Yucatán; and Braulio Maldonado Sánchez, federal deputy from Baja California del Norte.

†The idea of autonomy, according to most observers, was probably that of Emilio Portes Gil, who used it to meet student demands and won some concessions for the government.

Table 6.4

Students and Professors Who Supported the University
Autonomy Movement in 1929[a]

Name of Supporter		Year, Degree & University		Highest Public Office Held
Azuela, Salvador	1931	Law	UNAM	Director General of the Fondo de Cultura Económica
Brito Rosado, Efraín	1935	Law	UNAM	Senator from Yucatán
De Alba, Pedro	1913	Med.	UNAM	Senator from Aguascalientes
De Gortari, Alfonso	NI	Med.	NI	Cardiologist
Del Campo, Germán	DNA	DNA	UNAM	Assassinated in 1929
De los Reyes, José María	1932	Law	UNAM	Federal Deputy from Hidalgo
Dromundo, Baltasar	1924	ENP	DNA	Federal Deputy from Chihuahua
Elorduy, Aquiles	1899	Law	UNAM	Senator from Aguascalientes
Flores Sánchez, Oscar[b]	1930	Law	UNAM	Governor of Chihuahua
García Villalobos, Ricardo	1932	Law	UNAM	Dean of the National School of Law
Garizurieta, César	1931	Law	UNAM	*Oficial Mayor* of Agrarian Affairs
Gómez Arias, Alejandro	1931	Law	UNAM	Vice President of the PPS
González Lugo, Hugo Pedro	1932	Law	UNAM	Governor of Tamaulipas
Guzmán Neyra, Alfonso	1933	Law	UNAM	Chief Justice of the Supreme Court
Henestrosa, Andrés	1924	ENP	DNA	Federal Deputy from Oaxaca
Landa, Rafael	1929	Law	UNAM	Died very young
Leduc, Renato	1929	Law	UNAM	Author and Poet
López Arias, Fernando	1934	Law	UNAM	Attorney General of Mexico
López Mateos, Adolfo	1934	Law	UNAM	President of Mexico
Martínez Mezquita, Luis F.	1932	Law	UNAM	Leader of the PPS
Miranda Fonseca, Donato	1935	Law	ELD	Secretary of the Presidency
Moreno Sánchez, Manuel	1932	Law	UNAM	President of the Senate
Pérez Martínez, Hector	1928	Den.	UNAM	Secretary of Government
Ramírez Cabañas, Joaquín	1902	ENP	DNA	Journalist, Poet and Professor
Ramírez Guerrero, Carlos	1932	Law	UNAM	Governor of Hidalgo
Ramírez y Ramírez, Enrique	1933	ENP	DNA	Federal Deputy from the Federal District
Romano Muñoz, José	NI	NI	NI	Director General of Higher Education
Serrano Castro, Julio	1930	Law	UNAM	Subsecretary of Labor
Sierra, Santiago X.	1932	Law	UNAM	Secretary General of Durango
Vallejo Novelo, José	1934	Law	UNAM	Federal Deputy from Yucatán
Zapata Vela, Carlos	1931	Law	UNAM	Federal Deputy from the Federal District

[a]This table only contains those names of supporters about whom we have some career information.
[b]Oscar Flores Sanchez is one of those Mexicans who has successfully obtained high political office in more than three administrations. In 1976 Lopez Portillo appointed him Attorney General of Mexico.
Key: NI = No information; DNA = Does not apply; ENP = National Preparatory School; and ELD = Free Law School.

several weeks, schools and universities throughout Mexico and even outside of Mexico became supporters of the autonomy movement. Even private schools, like the well-known Colegio Francés de Morelos, operated by the Brothers of Mary, joined the student movement.[38] As can be seen from Tables 6.3 and 6.4 among the more prominent leaders of the autonomy movement in 1929 there were many students who participated in the Vasconcelos campaign. Again, various generations of students were brought together by the strike,* especially the 1929, 1931, and 1932 groups (Table 6.4).[39]

If we were to examine all of the members of the 1920s generations who overlapped their education with Alemán, as I have done in great detail elsewhere,[40] we could see the results of many preparatory school and university friendships on political careers.[41] I concluded that all of the members of the Alemán administration (1946–52) listed in Table 6.5 knew each other or the president himself as preparatory students, university students, or professors. An excellent example of a student in Table 6.5 whose political career was influenced by his co-students and his professors is Víctor Manuel Villaseñor, who had the unusual experience for his generation of being educated in both the United States and Mexico. He attended the University of Michigan, graduating in 1926, and returned to Mexico City, where he became a member of the Alemán generation in 1927, graduating with most of that group two years later. During his law school days at the National University, he became good friends with Luis Cabrera, a noted professor and intellectual thinker of the Mexican Revolution. He practiced law with Cabrera for two years, but became interested in those issues which were being disputed between Mexico and the United States. With the help of Cabrera, he obtained an appointment to the Mexican-United States General Claims Commission and went to Washington, D.C., just before the Great Depression. In 1930, he completed his thesis on the "Nationality of Companies and the Protection of Foreign Interests in Mexico," dedicating it to his mentor.

Several years later, after becoming a Marxist, he began writing and giving various conferences on subjects relating to the Soviet Union. As a result of one conference in 1932, Narciso Bassols, under whom he had studied at law school and who was then Secretary of Public Education, asked him if he could publish one of his speeches. They became close friends, and in 1934, when Lázaro Cárdenas became president, he appointed Bassols as Secretary of the Treasury. Bassols asked Villaseñor to become Director of the Department of Economic Archives. In 1940, Bassols, Villaseñor, and other former students of Bassols founded a review to oppose the government of President Manuel Ávila Camacho. In 1943, Villaseñor and Bassols were candidates for federal deputy, but both men, without official party support,

---

*This is illustrated by the student membership on the first Council of the National University in July, 1929, which has served as an executive board of that institution. Among the students were Alejandro Gómez Arias and Julio Serrano Castro (law school); Salvador Aceves Parra (medical school); Bruno Mascanzoni (engineering school); and Efraín Brito Rosado and José Vallejo Novelo (preparatory school). All were members of the strike committee.

Table 6.5

Students and Professors of the "Alemán Generation" Who Followed Public Careers

Name of Generation Member	Attended ENP	Law Graduate or Other at UNAM	Position in the Alemán Administration
Aceves Parra, Salvador	X	1928 Medicine	None
Aranda Osorio, Efraín	X	1932	Senator from Chiapas
Armendáriz, Antonio	X	1932	President of the National Securities Commission
Arteaga y Santoyo, Armando	X	1930	Director of IEPES of PRI
Azuela, Mariano	X	1928	Justice of the Supreme Court
Azuela, Salvador	X	1934[a]	Delegate to UNESCO
Beteta, Ramón	X	1926	Secretary of the Treasury
Burguete, Ezequiel	X	1929	None
Bustamante, Eduardo		1926	Subsecretary of the Treasury
Canudas O., Luis Felipe	X	1932	Assistant Attorney General
Carrillo Durán, Ricardo	X	1929	None
Carrillo Flores, Antonio	X	1929	Director General of the National Finance Bank
Carvajal, Angel	X	1928	Governor of Veracruz
Casas Alemán, Fernando		1926	Head of the Federal District
Castro Estrada, José	X	1929	Subsecretary of Agriculture
Chávez, Leopoldo		Medicine	Subsecretary of Education
De la Selva, Rogerio		1933	Secretary of the Presidency
Dovalí Jaime, Antonio	X	1929 Engineering	Subsecretary of Public Works
Fernández Robert, Raúl		1929	Attorney General of Military Justice
Franco Sodi, Carlos		1927	Attorney General of Mexico
García González, Alfonso	X	1931	Governor of Baja California del Norte
García López, Agustín		1925	Secretary of Public Works
Garizurieta, César	X	1931	Federal Deputy from Veracruz
González Blanco, Alberto	X	1927	Justice of the Superior Court of the Federal District
González Blanco, Salomon	X	1927	*Oficial Mayor* of Labor
Gual Vidal, Manuel		1926	Secretary of Public Education
Guzmán Neyra, Alfonso	X	1933	President of the Federal Conciliation & Arbitration Board
Huerta Sánchez, Luciano	X	1925 Medicine	None
Iturriaga A., Bernardo		1926	Subsecretary of the Treasury
López Sánchez, Raúl		1929	Governor of Coahuila
Magdaleno C., Mauricio	X	1928	Federal Deputy from Zacatecas
Maldonado, Braulio	X	1928	Federal Deputy from Baja California del Norte
Martínez Báez, Antonio		1926	Secretary of Industry & Commerce
Noriega, Alfonso		1929	None
Noriega O., Raúl		1947[a]	*Oficial Mayor* of the Treasury
Novo, Salvador	X	Some Literature	Director of Theater, Bellas Artes
Novoa, Carlos	X	1926	Director General Bank of Mexico
Orive Alba, Adolfo	X	1927 Engineering	Secretary of Hydraulic Resources
Ortiz Mena, Antonio	X	1928	Subdirector National Mortgage Bank

Table 6.5 *(continued)*

Students and Professors of the "Alemán Generation"
Who Followed Public Careers

Name of Generation Member	Attended ENP	Law Graduate or Other at UNAM	Position in the Alemán Administration
Palacios, Manuel R.	X	1926	Director General National Railroads
Pérez Martínez, Héctor	X	1928 Dentistry	Secretary of Government
Ramírez Vázquez, Manuel	X	1929	Secretary of Labor
Ramírez Vázquez, Mariano	X	1926	Justice of the Supreme Court
Ramos Millán, Gabriel	X	None Free Law School	Director of the National Maize Commission
Rivera Pérez C., José	X	1931	Senator from Guanajuato
Romandia F., Alfonso	X	1927	*Oficial Mayor* of Agriculture
Sánchez Cuen, Manuel	X	1929	Subsecretary of Industry and Commerce
Serra Rojas, Andres	X	1928	Secretary of Labor
Serrano Castro, Julio		1930	Subdirector of PEMEX
Solorzano, Roberto A.	X	1930	Federal Deputy from Colima
Soto Máynez, Oscar		1927	Governor of Chihuahua
Sousa Gordillo, Mario		1925	Head of the Agrarian Affairs Department
Terán Zozaya, Horacio		1927	Governor of Tamaulipas
Uruchurtu, Ernesto P.	X	1931	Secretary of Government
Zamora, Adolfo	X	1931	Director General of the National Mortgage Bank

[a]Both of these individuals were co-students of Miguel Alemán, but had very erratic student careers.

lost the election. Much later, in 1944, he accompanied Bassols as Ambassador to the USSR on a trip to the Eastern European countries. In 1948, both Bassols and Villaseñor became active again in politics, this time as founders of the Popular Party (later the PPS). However, they resigned in 1949 after becoming disillusioned with the party leadership.

It was at this point that Villaseñor decided to leave all political activities, since he believed the left was divided in Mexico and his experiences were sterile and frustrating. During this interlude in 1951, he had lunch with Miguel Alemán, and proposed to him that he would like to demonstrate to Mexicans that a government-controlled and operated enterprise could be as efficiently operated as a private one. Alemán, who had been his classmate at the law school, offered him the choice of several agencies that were in the planning stages, and Villaseñor accepted the directorship of the new agency designed to produce railroad cars for the National Railroads of Mexico. He later became director of the National Diesel Company and then of the National Railroads of Mexico.[42] Villaseñor's contact with President Alemán is an excellent illustration of the persistent importance of a friendship made during their student days. It was his friendship with Alemán that gave Villa-señor access to the President. Politically, they had long been on opposing sides, and it could hardly be argued that Alemán, at the end of his administration, would receive any benefits by appointing Villaseñor, who while a man of many talents had not demonstrated any previous administrative experience. Without this access to Alemán, Villaseñor would probably have never become the director of several of Mexico's most important public industries.

Despite the special circumstances of the decade that fomented contact, various students have indicated to the author that because of class size they had the opportunity to know most of their student companions from various generations.[43] These did not just include persons at the law school, but the prominent future writers, artists, historians, engineers, and doctors who influenced Mexico in all fields.[44]

The National School of Law, 1931–40

The 1930s, like the previous decade, was characterized by several factors that increased student and student-faculty contact. First, there was a carry-over among the preparatory students and first- and second-year law students who participated in any of the events of 1929. Second, similar to the 1920s, a president, Adolfo López Mateos, graduated from the law school during the middle of the decade. Third, there were several strikes, particularly the 1933 strike, which, like that of 1929, contributed to student and professor interchange and activity. And last, as Manuel Rivera Silva has suggested, the students of this era saw the law profession paralleling the career of being a politician. Therefore, many law students felt it necessary to participate in student and national politics.[45]

Rather than enumerate the contacts and careers of most students in the 1930s, let us examine the careers of an entire generation, the 1928–32 group, for which we have fairly complete information (Table 6.6). Of the 116 living members of that law class (as of 1973), 29 were practicing lawyers in various fields, 57 (49 percent) were public officials, 9 worked for or were officials of private firms, one became a career military judicial officer and another a priest. We could not determine the main occupation of the remaining 17 graduates. Of those with known careers, 18 or slightly over 18 percent held important public positions ranging from federal deputy to cabinet member. This generation would not be considered remarkable for the number of graduates in public service, since it did not produce a president nor a group of cabinet secretaries. Therefore, it is revealing that nearly half of the graduates went into public life, while so few were recruited by private enterprise. These figures show the extent to which law school graduates were recruited into electoral and administrative positions in the public sphere.

Table 6.6

Graduates of the National School of Law Generation of 1928–1932

Name of Graduate	Profession or Public Office	Residence in 1973
Acedo Romero, Guillermo	Notary Public	Sonora
Acevedo Astudillo, Rubén	Lawyer	Mexico, D.F.
Acuña Pardo, Daniel	Court Secretary	Mexico, D.F.
Aguilar Alvarez, Ernesto	Justice of the Supreme Court	Mexico, D.F.
Aguilar Borges, Joaquín	Department Head, Treasury	Mexico, D.F.
Aguilar Pico, Saúl	Justice of State Superior Court	Sinaloa
Aguirre del Castillo, Vicente	Governor of Hidalgo	Mexico, D.F.
Algaba, Horacio	Lawyer	Coahuila
Alvarado Belmont, León	Tax Lawyer, Treasury of DF	Mexico, D.F.
Alvarez Arellano, Vicente	Lawyer	Mexico, D.F.
Alvarez Salas, Leopoldo	State Judicial Agent	Chihuahua
Andrade González, José	Secretary General of Jalisco	Jalisco
Arceo Cortes, Manuel	Court Secretary	Mexico, D.F.
Arías Soria, Roberto	Lawyer	Hidalgo
Armendáriz, Antonio	Subsecretary, Treasury	Mexico, D.F.
Arnoux Siqueiros, Ernesto	Director, National Savings Bank	Mexico, D.F.
Balderas Pérez, Manuel	....	Mexico, D.F.
Beltrán Beltrán, Amando	President, Federal Arbitration Board	Mexico, D.F.
Bernal Pérez, Manuel	Lawyer, PEMEX	Mexico, D.F.
Blanco Sánchez, Jaime	Lawyer	Mexico, D.F.
Calvo Marroquín, Octavio	Treasurer, DDF	Mexico, D.F.
Canales Valverde, Tristán	Subsecretary, Labor	Mexico, D.F.
Capdevielle Ochoa, Gontrand	Lawyer, Mexican Light & Power	Mexico, D.F.
Carrillo Azcarate, Alberto		Mexico, D.F.
Carrillo Díaz, Roberto	Lawyer, Secretary of Government	Mexico, D.F.
Carillo Fernández, Abel	Archivist, Treasury	Mexico, D.F.
Castillo López, Jesús	Governor of Morelos	Mexico, D.F.
Castro Reguera, Carlos	....	Mexico, D.F.
César Pasos, Emilio	President, Superior Court DF	Mexico, D.F.
Cruz Manjarrez, Rafael	....	Baja California (Norte)
Dávila Valdéz, José	....	Mexico, D.F.
De Ibarrola, Antonio	Practicing Lawyer & Professor	Mexico, D.F.
De Otaduy, Augusto	....	Mexico, D.F.
Del Arenal Ordóñez, Lucas	Civil Judge	Mexico, D.F.
De los Reyes T., José María	Federal Deputy & PRI Official	Mexico, D.F.
Enríquez Vidal, Rafael	....	
Escudero, J. Agustín	Priest	Baja California (Norte)
Espinosa y Cossio, Héctor E.	President, Private Firm	Mexico, D.F.
Fernández Anaya, Francisco	Tax Attorney, Treasury DF	Mexico, D.F.
Fernández del Campo, Luis	Lawyer and Poet	Mexico, D.F.
Flores Zavala, Ernesto	Lawyer and Dean of the Law School	Mexico, D.F.

Table 6.6

Graduates of the National School of Law Generation of 1928–1932

Name of Graduate	Profession or Public Office	Residence in 1973
Gálvez de Forbes, Mauricio	....	Mexico, D.F.
García González, Pastor	Lawyer	Mexico
García Ramos, Feliciano	Attorney, Tax Department	Mexico, D.F.
Gaytan Medina, Ramón	Lawyer	Mexico, D.F.
González, Hugo Pedro	Governor of Tamaulipas	Tamaulipas
González García, Eleazar	Lawyer	Mexico, D.F.
González Millan, Héctor	Lawyer, National Banking Comis.	Mexico, D.F.
González Treviño, Rodolfo	Lawyer	Coahuila
Greaves, José Antonio	Vice-President, Import Business	Mexico, D.F.
Guerrero Reyes, Angel	....	Mexico, D.F.
Haces Gil, Lucas	Lawyer	Coahuila
Hernández Partida, Leopoldo	Secretary of CEN of PRI	Guanajuato
Jurado Domínguez, José	Lawyer, Federal Automobile Registry	Mexico, D.F.
L., Mercedes Pons Galindo de	(only woman graduate)	Mexico, D.F.
Landero Alamo, Francisco	Subtreasurer, Puebla	Puebla
Ledesma, J. de Jesús	Lawyer and Professor	Mexico, D.F.
Legorreta B., Gustavo	Lawyer	Mexico, D.F.
López Clares, Xavier	Lawyer	Mexico, D.F.
Loustau, Mario R.	Mayor, Ciudad Valles, San Luis Potosí	San Luis Potosí
Luna, Cirilo R.	Lawyer, National Public Works Bank	Mexico, D.F.
Luna y Parra, José	Lawyer and Professor	Mexico, D.F.
Manzano Osorno, Javier	Secretary General of Hidalgo	Hidalgo
Martínez Mezquida, Luis F.	Leader of the PPS	Mexico, D.F.
Meixueiro Hernández, Ernesto	....	Mexico, D.F.
Mestre Martínez, Eduardo	Subdirector Dept, National Savings Bank	Mexico, D.F.
Minvielle Roca, Carlos	Lawyer	Veracruz
Montaño, José A.	Director of Government-DDF	Mexico, D.F.
Moreno Uruchurtu, Gustavo	....	Mexico, D.F.
Muldoon Saury, Francisco	....	Mexico, D.F.
Muro Méndez, José	....	Mexico, D.F.
Nadal, Filiberto	Notary Public	Veracruz
Nataren Castellaños, Ernesto	....	Mexico, D.F.
Olvera Castillo, Antonio P.	....	Mexico, D.F.
Ontiveros Chávez, Federico	Director, Federal Treasury Office	Guanajuato
Oreza Jordan, Octavio	Conciliator, Labor Department	Mexico, D.F.
Orive Alba, Armando	Lawyer	Mexico, D.F.
Ortega y Aviles, Antonio	Dept Head, National Public Works Bank	Mexico, D.F.
Parra Hernández, Enrique	Director General, National Foreign Trade Bank	Mexico, D.F.
Pascal del Campo, Fausto	Lawyer	Mexico, D.F.
Pavia Suñol, Jaime	Lawyer, Cervecería Modelo	Mexico, D.F.
Pérez Nieto Priego, Leonel	Lawyer	Mexico, D.F.
Pérez Ortiz, José	Lawyer	Sonora

Table 6.6 (*continued*)

Graduates of the National School of Law Generation of 1928–1932

Name of Graduate	Profession or Public Office	Residence in 1973
Pérez Verdia, Enrique	Lawyer, Secretary of the Mexican Bar	Mexico, D.F.
Pimentel Pimentel, José María	Lawyer and Poet	Mexico, D.F.
Ponce del León, Salvador	Lawyer	Mexico, D.F.
Quiroz Barranco, Gustavo	Dept Head, PEMEX	Mexico, D.F.
Ramírez Guerrero, Carlos	Governor of Hidalgo	Mexico, D.F.
Ramírez Reyes, Horacio	Lawyer, National Agricultural Credit Bank	Mexico, D.F.
Ramos Rodríguez, Agapito	Lawyer	Mexico, D.F.
Rebollar Sánchez, Daniel	Asst. Legal Director, Private firm	Mexico, D.F.
Reyeros M., José Aurelio	Judge, First Penal Appeals Court	Mexico, D.F.
Reynaud, Luis	Notary Public	Veracruz
Reynoso Márquez, Virgilio	....	Hidalgo
Roqueñi, Antonio	Director Federal Treasury Office	Hidalgo
Rosales Piña, Mario	Notary Public	Morelos
Rubio Rubio, Ernesto	Director Federal Treasury Office	Mexico, D.F.
Ruiz de Chávez Salazar, Jesús	Lawyer, Construction Firm	Mexico, D.F.
Sahagun Arreola, Salvador	Director Federal Treasury Office	Sonora
Saldaña Villalaba, Adalberto	Director General, National Finance Bank	Mexico, D.F.
Santos Galindo, César	Director General, Film Company	Mexico, D.F.
Solis Guillén, Eduardo	Career Navy Officer	Mexico, D.F.
Taladrid, José de Jesús	Lawyer	Mexico, D.F.
Toral Moreno, Jesús	Judge, Second Admin. Collegiate Court	Mexico, D.F.
Torres Araiza, Juvenal	Actuary, Civil Court	Mexico, D.F.
Torres Rivas, Jesús	....	Mexico, D.F.
Treviño D., José María	Lawyer	Chihuahua
Ulloa Ortiz, Manuel	Member of the CEN of PAN	Mexico, D.F.
Urbiola Olvera, Edmundo	Lawyer	Mexico, D.F.
Váldez Barahona, Joaquín	Regional Delegate, Treasury	Puebla
Varela Quezada, Manuel	Notary Public and Poet	Aguascalientes
Vargas Díaz, Eduardo	Federal Deputy from Puebla	Mexico, D.F.
Vega Miner, Luis	Dept Head, Government	Mexico, D.F.
Viramontes P., Guillermo H.	Director General, National Mortgage Bank	Mexico, D.F.
Visoso Aramburo, José	Lawyer, Private Bank	Mexico, D.F.
Zarazua Licona, Jenaro	Secretary, Supreme Court, & Poet	Mexico, D.F.

Key: DF = Federal District; DDF = Department of the Federal District.

A close examination of the career patterns of those participating in public life reveals quite clearly that student friendships were again important to individual career patterns. For example, in the Secretariat of the Treasury in 1953, Antonio Carrillo Flores (1929), Antonio Armendáriz (1932), and Raúl Noriega (1929) held the top three positions. All three were members of the 1920–24 National Preparatory School generation, and Antonio Armendáriz, for financial reasons, extended his preparatory education through 1927, entering law school in 1928. Other members of the 1928–32 law class, like Armendáriz, became friends with, or their abilities were known to, members of the earlier 1925–29 law generation.[46] In 1953, four of the directors of Federal Treasury regional offices were members of the 1928–32 generation. If one member of the 1928–32 generation succeeded in obtaining a high position in the federal bureaucracy, he often appointed other co-students to positions of responsibility. An excellent example is Octavio Calvo Marroquín, a career employee of the Department of the Federal District, who ultimately became Treasurer of the Federal District. During the Echeverría administration two of Calvo's classmates, León Alvarado Belmont and Francisco Fernández Anaya, served under him.

Sometimes, certain regional patterns became apparent, largely because of the successful career of one or two individuals. The state of Hidalgo was well represented among this generation, and including one of the deceased members of the 1928–32 generation, it produced two governors, a secretary general, a district judge, and a noted local historian. Roberto Arias, also a native of Hidalgo, has written to me that his classmate, Vicente Aguirre del Castillo, governor from 1946–51, offered him the position of president of the State Superior Court, which he turned down.[47] Again, these examples are duplicated elsewhere by other members of this generation.

Lastly, in relation to Table 6.6, it is important to note the attractiveness of Mexico City for the graduates. Of the 116 graduates, an overwhelming number, 91 or 78 percent now live in the Federal District, even though at one time they may have held regional positions in business or public life. This figure is important because most graduates recall that the majority of their classmates came from the provinces, yet few have returned to their native states. For whatever reason, psychological, economic, and political, Mexico City is a magnet for law school graduates, a pattern duplicated among the earlier generations. Furthermore, of the 24 persons living outside of Mexico City, only four were living in cities which were not state political capitals. The university not only serves to recruit men and women into public life, but it attracts the better students from the provinces, and often keeps them and their skills in Mexico City, thus contributing to the social, economic, intellectual, and political imbalance between Mexico City and the provinces.

Student life in the 1930s still provided the same degree of contact encountered by earlier, somewhat smaller generations. Hugo Pedro González, a student from the provinces, describes it as follows:

They listened with interest to the conferences and explanations of the professors; they consulted orthodox texts in the libraries; they were heard conversing with their companions over legal and philosophical theories and commenting on recent literary works. They prepared themselves earnestly at the end of the academic year. We attended the oral examinations at the end of the year to listen to our companions and to the professional examinations of distinguished students in higher years.[48]

Most of the students during the 1930s lived in the Pink Zone or *Zona Rosa*. There were a number of homes in this area that were owned by formerly wealthy members of the Díaz society who needed income to maintain these residences. They rented rooms out to students, and therefore there was never a problem in making friends from all social classes, since students with various backgrounds came together in these private homes. Furthermore, there existed a student dormitory which was known as the House of Students, originally founded by the Secretary of the Treasury under the Díaz regime, José Limantour. This house served as a guest home for students from the states and territories. Social and geographic diversity melted away because of the unity provided by student housing.[49] Other students came together because of intellectual activities. For example, the Center for Law Students, through the efforts of Ernesto Santiago López, Salvador Urbina, Jr, and Manuel Ulloa Ortiz, produced a short-lived journal called *Jus* in 1933.[50]

In 1933, the university was confronted by another strike, and this time, professors were very much involved.[51] In 1932, some political leaders, notably Vicente Lombardo Toledano, with the support of various student groups, began a campaign to introduce a Marxist ideological emphasis in all levels of education.* The battle reached the university and became a question of socialist education versus the freedom to teach and do research as the individual professor saw fit. A large number of professors of various political

---

*Another important event taking place in 1935, but having some antecedents in 1933, was the role of university students in the Rodulfo Brito Foucher expedition to Tabasco. This event was previously tied to student politics by the fact that Alonso Garrido Canabal, a nephew of the dictator of that state, ran for president of the Confederation of University Students in 1933 with the support of Vicente Lombardo Toledano. He defeated José Vallejo Novelo, leader of the exiled Tabascan students, who had the support of Brito Foucher. However, because of the disputed results, Garrido Canabal was forced to resign from this student position in October, 1933.

ideologies,* but staunch defenders of the principle of academic freedom, resigned to indicate their opposition to the introduction of such a program.[52] Antonio Caso became the most prominent leader of the group supporting academic freedom, whereas Vicente Lombardo Toledano became the ideological leader of the opposition group. Some of Caso's and Lombardo Toledano's student followers at the National University became prominent in public life.[53]

Student activity and contact was also heightened by this ideological debate in the 1930s.† The 10th National Student Congress met in 1933, and the students competing for leadership stood on separate sides of the socialist education issue.[54] Guillermo Ibarra, in a conversation with me, suggested that students from the provinces had considerable contact with student leaders from the Federal District because of the activities of the national student congresses, of which he was a leader.[55] Another student leader during this period, but already within the official party, was Adolfo López Mateos. During the 1940s, he worked under co-student Benito Coquet Laguna in the Youth Department of the Federal District, and co-student Carlos Madrazo served as Director of Social Action.‡ All three knew each other as student

---

*Some of the participants among the professors included: Antonio Caso, Roberto Esteva Ruiz, Manuel Gómez Morín, Luis Chico Goerne, Mariano Azuela, Trinidad García, Miguel Palacios Macedo, Gabriel García Rojas, Manuel Borja Soriano, Octavio Medellín Ostos, Ricardo J. Zevada, Francisco González de la Vega, Enrique González Aparicio, Antonio Carrillo Flores, Agustín García López, Manuel Gual Vidal, Daniel Cosío Villegas, Andrés Serra Rojas, Manuel Sánchez Cuen, Luis Garrido, José Rivera Pérez, Salvador Azuela, Eduardo Villaseñor, José Hernández Delgado, Mario Sousa, Hilario Medina, Jesús Castorena, Alfonso Caso, and Rodulfo Brito Foucher, most of whom distinguished themselves in public life.

†Among the more prominent student leaders who were active in this period were Gillermo Ibarra Ibarra, president of the National Student Federation, 1933; Carlos Madrazo, president of the Student Society of the National Preparatory School, 1933; Norberto Treviño Zapata, president of the Student Society of the School of Medicine, 1933; Manuel González Cosío, president of the Student Federation of the Federal District, 1934; and Benito Coquet Laguna, president of the National Student Federation, 1934. All of these men became prominent public figures in the 1950s and 1960s.

‡Benito Coquet Laguna had a more consistent, and during his initial career, more successful trajectory than his friend, Adolfo López Mateos. A native of Veracruz, he came to the attention of Adolfo Ruiz Cortines, who served as Manuel Avila Camacho's presidential campaign treasurer. Coquet was an orator in the same campaign, and was rewarded with the directorship of the Youth Department, bringing López Mateos along as his subordinate. López Mateos himself became known to Miguel Alemán because he was López Mateos' mother's lawyer. But López Mateos' rise to power actually received a boost into national prominence through the efforts of Isidro Fabela, an influential leader from López Mateos' home state. When Fabela ran for senator in 1946, he asked López Mateos to become his alternate. After winning the office, he left the Senate to become a judge on the International Court of Justice. Although Alemán offered López Mateos the ambassadorship to Costa Rica, he wisely remained in Mexico and replaced his mentor as senator. See *Enciclopedia de México 8,* p. 147; and Robert E. Scott, *Mexican Government in Transition,* 2nd edition (Urbana: University of Illinois Press, 1964), p. 218.

leaders in the 1930s. When López Mateos graduated from the National University in 1934, and as did Miguel Alemán, he affected the career patterns of many of his classmates (Table 6.7). However, he did not have a significant impact on initially recruiting co-students into public life, since he himself was first in an opposition party, then became private secretary to the president of the official party, a powerful political leader who lost his influence in the Calles-Cárdenas break of 1934–35. In short, López Mateos' political rise was delayed some years until he attracted the attention of Alemán in the early 1940s. Therefore, his impact occurred at the later stages of his co-students' careers, when he had the ability to appoint friends to subordinate positions.

Table 6.7

Graduates of the National School of Law in 1934–35 Who Held High Public Office Under Adolfo López Mateos (1958–64)

Name of Graduate[a]	Position During 1958–1964
Amorós Guiot, Roberto	Director General of CONASUPO
Carrillo Marcor, Alejandro	Ambassador to the United Arab Republic
Coquet Laguna, Benito	Director General of the Mexican Social Security Institute
Encinas Johnson, Luis	Governor of Sonora
García Reynoso, Placido	Subsecretary of Industry and Commerce
Huitrón y Aguado, Abel	Senator from México
Ibarra Ibarra, Guillermo	Senator and Director General of PIPSA
López Arias, Fernando	Attorney General of Mexico
Luque Loyola, Eduardo	Federal Deputy from Querétaro
Ramírez Valadez, Guillermo	Senator from Jalisco
Ruiz Vasconcelos, Ramón	Senator from Oaxaca
Suárez Torres, Gilberto	Assistant Attorney General of Mexico
Tapia Aranda, Enrique	Federal Deputy from México
Torres Landa, Juan José	Governor of Guanajuato
Treviño Rios, Oscar	Assistant Attorney General of Mexico
Vallejo Novelo, José	Federal Deputy from Yucatán
Vázquez Pallares, Natalio	Senator from Michoacán

[a]Only those graduates who were definitely known to have graduated during this two-year period were included.

The National School of Law, 1941–50

During the 1940s, the number of law degrees granted by the National Law School began to average over 150 per year.[56] Despite the increase in the number of students both attending the law school and graduating from it, the numbers were still quite small in comparison to later decades. This fact permitted most of the students to know each other, regardless of their year of study.[57] Equally important was the physical location of the university in various buildings in downtown Mexico City. Most of the students and the

Table 6.8

**Graduates of the National School of Law From 1931 to 1940
Who Held High Public Office From 1935 to 1976**[a]

Name of Graduate	Year	Highest Position in Public Life Since 1935
Altamirano Herrera, Rafael	1931	Senator from Querétaro
Galván Campos, Fausto	1931	Senator from Morelos
García González, Alfonso	1931	Director General of Tourism
Garizurieta, César	1931	*Oficial Mayor* of Agrarian Affairs
Martínez Ostos, Raúl	1931	Subdirector General of *Nacional Financiera*
Moreno Sánchez, Manuel	1931	President of the Senate
Pizarro Suárez, Nicolás	1931	Director General of the ISSSTE
Alavéz Flores, Rodolfo	1933	Federal Deputy from Oaxaca
Canudas Orezza, Luis Felipe	1933	Secretary General of Agrarian Affairs
Guzmán Araujo, Roberto	1933	*Oficial Mayor* of Government
Lomeli Garduño, Antonio	1933	Federal Deputy from Guanajuato
Luna Arroyo, Antonio	1933	Assistant Attorney General of Mexico
Mondragón Guerra, Salvador	1934	Justice of the Supreme Court
Rocha, Antonio	1934	Attorney General of Mexico
Aguilar y Maya, Guillermo	1935	Attorney General of the Federal District
Benhumea, Sergio L.	1935	*Oficial Mayor* of the Presidency
Osorio Ramírez, Miguel	1935	Secretary General of the CEN of PRI
Cisneros Molina, Joaquín	1936	Governor of Tlaxcala
Flores Betancourt, Dagoberto	1936	Secretary General of the FSTSE
Landerreche Obregón, Juan	1936	Federal Deputy from the Federal District
Palomares, Noé	1936	Subsecretary of Agriculture
Acosta Romo, Fausto	1937	Assistant Attorney General of Mexico
Calleja García, J. Moises	1937	Federal Deputy from the Federal District
Casahonda Castillo, José	1937	Federal Deputy from Chiapas
Castillo Tielemans, José	1937	Governor of Chiapas
Corona del Rosal, Alfonso	1937	President of the CEN of PRI
Hinojosa Ortiz, Manuel	1937	Subsecretary of Agriculture
Madrazo, Carlos	1937	President of the CEN of PRI
Margaín, Hugo B.	1937	Secretary of the Treasury
Ramírez Acosta, Abel	1937	Secretary of the CEN of PRI
Rángel Frias, Raúl	1937	Governor of Nuevo León
Rivera Silva, Manuel	1937	Justice of the Supreme Court
Sánchez Piedras, Emilio	1937	Governor of Tlaxcala
Campillo Saínz, José	1938	Secretary of Industry and Commerce
González Saenz, Leopoldo	1938	Secretary of the CEN of PRI
Iñarritu, Jorge	1938	Justice of the Supreme Court
Rivera Uribe, Diodoro	1938	Senator from Morelos
Román Lugo, Fernando	1938	Attorney General of the Federal District
Terán Mata, Juan Manuel	1938	Senator from Tamulipas
Telleache, Ramón	1939	Subsecretary of Agriculture
Barros Sierra, Manuel	1940	Subdirector General of PEMEX
Christlieb Ibarrola, Adolfo	1940	President of the CEN of PAN
Lanz Duret, Fernando	1940	Senator from Campeche
León Orantes, Gloria	1940	Justice of the Superior Court of the Federal District
López Portillo B., Arturo	1940	Federal Deputy
Rosas Magallón, Salvador	1940	Federal Deputy from Baja California del Norte

[a]Excludes those graduates of the National School of Law included in tables 6.6 and 6.7.

professors did not use automobiles, and they travelled from one building to another on foot, meeting friends and conversing between classes. Furthermore, most of the students who worked did so in places very close to the university buildings.[58]

The majority of students were from the middle and popular classes. There were not many scholarships for poorer students, although some existed from individual states and from the Secretariat of Public Education. Classes lasted until 6:00 pm, but many of the students worked mornings in offices or government jobs.[59] The university aided poorer students by allowing them to pay in installments, similar to the system of deferred tuition payments widely used in colleges and universities in the United States. As in some earlier generations, students who demonstrated a superior intellectual capacity had the opportunity to work as assistants to professors. María Emilia Téllez Benoit, who was a co-student with Presidents Luis Echeverría and José López Portillo, served as an assistant to Professor Manuel Pedroso.[60]

Other students, such as Luis Echeverría and Wilberto Cantón (later a federal deputy in Echeverría's administration), attracted student support and interest by editing a newspaper.[61] Still other students had the opportunity to develop closer relationships with professors and intellectuals by working for the official paper *Universidad de México* in the late 1940s, whose editors included Agustín Yáñez (later secretary of Public Education and governor of Jalisco), and Rafael Corrales Ayala (later assistant attorney general of Mexico and secretary general of PRI).[62]

For the 1940s generations, political activity was confined to participation in national political campaigns, particularly those of 1940 and 1946, and elections for student representatives. There were few strikes during these years, and most were in the cause of improved curriculum. Although several members of these generations mentioned the important group known as *Medio Siglo*, organized intellectual activities were reduced.

Student friendships remained equally important to future public leaders of the 1940s classes and will continue to be so in the immediate future, since José López Portillo, the new president of Mexico, also comes from this group (Table 6.9). In fact, in discussing the unusual cabinet shakeup which took place after López Portillo's nomination as the PRI candidate in 1975, Hugo Cervantes del Río explained to a reporter his relationship to López Portillo and the reason why he left a cabinet secretaryship to serve as his campaign director in the Federal District. "I was his student in General Theory of the State in 1947 at the School of Law. From that point on I have liked him and had a great respect for him."[63]

Ignoring the fact of whether or not Cervantes del Río liked or respected López Portillo, the importance of this information is that he has been known to López Portillo since his student days. López Portillo, who did not have a lengthy political career prior to his nomination, had an equally small political clique surrounding him, and needed collaborators with the political experience and skill of Cervantes del Río (also one of the contenders for the presidential nomination in 1976). Furthermore, from Cervantes del Río's point of view, this was a clever move designed to promote his own political career by changing *camarilla* affiliations from Echeverría's group, whose influence would be short lived, to López Portillo's, whose was in ascendancy. His service to López Portillo was well rewarded when his former professor appointed him as Director General of the Federal Electric Commission in

Table 6.9

**Graduates of the National School of Law From 1941 to 1950
Who Held High Public Office From 1935 to 1976**

Name of Graduate	Year	Highest Position in Public Life Since 1935
Hernández González, Octavio	1941	Secretary General of the Federal District
Hernández Ochoa, Rafael	1941	Governor of Veracruz
Mena Brito, Antonio	1941	Secretary of the CEN of PRI
Senties, Octavio	1941	Head of the Federal District Department
Trujillo García, Mario	1941	Governor of Tabasco
Rodríguez y Rodríguez, Jesus	1942	Subsecretary of the Treasury
Castellanos Everardo, Milton	1943	Governor of Baja California del Norte
González Torres, José	1943	President of the CEN of PAN
Llorente González, Arturo	1943	Subsecretary of Labor
López Portillo, José	1943	President of Mexico
Reyes Heroles, Jesús[a]	1943	President of the CEN of PRI
Romero Pérez, Humberto	1943	Private Secretary to the President of Mexico
Salvat Rodríguez, Agustín	1943	Treasurer of the CEN of PRI
Dzib Cardozo, José	1944	Assistant Attorney General of Mexico
Echeverría, Luis	1944	President of Mexico
Echeverría, Rodolfo	1944	Director of the National Cinema Bank
Farell Cubillas, Arsenio	1944	Director General of the CFE
Gálvez Betancourt, Carlos	1944	Director General of the IMSS
Heredia Ferraez, Jorge	1944	*Oficial Mayor* of the CFE
Ibañez Llamas, Santiago	1944	Director General of INPI
Pérez Abreu, Juan	1944	*Oficial Mayor* of Communications
Téllez Benoit, Emilia[a]	1944	*Oficial Mayor* of Foreign Relations
Apodaca Osuna, Francisco	1945	Ambassador to France
Farias Martínez, Luis	1945	Governor of Nuevo León
Rios Elizondo, Roberto	1945	Secretary General of the Federal District
Salmorán de Tamayo, María C.	1945	Justice of the Supreme Court
Colín Sánchez, Mario	1946	Federal Deputy from Mexico
De Lara Issacs, Alfredo	1946	Senator from Aguascalientes
Gómez Morín Torres, Juan M.	1946	Secretary General of the CEN of PAN
González Casanova, Rablo	1946	Rector of UNAM
González Sosa, Ruben	1946	Subsecretary of Foreign Relations
Manzanilla Schaffer, Víctor	1946	Secretary of the Senate Great Committee
Rabasa, Emilio	1946	Secretary of Foreign Relations
Beteta, Mario Ramón	1948	Secretary of the Treasury
Cervantes del Río, Hugo	1949	Secretary of the Presidency
González Pedrero, Enrique	1950	Secretary General of the CEN of PRI
Sánchez Vite, Manuel	1950	President of the CEN of PRI

[a]Jesús Reyes Heroles was appointed Secretary of Government and Emilia Téllez Benoit Subsecretary of Foreign Relations under President López Portillo. Both positions are more important than those they held previously.
Key: IMSS = Mexican Social Security Institute; CFE = Federal Electric Commission; and INPI = National Institute for the Protection of Infants.

1976. Skillful switching of *camarillas*, as long as it is not engaged in too frequently or too soon, is part of surviving in the Mexican political system. Such moves ultimately can benefit the original *camarilla* leader, who often sees a member of his group rise above his own level of political influence. A case in point was the appointment of Emilio Martínez Manatou as Secretary of Health by José Lopez Portillo. This appointment was not, as some journalists claimed, a return of President Díaz Ordaz's influence, rather it was an example of a former *camarilla* member reciprocating favors back to his mentor.

López Portillo's own career, particularly since 1970, has depended to a great extent on his long friendship with Luis Echeverría, a friendship begun as playmates in the Colonia del Valle of the Federal District, and later enhanced by their law school days together. He also accompanied Echeverría to Santiago, Chile, on a Chilean scholarship to study at the University of Santiago. While in politics, each developed his own career independent of the other, and López Portillo became part of the *camarilla* of Emilio Martínez Manatou, who opposed Echeverría for the presidential nomination in 1969. Despite this, they retained their close friendship and López Portillo received an appointment in the subcabinet.[64] Many of Echeverría's other appointees were co-students from the law school in the 1940s (Table 6.9).

The National School of Medicine

In describing the educational background of public men in Mexico, several other schools at the National University were important, in addition to the law school. These were the schools of medicine, engineering, and economics. In addition to these schools, a number of state universities have graduated future public men.

Historically, the single most important school graduating future public men in Mexico, after the National Law School, has been the National School of Medicine.[66] This is not surprising, since the school has a long history in Mexico and a large enrollment since 1911, and since medicine has been a traditionally important profession in Mexico. During the Revolution itself, as a result of the armed struggles, there were years when the medical school remained closed because provincial students were unable to come to Mexico City.[67] In 1917, when the school again started its program, 300 students enrolled as first-year medical students. Following the practice used at the preparatory school, these students were divided by alphabetical order and attended required courses as groups.[68] Therefore, students had repeated contact with members of their alphabetical group. However, such student groups at the medical school did not prevent students from meeting and knowing students outside of their group or from different years, especially in the advanced classes, where alphabetical and class groups were not adhered to. For example, Ignacio Chávez, who graduated in 1920, knew Salvador Zubirán quite well, despite the fact they were in different groups.[69] Both Chávez and Zubirán recall close friendships with older and younger medical students.[70] As was true of the preparatory schools we have examined, as well as the National Law School, students had a wide range of friends beyond their own graduating classes.

Although most medical students readily made friends who were outside their classes within the medical school, some developed friendships with professional students from other schools, even though during the years of our study the professional schools of the National University were located in separate buildings throughout Mexico City.[71] Such friendships were developed and maintained among students from various schools through several means. First, a sizeable group of students had attended the National Preparatory School. Although students often grouped together at the preparatory school according to the professional curriculum they would follow, they all took liberal arts courses. Furthermore, some majored in one professional preparatory curriculum, then changed their minds and switched to a different degree program at the professional school level.* For example, Samuel Ramos, the distinguished Mexican philosopher and a contemporary of Ignacio Chávez, started his career in medicine but later changed to philosophy.[72] An even smaller group followed a consistent program through preparatory school and into professional school, later changing their minds once into their third or fourth year of professional school. An excellent example of this was Jaime Torres Bodet, who gave up law school to attend the school of philosophy.

A second factor contributing to contact across professional schools was geographic background. The majority of the students attending all professional schools during the 1910s, 1920s, and 1930s were from the provinces. Of the 132 medical students who graduated in 1924–25, 21, or 16 percent, were from Mexico City; three, or 2 percent, were from foreign birthplaces; and the rest, or 82 percent, were from other areas in Mexico.[73] A good example of students who retained friendships after entering different professional schools is the group of distinguished preparatory graduates from the Colegio de San Nicolás, who included Ignacio Chávez (medicine), Salvador González de Rejón (medicine), Manuel Martínez Báez (medicine), Gabino Fraga (law), Antonio Martínez Báez (law), Rodolfo Chávez (law), and Samuel Ramos (philosophy). Such friendships developed among students from the same town or regions because often boarding houses in Mexico City grouped students together on the basis of provincial orgin.

---

*This also occurred at private schools. Adolfo López Mateos, who attended the Colegio Francés Morelos on a scholarship, became good friends with José Alvarez Amezquita. López Mateos went on to law school, and Alvarez Amezquita into medicine. They each followed separate careers until 1956, when López Mateos appointed his friend as the director general of medical services for the Secretariat of Labor. In 1958, when he became president, Alvarez Amezquita became his secretary of Public Health.

Other professional students became friends through formal student structures such as the university board, which had student representation, and the national student organizations, which had student delegates from various schools. These activities attracted students who were already interested in politics and who were likely to go into public life. For example, Héctor Pérez Martínez, who received his degree from the School of Dentistry, knew many of the prominent student leaders of the Alemán generation through his activities in university government and as a member of the National Youth Congress in 1926. He later became Alemán's secretary of government in 1946. The intellectual and social clubs we discussed earlier also provided a meeting place for students from different professional schools.[74]

Medical school students, when compared with law school students, had greater opportunities to know individual professors intimately. As young medical students, they had to intern with their professors in the major hospitals in Mexico City.[75] Unlike law school students, there were many students serving as assistants to their professors at medical school. Medical students had a greater tendency to take on mentors in professional school who contributed to their career development. Some of the notable physicians who attracted such students from medical school were Fernando Ocaranza (later rector of UNAM); Ignacio Chávez (later rector of UNAM); Gustavo Baz (later rector of UNAM and secretary of Public Health); Salvador Zubirán (later rector of UNAM and subsecretary of Public Health); and Salvador González de Rejón (later dean of the medical school). All except Zubirán were deans of the medical school. These professors helped each other and their students in medical careers in the field of public health.[76]

Although a much smaller number of students who became public men were in the natural sciences, they too had considerable interchange with their professors, serving as student assistants and obtaining help from their professors in acquiring initial employment opportunities.[77] Enrique Beltrán, who was such a student in the 1920s, obtained his first employment as a lab assistant to his mentor Guillermo Gándara, a distinguished Mexican botanist. He reciprocated in 1934, appointing Professor Gándara as Director of the Department of Botany in the Biotechnical Institute.[78] Of the 31 medical students in Table 6.10, seven are known to have appointed or received appointments to high-level public offices because of student-professor friendships.*

---

*José Alvarez Amézquita appointed two of his professors, who were his intern supervisors, in succession, as subsecretaries: José Castro Villagrana, 1958–60, and Conrado Zuckermann Duarte, 1960–64. Rafael P. Gamboa appointed his student companion as *Oficial Mayor* of Health in 1946, and then to subsecretary in 1948. Gustavo Baz was responsible for the public career of Jorge Jiménez Cantu, who became known to Baz when he was Dean of the School of Medicine as a student activist and founder of the military pentathelon at the University in 1938. Later, in 1957, he served as Baz's Secretary General of Government of the state of Mexico. In 1975, Jiménez Cantu became governor of Mexico.

The graduates from the medical school and the natural sciences had the opportunity to contribute to the direction of Mexico's health program, and a relatively small number of graduates from the 1910s and 1920s had a significant impact on public medicine.[79] Although some of the graduates of the medical school went into politics first, then practiced medicine, the majority seem to have made a reputation within the major Mexico City hospitals and then achieved high-level administrative positions in the Secretariat of Public Health or at the National University. The career of Salvador Zubirán typifies this latter pattern. He graduated from medical school in 1922, carrying on advanced work at Harvard University. With the help of his mentor, Professor Gaston Melo, Director of the Department of Health, he received his first public appointment as head of the Office of Food and Drink in 1931. Melo, a distinguished surgeon, was the personal physician to President Calles. When Melo died, Zubirán took over as personal physician to Calles, and several years later to other influential public figures, including presidents Cárdenas

Table 6.10

**Graduates of the National School of Medicine From 1911 to 1948
Who Held High Public Office After 1935**

Name of Graduate	Year	Highest Position in Public Life Since 1935
De Alba, Pedro	1913	Senator from Aguascalientes
Támez, Ramiro	1913	Senator from Nuevo Leon
Castro Villagrana, José	1914	Subsecretary of Public Health
Del Valle, Alberto	1917	Governor of Aguascalientes
Alamazán, Leonides	1920	Secretary of Public Health
Bautista, Gonzalo	1920	Governor of Puebla
Baz, Gustavo	1920	Secretary of Public Health
Chávez Sánchez, Ignacio	1920	Rector of UNAM
Martínez, Pedro Daniel	1920	Subsecretary of Public Health
Ruiz Castañeda, Maximiliano	1920	Senator from Mexico
Zubirán, Salvador	1920	Subsecretary of Public Health
Argil Camacho, Gustavo	1923	Subsecretary of Public Health
Gamboa, Rafael P.	1923	Secretary of Public Health
Huerta Sánchez, Luciano	1924	Governor of Tlaxcala
Bustamante, Miguel	1925	Subsecretary of Health
Fonseca García, Francisco	1925	Subdirector General of Medicine of ISSSTE
Uruchurtu, Gustavo A.	1925	Senator from Sonora
Zuckermann Duarte, Conrado	1925	Subsecretary of Public Welfare
Aceves Parra, Salvador	1928	Secretary of Public Health
Pérez Martínez, Héctor	1928[a]	Secretary of Government
Aguirre Beltrán, Gonzalo	1931	Subsecretary of Public Education
Alvarez Amezquita, José	1934	Secretary of Public Health
Ortega Martínez, Lauro	1935	President of the CEN of PRI
Treviño Zapata, Norberto	1935	Governor of Tamaulipas
Jiménez Cantú, Jorge	1939	Secretary of Public Health
Navarro Díaz de Leon, Ginés	1940	Secretary of Public Health
Campillo Saínz, Carlos	1941	Subsecretary of Public Health
Pérez Vela, Juan	1941	*Oficial Mayor* of Agriculture
Guzman Orozco, Renaldo	1944	Subsecretary of Public Health
Martínez Manatou, Emilio	1944	Secretary of the Presidency
Soberón, Guillermo	1948	Rector of UNAM

[a]Degree in dentistry.

and Ávila Camacho. During the 1930s, he began a long teaching career at the National School of Medicine and served in several administrative positions in public health and at the General Hospital in Mexico City. In 1938, through his friendship with President Cárdenas, he became subsecretary of Public Assistance. In 1940, his close friend from medical school, Gustavo Baz, became the new secretary of Public Health, and he continued his tenure as subsecretary.[80]

The National School of Medicine, after the law school, has produced the greatest number of high-level public men in Mexico. However, as indicated by the total number of graduates in Table 6.10, medical students have not played a large role in public life on all levels, and most have confined their careers to one ministry, Public Health. Proportionately, students from the National School of Medicine who were successful in public life, have been a much smaller percentage than students from some of the other professional schools at UNAM. For example, in 1925, 1060 students were enrolled in the five-year program at the National School of Medicine, and during the same year, 132 medical students graduated.[81] Of these, four or 3 percent are known to have become high-level officeholders after 1935. At the law school, however, there were only 385 students enrolled, of which 52 graduated in 1925. Of these, four or 8 percent were prominent in public life after 1935.[82] Proportionately, the medical school produces far fewer successful public men than do the law, economics, or engineering schools at UNAM, and therefore is not a professional school that attracts students already interested in seeking public careers.

The National School of Engineering, 1911–54

The National School of Engineering, when examined in terms of its contributions to public life in Mexico, has certain similarities to the medical school. At the beginning of the second decade of the 20th century, enrollment at the School of Engineering was over 200 students. Unlike the law school, students since 1911 have been divided into various subdisciplines, including civil engineering, mining, topography, assaying, electrical engineering, and metallurgy. Most students majored in civil engineering, and the number of students graduating in each of the other subdisciplines during the 1910s through the 1940s was generally a handful.[83] Through the 1940s, the maximum number of students in each specialized class was ten.[84] Therefore, students in the subdisciplines had considerable contact with each other and their professors. The general classes taken by first, second, and third-year students were relatively small, remaining at approximately 30–35 through the 1940s.

Like the medical students during these years, the engineering students worked with their professors in various government agencies. Although they were not required to intern in the same sense as medical students, practically all of the engineering students attempted to obtain practical experience during vacations.* Given the limited opportunities for engineering graduates in private enterprise, most students worked for government agencies, primarily the National Irrigation Commission (later the Secretariat of Hydraulic Resources), the Secretariat of Public Works, and the National Railroads of Mexico.[85] The implementation of laws concerning the nationalization of natural resources and the Mexicanization of sectors of the economy requiring the expertise of engineers opened up new areas to engineering students. Graduates of the school were significantly involved in the expropriation of the oil companies in 1938, and the establishment of the government-operated Mexican Petroleum Company.[86]

The background of engineering students was similar to that of law and medical students. José Hernández Terán, a graduate of the school in 1946, believes approximately three-fourths of his co-students graduated from the National Preparatory School, while the remainder were educated in private schools and in state preparatory schools.[87] This distribution of students accounts for the fact that engineering students from the National Preparatory School made many friends among students who entered other professional schools at the National University.† For those students who were representative of their school on the all university student-faculty council, these friendships were supplemented after entering the engineering school.[88]

Most of the prominent professors at the engineering school during these years were involved in public life, either in technical departments or high-level administrative positions. Engineering students who became public men regarded their contact with professors as extremely close because of small class size and practical laboratory experiences. Hernández Terán noted the following professors as having frequent contact with their students: Antonio Correo, Professor of Hydraulic Resources, who was director general of engineering for the National Irrigation Commission, Pedro Martínez Tornel, Secretary of Public Works, Antonio Dovalí Jaime, Professor of Bridges and later subsecretary of Public Works and director general of PEMEX.[89]

All of these professors were responsible for initiating public careers for some of the graduates listed in Table 6.11. A number of them held positions under one another in those government agencies dominated by engineering

---

*José Hernández Terán argues that his practical experience was instrumental in his becoming acquainted with students from older generations. He worked on such a program in topography with five students, four of whom became cabinet-level secretaries in the 1960s.

†For example, Hernández Terán knew Jesús Reyes Heroles, Luis Echeverría, and Ernesto Fernández Hurtado before he entered the National School of Engineering. All of them held cabinet-level positions under President Díaz Ordaz.

graduates. Like medical students, most successful engineering students entering public careers have followed career patterns of successive technical positions within the same agencies. As a group, they have been more dominant in top-level positions because more than one government agency requires engineering skills. Proportionately, this demand shows up in the number of graduates actually holding high-level public offices. Although engineering degrees from UNAM are behind law and medical degrees among high-level public officials during the years of our study, engineering students were proportionately from a much smaller group. During the 1920s and 1930s they often were half the size of the law school group and a fifth the size of the medical school group. Successful public men were proportionately far more common among engineering school graduates than those graduating from Medical School.

Table 6.11

Graduates of the National School of Engineering From 1911 to 1953 Who Held High Public Office After 1935

Name of Graduate	Year	Highest Position in Public Life Since 1935
Ortiz, Andrés	1912 (T)[a]	Director General of PEMEX
Cortés Herrera, Vicente	1913 (C)	Director General of PEMEX
Barocio Barrios, Alberto	1914 (T)	Subsecretary of National Properties
Santillán, Manuel	1916 (M)	Subsecretary of Public Works
Angulo, Melquiades	1917 (M)	Secretary of Public Works
Martínez Tornel, Pedro	1918 (C)	Secretary of Public Works
Colomo Corral, José	1920 (M)	Subdirector of PEMEX
Gutiérrez R., Efraín A.	1921	Governor of Chiapas
Chávez Ramírez, Eduardo	1922	Secretary of Hydraulic Resources
Orive Alba, Adolfo	1927	Secretary of Hydraulic Resources
Dovalí Jaime, Antonio	1928 (C)	Director General of PEMEX
Paéz Urquidi, Alejandro	1929 (E)	Director General of the Federal Electric Commission
Esquivel Méndez, Eligio	1933 (T)	Governor of Baja California del Norte
Gutiérrez Lascuráin, Juan	1933	President of the CEN of PAN
Aguilar Chávez, Salvador	1936	Subsecretary of Hydraulic Resources
Dupré Ceniceros, Enrique	1936	Governor of Durango
Hiriart B., Fernando	1938	Subdirector of the Federal Electric Commission
Carrillo Flores, Nabor	1939 (C)	Rector of UNAM
Barros Sierra, Javier	1940 (C)	Secretary of Public Works
Padilla Segura, José A.	1941 (E)	Secretary of Communications and Transportation
Espinosa G., Fernando	1942	Subsecretary of Public Works
Rovirosa Wade, Leandro	1942	Secretary of Hydraulic Resources
De la Peña Porth, Luis	1943	Subsecretary of National Properties
Franco López, Manuel	1944 (M)	Secretary of National Properties
Bracamontes, Luis E.	1945 (C)	Secretary of Public Works
Hernández Terán, Jose	1946	Secretary of Hydraulic Resources
Félix Valdes, Rodolfo	1947	Subsecretary of Public Works
Valenzuela, Gilberto	1947	Secretary of Public Works
Díaz de Cossio, Roger	1953	Subsecretary of Public Education

[a]The letters behind the class date indicate the specialty followed in the engineering program: (T) = topographical, (C) = civil, (M) = mechanical, and (E) = electrical.

The National School of Economics, 1929–52

Of the four professional schools at the National University contributing most to the education of future public men, the National School of Economics has been the newest school with *proportionately the greatest percentage* of graduates in public life.[90] We can substantiate the role of economists in public life and the recruitment of students from the National School of Economics by using a complete population of all graduates from the founding of the school in 1929 to 1952. During this period, only 174 persons obtained their degree.

The National School of Economics had a tenuous beginning. In 1929, an economics division was established as part of the School of Law. This marked the first formal economics training and degree-granting program at the university level in Mexico.[91] However, the division nearly floundered when, during the second year, only three students registered for the economics curriculum.* The lack of student interest had several causes.[92] First, people were ignorant of the necessity for the discipline in Mexico, and of the careers that could be pursued by a professional economist.[93] Second, there were not enough professors trained in economics to handle a second class in 1930. Because there had been no economics program in Mexico before 1929, the professors in this division were trained in other fields† and held no university degrees in economics.[94] Third, public accountants opposed the program as an encroachment on their own profession.[95] However, both professors and students of the first generation were able to sustain enough interest in the program to support a larger group of students in 1931.‡ The

---

*Daniel Cosío Villegas replaced Jesús Silva Herzog as professor of economic policy in the economics section at the School of Law. He was named director of the economics section by Manuel Gómez Morín, but encountered many difficulties in getting good professors for this program. He then proposed to eliminate the program and to send good students on scholarships to foreign programs. Silva Herzog and Mario Sousa opposed this plan, along with such early students as Emigdio Martínez Adame, Sealtiel Alatriste, and Alfonso Pulido Islas. Tobether, they saved the program for a second time in 1933.

†In support of this statement, it should be noted that the founders of the economics program included Antonio Castro Leal and Narciso Bassols, Rector of the National University and Dean of the Law School, respectively; and Daniel Cosío Villegas, Jesús Silva Herzog, Fritz (Federico) Bach, Manuel Palacios Macedo, Eduardo Villaseñor, Manuel Gómez Morín, Antonio Espinosa de los Monteros, and Manuel Mesa Andraca, professors who designed the curriculum for the program. All were public men, and all, except Espinosa de los Monteros and Cosío Villegas, who studied at Harvard University, and Bach and Villaseñor, who studied at the Sorbonne and London, respectively, had degrees in law, philosophy, and engineering.

‡This was in part due to the reputations of the first professors who included Jesús Silva Herzog, founder and Director of the Office of Economic Studies, National Railroads of Mexico, 1931; Mario Sousa, Director of the Institute of Rural Economy, Secretariat of Agriculture in the 1930s. Miguel Othón de Mendizábal, professor and first Director of the Institute for Economic Research, UNAM, and Joaquín Ramírez Cabañas, distinguished professor at the National Preparatory School.

economics program remained a division of the law school until 1935, when it became a full-fledged school of the National University.

The educational environment during the early years of the school's development permitted considerable student-faculty contact.[96] A special characteristic that promoted intellectual exchange was the age and experience of the early students: most had degrees in law or accounting, and held middle-level positions in government.* Classes were small and each student knew his co-students, as well as students from the law school who were taking selected courses. Even until 1952, such contact among economics students was facilitated since the total number of students enrolled at the school did not exceed 250. Professors and students had numerous social as well as intellectual contacts. During the May vacations, many of the economics professors took their students on field trips to private and government-owned industries as far away as Monterrey.[97]

If we examine in some detail the backgrounds of all graduates from the School of Economics and compare them with a selected group of economics professors, we encounter several distinct characteristics (Table 6.12 and Table 6.13). Both students and professors come from urban backgrounds, from middle-class parents, and are disproportionately from the Federal District. But most important, these tables reveal that both professors and students are oriented to public careers. Both pursue public careers, and I believe that professors have been largely responsible for students following their career patterns. Since 1929, the National School of Economics has developed several generations of professors and students who are tied to one another because they in turn produced a generation of students who became the future professors of the National School of Economics.

Both notable professors and successful students provide numerous examples of the recruitment process in action. For example, Jesús Silva Herzog, one of the founding professors of the Economics School, helped found or directed a number of technical agencies in the 1930s that he staffed with many of his prominent students. Among them, he describes the staffing of a new government commission designed to make subsidies for certain imports and to watch exchange rates: "I took to the offices of the Commission various young students in their last years of an economics major, among them those who later distinguished themselves in public service or private enterprise."[98] In the 1940s, as a high-level official of the Secretariat of the Treasury, Silva Herzog was able to obtain funds to send many of his best students to study in graduate institutions in the United States. Most of the economists

---

*For example, Alatriste already had a CPA degree; Estela San Inéz, the first woman economist in Mexico, also had a degree in public accounting; Hugo Rangel Couto and Juan Torres Vivanco were lawyers. All were members of the first or second class of economists.

in public life whom I interviewed indicated that their first jobs in government were the results of the efforts of their professors. Those who became professors, and 19 or 79 percent of the 24 graduates who became prominent public figures did teach, helped their best students to obtain positions. As in the case of public men who taught in other professional schools, several admitted that one of the bonuses of teaching at the university was the chance to recruit the finest students.

Graduates of the National School of Economics have tended to concentrate heavily in two government agencies: the Secretariat of Industry and

Table 6.12

Background Data for All Graduates of the National School of Economics, 1929–51[a]

Region of Birth	No.	Percent	Percent of General Population from that Region[b]
Federal District	58	36.0	4.7
West Central	20	12.4	21.3
East Central	15	9.3	21.6
Gulf	12	7.5	11.6
North	21	13.0	11.1
West	11	6.8	16.0
South	14	8.7	13.7
Foreign	10	6.2	0.0
Subtotal	161		
No Information	17		
	178		

Urban-Rural Birthplace	No.	Percent	
Urban	125	79.6	
Rural	32	20.4	
Subtotal	157		
No Information	21		
	178		

Employment	No.	Percent	
Public Careers[c]	164	92.6	
Private Careers	13	7.3	
Subtotal	177		
No Information	1		
	178		

[a]Our sample includes all 178 students who completed their studies between the years 1929–51 and received their degree prior to 1959. Most students complete their studies in five years and finish their thesis within six years following their last year of study. This population has probably omitted several students who finished their studies but did not complete their thesis by 1959. If the average time lapse between completion of studies and submission of thesis is a valid indicator, then no more than three students have been omitted.

[b]1910 census data, since most graduates were born between 1900 and 1925.

[c]In cases where public and private careers were combined, I credited persons with public careers only if they had become department heads in a federal agency.

Commerce, and the Secretariat of the Treasury. There are several reasons for this concentration. As is evident in Table 6.13, leadership of those agencies has been dominated by professors or graduates of the National School of Economics from 1929 to 1951. Gilberto Loyo, who became Dean of the School of Economics in 1944, gave a great impetus to the career of being an economist by encouraging the employment of economists in the Secretariat of Industry and Commerce, which he headed in 1952 after leaving the deanship. Control of this agency by National School of Economics graduates continued until 1974. The establishment of a Federal Income Tax Department in the Secretariat of the Treasury, which almost exclusively employed economists (ten from our sample), was soon directed consecutively by National Economics School graduates.

Of the 159 students who graduated from the School of Economics between the years 1929 to 1951 about whom we have fairly complete information, 24, or 15 percent, held middle- or high-level positions in public life. Seventeen, or 11 percent, held high-level positions, indicating that the Economics School, not the Law School, has produced *proportionately* the greatest number of successful public men in Mexico.* While law students will continue to predominate in Mexican government for years to come, I believe economists will increase among top-level officeholders.

Conclusions

The professional schools of medicine, engineering, and economics have been shown to be influential in the process of recruitment and career mobility of their graduates in public life. The same relationships among students and professors were encountered in each of these schools. Important to the success of many of the graduates of the professional schools has been their ability to make and sustain friendships at the preparatory school or, after entering their professional school, with students at the law school. Numerically, the law school has contributed the greatest number of successful public men, but because of its size, compared with the other schools, the economics and engineering schools have proportionately contributed greater percentages of their graduates to public life. Since the opportunities for economists in government are greater than those for engineers, it is not surprising that they are found in even greater percentages in public life. The medical school, because of limited opportunities in public life, has contributed a very small proportion of its graduates. All professional schools, except the law school, are similar in the sense that the majority of their graduates entering public careers have

---

*The same experience, on a much smaller scale, is being duplicated by the School of Political and Social Science, which developed from the law school in the early 1950s.

Table 6.13

Public Careers of Teachers and Graduates of the National School of Economics (ENE)[e]

Primary Government Agencies Employing Notable Professors and Graduates of ENE[a]	No.	Percent	Primary Government Agencies Employing Ordinary Graduates of the ENE[b]	No.	Percent
Secretariat of Industry 1970–74 Torres Manzo 1964–70 Campos Salas 　1964–65 Espinosa de 　los Reyes[f] 1958–64 Salinas Lozano 1961–64 Espinosa de 　los Reyes 1952–58 Loyo (P)[d] 　1946–53 Torres Gaytán 1940–46 Sousa (P)	8	22.2	Secretariat of Industry 1964–74 Four 　director generals[c]	33	20.1
Secretariat of Treasury 1952–58 Carrillo Flores (P) 1952–58 Ortiz Mena, R. 1946–52 Beteta, R. (P) 1946–49 Bustamante (P) 　1946–52 Loyo (P) 1945–46 Silva Herzog (P) 1940–45 Beteta, R. (P) 　1941–45 Carrillo Flores (P) 1935–35 Silva Herzog (P)	8	22.2	Secretariat of Treasury 1946–70 Two 　director generals	33	20.1
Secretariat of National 　Patrimony 1970–75 Flores de la Peña 1958–64 Bustamante, E. (P) 1958–64 Alatriste 1949–51 Rangel Couto 1946–49 Rangel Couto	4	11.1	Secretariat of National 　Patrimony 1946–64 Two 　director generals	12	7.3
National Finance Bank 1974–76 Romero Kolbeck 1970–72 Díaz Arias 1965–70 Díaz Arias 1950–52 Ortiz Mena, R. 1946–52 Carrillo Flores (P)	4	11.1	National Finance Bank	6	3.7

[a]Thirty-six graduates of the ENE who held positions of *Oficial Mayor* or higher, and/or were selected by public men as notable professors. (Persons in both categories were counted once, and professors without public careers were not included.)

[b]This sample is taken from 164 economists who graduated from ENE during this period and followed public careers.

[c]Director generals in cabinet agencies are fourth-ranked positions.

[d](P) = notable professors.

[e]This table is adapted from Table 7, from my "The National School of Economics and Public Life in Mexico," *Latin American Research Review* (Fall 1975): 148.

[f]Indented dates and names indicate second & third-level positions of importance.

followed administrative careers confined to several agencies. This pattern results not only from the functions of the agency, but more important, because generations of professors and students who recruited students to public careers were responsible for the growth and leadership of the respective agencies in public health, public works, hydraulic resources, banking, finance, and communications in Mexico.* Professors, more than students, have been responsible for initiating public careers. Students, on the other hand, have had a significant impact on the later career patterns of their co-students. While I do not believe that the university has an exclusive influence over recruitment and career mobility, it does have a more substantial role than any other *single* institution or organization in Mexico.

NOTES TO CHAPTER 6

[1]Luis Calderón Vega, *Los 7 sabios de México* (Mexico, 1961), p. 26; and Baltasar Dromundo, *Mi Barrio de San Miguel* (México: Antigua Librería Robredo, 1951), p. 62ff.
[2]Lucio Mendieta y Núñez, *Historia de la Facultad de Derecho* (México: UNAM, 1956), p. 267.
[3]Personal interview with Francisco González de la Vega, Mexico City, July 23, 1974.
[4]Luis Calderón Vega, *Los 7 sabios de México*, p. 26.
[5]Personal interview with Lucio Mendieta y Núñez, Mexico City, July 27, 1974.
[6]James Wilkie and Edna Monzón de Wilkie, *México visto en el siglo xx* (México: Instituto Mexicano de Investigaciones Económicas, 1969), p. 146, for Manuel Gómez Morin's commentary on this in an interview with the Wilkies.
[7]Personal interview with Francisco González de la Vega.
[8]Personal interview with Daniel Cosío Villegas, Mexico City, June 30, 1975; interview with Lucio Mendieta y Núñez; interview with Francisco González de la Vega.
[9]Luis Calderón Vega, *Los 7 sabios de México*, p. 27, in an interview with Alfonso Caso.
[10]See *Hispano Americano*, December 28, 1945.
[11]Personal interview with Daniel Cosío Villegas June 30, 1975; letter from Jaime Torres Bodet, Mexico City, August 1, 1972.
[12]*Excélsior*, July 16, 1973, p. 4; also see Calderón Vega, *Los 7 sabios de México*, pp. 46–7 for an interview with Vicente Lombardo Toledano.
[13]John S. Innes, "The Universidad Popular Mexicana," *The Americas 30* (July 1973): 111.
[14]*Ibid.*, p. 112.
[15]*Ibid.*, p. 115.
[16]Valdemar Rodríguez, "National University of Mexico: Rebirth and Role of the Universitarios, 1910–1957" (unpublished Ph.D. Dissertation, University of Texas, 1958, p. 39) claims the Free Law School reduced the number of degrees from the National Law School by one half.
[17]Letter from Emilio Portes Gil, Mexico City, October 20, 1972; interview, Mexico City, August 1, 1974.

---

*It is possible that Mexican presidents make a conscious effort to represent certain professional schools in the leadership positions of various agencies. Graduates of professional schools are generally members of influential professional organizations.

[18]Valdemar Rodríguez, "National University," pp. 87–8.

[19]Luis Calderón Vega, *Los 7 sabios de México*, p. 69. Among those were Alberto Vázquez del Mercado, Antonio Castro Leal, Pedro Henríquez Ureña, Alfonso Caso, Vicente Lombardo Toledano, and Ramón López Velarde.

[20]Luis Calderón Vega, *Los 7 sabios de México*, p. 76, in an interview with Manuel Gómez Morín.

[21]James Wilkie and Monzón de Wilkie, *México visto*, p. 264.

[22]Luis Calderón Vega, *Los 7 sabios de México*, note 3, p. 8.

[23]*Ibid.*, pp. 60–1.

[24]Some professors taught more than one class. We only counted each professor once, regardless of the number of classes taught by that professor.

[25]Eduardo Villaseñor, *Memorias-Testimonio* (Mexico: Fondo de Cultura Económica, 1974), p. 123.

[26]Personal interview with Eduardo Bustamante, Mexico City, July 24, 1974.

[27]Personal interview with Antonio Martínez Báez, Mexico City, June 27, 1975.

[28]Letter from Ricardo J. Zevada, Mexico City, May 4, 1973; interview with Antonio Carrillo Flores, Mexico City, June 26, 1975.

[29]Valdemar Rodríguez, "National University," p. 127.

[30]Ciriaco Pacheco Calvo, *La organización estudiantil en México* (México: Confederación Nacional de Estudiantes, 1934), pp. 19–20.

[31]Valdemar Rodríguez, "National University," pp. 99–100.

[32]Pacheco Calvo, *La organización estudiantil*, pp. 30–3.

[33]Letter from Manuel R. Palacios, Mexico City, February 1, 1973.

[34]Personal interview with Efraín Brito Rosado, Mexico City, August 11, 1974.

[35]The Casa de la Troya, a student dormitory, became a center for students involved in both activities. See Baltasar Dromundo, *La Escuela Nacional Preparatoria Nocturna y José María de los Reyes* (México: Porrúa, 1973), p. 35.

[36]Baltasar Dromundo, "Balance de la generación de 29," in *En Torno de una generación* (México, 1949), p. 66; also see his *Los Oradores de 29* (México: Ediciones "Una Generación," 1949).

[37]Antonio Damiano, "Prolegomenos de la huelga universitaria," in *En Torno de una generación* (México, 1949), p. 14.

[38]*Ibid.*, p. 16.

[39]Jorge Vallejo y Arizmendi, *Testimonio 1930–34* (México: Editorial Stylo, 1947), pp. 53–4.

[40]See my "Education and Political Recruitment in Mexico: The Alemán Generation," *Journal of Inter-American Studies and World Affairs* 8 (August 1976).

[41]Manuel González Ramírez, a member of the 1925–29 group, has called his generation a political one. See his *Mexico, Litografía de la ciudad que se fue México* (México: Private edition, 1962), p. 82.

[42]Personal interview with Víctor Manuel Villaseñor, Mexico City, June 26, 1975; also see his autobiography, *Memorias de un hombre de izquierda*, 2 vols (Mexico: Editorial Grijalbo, 1976).

[43]Letter from Carlos Nova, Mexico City, January 13, 1975.

[44]Letter from Alejandro Gómez Arias, Mexico City, September 27, 1973.

[45]Manuel Rivera Silva, *Perspectivas de una vida, biografía de una generación* (México: Porrúa, 1974), p. 143.

[46]Letters from Roberto Arias, Pachuca, August 16, 1974, and December 4, 1975.

[47]Letter from Roberto Arias, August 16, 1974.

[48]Letter from Hugo Pedro González, Ciudad Victoria, August 15, 1974.

[49]Personal interview with Raúl Rangel Frías, Monterrey, July 18, 1974. Rangel Frías was a student leader during the 1930s.

[50]Vallejo y Arizmendi, *Testimonio*, p. 46.

[51]Alan M. Kirshner, "Tomás Garrido Canabal and the Mexican Red Shirt Movement" (unpublished Ph.D. dissertation, New York University, 1970), pp. 76–7.

[52]Sebastian Mayo, *La Educación socialista en México: el asalto a la universidad nacional*

(Rosario, Argentina: Editorial Bear, 1964), p. 124; and Octavio González Cárdenas, *Los Cien años de la Escuela Nacional Preparatoria* (México: Editorial Porrúa, 1972), pp. 195–6.

[53]Personal interview with Roberto Mantilla Molina, Mexico City, June 19, 1974, a student leader in 1933 and president of the Student Society of the School of Philosophy at the National University.

[54]Valdemar Rodríguez, "National University," p. 224.

[55]Personal interview with Guillermo Ibarra, Mexico City, August 6, 1974.

[56]Lucio Mendieta y Núñez, *Historia,* p. 268.

[57]Personal interview with Mario Colin Sánchez, Mexico City, June 26, 1975; letter from Mario Colin Sánchez, Mexico City, May 3, 1974.

[58]Letter from César Sepulveda, Mexico City, August 7, 1974.

[59]Personal interview with Mario Colin Sánchez, June 26, 1975.

[60]Personal interview with María Emilia Téllez Benoit, Mexico City, July 28, 1974.

[61]Mario Colin Sánchez, *Una semblanza de Luis Echeverría* (México: Testimonios de Atlacomulco, 1969), pp. 8–9. For details of a student congress in which many members of the Echeverría administration participated, see Horacio Labastida and Antonio Pérez Elias, eds, *Congreso de crítica de la revolución mexicana, 1910–1945–1970* (México: Editorial Libros de México, 1972).

[62]*Universidad de México,* May, 1949, p. 15.

[63]*Excélsior,* October 10, 1975, p. 20A.

[64]*Latin America,* September 26, 1975, p. 297.

[65]Daniel Cosío Villegas, *La Sucesión presidencial* (México: Joaquín Mortiz, 1975), p. 68, strongly emphasizes this relationship.

[66]For a description of the development of professional schools in Mexico, see Porfirio Muñoz Ledo, "La Educación Superior," in *México, Cincuenta Años de Revolucion* **2** (Mexico: Fondo de Cultura Económica, 1963).

[67]Other students from the medical school joined the Revolution reports Ramiro Támez Cavazos, Monterrey, Nuevo León, in a letter to me, Feburary 26, 1974. Támez Cavazos and his friends joined the Maderista movement in 1911.

[68]*Salvador, Zubirán, 50 Años de Vida Professional* (México, 1973).

[69]Personal interview with Ignacio Chávez, Mexico City, August 15, 1974.

[70]*Salvador, Zubirán,* p. 25.

[71]The only exception was the law school and the economics school, since the latter was originally part of the former.

[72]José López Escalera, *Diccionario biográfico y de historia de México* (Mexico: Editorial del Magistrado, 1964), p. 913; Ronald Hilton, ed., *Who's Who in Latin America:* Mexico (Stanford: Stanford University Press, 1946), p. 98.

[73]Mexico City, Universidad Nacional, *Catálogo de la Universidad Nacional de México, 1926–27* (México: Talleres Gráfico de la Nación, 1926), pp. 61–4.

[74]Dr Julián Garza Tijerina, a 1925 graduate of the Military Medical School, indicated to me that students from his alma mater were able to meet students from other professional schools in Mexico City through social events held at the main student boarding houses. Although Dr Pedro Daniel Martínez, who came from a humble background, has argued that poorer students were neglected socially in interchanges with other students, other contemporaries disagree. Dr Martínez also believes that middle-class students had greater access to their professors (letter to me, Mexico City, February 13, 1974).

[75]Dr Salvador Aceves Parra said that during the 1920s students had to intern in hospital clinics for at least half a day. As a clinical doctor, he established a number of student relationships as a professional and a professor (personal interview, Mexico City, July 22, 1974).

[76]Personal interview with Daniel Pedro Martínez, Mexico City, June 20, 1975.

[77]Personal interview with Enrique Beltrán, Mexico City, August 13, 1974.

[78]Letter from Enrique Beltrán, Mexico City, January 28, 1974; and "Veinticinco Años de Ciencias Biológicas en México," *Revista de la Sociedad Mexicana de Historia Natural* **10** (December 1949): 19–20.

[79]See Xavier de la Riva Rodríguez, "Salubridad y Asistencia Médico-Social en México," in *Mexico, 50 años de revolución* II (Mexico: Fondo de Cultura Económica, 1963), pp. 383–442.

[80]*Zubirán, Salvador*, p. 36ff.

[81]Mexico City, Universidad Nacional, *Catálogo . . . 1926–27*, pp. 61–4, 214.

[82]*Ibid.*, pp. 82–3.

[83]*Ibid.*

[84]Personal interview with Luis de la Peña Porth, Mexico City, June 23, 1975.

[85]Personal interview with a former cabinet secretary and graduate of the National School of Engineering, 1944.

[86]Jorge Tamayo, *Breve reseña sobre la Escuela Nacional de Ingeniería* (México: Universidad Nacional Autónoma de México, 1958), p. 65.

[87]Personal interview with José Hernández Terán, Mexico City, July 28, 1974.

[88]Letter from Antonio Dovalí Jaime, Mexico City, May 9, 1972.

[89]Personal interview with José Hernández Terán.

[90]Much of the following discussion is taken from my article "The National School of Economics and Public Life in Mexico," *Latin American Research Review* 10 (Fall 1975): 137–51.

[91]UNAM, Escuela Nacional de Economía, *Anuario, 1959* (México: UNAM, 1959), p. 17.

[92]See Jesús Silva Herzog, *Una vida en la vida de México* (México: Siglo XXI, 1972), p. 148.

[93]*Ibid.*, p. 18.

[94]Personal interview with Sealtiel Alatriste, Mexico City, July 23, 1974.

[95]Jesús Silva Herzog, *Una vida*, p. 132.

[96]Personal interview with Sealtiel Alatriste July 23, 1974; interview with Alfonso Pulido Islas, Mexico City, August 12, 1974.

[97]Personal interview with Rubén Gleason Galicia, Mexico City, August 15, 1974, a member of the 1947 generation.

[98]Jesús Silva Herzog, *Una vida*, p. 215.

7. Professors
and Administrators
at the
National University

In the preceding chapters, I have provided considerable evidence to support my original contention that professors and students are important in the recruitment process of one another into Mexican public life. Since professors have been more significant than students as far as initial recruitment into public careers is concerned, it is important to show the degree to which public men were involved in teaching and university administration; to identify those who were most notable in the eyes of future public men; and to illustrate the homogeneity of the backgrounds of professors, academic administrators, and public men in Mexico.

Educators as Public Men

One of the most interesting characteristics of public men in Mexico is that many of them teach. This is possible because most professors at the National University are part-time, making it necessary for the university to depend on teachers who are employed elsewhere. Prospective professors, as I suggested earlier, are recruited to the university by their own professors and deans. Frequently, older professors, who themselves are often public men, will be responsible for recruiting competent students into teaching as well as government. Since 1935, there has been an increase of high-level officeholders who teach, beginning with 28 percent of the public men during the Cárdenas administration, but encompassing 44 percent in the Echeverría administration (Table 7.1). The higher the political office, the more likely it is that its occupant will have taught at the university. For example, an earlier examination of cabinet officers revealed that approximately 50 percent between 1940 and 1970 had taught.[1]

[168]

Table 7.1

Teaching Experience of High-Level Officeholders From 1935 to 1976[a]

Administration in Which Position Was Held	Teaching Experience and Institution		
	None	National University	Other Institutions
1935 to 1940			
No. of high-level officeholders	131	26	24
% of high-level officeholders	72.4	14.4	13.2
1940 to 1946			
No. of high-level officeholders	72	30	9
% of high-level officeholders	64.9	27.0	8.1
1946 to 1952			
No. of high-level officeholders	58	37	17
% of high-level officeholders	51.8	33.1	15.1
1952 to 1958			
No. of high-level officeholders	44	20	20
% of high-level officeholders	52.4	23.8	23.8
1958 to 1964			
No. of high-level officeholders	52	22	18
% of high-level officeholders	56.5	23.9	19.6
1964 to 1970			
No. of high-level officeholders	54	28	19
% of high-level officeholders	53.5	27.7	18.8
1970 to 1976			
No. of high-level officeholders	59	38	32
% of high-level officeholders	45.7	29.5	24.8

[a]This table excludes opposition party leaders and federal deputies. Data are from the MPBP.

Of the more than 40 percent of all high-level public men in Mexico who have taught, the largest number have done so at the National University and to a lesser extent at state universities (see Table 7.1). More than one out of every four public leaders in Mexico has taught at the National University, making UNAM almost as important as an employer of future public men as it is an educator. Further, if we look at public men as college administrators, we find that approximately 9 percent of the high-level officeholders were deans or rectors at the National University, IPN, or other major state universities (Table 7.2).

Table 7.2

High-Level Officeholders From 1935 to 1976 Who Were Rectors and Deans[a]

Administration in Which They Served	Rectors[b]		Deans[c]	
	No.	Percent	No.	Percent
1935 to 1940	10	5.5	9	4.9
1940 to 1946	12	10.6	6	5.3
1946 to 1952	7	6.2	6	5.3
1952 to 1958	3	3.5	5	5.9
1958 to 1964	6	6.5	6	6.5
1964 to 1970	7	6.9	2	2.0
1970 to 1976	5	3.8	8	6.1

[a]This table excludes opposition party leaders and federal deputies. Data are from the MPBP.
[b]Rectors include only those persons who were presidents of the National University, the National Polytechnic Institute, or any public regional university.
[c]Deans include only those persons who held this position at the National University.

Obviously, then, educators who are public men are very much involved in the university. But as educators, do they influence their students, or as most students of education in Latin America would suggest, are part-time professors generally mediocre?[2] A study of the National University in the 1960s indicated that 97 percent of the professors were part-time, yet 50 percent of the students rated their professors as excellent and 70 percent rated their university experience as satisfactory or very satisfactory.[3] My own interviews with former students turned public men indicates that their most notable professors were often part-time educators and full-time professional persons or public men.

Among the schools that have been most influential in the education of future public leaders are the National Preparatory School, and the schools of law, economics, and engineering at the National University. In interviews and correspondence with approximately 100 public men who were graduates of these schools, a list of notable professors who taught at these institutions between 1911 and 1950 has been compiled. Each person who appears in the following tables of notable professors received at least three votes as an influential professor from his former students who became public men.*

National Preparatory School Teachers

The professors at the National Preparatory School who were considered by our sample of public men to have been notable educators are distinguished by three qualities: of those about whom we have complete information, only three graduated from institutions other than the National Preparatory School or the National University. Secondly, all except three graduated before 1920, suggesting that older and more experienced professors were influential at the National Preparatory School. Lastly, an overwhelming majority of them taught for more than 20 years[4] (Table 7.3). The subjects taught by these distinguished educators represented the wide range of subjects taught at the preparatory school. In terms of their education, they were a homogeneous group, having gone back to teach at their alma mater. These professors, then, were very much like public men in general, having received their educations from the same institutions. If we go beyond similarities in educational background between professors and public men, we find other similar characteristics. Preparatory professors, like political leaders, were overwhelmingly from urban backgrounds, even exceeding the proportion among public men (Table 7.4). Although we had economic information on only slightly more than half of the notable preparatory professors, all of them came from

---

*Therefore, professors who impressed students who did not go into public life may not be in the list, nor are professors who influenced generations of students after 1950, since these generations included few public men in the MPBP.

middle-class or well-to-do backgrounds, compared to 63 percent of the political leaders. The number of notable preparatory professors is too small to allow us to evaluate the distribution of home states or geographic regions in Mexico, but it is apparent that the Federal District is heavily represented as a birthplace (Table 7.4). As a group, however, these professors seem to be more homogeneous and selected from a smaller proportion of the population than are political elites in general, since most came from an urban environment characteristic of only about 15 percent of the population and from a socioeconomic background even less characteristic of the general population.

Distinguished preparatory professors have other characteristics similar to those of political leaders. While our information is incomplete concerning professors' activities as students, it does show that they were involved in a wide range of student intellectual and political activities. Those who studied under professors during the years covered by our study (1911 to 1950), also had teachers in this same list of notable professors. Notable professors are prominent students of older distinguished professors, and have been encouraged by them to pursue teaching careers. Given the size of the teaching staff at the preparatory school, older and younger professors form a fairly small,

Table 7.3

Notable Professors of the National Preparatory School From 1911 to 1950

Name of Professor	Institution & Year Graduated		Subject and Years Taught	
Aragón, Enrique Octavio	UNAM (med)	1904	Psychology	30
Argüelles, General Pedro	Durango	1870s	World History	40
Caso, Alfonso	UNAM (law)	1919	Philosophy	20
Caso, Antonio	UNAM (law)	1906	Sociology & Philosophy	20
Castellanos Quinto, Erasmo	UNAM (law)	1903	Spanish Literature	50
Chávez, Ezequiel A.	UNAM (law)	1891	Psychology	50
Chico Goerne, Luis	UNAM (law)	1918	Sociology	20
Guillén y Sánchez, Palma	UNAM	1919	Spanish	30
Fernández Granados, Enrique	UNAM	1880s	Spanish Literature	20
Fierro, Otilio	NI[a]	NI	Algebra	NI
Jiménez Rueda, Julio	UNAM (law)	1920	Mexican Literature	25
Loera y Chávez, Agustín	UNAM & Paris	1915–20	Mexican History	40
Lombardo Toledano, Vicente	UNAM (law)	1919	Ethics	15
López Aguado, Manuel	UNAM (eng)	NI	Mathematics	50
López Velarde, Ramón	Aguas (law)	1911	Spanish Literature	5
Maas de Serrano, Ana	UNAM (philos)	1930	Ethics	20
Ramírez Cabañas, Joaquín	ENP	1900s	Mexican History	30
Ramos, Samuel	UNAM (philos)	1922	Logic & Philosophy	30
Reyes, Alfonso	UNAM (law)	1913	Spanish Literature	NI
Romano Muñoz, José	NI	NI	Ethics & Civics	20
Schultz, Enrique	UNAM (eng)	1895	World Geography	20
Urbina, Luis G.	ENP	1880s	Spanish Literature	20
Vasconcelos, José	UNAM (law)	1907	Philosophy	NI
Yáñez, Agustín	Guad (law)	1929	World History	10

[a]NI = No information

cohesive group. It also is of interest to note that of the 24 prominent teachers, there are two women—Palma Guillén y Sánchez and Ana Maas de Serrano.

Preparatory professors can be distinguished from teachers at the other schools frequented by public men because of their careers: they have not been, on the whole, successful public men. In fact, of all the schools examined, notable professors of the National Preparatory School were more likely to have followed careers as full-time professors and distinguished

Table 7.4

**Background Data on Notable Professors at the National Preparatory School
From 1911 to 1950**

Name of Professor	Home State & Urban-Rural Birth	Socio-economic status[a]	Student Political Activity	Notable Professor as a Student
Aragón, Enrique Octavio	NI[c]	NI	NI	DNA
Argüelles, General Pedro	Durango (R)	NI	NI	DNA[b]
Caso, Alfonso	Federal District (U)	H	Seven Wise Men	Antonio Caso
Caso, Antonio	Federal District (U)	H	Ateneo	DNA
Castellanos Quinto, Erasmo	Veracruz (R)	H	NI	DNA
Chávez, Ezequiel A.	Aguascalientes (U)	H	None	DNA
Chico Goerne, Luis	Guanajuato (U)	H	NI	NI
Fernández Granados, Enrique	Federal District (U)	NI	Student Journalist	DNA
Fierro, Otilio	NI	NI	NI	DNA
Guillén y Sánchez, Palma	Federal District (U)	NI	Seven Wise Men	Vasconcelos
Jiménez Rueda, Julio	Federal District (U)	NI	Catholic Student Leader	NI
Loera y Chávez, Agustín	Aguascalientes (U)	H	NI	NI
Lombardo Toledano, Vicente	Puebla (R)	H	Seven Wise Men	Antonio Caso
López Aguado, Manuel	NI	NI	NI	DNA
López Velarde, Ramón	Aguascalientes (R)	NI	NI	Antonio Caso
Maas de Serrano, Ana	Puebla	H	Student Repres.	Samuel Ramos
Ramírez Cabañas, Joaquín	Veracruz (R)	H	Literary Activities	NI
Ramos, Samuel	Michoacán (U)	H	Literary Activities	Antonio Caso
Reyes, Alfonso	Nuevo León (U)	H	Ateneo	DNA
Romano Muñoz, José	NI	NI	NI	NI
Schultz, Enrique	Federal District (U)	H	NI	DNA
Urbina, Luis G.	Federal District (U)	NI	Literary Activities	DNA
Vasconcelos, José	Oaxaca (U)	H	Ateneo	DNA
Yáñez, Agustín	Jalisco (U)	H	Catholic Student Leader	NI

[a]Under SES (socio-economic status), anyone coming from middle or upper class backgrounds was given the designation of H.
[b]DNA (does not apply) refers to those notable professors from the 1911 to 1950 period who were too old to have been students of notable colleagues after 1911.
[c]NI = No information

academic administrators, than as public men (Table 7.5). Six ultimately became rectors of the National University, the most prestigious academic position in Mexico, and three became secretaries general or deans at the same institution. While a sizeable number of preparatory professors have had no public careers, an equal number have been moderately successful and a third group has been eminently successful in public life. What is significant to note about the careers of notable professors is that those who were successful in public life, were equally successful in academia. The abilities and skills that produced competent public men in Mexico are also characteristic of academic leaders. Although public men were substantially represented among notable preparatory professors, very successful public men were not teaching in great numbers at the preparatory school. Of the 139 professors at the preparatory school in 1930, only 11 had careers as high-level officeholders.

A typical example of the full-time professor at the preparatory school who did not involve himself in public life was Erasmo Castellaños Quinto. Castellaños Quinto was born in Veracruz in the late 1870s, and did his

Table 7.5

Career Patterns of Notable Professors at the National Preparatory School, 1911 to 1950

Name of Professor	Level Reached in Government Service	Years in Government	Level Reached in Academic Career
Aragón, Enrique Octavio	None	None	Rector of UNAM
Argüelles, General Pedro	None	None	Full-time Professor
Caso, Alfonso	High-level	30	Rector of UNAM
Caso, Antonio	Middle-level	2	Rector of UNAM
Castellaños Quinto, Erasmo	None	None	Full-time Professor
Chávez, Ezequiel A.	High-level	16	Rector of UNAM
Chico Goerne, Luis	High-level	22	Rector of UNAM
Fernández Granados, Enrique	Low-level	NI	Professor at UNAM
Fierro, Otilio	NI[a]	NI	Professor at ENP
Guillén y Sánchez, Palma	Middle-level	15	Professor at ENP
Jiménez Rueda, Julio	Middle-level	NI	Secretary General of UNAM
Loera y Chávez, Agustín	Middle-level	NI	Dean at UNAM
Lombardo Toledano, Vicente	High-level	40	Director of ENP
López Aguado, Manuel	None	None	Professor Emeritus
López Velarde, Ramón	Middle-level	5	Professor at ENP
Maas de Serrano, Ana	None	None	Professor at ENP
Ramírez Cabañas, Joaquín	None	None	Professor at UNAM
Ramos, Samuel	High-level	5	Dean at UNAM
Reyes, Alfonso	Middle-level	23	Secretary at UNAM
Romano Múñoz, José	Middle-level	NI	Professor at ENP
Schultz, Enrique	None	None	Full-time Professor
Urbina, Luis G.	Middle-level	7	Professor at ENP
Vasconcelos, José	High-level	12	Rector of UNAM
Yáñez, Agustín	High-level	40	Professor at UNAM

[a]NI = No information

preparatory studies in Orizaba. After teaching Latin in Orizaba, he went to study in Mexico City, where he completed a law degree and began practicing with several other lawyers. He soon left that profession to teach Spanish, Spanish literature, and general literature at the National Preparatory School and the National University. He served briefly as Subdirector of the National Preparatory School, and as interim director in 1915. He published several critical works on poetry and literature. He was non-political in his philosophy and his activities as an educator. Although he had hundreds of prominent public figures as his students, his most successful protegé was Ángel Carvajal, pre-candidate for president of Mexico in 1958. However, Castellaños Quinto never accepted a public position from a former student.[5]

Equally popular as a teacher, but one of the foremost public men of this century, was Vicente Lombardo Toledano. A student of Antonio Caso, he became a member of the famous 1911–15 group at the National Preparatory School, and graduated from the National University in 1919. Despite numerous political activities, he taught for most of the years between 1918 and 1933. His academic career, like his public career, was extraordinary. He served as secretary of the law school, director of the preparatory school, director of the night preparatory school, and director of the Worker's University. Among his prominent student assistants were Manuel R. Palacios, José de Jesús Castorena, and Alejandro Carrillo, all of whom followed distinguished public careers.[6]

National School of Law Teachers

Notable professors at the National Law School were similar to those at the preparatory school. Former students selected 34 of their professors as deserving of praise (Table 7.6). There is an even more remarkable homogeneity in the education of these law school professors than was true of preparatory school educators. Of the native-born professors, all except two graduated from the National University.* Three generations of graduates were particularly well-represented among these professors: 1918–19; 1925–26, and 1928–29. As a group, they tended to be much younger than the preparatory professors, and the majority of them graduated after 1910.[7] While most of these law professors had shorter teaching careers than their counterparts at the preparatory school, the majority taught for 20 or more years. This is much longer than the average professor at the national university, where the typical tenure was seven years.[8] Lastly, three of the law professors were also listed as

---

*King suggests the same pattern among regional schools: "Recruitment from among an institution's own graduates (and promotion from within) seems very much to be the rule, a finding that squares with the analysis of the source of professional training of professors" (*The Provincial Universities of Mexico* [New York: Praeger, 1971], p. 64).

notable preparatory professors. Interestingly, those who were able to obtain success in both schools graduated before 1920, indicating the shortage in those early years of competent instructors. Since that time, few part-time professors have taught in both schools for any length of time, since a much larger pool of graduates is now available as part-time instructors, and since public men who teach prefer to do so at the university.

Otherwise, the distinguished law school professors are as homogeneous as the preparatory teachers, and like them, come from a comparably select group of Mexicans. Like their preparatory counterparts, law professors come from urban backgrounds (Table 7.7). While 81 percent had urban birthplaces, nearly a third were born and raised in the Federal District. Of the known economic backgrounds of these professors, 16 came from middle-class and

Table 7.6

Notable Professors of the National School of Law From 1911 to 1950

Name of Professor	Institution & Year Graduated		Subject and Years Taught	
Bassols, Narciso	UNAM (law)	1919	Guarantees & Amparo	15
Beteta, Ramón	UNAM (law)	1926	Sociology & Economics	20
Borja Soriano, Manuel	UNAM (law)	1897	Civil Law	45
Brito Foucher, Rodulfo	UNAM (law)	1923	General Theory	20
Carrillo Flores, Antonio	UNAM (law)	1929	Administrative Law	15
Caso, Alfonso	UNAM (law)	1919	Philosophy of Law	20
Caso, Antonio	UNAM (law)	1906	Sociology	20
Chico Goerne, Luis	UNAM (law)	1918	Sociology	20
Cossio y Cossio, Roberto	UNAM (law)	1929	Business Law	20
De la Cueva, Mario	UNAM (law)	1925	General Theory	30
Esteva Ruiz, Roberto A.	UNAM (law)	1908	International & Constitutional Law	20
Fraga, Gabino	UNAM (law)	1920	Administrative Law	20
García, Julio	UNAM (law)	1880s	Civil Law	30
García, Trinidad	UNAM (law)	1919	Roman Law	30
García Máynez, Eduardo	UNAM (law)	1931	Ethics & Philosophy of Law	30
García Rojas, Jorge Gabriel	UNAM (law)	1920	Contract Law	20
Gómez Morín, Manuel	UNAM (law)	1919	Public Law	30
González Aparicio, Enrique	UNAM (law)	1928	Economic Theory	10
González Roa, Fernando	Gto (law)	1904	Agrarian Law	10
Guerrero, Julio	UNAM (law)	1889	International Public Law	15
Herrasti, Francisco de P.	UNAM (law)	1903	Roman Law	25
Herrera y Laso, Manuel	ELD (law)	1915	Constitutional Law	22
Lanz Duret, Miguel	UNAM (law)	1901	Constitutional Law	10
Lombardo Toledano, Vicente	UNAM (law)	1919	Labor Law	15
López Portillo, José	UNAM (law)	1943	General Theory	11
Martínez Baez, Antonio	UNAM (law)	1925	Constitutional Law	30
Pedroso, Manuel	Madrid (law)	1910	General Theory	20
Pérez Abreu, Juan	NI	NI	Sociology	20
Recasens Siches, Luis	Madrid (law)	1925	Private International Law	30
Reyes Heroles, Jesús	UNAM (law)	1943	General Theory	15
Serra Rojas, Andrés	UNAM (law)	1928	General Theory	20
Sousa, Mario	UNAM (law)	1925	Business Law	15
Suárez, Eduardo	UNAM (law)	1917	Public International Law	15
Vázquez del Mercado, Alberto	UNAM (law)	1919	NI	5

Key: Gto = Guanajuato; ELD = Free Law School; and NI = No information.

upper-class families, and only one, Manuel Gómez Morín, came from a working-class family.[9] Law professors come from a much more select group than do public men, and appear to be slightly more homogeneous in terms of education, birthplace, and family circumstances than do preparatory professors. As young students, they too were active in some of the well-known

Table 7.7

Background Data on Notable Professors at the National School of Law From 1911 to 1950

Name of Professor	Home State & Urban-Rural Birth	Socio-economic Status	Student Political Activity	Notable Professor as a Student
Bassols, Narciso	Mexico (R)[a]	H[c]	Seven Wise Men	Antonio Caso
Beteta, Ramón	Sonora (R)	H	Student Leader	Gómez Morín
Borja Soriano, Manuel	Fed. Dist. (U)[b]	NI[d]	NI	DNA[e]
Brito Foucher, Rodulfo	Tabasco (U)	H	Student Leader	NI
Carrillo Flores, Antonio	Fed. Dist. (U)	H	Student Oratory	Bassols
Caso, Alfonso	Fed. Dist. (U)	H	Seven Wise Men	Antonio Caso
Caso, Antonio	Fed. Dist. (U)	H	Ateneo	DNA
Chico Goerne, Luis	Guanajuato (U)	H	NI	NI
Cossío y Cossío, Roberto	Fed. Dist. (U)	H	NI	Gómez Morín
De la Cueva, Mario	Fed. Dist. (U)	NI	NI	NI
Esteva Ruiz, Roberto A.	Fed. Dist. (U)	H	NI	DNA
Fraga, Gabino	Michoacán (U)	NI	NI	Antonio Caso
García, Julio	Guanajuato (U)	NI	NI	DNA
García Trinidad	Fed. Dist. (U)	H	Seven Wise Men	NI
García Máynez, Eduardo	Fed. Dist. (U)	NI	NI	Antonio Caso
García Rojas, Jorge Gabriel	Fed. Dist. (U)	NI	NI	NI
Gómez Morín, Manuel	Chihuahua (R)	L[f]	Seven Wise Men	Luis Cabrera
González Aparicio, Enrique	Veracruz (U)	NI	Student Leader	NI
González Roa, Fernando	Guanajuato (U)	NI	NI	NI
Guerrero, Julio	Fed. Dist. (U)	NI	NI	DNA
Herrasti, Francisco de P.	Fed. Dist. (U)	H	NI	DNA
Herrera y Laso, Manuel	San Luis Potosí	H	Co-founder ELD	Rodríguez, A.
Lanz Duret, Miguel	Campeche (U)	H	NI	NI
Lombardo Toledano, Vicente	Puebla (R)	H	Seven Wise Men	Antonio Caso
López Portillo, José	Fed. Dist. (U)	H	Co-founder University Extension	Manuel Pedroso
Martínez Báez, Antonio	Michoacán (U)	H	Student asst	Bassols
Pedroso, Manuel	Cuba (U)	H	Student Journalist	DNA
Pérez Abreu, Juan	Campeche	NI	NI	NI
Recasens Siches, Luis	Guatemala (U)	H	NI	DNA
Reyes Heroles, Jesús	Veracruz (U)	NI	Member of PRI	Manuel Pedroso
Serra Rojas, Andrés	Chiapas (R)	NI	Student Leader	Antonio Caso
Sousa, Mario	Veracruz (U)	NI	Student asst	Gómez Morín
Suárez, Eduardo	Mexico (R)	NI	NI	Julio García
Vázquez del Mercado, Alberto	Guerrero (U)	H	Seven Wise Men	Henríquez Ureña

[a](R) = Rural birthplace (town of 5,000 or less).
[b](U) = Urban birthplace (town of more than 5,000).
[c]H = Middle and upper class background.
[d]NI = No information.
[e]DNA = Does not apply.
[f]L = Lower class background.

student organizations, both political and intellectual, and six were members of the "Seven Wise Men" group. Since nearly all of them graduated from the National University, it is not surprising that their mentors were also graduates and distinguished professors: Antonio Caso, Narciso Bassols, and Manuel Gómez Morín (Table 7.7). Antonio Rodríguez, who was also a mentor, was a distinguished lawyer and professor, but he became a founder and rector of the Free Law School, limiting his influence on national university graduates. Luis Cabrera, the other mentor of one of our professors, was one of the most distinguished thinkers of the Revolution, but influenced only pre-1920s generations and did so mostly outside of the classroom.

The most striking quality of notable law professors, unlike preparatory professors, is that nearly *all* were public men holding middle-level or high-level positions during their lifetimes (Table 7.8). In 1930, of the 49 faculty members teaching at the law school, 29 had held, or would hold, high-level public positions.[10] Even in 1954, of the approximately 175 faculty members at the law school, 39 had held or would hold high-level public offices.[11] Furthermore, as late as 1966, there were only four professors emeritus, all of whom were distinguished public men and all of whom appear in Table 7.8: Gabino Fraga, Antonio Martínez Báez, Mario de la Cueva, and Andrés Serra Rojas.[12]

Typical of the eminently successful public man and professor was Alfonso Caso, the younger brother of another distinguised Mexican educator and thinker, Antonio Caso. Alfonso, the son of an engineer, was a member of the 1915–19 generation. During the years 1918 to 1940 he taught at the School of Philosophy, the National Preparatory School, and the School of Law. He exemplifies the person who distinguishes himself in academia, and then moves into public affairs. While holding only minor positions in government in the 1920s, he became director of the National Preparatory School in the late 1930s; he then served as Director General of Higher Education for the Secretariat of Public Education in 1944. He was asked to serve as Rector of the National University in a time of crisis, and during his interim tenure from 1944–45 reorganized the legal basis for the university. He did an admirable job and his former student Miguel Alemán asked him to serve as coordinator for educational affairs during his presidential campaign in 1946. When Alemán became President, he appointed Caso as the first secretary of the new cabinet department responsible for national properties. Caso took many of his former students with him to establish and operate this new government agency.[13]

The law school has been dominated by professors from public life. While most studies might suggest that public men who are generally only part-time professors are not among the significant teachers, that is not the case, especially in the eyes of former students who themselves followed distinguished public careers. The tables on the law school faculty reveal, to a much greater degree than those tables dealing with preparatory professors, that public men are very much involved at the National School of Law, and that they, and not the full-time professors, are responsible for the education of most future political leaders in Mexico. They have not only been successful

Table 7.8

Career Patterns of Notable Professors at the National School of Law, 1911 to 1950

Name of Professor	Level Reached in Government Service	Years in Government	Level Reached in Academic Career
Bassols, Narciso	High-level	20	Dean UNAM
Beteta, Ramón	High-level	30	Professor
Borja Soriano, Manuel	Low-level	20	Professor Emeritus
Brito Foucher, Rodulfo	High-level[a]	3	Rector UNAM
Carrillo Flores, Antonio	High-level	42	Dean UNAM
Caso, Alfonso	High-level	30	Rector UNAM
Caso, Antonio	Middle-level	2	Rector UNAM
Chico Goerne, Luis	High-level	22	Rector UNAM
Cossío y Cossío Roberto	High-level[b]	15	Professor
De la Cueva, Mario	High-level	7	Rector UNAM
Esteva Ruiz, Roberto A.	High-level	15	Dean UNAM
Fraga, Gabino	High-level	25	Governing Board UNAM
García, Julio	High-level	20	Professor
García, Trinidad	High-level[b]	10	Dean UNAM
García Máynez, Eduardo	None	None	Secretary General UNAM
García Rojas, Jorge Gabriel	High-level	15	Professor
Gómez Morín, Manuel	High-level	10	Rector UNAM
González Aparicio, Enrique	Middle-level	10	Dean UNAM
González Roa, Fernando	High-level	20	Professor
Guerrero, Julio	Middle-level	15	Secretary UNAM
Herrasti, Francisco de P.	None	None	Full-time Professor
Herrera y Laso, Manuel	Middle-level	20	Professor Emeritus
Lanz Duret, Miguel	None[c]	None	Professor
Lombardo Toledano, Vicente	High-level	40	Director of ENP
López Portillo, José	High-level	15	Professor
Martínez Baéz, Antonio	High-level	20	Governing Board UNAM Profesor Emeritus
Pedroso, Manuel	Middle-level (Spain)	3	Vice-Rector Seville
Pérez Abreu, Juan	Middle-level	5	Professor
Recasens Siches, Luis	High-level (Spain)	6	Professor
Reyes Heroles, Jesús	High-level	35	Professor
Serra Rojas, Andrés	High-level	30	Appt. Rector UNAM[d]
Sousa, Mario	High-level	15	Dean UNAM
Suárez, Eduardo	High-level	20	Professor
Vázquez del Mercado, Alberto	High-level	10	Professor

[a]Brito Foucher served in a subcabinet capacity, but in the Adolfo de la Huerta government of 1923.

[b]These persons held high-level positions, but in opposition party bureaucracies.

[c]Miguel Lanz Duret, as Director General of *El Universal,* the most influential government newspaper, might be considered by some scholars to have a high-level position. Since the real relationship between the government and the newspaper is unknown to the author, I have not credited him with government service.

[d]Andrés Serra Rojas, a professor emeritus, was offered the rectorship in 1948. He accepted, but then made his acceptance on the condition that students publicly support him. This could not be done, and he refused the appointment.

as public men and as professors, but they have achieved prominent careers within the University. Six of these men have been rectors, and seven have served as deans or other high-level administrators.

National School of Economics Teachers

The National School of Economics, which is the youngest of the four schools examined in this chapter, is an offshoot of the law school. The School of Economics professors were a young group of law school graduates in the 1920s who became interested in the study of economics, and four of them were also remembered as outstanding professors at the law school (Table 7.9). It is not surprising that most of them had law degrees, since before 1929 no institution in Mexico granted economics degrees. Originally, many of these men helped to initiate and sustain the program at the law school, but since 1930 economics professors have been, for the most part, graduates of the School of Economics (Table 7.10).

Considering the number of notable professors selected by graduates of the School of Law and the School of Economics, the influence of two professors, Narciso Bassols and Manuel Gómez Morín, is remarkable. These two men deserve some comment. Twelve of the more than 30 public men interviewed by the author who attended either school during this period considered Narciso Bassols to have significantly influenced their formation as students and that of their co-students. As mentioned earlier, he was a member of the "Seven Wise Men" generation of the National Preparatory School, later completing his education at the National School of Law. A prominent student of Antonio Caso, he ran for and won the election as president of the Student

Table 7.9

Notable Professors of the National School of Economics, 1929 to 1950[a]

Name of Professor	Institution & Year Graduated		Subject and Years Taught	
Bach, Federico (Fritz)[b]	Europe (law)	NI	Industrial Economics Economic History	12
Beteta, Ramón	UNAM (law)	1926	Political Economics	18
Bustamante, Eduardo	UNAM (law)	1926	Public Finance	14
Carrillo Flores, Antonio	UNAM (law)	1929	Administrative Law	15
González Aparicio, Enrique	UNAM (law)	1928	Population	12
Loyo, Gilberto	UNAM (law)	1922	Economic History	24
Martínez Adame, Emigdio	UNAM (econ)	1930	NI	NI
Martínez Sobral, Enrique	Guat. (law)[b]	1895	Economic Policy	NI
Silva Herzog, Jesús	UNAM (cpa)	1924	Economic Doctrines	40
Sousa, Mario	UNAM (law)	1925	Economic Theory	15
Torres Gaytán, Ricardo	UNAM econ)	1941	International Trade	15
Zamora, Francisco	UNAM (law)	1916	Economic Theory	25

[a]Adopted from Roderic A. Camp, "The National School of Economics and Public Life in Mexico," *Latin American Research Review* **10** (Fall 1975): 140, Table 1.
[b]Enrique Martínez Sobral also received a law degree in Chile in 1897 and a doctorate in laws in Mexico.

Law Society. Before graduating from the law school, he wrote campaign literature for a gubernatorial election in Aguascalientes. In 1924, he served as Secretary General of the state of México under the prominent politician Carlos Riva Palacio.

His reputation as a professor, his authorship of the 1927 Agrarian Law, and his friendship with co-student Antonio Castro Leal (who became Rector of the National University in 1928) were factors in his selection as Dean of the law school at the age of 34. As dean, he attempted to introduce changes in the calendar and curriculum, alienating students in the process. He resigned after the student strike in 1929. Bassols' talents were very much appreciated by General Calles, and beginning with the administration of Pascual Ortiz Rubio, who followed Calles' tutelage, Bassols was named to the position of Secretary of Public Education. He was considered by Calles as a possible successor to Ortiz Rubio as president of Mexico. During his teaching career in the 1920s and early 1930s, he was a moderate socialist in his philosophy, and it was only in the 1930s that he moved further left to become a Marxist. He continued to serve in high-level positions, as Secretary of Government in 1934, Secretary of Finance the following year, and Ambassador to Great Britain, France, and then the Soviet Union in the late 1930s and 1940s. Ultimately he involved himself in Marxist intellectual activities in support of leftist parties opposed to the official party in Mexico. His students continue

Table 7.10

Background Data on Notable Professors at the National School of Economics From 1929 to 1950[a]

Name	Home State & Urban-Rural Birthplace	Socio-economic Status	Student Political Activity	Notable Professor as a Student
Bach, Federico (Fritz)	Foreign	NI	NI	NI
Beteta, Ramón	Federal District (U)	H	Student Leader Internat. Cong.	Gómez Morín
Bustamante, Eduardo	Oaxaca (U)	H	NI	Gómez Morín
Carrillo Flores, Antonio	Federal District (U)	H	Student Oratory Champion	Suárez, E.
González Aparicio, Enrique	Veracruz (U)	H	NI	Gómez Morín
Loyo, Gilberto	Veracruz (U)	H	NI	Gómez Morín
Martínez Adame, Emigdio	Guerrero (U)	H	Student Leader	Bassols
Martínez Sobral, Enrique	Foreign	H	Opposition Leader in Guatemala	DNA
Silva Herzog, Jesús	San Luis Potosí (U)	H	Supported the Revolution	Goldschmit (German)
Sousa, Mario	Veracruz (U)	NI	NI	NI
Torres Gaytán, Ricardo	Michoacán (R)	NI	NI	NI
Zamora, Francisco	Foreign	H	Student Journalist	NI

[a]Adapted from Roderic A. Camp, "The National School of Economics and Public Life in Mexico," *Latin American Research Review* **10** (Fall 1975): 143, Table 3.

Key: H = Middle & upper class background; NI = No information; DNA = Does not apply; (U) = Urban; and (R) = Rural.

to be influential as teachers and public men in contemporary Mexico, and two—Hugo Margáin and Antonio Carrillo Flores—followed in his footsteps as Treasury secretaries.[14]

The teaching career of Manuel Gómez Morín was equally influential on notable law and economics professors as students. Born the same year as Bassols, Gómez Morín had certain similarities to Bassols. Both were singled out as distinguished members of the ''Seven Wise Men'' generation, and both were part of the same law school class, although Gómez Morín completed his studies first. His successful academic and public career preceded that of Bassols. At the age of 24, he became Subsecretary of Finance, in charge of the ministry when the secretaryship was vacant. A year later he was appointed Dean of the National Law School. After leaving the deanship in 1924, he became the founder and director of the Bank of Mexico, equivalent to the Federal Reserve Board in the United States. During that same period he contributed to Mexico's legal legislation as the author of the first Agricultural Credit Law. As an educator, he was not known for the conservative views he later acquired. In fact, in 1928, he was a lawyer for the Soviet Commercial Delegation in Mexico. He culminated a distinguished academic career by serving as Rector of the National University during part of Bassols' tenure as Secretary of Education. Like Bassols, he became increasingly disillusioned with the political system and government policies. He taught until 1939, and then founded the National Action Party, which at that time, represented a conservative, Catholic ideology.[15] Although Gómez Morín and Bassols went in opposite political directions in later years, both left prominent public careers in order to stimulate opposition parties in Mexico. Their political ideologies and opposition careers did not adversely affect their influence as professors of future generations.

Influential economics professors, like the law professors, were very much involved in public careers, and most held high-level positions (Table 7.11). In 1930, four of the regular 12 faculty members had or would hold high-level public office. A detailed examination of all faculty members at the School of Economics in 1952 reveals the extent to which public men were involved.[16] There were 56 persons teaching, of whom 39 were professors, 14 were provisional professors, and nine were interim instructors. Nineteen of those educators had held or were holding top-level positions in government. Another ten served as department heads or bureau chiefs in government agencies. Therefore, 29, or well over half of the professors, were in a position to hire or assist students in obtaining public employment.[17]

National School of Engineering Teachers

The third important school at the National University making an important contribution to the education of public men is the School of Engineering.

Since the School of Engineering has had a long history in Mexico, it is not surprising that many of its educators were its own graduates, even in the 19th century. The only notable professor who was an exception was Juan Salvador Agraz, who received his professional training in Paris and Berlin. Educationally, the engineering faculty was a very homogeneous group, and all but two of these professors taught for 15 or more years (Table 7.12). While we have less information about engineering professors than law or economics professors, they do seem to be a more representative group than the other professors, when classified by birthplace. Many of the notable professors came

Table 7.11

**Career Patterns of Notable Professors at the National School
of Economics, 1929 to 1950**

Name of Professor	Level Reached in Government Service	Years in Government	Level Reached in Academic Career
Bach, Federico (Fritz)	Middle-level	12	Professor
Beteta, Ramón	High-level	30	Professor
Bustamante, Eduardo	High-level	41	Professor
Carrillo Flores, Antonio	High-level	42	Dean UNAM
González Aparicio, Enrique	Middle-level	10	Dean UNAM
Loyo, Gilberto	High-level	40	Dean UNAM
Martínez Adame, Emigdio	High-level	24	Professor
Martínez Sobral, Enrique	Middle-level	20	Professor
Silva Herzog, Jesús	High-level	22	Governing Board UNAM
Sousa, Mario	High-level	27	Dean UNAM
Torres Gaytán, Ricardo	High-level	19	Dean UNAM
Zamora, Francisco	None	None	Full-time Professor

Table 7.12

Notable Professors of the National School of Engineering From 1911 to 1950

Name of Professor	Institution & Year		Subject and Years Taught	
Agraz, Juan Salvador	Paris-Berlin	1903	Chemistry	45
Aguilera S., José Guadalupe	UNAM (eng)	1880	Geology	30
Barros Sierra, Javier	UNAM (eng)	1943	Mathematics	15
Carrillo Flores, Nabor	UNAM (eng)	1939	Mechanics (structural)	21
Colomo, José	UNAM (eng)	1920	Petroleum Engineering	25
Contreras C., David	UNAM (eng)	NI[a]	Metallurgy	15
De la O. Carreño, Alfonso	UNAM (eng)	NI	Petroleum Engineering	15
Dovalí Jaime, Antonio	UNAM (eng)	1928	Bridges	30
Flores, Alberto J.	UNAM (eng)	1929	Concrete (structural)	20
Gama, Valentín	UNAM (eng)	1893	Topography	25
Larios Torres, Hermión	UNAM (eng)	1914	Chemistry	20
Martínez Tornel, Pedro	UNAM (eng)	1918	NI	20
Moctezuma, Mariano	UNAM (eng)	1905	Geology	20
Ortiz, Enrique	UNAM (eng)	NI	Metallurgy	10
Vega Argüelles, Oscar	UNAM (eng)	NI	NI	10

[a]NI = No information.

from various states in Mexico, and in equal numbers from rural and urban communities. Although our information concerning family background is limited to five of the 16 professors, they, like law and economics professors, seem to have been from middle- and upper-class families (Table 7.13). There is insufficient information to permit comment concerning their student activities or their professors at the university.

All of the engineering professors were involved in public careers, though more were in middle-level positions as department heads of technical agencies than were prominent public leaders. Of the three schools we have discussed at the National University, the engineering school has the smallest proportion of notable professors in high-level public positions (Table 7.14). This is clearly indicated, for example, by our data for all teaching staff at the School of Engineering in 1930, when none of the 48 professors could be classified as a high-level public officials. Despite smaller proportions of high-level officeholders, it is obvious from Table 7.14, however, that most had long careers in public service; furthermore, they too were eminently successful in academia.

The previous data, and an analysis of that data, confirm the influence of public men who are professors. It is important to understand who the university professors are because of the role they play in the education and recruitment of students who later enter public careers, but as I suggested earlier,

Table 7.13

**Background Data on Notable Professors at the National School
of Engineering From 1911 to 1950**

Name of Professor	Home State & Urban-Rural Birthplace	Socio-economic Status	Student Political Activity	Notable Professor as a Student
Agraz, Juan Salvador	Jalisco (R)	H	NI	DNA
Aguilera S., José Guadalupe	Durango (R)	NI	NI	DNA
Barros Sierra, Javier	Federal District (U)	H	Student Assistant	Dovalí Jaime
Carrillo Flores, Nabor	Federal District (U)	H	Student Assistant	NI
Colomo, José	Chihuahua (R)	NI	NI	NI
Contreras C., David	NI	NI	NI	NI
De la O. Carreño, Alfonso	NI	NI	NI	NI
Dovalí Jaime, Antonio	Zacatecas (U)	NI	Student Rep.	Martínez Tornel
Flores, Alberto J.	NI	NI	NI	NI
Gama y Cruz, Valentín	San Luis Potosí	H	NI	DNA
Larios Torres, Hermión	Jalisco (U)	NI	NI	NI
Martínez Tornel, Pedro	Veracruz (U)	NI	NI	NI
Moctezuma, Mariano	San Luis Potosí (R)	NI	NI	DNA
Ortiz, Enrique	NI	H	NI	NI
Vega Arugüelles, Oscar	NI	NI	NI	NI

Key: (R) = Rural birthplace; (U) = Urban birthplace; H = Middle and upper class background; NI = No information; and DNA = Does not apply.

professors are also crucial in the recruitment of brilliant students to professorships at major schools in the National University.[18] As a former law school dean noted in the 1920s, school administrators were unable to get eminent lawyers to become professors, so they often got young people to take these positions instead. A number of fifth-year students became professors: Antonio Carrillo Flores, Antonio Martínez Báez, Manuel Sánchez Cuen, Daniel Bello, Andrés Serra Rojas, and others. The professors were important in choosing these students because they often picked among the distinguished young men who gave brilliant professional examinations.[19]

Administrators

In order to have a complete understanding of the influence of public men on the university, we need to examine the role of university administrators and the process by which they are selected. The relationship between the university and the federal government has changed during the years of our study. Initially, in 1910, article 4 of the Constitutive Law of the National University stated: the rector of the University will be named by the President of the Republic; will remain in office three years; but could be reappointed for one or various periods.[20] But, in 1929, the process for appointing the rector changed. The President of Mexico would provide the University Council with three nominees, from which the Council would have to choose.[21] Although he could not appoint a specific individual, the President could still insure that

Table 7.14

**Career Patterns of Notable Professors at the National School
of Engineering, 1911 to 1950**

Name	Level Reached in Government Service	Years in Government	Level Reached Academic Career
Agraz, Juan Salvador	Middle-level	25	Director National School of Industrial Chemistry
Aguilera S., José Guadalupe	High-level	5	Director Geological Institute
Barros Sierra, Javier	High-level	12	Rector UNAM
Carrillo Flores, Nabor	Middle-level	15	Rector UNAM
Colomo, José	Middle-level	30	Professor & Founder of Petroleum Curriculum
Contreras C., David	Middle-level	NI	Professor
De la O. Carreño, Alfonso	Middle-level	15	Professor
Dovalí Jaime, Antonio	High-level	40	Dean UNAM
Flores, Alberto J.	Middle-level	15	Dean UNAM
Gama y Cruz, Valentín	Middle-level	10	Rector UNAM
Larios Torres, Hermión	Middle-level	17	Professor
Martínez Tornel, Pedro	High-level	30	Dean UNAM
Moctezuma, Mariano	High-level	6	Dean UNAM
Ortiz, Enrique	NI[a]	NI	Professor
Vega Argüelles, Oscar	Middle-level	12	Professor

[a]NI = No information.

someone in whom he had confidence would be selected.[22] In political terms, the university was not separate from the federal government, and the President retained his influence over the choice of a rector until 1933, when a new internal law was passed, making the University Council the supreme authority of the university, and giving it the responsibility for selecting a rector to serve a four-year term.[23] Deans and other personnel would also be designated by the council. In 1945, the internal government of the university was once again reorganized, and this law remained effective through the end of our study. A new Governing Board of distinguished university graduates who had been teachers or researchers were selected. This new board became responsible for designating the rector, the same role performed by the University Council from 1933 to 1944. In turn, the rector was responsible for nominating a slate of three individuals to serve as deans and directors of schools and institutes at the National University, with the final selection being made by the Governing Board.[24]

Since 1945, there has been no evidence that the President or other members of the government have pressured the Governing Board in its selection of a rector.[25] On the other hand, several sources indicate that a rector, once designated, cannot serve without the support of the President of Mexico.[26] If we accept the contention that the President has not been directly involved in the designation of the rector since 1933, the importance of the University Council, and later the Governing Board, becomes apparent. An examination of the membership of the latter organization during the period covered by this study reveals the prominence of former deans as well as public men (Table 7.15). We are not arguing that public men who are members of the governing board are influenced by political considerations in their choice of rectors and deans, but only that public men are well represented and play a large part in the selection process. Furthermore, deans are responsible for the selection of new professors in their schools. Therefore, both deans and rectors need to be examined to determine who they are and the extent to which they have had careers outside of academia.

The directors of the National Preparatory School, like its notable professors, are similar in educational backgrounds, having graduated, for the most part, from the National University. Like the professors, they came from the pre-1920s generations, only two graduating after 1920 (Table 7.16). Public men were predominant among these directors, but, as was true of notable preparatory professors, a sizeable minority had no public careers. Not surprisingly, many of the National Preparatory School directors were singled out by students as notable professors. Professors who influenced their students and administrators who influenced the careers of professors and students, were often one and the same. Educational leaders, because they must have degrees in order to succeed, are by definition a small elite in Mexican society. That elite is drawn from the same group which produces public men in Mexico. Furthermore, within this group, certain families produce more than one prominent academician or public man, such as Antonio and Alfonso Caso, Miguel and Enrique Schultz, or Nabor and Antonio Carrillo Flores.

If we examine other prestigious academic positions in Mexico, in particular that of rector and secretary general of the National University, we again encounter a homogeneous background. Since 1910, all rectors of the National University have been graduates of UNAM. Two groups have pro-

Table 7.15

Governing Boards of the National University, 1945 to 1966

Name of Member	1945	Boards Served On 1948	1952	1954	1966	Level Reached in Government Service
Aceves Parra, Salvador					*X*	High-level
Ayala González, Abraham		X		X		High-level
Baz, Gustavo			X	X		High-level
Carrillo Flores, Antonio		X				High-level
Casas Alatriste, Roberto			X	X		High-level
Caso, Alfonso		X		X		High-level
Caso, Antonio	X					Middle-level
Castillo Miranda, Wilfrido					X	NI[a]
Castro Estrada, José					X	High-level
Chávez, Ignacio	X	X				Middle-level
De la Cueva, Mario		X				High-level
Fraga, Gabino	X	X	X	X		High-level
García, Trinidad		X				High-level
Garrido Díaz, Luis			X	X	X	Middle-level
Gómez Morín, Manuel	X					High-level
González Herrejón, Salvador			X			None
Hernández, Mariano		X				NI
Hiriart Balderrama, Fernando					X	High-level
Mariscal, Federico	X	X				None
Martínez Báez, Antonio	X	X	X	X	X	High-level
Martínez Tornel, Pedro		X				High-level
Mascanzoni, Bruno			X			None
Millán, Alfonso			X		X	NI
Noriega, Alfonso			X		X	Middle-level
Ocaranza, Fernando	X					None
O'Gorman, Edmundo			X	X	X	None
Orozco, Fernando			X		X	NI
Pous Ortiz, Raul					X	Middle-level
Quijano, Alejandro		X				None
Reyes, Alfonso		X				Middle-level
Sandoval Vallarta, Manuel	X	X		X		High-level
Sepulveda, Bernardo					X	NI
Silva Herzog, Jesús	X	X	X	X		High-level
Torres Gaytan, Ricardo					X	High-level
Vázquez, Mariano			X			NI
Villagran García, José				X	X	None
Zavala, Silvio				X		High-level
Zubirán, Salvador			X			High-level

[a]NI = No information.

vided an important number of rectors: the Ateneo graduates of 1907–09, and the "children" of the Ateneo or the 1918–20 graduates (Table 7.17). While the law school has contributed the vast majority of rectors, the medical school has contributed a noteworthy number of rectors as well, including the most recent. The only other school represented among the rectors during this period is the School of Engineering. Again, we can readily recognize the names of many rectors, notable professors in their respective fields and directors of the National Preparatory School. Four of the rectors held this latter position during the years 1911 to 1944, and nine were deans at the National University. The majority who repeated high-level academic positions were high-level officeholders in public life as well. Although our data are less complete for secretaries general, the second ranking academic position at the National

Table 7.16

Education and Public Careers of Directors of the National Preparatory School, 1911 to 1944[a]

Dates as Director	Name of Professor	Institution & Year Graduated	Level Reached in Government Service	Years in Government
1910–1911	Manuel Flores	UNAM 1880	High-level	20
1911–1912	Francisco Echegaray y A.	UNAM 1860s	Low-level	NI
1912–1913	Valentín Gama	UNAM 1893	Middle-level	10
1913–1913	Miguel V. Avalos	NI[e] NI	NI	NI
1913–1914	Genaro García	UNAM 1891	Middle-level	6
1914–1914	José Vasconcelos[b]	UNAM 1907	High-level	12
1915–1915	Antonio Caso	UNAM 1906	Middle-level	2
1915–1915	Erasmo Castellaños Quinto	UNAM 1903	None	None
1915–1915	Enrique Octavio Aragón[c]	UNAM 1904	None	None
1915–1915	Miguel E. Schultz[d]	UNAM 1876	None	None
1915–1916	Mariano Lozano	NI NI	NI	NI
1916–1917	Rodrigo Cárdenas	NI NI	NI	NI
1917–1920	Moisés Sáenz	Columbia U.	High-level	20
1920–1921	Ezequiel A. Chávez	UNAM 1891	High-level	16
1922–1924	Vicente Lombardo Toledano	UNAM 1919	High-level	40
1924–1928	Ángel Vallarino	NI NI	NI	NI
1929–1929	Alfonso Caso	UNAM 1919	High-level	30
1929–1933	Pedro de Alba	UNAM NI	High-level	15
1933–1935	José Luis Osorio Mondragón	Military College	None	None
1935–1937	Manuel García Pérez	NI NI	NI	NI
1937–1938	José de Lille	UNAM 1929	None	None
1938–1942	Samuel García	UNAM 1896	None	None
1942–1944	Francisco Villagran	UNAM 1922	Middle-level	NI

[a]After 1944, the director of the National Preparatory School became the director general of Preparatory Education. Later, in the 1950s, the preparatory school began expanding into different locations.
[b]José Vasconcelos also served as an interim director in February, 1922.
[c]Enrique Octavio Aragón also served as interim director from December, 1921 to February, 1922.
[d]Miguel E. Schultz is the father of the distinguished professor of ENP, Enrique Schultz.
[e]NI = No information.

University, they show patterns similar to those found among rectors (Table 7.18). The position of secretary general has seldom led men to the position of rector, since deanships have been far more useful as stepping stones to the rectorship.

Looking at the other public university most responsible for the education of future public leaders, the National Polytechnic Institute, we find its directors have been younger, recent graduates, with fewer years in public service (Table 7.19). Because of the emphasis on technical subjects at IPN, particularly in all fields of engineering, most of the administrators have had engineering degrees. However, IPN is too young to have built up a pattern of recruiting its own graduates as directors. Typical of recent administrators is José Antonio Padilla Segura, Director General of the national steel company Altos Hornos under Luis Echeverría and José López Portillo. Padilla Segura

Table 7.17

**Education and Public Careers of Rectors of the National University
From 1911 to 1976**

Dates as Rector	Name of Rector	Institution & Year Graduated	Level Reached in Government Service	Years in Government
1910–13	Joaquín Eguía Lis	UNAM 1861	Middle-level	5
1913–14	Ezequiel A. Chávez	UNAM 1891	High-level	6
1914–15	Valentín Gama	UNAM 1893	Middle-level	10
1915–20	José Natividad Macias	UNAM NI	High-level	8
1920–20	Balbino Dávalas	UNAM 1880s	Middle-level	10
1920–21	José Vasconcelos	UNAM 1907	High-level	5
1921–23	Antonio Caso	UNAM 1909	High-level	30
1923–24	Ezequiel A. Chávez	UNAM 1891	High-level	6
1924–28	Alfonso Pruneda	UNAM 1903	Middle-level	8
1928–29	Antonio Castro Leal	UNAM 1919	Middle-level	10
1929–31	Ignacio García Téllez	UNAM 1921	High-level	24
1931–33	Roberto Medellín Ostos	UNAM 1908	High-level	6
1933–34	Manuel Gómez Morín	UNAM 1919	High-level	10
1934–35	Fernando Ocaranza	UNAM 1900[a]	None	None
1935–39	Luis Chico Goerne	UNAM 1918	High-level	22
1939–40	Gustavo Baz	UNAM 1920	High-level	25
1940–42	*Mario de la Cueva y de la R.*	UNAM 1925	High-level	7
1942–44	Rodulfo Brito Foucher	UNAM 1923	High-level	3
1944–45	Alfonso Caso	UNAM 1919	High-level	30
1945–46	Genaro Fernández MacGregor	UNAM 1907	Middle-level	20
1946–48	*Salvador Zubirán Anchondo*	UNAM 1922	High-level	28
1948–52	*Luis Garrido Díaz*	UNAM 1922	Middle-level	24
1952–61	Nabor Carrillo Flores	UNAM 1939	Middle-level	15
1961–66	*Ignacio Chávez Sánchez*	UNAM 1920	Middle-level	20
1966–70	Javier Barros Sierra	UNAM 1943	High-level	6
1970–72	Pablo González Casanova	UNAM 1945	None	None
1973–76	Guillermo Soberón Acevedo	UNAM 1948	None	None

[a]Fernando Ocaranza completed three years of study at the National Medical School and two years at the Military Medical School. It is unclear whether he graduated from the latter college.

was educated in various locales because of the travels of his father, a middle-class entrepreneur in agriculture and commerce. He attended secondary school at the Higher School of Mechanical and Electrical Engineering of IPN, but completed his degree at the National University. Despite the fact that he worked at Mexican Electrical Laboratories while in school, he was an exceptional student. After completing his degree in electrical engineering in 1942, he became a professor at both IPN and UNAM. He worked as an engineer for the National Irrigation Commission, as was typical of his generation, but he soon emphasized his academic career as Chief of Laboratories for the Higher School of Mechanical and Electrical Engineering of IPN. After being appointed as Director of IPN in 1963, he left to serve as the Secretary of Communication and Transportation in the Díaz Ordaz administration. This ministry has been a home for several distinguished IPN administrators, including Eugenio Méndez Docurro, who preceded Padilla as Director of IPN but served as his Subsecretary in the Secretariat of Communication and Transportation.

Table 7.18

Education and Public Careers of Secretaries General of the National University, 1929 to 1976

Dates as Secretary General	Name of Administrator	Institution & Year Graduated	Level Reached in Government Service	Years in Government
1929	*Daniel Cosío Villegas*	San Nicolás 1925	Middle-level	8
1930	José López Lira	Guanajuato NI	High-level	30
1932	Joaquín Gallo	UNAM 1904	Low-level	30
1932–33	Julio Jímenez Rueda	UNAM 1920	Middle-level	NI
1933	*Salvador Azuela*	UNAM 1930	Middle-level	11
1934	*Antonio Armendáriz*	UNAM 1932	High-level	30
1935–38	Manuel Gual Vidal	UNAM 1926	High-level	15
1938–40	*Mario de la Cueva*	UNAM 1925	High-level	7
1940–42	José Torres Torrija	NI NI	NI	NI
1942	*Alfonso Noriega*	UNAM 1929	Middle-level	15
1942–44	Samuel Ramírez Moreno	NI NI	NI	NI
1944	Julio Jímenez Rueda	UNAM 1920	Middle-level	NI
1944–46	Eduardo García Máynez	UNAM 1931	None	None
1946–47	Francisco González Castro	NI NI	NI	NI
1947–48	José Rivera Pérez Campos	UNAM 1931	High-level	40
1948–52	Juan José González Bustamante	ELD 1929	High-level	36
1952–53	Raúl Carrancá y Trujillo	Madrid 1920s	High-level	15
1953–61	Efrén C. del Pozo	NI NI	NI	NI
1961–66	*Roberto Mantilla Molina*	UNAM 1933	Middle-level	8
1966–70	*Fernando Solana Morales*[a]	UNAM 1964	Middle-level	10
1970–72	Manuel Madrazo Garamendi	NI NI	NI	NI
1972–76	Fernando Pérez Correa	NI NI	NI	NI

[a]Solana was appointed as Secretary of Industry & Commerce by President López Portillo. In 1977, he became Secretary of Public Education.

The deans of the National University, as represented by the schools of law, economics, and engineering, have been very much involved in public careers. Well over half of the law school deans have held top-level public offices. They have been UNAM educated, graduates from the classes that produced important public and academic generations: 1919, 1925, 1929, and 1932 (Table 7.20). While deans of the national engineering school often had active public careers, even at high levels, public men were not as well represented in the deanship of engineering as in the schools of law and economics (Table 7.21). These deans are well represented among the notable professors who taught at the School of Engineering.

Deans from the National School of Economics, with the exception of the most recent dean, have consistently had lengthy and important public careers, more so than men in any other academic post we have examined in this chapter. This may be true because of the 178 students who graduated from this school between the years 1929 and 1951, 93 percent followed careers in the public sector.[27] Since deans generally serve at the school from which they graduate, it would be surprising to find someone without a public career. It is still significant, however, that these deans have been prominent as public men and notable professors (Table 7.22).

Table 7.19

Education and Public Careers of Directors General of the National Polytechnic Institute, 1937 to 1976

Dates as Director	Name of Director	Institution & Year Graduated	Level Reached in Government Service	Years in Government
1937–1937	Roberto Medellín Ostos	UNAM 1908	High-level	5
1938–1939	Miguel Bernard	Military College 1889	High-level	8
1940–1940	Manuel Cerrillo Valdivia	NI NI	NI	NI
1940–1942	Wilfrido Massieu[a]	Military College 1903	Low-level	20
1942–1943	José Laguardia	NI NI	NI	NI
1943–1946	Manuel Sandoval Vallarta	MIT 1921	High-level	9
1946–1948	Gustavo Alvarado Pies	NI NI	NI	NI
1948–1950	Alejandro Guillot Schiaffino	UNAM 1937	Middle-level	8
1950–1953	Juan Manuel Ramírez Caraza	NI NI	High-level	14
1953–1956	Rodolfo Hernández Corzo	IPN 1940	Middle-level	10
1956–1959	Alejo Peralta Díaz	NI NI	NI	NI
1959–1963	Eugenio Méndez Docurro	IPN 1948	High-level	14
1963–1964	José Antonio Padilla S.	UNAM 1942	High-level	12
1964–1970	Guillermo Massieu H.	IPN 1946	None	None
1970–1973	Manuel Zorrilla Carcaño	NI NI	None	None
1973–1976	José Gerstl Valenzuela	NI NI	NI	NI

[a]Wilfrido is the father of Guillermo Massieu Helguera.
Key: NI = No information; IPN = National Polytechnic Institute.

Table 7.20

Education and Public Careers of National School of Law Deans
From 1911 to 1976

Dates as Dean	Name of Dean	Institution & Year Graduated	Level Reached in Government Service	Years in Government
1903–11	Pablo Macedo	UNAM 1870s	Middle-level	5
1911–12	Julio García	UNAM 1880s	High-level	20
1912–12	Pedro Lascuraín Paredes	UNAM 1880	High-level	10
1912–13	Luis Cabrera	UNAM 1901	High-level	10
1913–14	Julio García	UNAM 1880s	High-level	20
1914–14	José Natividad Macias	UNAM 1890s	High-level	6
1914–15	Julio García	UNAM 1880s	High-level	20
1915–16	Juan N. Frías	NI[a] NI	High-level	NI
1916–16	Fernando Lizardi	UNAM 1906	High-level	30
1916–17	Antonio Alcocer	NI NI	NI	NI
1917–19	Fernando Lizardi	UNAM 1906	High-level	30
1919–20	Manuel Mateos Alarcón	UNAM 1870s	None	None
1920–22	Alejandro Quijano	UNAM 1907	None	None
1922–25	Manuel Gómez Morín	UNAM 1919	High-level	10
1925–25	Aquiles Elorduy	UNAM 1890s	High-level	15
1925–25	Julio Guerrero	UNAM 1889	Middle-level	15
1927–27	Luis Sánchez Ponton	Puebla 1913	High-level	35
1927–29	Aquiles Elorduy	UNAM 1890s	High-level	15
1929–29	Narciso Bassols	UNAM 1919	High-level	20
1929–33	Luis Chico Goerne	UNAM 1918	High-level	22
1933–34	Rodulfo Brito Foucher	UNAM 1923	High-level	3
1934–35	*Trinidad García*	UNAM 1919	High-level	10
1935–38	Emilio Pardo Aspe	NI NI	NI	NI
1938–39	Agustín García López	UNAM 1923	High-level	15
1939–41	Manuel Gual Vidal	UNAM 1926	High-level	15
1941–43	Vicente Peniche López	Yucatán 1920	Low-level	10
1943–44	*Alfonso Noriega*	UNAM 1929	Middle-level	15
1944–45	*Antonio Carrillo Flores*	UNAM 1929	High-level	42
1945–48	Virgilio Domínguez	UNAM 1929	NI	NI
1949–51	José Castillo Larranaga	UNAM 1922	High-level	25
1951–53	*Mario de la Cueva*	UNAM 1925	High-level	7
1953–58	*Roberto Mantilla Molina*	UNAM 1933	Middle-level	8
1958–62	Ricardo García Villalobos	UNAM 1932	Middle-level	30
1962–66	*Cesár Sepulveda*	UNAM 1944	Middle-level	14
1966–66	Ignacio Medina	NI NI	NI	NI
1966–70	Ernesto Flores Zavala	UNAM 1932	Low-level	5
1970–73	Fernando Ojesto	NI	NI	NI
1973–76	Pedro Astudillo Ursua	NI NI	NI	NI

[a]NI = No information.

Conclusions

Public men dominate among university administrators and notable professors at the National University. Because the large majority of professors seen as most important by students who became political leaders were middle-level and upper-level public leaders, and because the administrators at the schools most important in the education of political leaders also had public careers, it is impossible to separate the National University and public life when looking at leadership and recruitment in academia and in politics. While political considerations have at times affected the careers of students or professors, the most important effect of this interrelationship is structural. This structural impact is illustrated through a review of several of the important elements of

Table 7.21

Education and Public Careers of Deans of the National School of Engineering From 1914 to 1970

Dates as Dean	Name of Dean	Institution & Year Graduated		Level Reached in Government Service	Years in Government
1914	Alfonso de Ibarrola	NI[a]	NI	NI	NI
1914–15	Carlos Daza	NI	NI	NI	NI
1915–23	Mariano Moctezuma	UNAM	1905	High-level	6
1923–25	Valentín Gama	UNAM	1893	Middle-level	10
1925–29	José A. Cuevas	UNAM	1916	NI	NI
1929–33	Mariano Moctezuma	UNAM	1905	High-level	6
1933	Claudio Castro	UNAM	1892	None	None
1934	Valentín Gama	UNAM	1893	Middle-level	10
1934–35	Ignacio Avilez	UNAM	1914	None	None
1935–38	Federico Ramos	UNAM	1903	Middle-level	31
1938–42	Mariano Moctezuma	UNAM	1905	High-level	6
1942–46	Pedro Martínez Tornel	UNAM	1918	High-level	30
1946–51	Alberto J. Flores	UNAM	1929	Middle-level	15
1951–55	José L. de Parres	UNAM	1920	Middle-level	20
1955–59	Javier Barros Sierra	UNAM	1943	High-level	12
1959–66	*Antonio Dovalí Jaime*	UNAM	1929	High-level	40
1966–70	Manuel Paulín Ortiz	NI	NI	NI	NI

[a]NI = No information.

Table 7.22

Education and Public Careers of Deans of the National School of Economics From 1929 to 1976

Dates as Dean	Name	Institution & Year Graduated		Level Reached in Government Service	Years in Government
1929–38	Enrique González Aparicio	UNAM	1928	Middle-level	10
1938–40	Mario Sousa	UNAM	1925	High-level	27
1940–42	Jesús Silva Herzog	UNAM	1919	High-level	22
1942–44	*Alfonso Pulido Islas*	UNAM	1939	High-level	40
1944–53	*Gilberto Loyo*	UNAM	1923	High-level	40
1953–59	Ricardo Torres Gaytán	UNAM	1941	High-level	19
1959–65	Octaviano Campos y Salas	UNAM	1944	High-level	30
1965–67	Horacio Flores de la Peña	UNAM	1946	High-level	30
1967–69	Gustavo Romero Kolbeck	UNAM	1946	High-level	20
1969–71	Ifigenia Martínez de N.	UNAM	1945	Middle-level	20
1971–76	José Luis Ceceña	NI	NI	NI	NI

[a]NI = No information.

the recruitment process. The National University and in particular the professional schools that have graduated public men are the locus of much of the political recruitment and contribute to later career mobility of political leaders. Attendance at the National University automatically enhances the ability to get into the political system and to succeed in it. In this sense, the National University is both a funnel and a sieve for future political leaders, giving professors-public men a chance to measure the abilities of their students and to promote individual careers. A person cannot be recruited through the university if he is not in the university to begin with.

The university environment also tends to have a homogenizing influence, not in the sense that it makes all students and professors think alike, but that professors and public men, as well as the majority of students who become public men and who actually complete their education, have urban, middle-class backgrounds, and emerge from their university experiences with a number of values that tie them together.[28] These socializing elements help to cement together different generations of Mexican political leaders, providing for a thread that is not obvious in the continuity of Mexico's political leadership. Thus, because students who become political leaders are most influenced by political leaders who are part-time but often long-term educators, they can pass on their experiences and values to a younger generation of leaders who, in turn (following the path of their mentors as teachers-public men), pass on these or similar beliefs to the succeeding generation. Perhaps what is most important here is not an ideological education in terms of radical or conservative political beliefs, but rather the style or pragmatic behavior learned from mentors. Those who want to succeed in the Mexican political system, by their third or fourth year in professional school, have allowed themselves, in terms of their behavior, to conform to the practices of that system, rather than to challenge it. They do not mold the system; it molds them. Ideological differences, within certain boundaries, have always been tolerated among political leaders within the official party system, and have rarely been the focus for promotion within the political structure since the views of many successful leaders are not well known, nor do they appear to have had any major impact on the structure of agency bureaucracies or the political system itself. Instead, the emphasis is placed on interpersonal political skills, administrative abilities, individual discipline, and loyalty to upwardly mobile mentors.

Because the internal structure of the National University is very similar to the series of pyramids of political groups described in chapter ii, ascendency in academia often relies on many of the same patterns of recruitment and career mobility described for political leaders.[29] The interchange of public men in academia with professors and administrators in public life has created an environment whereby the university becomes a testing ground for the political skills of students as leaders, activists and intellectuals; and for professors who hope to use academic careers as a stepping stone to successful political careers. Future political leaders know that the university provides them with an alternate career route, and the right deanship or rectorship can and does often lead to public positions, provided few stumbling blocks are encountered during an individual's tenure. Because the rectorship of the National University involves one of the most complex political situations to manage, and has proved difficult to handle, many politically career-minded individuals have turned it down, rather than take the risk of ending their careers.[30] As long as the university continues to serve as an institution for recruiting political leaders and for promoting political careers, it is unlikely that the National University will make any progress in separating itself from political affairs.

NOTES TO CHAPTER 7

[1] See my article, "The Cabinet and the *Técnico* in Mexico and the United States," *Journal of Comparative Administration* 3 (August 1971): 206.

[2] See E. Wight Bakke, "Students on the March: The Cases of Mexico and Colombia," *Sociology of Education* 37 (Spring 1964), p. 216; and Arthur Liebman, et al, *Latin American University Students: A Six Nation Study* (Cambridge: Harvard University Press, 1972), p. 75.

[3] Liebman, *Latin American University Students*, pp. 80–3.

[4] In his study of regional universities, King found that 69 percent of the professors attended public junior high schools, and 78 percent attended public preparatory schools. See Richard G. King, *The Provincial Universities of Mexico* (New York: Praeger, 1971), p. 60.

[5] Baltasar Dromundo, *Mi calle de San Ildefonso* (Mexico: Editorial Guaranía, 1956), p. 139; Carlos Morales Díaz, *Quién es quién en la nomenclatura de la ciudad de México* (Mexico: Costa-Amica, 1971), pp. 113–14; and personal interview with Manuel R. Palacios, Mexico City, July 1, 1975.

[6] *Excélsior,* July 16, 1973, p. 4; Luis Calderón Vega, *Los 7 sabios de Mexico* (Mexico, 1961), p. 8; Enríque Krause, *Caudillos culturales en la revolución mexicana* (Mexico: Siglo XXI, 1976); James W. Wilkie and Edna Monzón de Wilkie, *Mexico visto en el siglo xx* (Mexico: Instituto Mexicano de Investigaciones Económicas, 1969), pp. 199–203; and Robert Paul Millon, "Vicente Lombardo Toledano: Critic of the Mexican Revolution" (unpublished Ph.D. dissertation, University of North Carolina, 1963).

[7] King also found that in provincial universities over half of the professors were under the age of thirty (*The Provincial Universities,* pp. 58–9).

[8] Lucio Mendieta y Núñez and José Gómez Robledo, *Problemas de la Universidad* (México: UNAM, 1948), p. 165.

[9] Even Gómez Morín's father was not a typical working-class member since he saved enough money to start his own store. Although he died when Gómez Morín was still an infant, Gómez Morín and his mother received some income after the sale of his father's store. See Enrique Krause, *Caudillos culturales,* p. 39.

[10] Mexico City, Universidad Nacional Autónoma de México, *Anuario, 1931–32* (México: UNAM, 1931), pp. 69–71.

[11]Mexico City, Universidad Nacional Autónoma de México, *Anuario General, 1954* (México: UNAM, 1954), pp. 135–9.

[12]Ernesto Flores Zavala, *El Estudiante Inquieto* (México, 1972), pp. 262–3.

[13]Luis Calderón Vega, *Los 7 sabios*, p. 58; *Hispano Americano*, May 28, 1956, p. 12; *Diccionario Porrúa* (Mexico: Editorial Porrúa, 1970), p. 2375; Ronald Hilton, ed., *Who's Who in Latin America: Mexico* (Stanford: Stanford University Press, 1946), p. 21; and Roderic A. Camp, *Mexican Political Biographies, 1935–1975* (Tucson: University of Arizona Press, 1976), pp. 59–60.

[14]Lucio Mendieta y Núñez, *Historia de la Facultad de Derecho* (Mexico: UNAM, 1956), pp. 244–45; Narciso Bassols, *Obras* (Mexico: Fondo de Cultura Económica, 1964), p. 2ff.; Jesús Silva Herzog, *Una vida en la vida de México* (Mexico: Siglo Veintiuno, 1972), pp. 139, 142; and letter from José Ricardo Zevada, Mexico City, May 4, 1973.

[15]Luis Calderón Vega, *Los 7 sabios*, p. 50; James W. Wilkie and Edna Monzón de Wilkie, *Mexico visto*, p. 144 ff.; *Hoy*, April 29, 1972, p. 3; *Hispano Americano*, April 24, 1972, p. 21; *Justicia*, January, 1973; Vicente Fuentes Díaz, *Los partidos políticos en México* (México: Editorial Altiplano, 1969), p. 296ff.; and Manuel Gómez Morín, *1915 y otros ensayos* (Mexico: Editorial Jus, 1973).

[16]Manuel Pallares Ramírez, *La Escuela Nacional de Economía, esbozo histórico 1929– 1952* (Mexico, 1952).

[17]Roderic A. Camp, "The National School of Economics and Public Life in Mexico," *The Latin American Research Review* **10** (Fall 1975): 139.

[18]Larissa Lomnitz, "Conflict and Mediation in a Latin American University," *Journal of Inter-American Studies and World Affairs* **19** (August 1977): 323.

[19]Ernesto Flores Zavala, *El estudiante inquieto*, pp. 265–6.

[20]Jesús Silva Herzog, *Una historia de la Universidad de México y sus problemas* (Mexico: Siglo Veintiuno, 1974), p. 19.

[21]*Ibid.*, pp. 55–6.

[22]See Ramiro Aguirre Santoscoy, *Historia y sociología de la educación* (México: Secretaria de Educación Pública, 1963), p. 210, for a comment on the significance of this relationship.

[23]Jesús Silva Herzog, *Una historia*, p. 63.

[24]*Ibid.*, p. 86.

[25]Luis Garrido Díaz, *El Tiempo de mi vida, memorias* (México: Porrúa, 1974), p. 370.

[26]See Silva Herzog for the example of Salvador Zubirán and President Alemán in 1948; and for Ignacio Chávez and President Díaz Ordaz in 1966 (*Una historia*, pp. 96, 143–4). Benveniste, in his *Bureaucracy and National Planning* (New York: Praeger, 1970), p. 44, suggests that the rector reports directly to the president.

[27]Roderic A. Camp, "The National School of Economics and Public Life in Mexico," p. 144.

[28]Roderic A. Camp, "The Values and Ideological Beliefs of Mexican Political Leaders Since 1946," paper presented at the Midwest Association of Latin Americanists, St Louis, 1977.

[29]Larissa Lomnitz, "Conflict and Mediation," p. 333.

[30]See Jesús Silva Herzog's statement that in 1948, many individuals refused the rectorship, including Francisco González de la Vega (*Una historia*, pp. 96–7). Furthermore, the president and his collaborators may make it difficult for a rector to survive his tenure by slowing down or cutting off the flow of funds to the university. See Javier Barros Sierra, *1968* (Mexico: Siglo XXI, 1972), p. 116.

8. Education and Public Life: Conclusions

In the introduction, I set forth a number of hypotheses concerning the relationship between education and public life in Mexico since 1911. In light of the data presented in the previous chapters, some comments can be made on the significance of those findings for understanding the Mexican political system in the past and in the future.

I have argued that the typical political leader in Mexico is geographically representative of the Mexican population by region, but that he comes predominantly from an urban background. Although some leaders are from humble backgrounds, the more typical political leader, especially in recent years, has come from a middle-class family. An urban birthplace and middle- or upper-class background has given the prospective Mexican political leader access to education, especially higher education, an essential prerequisite among recent political leaders. Even in the earlier years of Mexico's political development, most political leaders were educated at the major preparatory and university institutions in Mexico. This supposition is borne out by the data; more than three-fourths of Mexico's leadership has been so educated. However, since university education in general is limited to such a small number of Mexicans, political leadership has and will continue to come from a small pool of the population. Therefore, I would predict that political leaders in Mexico will continue to come increasingly from urban backgrounds and from middle-class parents. This prediction is supported by data from the National University over time, which indicate little change in the socio-economic status of the general student body from which Mexico recruits a sizeable number of its political leaders. In the 1940s, an examination of 505 students and their parents revealed that 17 percent came from professional families, and 37 percent from white-collar workers.[1] In the late 1960s, Lieb- man concluded that 15 percent came from professional families and 40 per- cent from white-collar parents. He notes that those students from professional families are disproportionately represented at the university when compared with the percentage of professional people in the Mexican labor force.[2]

Although the majority of political leaders are recruited from the Na- tional University, they are not recruited equally from each social-economic group represented at the National University.[3] The overwhelming majority of political leaders with an education from the National University came from middle-class backgrounds, and more than 15 percent had parents with profes- sional occupations. This can be explained, in part, by the fact that the com- position of the student body graduating from UNAM is different from that entering UNAM or attending the university at any one time. Students from higher socioeconomic backgrounds are more likely to graduate, and public men are recruited from among graduates. The importance of these conclu- sions is that they indicate that recruitment is being increasingly restricted to a certain type of individual. This has been illustrated recently by an interesting change in the state constitution of Chiapas, which in 1973 required that the governor have a university education.[4] In a country where no more than two percent of the population has such an education, viable candidates would automatically come from a tiny minority. There is no evidence presented in this book to suggest the significance of the homogeneity in the educational background of Mexico's political leadership on policy making. But given the availability of these data, scholars need to examine the relationship between background and educational characteristics of public men and their beliefs about policy issues to determine the effect, if any, of one upon the other. Furthermore, students of intellectual history should examine the educational environment at the National University to determine its impact on future public men.[5]

I further hypothesized that the National Preparatory School and the National University had become the single most important institutions for recruiting men and women who sought careers in Mexican public life. The majority of high-level public men passed through these two institutions. Pub- lic agencies have used the National University to find and recruit the best students. Greenberg describes how this was accomplished by the Ministry of Hydraulic Resources:

> Promising students would be approached by the Commission, and later the Ministry, as early as their sophomore or junior years in college, and told of the benefits which would be theirs if they chose the CNI [Na- tional Irrigation Commission] as the vehicle to launch their careers. Since the number of potential candidates was so small, the CNI found

itself engaged in heated competition with numerous other government agencies, most notably the Ministry of Public Works and the Federal Electric Commission.[6]

The student at the National University, before graduating, is already competing for a future career, and government agencies in turn are competing for the most promising students. The fact that the university can and does provide students with an opportunity to obtain the most promising careers in public life is known to knowledgeable Mexicans, and therefore, the competition is keen to get into the university—not because it offers the best education, but rather because it provides the best opportunity for a promising future. E. Wight Bakke, in his study of university students, confirms this point:

> Once the possibility of students serving their political "apprenticeship" in the university is established, the process feeds on itself. University life attracts those with political ambitions and *for this purpose*. Registration as a student becomes *the* accepted way of preparing for and entering political life. Virtually every political leader of note has been a student leader.[7]

The university is indeed an apprenticeship for public careers, but while we do not believe that all successful public men were student leaders *in the political sense*, most distinguished themselves in some manner at the university, whether in class, intellectual circles, literary activities, oratory, sports, or student politics. When public men were asked if their university education prepared them for public life, they often responded that the experience of being a student itself was equal to or more important than the formal process of learning, and that education at the public university was a microcosm of the experiences of public life in general.

It is obvious from the data that the military and Revolutionary contacts were responsible for the careers of only a small number of successful public men after 1935. And because political leaders with union careers are only a small minority of the prominent men in Mexico, only a small number of persons entered public life through that channel. The remaining institutions that served recruitment are difficult to separate; they are the official party and the federal bureaucracy. The official party has historically provided opportunities for greater numbers of men and women with rural backgrounds, humble parents, and low levels of education than those with urban backgrounds, middle-class parents, and higher education. The party has been responsible for recruiting political leaders at the state and local level, incorporating them in party or state organizations, where they have worked their way into party leadership positions and run for electoral offices. But the official party at the national level primarily recruits political leadership through its national youth sector at the university, most members of which fit the description of student leaders given by Wight Bakke. In reality, the largest group of students who follow successful public careers are incorporated directly into the federal bureaucracy, and are only nominally members of the official party, or do not become members until later in their careers.

Career patterns within the Mexican government are divided into a number of channels. While the men and women who are recruited by the official party often follow electoral careers as deputies, senators and governors, or party careers, a smaller number make their reputation in the federal bureaucracy, and then become agency heads and sometimes senators and governors. Our evidence shows that a larger number of students are recruited directly into the federal bureaucracy rather than into the official party by the agencies themselves, with the help of professors and co-students, and not through representatives of the official party. The university, rather than the party, has served as a recruiting ground for the greatest number of successful public men. This is significant because the political leadership is growing more homogeneous and the universities are becoming more important in this process. A careful analysis of political leadership in recent years would show that those political leaders who are in positions of public authority, and control the most resources in the public sector, are not the men recruited by the party, but instead, have been recruited at the university and have followed bureaucratic careers.*

The diversity in leadership to which the party has contributed in the past is rapidly declining. This change is illustrated in the leadership of the official party itself in the last four years. The selection by President Echeverría of Jesús Reyes Heroles as president of the CEN of PRI is indicative of such a change. Reyes Heroles attended the National University from 1939 to 1944, graduating with an honorable mention in law. He joined the official party as a first-year law student in 1939, beginning his political career the same year as an auxiliary secretary to the private secretary of the president of the official party. He held this position under two party presidents until 1944, when he graduated from the University and became an adviser to the Secretary of Labor. He then served as an Alternate President of the Federal Arbitration and Conciliation Board. For a short time, he became Mayor of Tuxpan, Veracruz, and then served as Director of the Mexican Book Institute from 1949–53. During the ensuing years, he held a number of important technical posts, culminating in his designation as technical Subdirector General of IMSS. In 1961, he was elected as a federal deputy from his home state of Veracruz. After completing his term, the President designated him Director General of PEMEX. He served as director during the entire period from 1964 to 1970, and

---

*See *Proceso's* recent statement that of the top 727 government officials in Mexico, only 75 had been active in PRI. August 7, 1978, p. 20.

in the following administration, became head of the new industrial complex of Ciudad Sahagún. He completed advanced work at the University of Buenos Aires, and while advancing through these bureaucratic positions, he taught general legal theory at the National University and wrote six books and 39 articles. He was not typical of past leaders of the official party, since he held only two minor electoral posts during a 32-year career in public life and was known for his intellectual pursuits.[8]

In 1975, Reyes Heroles left the presidency of the official party to become director general of the cabinet-level IMSS. He was replaced by an even more atypical party leader, Porfirio Muñoz Ledo, under the influence of the presidential candidate, José López Portillo. Porfirio Muñoz Ledo's career focuses entirely on the university and the federal bureaucracy. A member of the 1955 graduating class at the National Law School, and a student of Jesús Silva Herzog, he began teaching at the Women's University and the National Preparatory School in 1950. He obtained his first government job as an assistant in the press office of the Secretary of National Properties in 1950. He was co-editor, with several other prominent students who later became public men, of the magazine *Medio Siglo*. After graduating in 1955, he went to the University of Paris, where he studied politics and economics and served as a visiting professor in economic and social development. In 1960, he received a Ph.D. in law from the University of Paris. He returned to Mexico, where he held a variety of technical posts, becoming Secretary General of the IMSS in 1966. Under President Echeverría, he served as Subsecretary of the Presidency, and then moved to the Secretariat of Labor. He has never held *any* electoral position in Mexico, and his only position with the official party has been as an adviser to the political studies section of the Institute of Political, Economic, and Social Studies of PRI.[9]

His career confirms a trend that is occuring in Mexican political leadership, where for the first time, public leaders with primarily bureaucratic careers are taking over the highest party positions. This pattern is not confined to party leadership, but is reflected dramatically in the presidency itself, since Luis Echeverría became the first president without prior experience as a deputy, senator, or governor, although he held an important administrative position within the party. His successor, José López Portillo, has never held an electoral position nor a party position, but like Muñoz Ledo, has only been an adviser to IEPES.

Because the university has served as the recruiting ground for the largest number of successful public men in recent years, professors and co-students have played an essential role in that process. But it is professors, rather than students, who are more important in recruiting students into public careers, largely because they already have the contacts among public men who are able to appoint promising students to government positions, or because they themselves have held such positions. In fact, as Charles Myers suggests, "it is for the purpose of recruiting and grooming these students, rather than for the money involved, that many of the high-level government técnicos are willing to teach at the National University and other institutions in the Federal District."[10] This statement is confirmed by interviews with many public men who were professors. Professors with public careers know that the university provides them with these opportunities for recruiting bright young students. But students too realize the importance of the university experience to their careers.[11] Many also realize that student political activity is one of the most prominent means of achieving visibility among professors and co-students, and begin such activities long before arriving at the preparatory school or university, a characteristic Myron Glazer found true of student activists in Chile as well.[12]

The university is not only responsible for important recruitment activities in Mexico, but it provides an environment in which the *camarilla* is often initiated, sometimes among students, but more often among professors and students. Medical professors, such as Gustavo Baz, a prominent political leader from the state of Mexico and national figure in the public health field, has recruited dozens of prominent students who followed his lead in the government bureaucracy, eventually holding high-level public offices. Ties among students and professors go back even to primary school. Earlier, we gave examples of several presidents whose companions in grammar school became cabinet officers in their administrations. During the campaign for president of José López Portillo, his primary school companions at the Benito Juárez public school in Mexico City organized a party for the candidate, and the key speaker was Arsenio Farrell, successor to López Portillo as Director General of the Federal Electric Commission during the Echeverría administration, and his fellow student at primary school.[13] The law school generations of 1938, 1939, and 1940 also organized a banquet to honor López Portillo, a member of the 1939 generation.[14] Not to be outdone, the dean of the law school organized a party with 45 to 50 professors to greet the candidate at the home of Alfonso Noriega, a distinguished professor of many prominent public men, including López Portillo, Hugo B. Margáin, Emilio Rabasa, and Luis Echeverría.*

---

*This practice is widespread among many graduates and professors of the National School who enter public life. For example, in the September 30, 1976 issue of *Excélsior,* a large advertisement appeared announcing a banquet in honor of Octavio A. Hernández, a federal deputy from 1967 to 1970 and Secretary General of the Federal District Department from 1970 to 1976. The invitation was extended to "co-workers, professors, co-students, university students and friends of Dr Hernández." Daniel Cosío Villegas, in his work, *Labor Periodística* (México: Biblioteca ERA, 1972), mentions the many banquets hosted by co-students of Luis Echeverría during his pre-candidacy in 1969.

The university has become something more than a proving ground for students and a career marketplace where students search for opportunities and professors for good students. Young, brilliant students who become professors can use the university, rather than the party or the bureaucracy, to further their public careers. This may happen by choice, or, with some men, by accident. Jesús Silva Herzog, a distinguished economist, professor emeritus, and public man describes what happened very early in his career:

> I studied a lot and I believe that my classes were good. It is curious that the students of the Chapingo school in their trips to the capital began talking about my abilities as a teacher and this is how my name became known in the capital.[15]

I am not suggesting that all professors at the National University have public careers in mind. Many, although they have been respected by students who become prominent in public life, turn down opportunities to serve in the government.[16] But others realize that the university provides a career path by which they may enter public life. This is why our data concerning successful university deans and administrators shows a predominance of public men holding those positions, which often serve as stepping stones to high-level political positions. Evidence in this book shows that public men are prominent as professors in the major public universities in Mexico. Many of the rectors of state universities are public men, especially on the local level; and among pre-candidates for governors in Mexico, it is not unlikely to encounter a state university rector.[17]

The fact that the most influential professors, in the opinion of public men in Mexico, are themselves public men, supports my contention that it is difficult to separate academic and public careers, since the most successful in one are the most successful in another. The overall significance of this finding, combined with the other conclusions reached, is that a political recruitment process has emerged in Mexico, focusing on the university, which draws disproportionately from a very narrow segment of the population. If state universities are now serving this same role, and I believe they are, then the university throughout Mexico serves a very important political role beyond that of socializing most of Mexico's public leadership.* While the National University has grown tremendously since 1955, so that the inter-

---

*Carlos A. Biebrich Torres, Governor of Sonora, 1973 to 1975, was the fifth law student to graduate from the University of Sonora. As a prominent student leader at that university in the late 1950s, he became known to Luis Encinas Johnson, rector of the school. Biebrich Torres started his public career under Encinas Johnson when he left the rectorship to become Governor of Sonora in 1961. Upon his selection as Governor, he appointed mostly school companions as his closest collaborators. Carlos Moncada, *Años de violencia en Sonora, 1955–1976* (Mexico: Editorial V Siglos, 1977), p. 108.

change and relationships described as characteristic of the 1910s, 1920s, and 1930s will not be typical of the future, state universities today are similar in size to the National University in the 1910s. Furthermore, since the National Preparatory School divided into multiple campuses in the 1950s, some campuses have earned reputations as politically active, so students can choose a campus with an emphasis on either academic or political education. Schools within the National University, even in the 1960s, were still not too large to permit considerable interchange; among excellent students and professors who are public men, relationships reminiscent of those described for earlier periods are still quite common. All of this suggests that Mexico's political system is complemented by an educational system allowing Mexico's political cal leadership to socialize and groom future generations of educators and public men, a situation which will not be changing in the immediate future.

The relationship between public universities and the political system has significant implications for the future of Mexico's political continuity. The lack of permeability in the recruitment process raises an important question. Unlike the United States, where the practice is common, business leaders seldom interchange roles in public life in Mexico.[18] The children of successful businessmen are turning away from the National University because of the political activities and unrest which have become characteristic of some of its schools.[19] Young people from lower class backgrounds are excluded because they lack access to the primary and secondary education necessary to provide them with the credentials for admittance to the National University. Whether because of its environment or because of its requirements, the University is excluding these two important groups from its pool of eligible recruits. Of the two groups, the businessmen are more important to the continuity and stability of economic policy making by the government, because of their education and economic resources. It is increasingly apparent, particularly during the Echeverría administration, that the views of government leaders and business groups are not coinciding on many issues.[20] This antagonism may be due in part to socializing experiences and viewpoints that are established at different universities.[21] Because private universities are excluded from recruiting national political leaders, students who hope to follow careers in private enterprise have little opportunity to make the contacts necessary to exchange roles in the public sector.

The only other means by which a variety of individuals may be recruited is by cooptation, which in the Mexican experience seems to be the result of efforts by an individual prominent official, especially a president. The data in chapter ii indicates that except for the early revolutionary experiences that brought people back together after they had followed different political paths, reliance on University contacts has been almost universally the means for opposition political leaders to reintegrate themselves into the official political apparatus. Kinship ties further restrict the pool of eligible individuals. Kinship ties among political families are not unusual, as demonstrated in a recent study of United States congressmen since the First Congress.[22] This same study, however, found that kinship ties had decreased, and in fact represented an approximate measure of political modernization in the United States.[23] While our data are not as precise as the data used in that study, there is no indication that kinship ties are on the decline among Mexican political leaders.

Because representatives of each group in Mexican society are being recruited by political leaders within the single most important recruiting agency, the National University, children of the poor and the successful entrepreneurs are largely excluded from the pool of eligible recruits. Mexico has a recruitment system described by Kenneth Prewitt and Heinz Eulau as career sponsorship, a process that is relatively closed and generally under the control of persons in power.[24] All candidates for high political office, whether they are in the executive, legislative, or judicial branch are appointed by the president or his collaborators already in such positions; no officeholders, therefore, are selected by a competitive primary electoral process.

Our findings concerning the recruitment process in Mexico enable us to speculate about several questions concerning the ability of the Mexican political system to function successfully. What kind of an elite governs Mexico and is that elite responsive to the needs of Mexican development? The recruitment process in any political system tends to promote certain skills or credentials among the group it selects.[25] It can be argued that Mexico's elite, in terms of skills and specialized roles, is developing faster than the political system.

In recent years, Mexico's political leadership has put greater emphasis on interpersonal, small-group skills than on mass political skills.[26] Since the recruiters at the university are a homogeneous group they naturally tend to promote students having skills similar to their own.[27] Because promotion within the Mexican political leadership is dependent on interpersonal skills used among small, informal political cliques, and on technical and organizational skills in management positions, recruits with these talents are highly successful within the political system.[28] On the other hand, middle-class, urban university students are less and less experienced or even oriented to the political skills of dealing with large groups. The manipulation of large masses has been left to a minority of political elites, educated and uneducated, who have come up through the ranks of the party and its affiliate organizations. The administrative elite generally deals with a small number of political brokers representing these groups, rather than with lower level leaders representing diverse interests within these organizations.[29] Thus, the group which holds the majority of political positions managing public resources in Mexico may well be losing sight of an important political skill, the manipulation of large groups on a face-to-face basis. Instead, the emphasis today is on the sophisticated manipulation of media, such as television, the movie industry, and newspapers.*

Most political leaders have come from a public school environment. Many have gone there by choice because they believe it provides a valuable training ground in dealing with various classes in Mexican society. This is true, especially compared with the environment one would encounter at a private university in Mexico. But our data and data from the university itself suggest that the university has become a middle-class environment, attracting students already predisposed to learn in such an environment, and largely excluding those who do not fit the pattern.

Does such an education, experienced by many of the political leaders, make them more or less responsive to the demands of Mexican society? This is an extremely difficult question to answer, and scholars have hypothesized that certain background variables and experiences may produce political leaders who are disposed to favor certain groups or react to specific policies. The state of comparative studies today reveals little hard data and few consistent patterns between background variables and policy orientations of political leaders.† In Mexico, this is even more difficult to determine since the President becomes the initiator of all legislation, and it is impossible to know whether his collaborators are truly sympathetic to various policy directions.[30]

Although it is difficult to pierce the secrecy of the decision-making process, long-term analyses of the direction of federal programs since the 1930s indicate rather definitely that some groups have borne the burden more heavily than others to achieve industrialization in Mexico. These have been primarily labor and the small farmer.[31] These are the same groups largely excluded from the recruitment process. It cannot be conclusively determined that the lack of responsiveness of the political elite to the needs of the underdeveloped rural sector and labor in general is due to their homogeneous, urban, middle-class background, but the last president to have a strong interest in the numerous, passive groups within the agricultural sector was Cárdenas, a man with little formal education, from a rural environment, who spent most of his youth in the provinces. One way of examining how political

---

*Elite recognition of the importance of media is illustrated by the establishment of a Subsecretary of Information in 1970 in the Secretariat of the Presidency, and the appointment of Fausto Zapata Loredo, who was educated at the World Press Institute, to this post.

†There is evidence, however, that those Mexicans from poor backgrounds who become educated are more decisively against the system and in favor of change. Rosalio Wences Reza found that a higher percentage of students from poor families believed that PRI has not served its original mission, that it is necessary to change the political system, that violence is indispensable to accomplish a change, and that a leftist revolutionary party would be preferable. See *El Movimiento estudiantil·y los problemas nacionales* (Mexico: Editorial Nuestro Tiempo, 1971), pp. 124–5. These, of course, are the students who are often excluded from the political recruitment process.

elites have distributed federal revenues is to look at the volume of federal revenues collected from the states that are returned to the states. The most significant conclusion is that the long-term pattern has not changed in Mexico from the 1930s through the early 1970s, and that it is a pattern disproportionately favoring the more urbanized and economically developed states.[32] The most serious question facing Mexico's political elite is whether it has the ability and the resources to allow for adequate growth simultaneously in all sectors of the society and economy.[33]

Mexico's leaders must also respond to two groups which have received considerable benefits—business and the officer corps. The late Daniel Cosío Villegas, in the first of his series of popular analyses on the Mexican political system, suggested that there was a growing dissatisfaction as well as an antidemocratic philosophy prevalent among business leaders.[34] Since then, the antagonism between the business groups and the government has increased. Their views on the methods that Mexico must use to resolve its problems are not parallel.

The military poses yet another question for Mexico's future. Their political role is still important, particularly in crisis situations.[35] While their influence, measured by the number of important political offices they hold, has decreased, they have also decreased their interchange with civilian political leaders. The military has been recently placated with an expensive new academy, and the continuation of a per capita expenditure for each member of the armed forces that is quite high for Latin America. But military political and economic attitudes appear to be more conservative than those expressed by political leaders. The responsiveness of the political elite to all of these groups, and its ability to deal with them, will depend on the type of individual who is recruited in the future. A major crisis may or may not come, but a number of mini crises, stemming from the political elite's inability to respond and juggle the increased demands, will exacerbate the situation.[36]

A further question raised by the conclusions drawn from this study is why the university has been allowed to perform such an important role in the recruitment process? Educational institutions have been important to elite recruitment in Mexico for many years. In the 19th century, the National Preparatory School was organized by the liberals as an institution to educate and train a new mestizo elite to govern Mexico.[37] This institution did function along these lines, but the ideological orientation was subverted under the long reign of the Porfiriato. In the 20th century, with the reopening of the National University, a complementary institution was created. After the Revolution, there was a tremendous demand for individuals with a variety of organizational and technical skills, reflected in the numerous career patterns of young university graduates who filled positions in their twenties that earlier would have been filled by men with lengthy apprenticeships of a decade or more. The need for trained men, more than any single factor, contributed to the continued importance of the university graduate in the political elite.[38] Later generations of Mexican leadership have not done anything new; instead they have built on an elitist recruitment tradition.* Not surprisingly, the new liberals and the conservatives recognized the importance of the university as a training ground for future leaders, and repeatedly fought during the 1910s, 1920s, and 1930s for control over the curriculum and admission policies of the National University and the National Preparatory School.[39]

The Mexican dependence on trust in recruitment makes former fellow students a logical choice for collaborators. The built-in process of turnover, and rapid horizontal as well as vertical mobility from one position to another in the Mexican bureaucracy makes it difficult for a successful political leader to develop any deep sense of confidence in his co-workers during his bureaucratic career. Political leaders do recruit from among career contacts, but often they are renewing old friendships from school as well. Proportionately, the source of recruitment is like a funnel, with the largest number coming from contacts in earlier years, and decreasing as the years go by to the smallest number from among recent career contacts. Since a leader has less time during his career to develop a sense of trust and to measure the abilities of his many collaborators, he often feels compelled to go back to a group of individuals who were socialized at the same time and in the same environment.[40] Thus, in spite of constant turnover at a rate fairly comparable to other political systems, Mexico maintains continuity between the recruiter and the recruit and often in its general policy direction as well.[41] Those in power serve as the gatekeepers for the new political elite, thus extending over a long period of time the leadership of a previous government. In fact, the system has worked so well that many of the original recruiters, out of political office for some time, are re-selected for high public office by men who they themselves brought into the public sector.† In this sense, Mexico does have a

---

*Many Mexicans believe that university graduates and professors did not dominate politics until 1946. While our data show that President Alemán did contribute strongly to this trend, especially by emphasizing university backgrounds in his cabinet, the data also show conclusively that the presence of university graduates in the Cárdenas and Avila Camacho eras was substantial. Even in the 1920s, the men who contributed most to the development of modern Mexico (excluding presidents) were men like Manuel Gómez Morín, Narciso Bassols, and José Vasconcelos, all university graduates and professors. Such men were continuing an established tradition.

†Two classic examples of this in the López Portillo administration are Emilio Martínez Manatou, who was the President's boss from 1965 to 1970, and gave him his first prominent position as Subsecretary of the Presidency in 1968, but who lost out to Echeverría for the presidency in 1970; and Guillermo Rossell de la Lama, who was the President's first boss in the federal bureaucracy as *Oficial Mayor,* then Subsecretary of National Properties from 1958 to 1959 and 1959 to 1964 respectively. Rossell de la Lama held no further important positions in government until López Portillo ran for president in 1976 (*Excélsior,* March 4, 1977, p. 6; *Hispano Americano,* December 6, 1976, p. 24; *The New York Times,* October 6, 1969, p: 16; *Excelsior,* February 25, 1977, p. 6, 8; and Kenneth F. Johnson, *Mexican Democracy: A Critical View* [Boston: Allyn and Bacon, 1971], pp. 183–4).

power elite, a small group of men who are capable of transmitting political power by sponsoring careers for one generation, which in turn sponsors the careers of the next generation.[42]

Although the recruitment process has functioned quite effectively during the past four decades, the concentration of recruitment activity in the National University has made a weak link in the political system. If something were to disrupt the continuity of classes at the National University over a long period of time, political recruitment itself might suffer. This is why control over the university, and therefore the students, is essential to the maintenance of political stability in Mexico. Octavio Paz pointed out the importance of this link by suggesting that any alliance between students and peasants or labor would be potentially disrupting.[43] To placate the student unrest, and to give his regime a youth oriented image, Echeverría took the unusual step of skipping over many persons from his own generation and appointing individuals from the following generation as well as representatives of the 1968 strike group. In this way, he attempted to coopt an entire generation.* By doing so, he succeeded in relatively stabilizing the university environment after 1971.

One of the remarkable qualities of the Mexican political system has been its continuity and its ability to survive with a minimum of political violence since 1929. In part, this is due to the narrow recruitment pool and the similar experiences shared by so many of Mexico's political leaders. Despite wide ideological differences, there is a remarkable degree of friendship and unity among members of early university generations, so much so that personal friendship appears to have moderated many ideological conflicts.[44] Even Alemán's generation, which had its share of Marxists, Neo-Liberals, and Conservatives, impressed the former president because of its sense of unity over the years.[45]

As most recent scholars suggest, Mexico most closely fits the model of an authoritarian regime with certain atypical characteristics.[46] The role of educational institutions in Mexico's recruitment process, and its relatively closed nature support this interpretation. The role played by the university in Mexican political recruitment points to the importance of examining similar institutions and processes in other Latin American and developing countries.

---

*Although youth is an amorphous group with little political organization, more than 60 percent of Mexico's population is under 25, making Mexico one of the truly youthful nations of the world.

NOTES TO CHAPTER 8

[1]See Lucio Mendieta y Núñez and José Gómez Robeldo, *Problemas de la Universidad* (México: UNAM, 1948) for additional statistical background data about students in the 1940s.

[2]Arthur Liebman, Kenneth Walker, and Myron Glazer, *Latin American University Students: A Six Nation Study* (Cambridge: Harvard University Press, 1972), pp. 41–2.

[3]See E. Wight Bakke, who presents the following image of students in Mexico: a) a privileged member of the elite; b) a man with a title; c) a member of the professional class; d) a member of the fraternity of educated men; e) a man with influential contacts; and f) a symbol and pillar of his family's social status. See "Students on the March: The Cases of Mexico and Colombia," *Sociology of Education* (Spring 1964): 206.

[4]*Excélsior,* November 6, 1973, p. 13.

[5]For evidence of its effect see my "The Making of a Government: The Socialization of Political Leaders in Post-Revolutionary Mexico" (unpublished book-length manuscript).

[6]Martin H. Greenberg, *Bureaucracy and Development: A Mexican Case Study* (Lexington: D.C. Heath, 1970), p. 98.

[7]E. Wight Bakke, "Students on the March," p. 203.

[8]*El Día,* December 1, 1976, p. 1 ff; *Hispano Americano,* December 6, 1976, p. 22; *Excélsior,* February 21, 1972, p. 18; *Hispano Americano,* December 28, 1958, p. 8; and *The New York Times,* December 2, 1976, p. 3.

[9]*Enciclopedia de México* **9,** p. 278; *Excélsior,* February 4, 1977, p. 6; Carlos Fuentes, *Tiempo Mexicano* (Mexico: Joaquin Mortíz, 1972), pp. 56–7; *Hispano Americano,* December 6, 1976, p. 23; and Banco de México, *Programa de becas y datos de los becarios* (Mexico, 1961), p. 87.

[10]Charles N. Myers, *Education and National Development in Mexico* (Princeton: Princeton University Press, 1965).

[11]For example, see E. Wight Bakke "Students on the March," p. 203 and Arthur Liebman, et al., *Latin American University Students,* p. 177.

[12]Myron Glazer, "Chile" in Donald K. Emmerson, ed., *Students and Politics in Developing Nations* (New York: Praeger, 1968).

[13]*Hispano Americano,* October 20, 1975, p. 17.

[14]*Excélsior,* September 27, 1975, p. 16A.

[15]Jesús Silva Herzog, *Una Vida en la vida de México* (México: Siglo XXI, 1972), p. 79.

[16]Antonio Armendáriz, in his monograph, *Semblanzas* (México: 1968), p. 3, gives the example of Professor Carlos Trinidad Romero, who received offers from many former students to participate in the administrations from 1940 through 1958, but did not accept any such offers.

[17]Lawrence S. Graham, *Politics in a Mexican Community* (Gainesville: University of Florida Press, 1968), p. 23, provides an example of the importance of a school tie in local politics.

[18]Thomas R. Dye and John W. Pickering, "Governmental and Corporate Elites: Convergence and Differentiation," *Journal of Politics* **36** (November 1974): 900–25.

[19]The managers of private enterprise in Mexico and Latin America tend to be a self-perpetuating lot, largely because business is a family dominated field. College students from wealthy families favor business careers over government careers, thereby eliminating themselves from consideration for public positions. See Arthur Liebman, et al. *Latin American University Students: A Six Nation Study* for evidence of this pattern.

[20]Rafael Segovia, "Las tendencias políticas en México de los proximos diez años," paper presented at the American University, School of International Service, Washington, D.C., March 18, 1976, p. 13.

[21]David C. Schwartz, "Toward a Theory of Political Recruitment," *Western Political Quarterly* **22** (September 1969): 553.

[22]Alfred B. Clubok, Norman M. Wilensky, and Forrest J. Berghorn, "Family Relationships, Congressional Recruitment, and Political Modernization," *Journal of Politics* **31** (November 1969): 1035–62.

[23]*Ibid.*, p. 1038.
[24]Kenneth Prewitt and Heinz Eulau, "Social Bias in Leadership Selection, Political Recruitment, and Electoral Context," *Journal of Politics* **33** (May 1971): 311.
[25]David C. Schwartz, "Toward a Theory," p. 554.
[26]David Schers, "The Popular Sector of the Mexican PRI," (unpublished Ph.D. dissertation, University of New Mexico, 1972), p. 59.
[27]For evidence of this and its impact on agency decision-making, see Martin H. Greenberg, *Bureaucracy and Development: A Mexican Case Study,* p. 117.
[28]Dwaine Marvick, "Political Recruitment and Careers," *International Encyclopedia of the Social Sciences* **12** (New York: Crowell, 1968), p. 280.
[29]For evidence that Mexico will need such skills, see Kenneth M. Coleman, "Diffuse Support in Mexico: The Potential for Crisis," *Sage Professional Papers in Comparative Politics* **5** (Beverly Hills: Sage Publications, 1976), p. 7.
[30]For some discussion of this point, see Susan Kaufman Purcell, *The Mexican Profit-Sharing Decision, Politics in an Authoritarian Regime* (Berkeley: University of California Press, 1975), p. 136ff; and Merilee Grindle, "Policy Change in an Authoritarian Regime, Mexico Under Echeverría," *Journal of Inter-American Studies & World Affairs* **19** (November 1977): 527.
[31]See James W. Wilkie, *The Mexican Revolution, Federal Expenditure and Social Change Since 1910* (Berkeley: University of California Press, 1970) and Roger D. Hansen, *The Politics of Mexican Development* (Baltimore: Johns Hopkins University Press, 1971).
[32]Roderic A. Camp, "A Reexamination of the Political Leadership and Allocation of Federal Revenues in Mexico, 1935–1973," *Journal of Developing Areas* **10** (January 1976): 193–213.
[33]James W. Wilkie, *The Mexican Revolution,* p. 281.
[34]Daniel Cosío Villegas, *El Sistema político mexicano* (Mexico: Joaquín Mortiz, 1972), p. 105ff; Robert Scott thought elite consensus was growing in the 1960s ("Mexico: the Established Revolution," in Lucian Pye and Sidney Verba, eds, *Political Culture and Political Development* [Princeton: Princeton University Press, 1965], p. 380). Jack Womack believes that the entrepreneur's commitment to "a licensed democracy" would prevent a major crisis between the two groups ("The Spoils of the Mexican Revolution," *Foreign Affairs* **48** [July 1970]: 682).
[35]David Ronfeldt, *The Mexican Army and Political Order Since 1940* (Santa Monica: Rand, September, 1973); and Franklin D. Margiotta, "Changing Patterns of Political Influence: The Mexican Military and Politics," paper delivered at the Annual Meeting of the American Political Science Association, New Orleans, 1973.
[36]For an excellent discussion of these problems, see Roger D. Hansen, "PRI Politics in the 1970's: Crisis or Continuity," in James W. Wilkie, et al., eds, *Contemporary Mexico* (Berkeley: University of California Press, 1976), pp. 389–401.
[37]For examples, see Octavio González Cárdenas, *Los Cien años de la Escuela Nacional Preparatoria* (Mexico: Editorial Porrúa, 1972).
[38]See Lorenzo Meyer, "Continuidades e innovaciones en la vida política mexicana del siglo xx, el antiguo y el nuevo régimen," *Foro Internacional* **16** (July–September 1975): 37–63.
[39]Alfonso Portuondo, "The Universidad Nacional Autonoma de Mexico in the Post-Independence Period: A Political and Structural Review," (unpublished MA Thesis, University of Miami, Coral Gables, Florida, 1972), superbly identifies the elements of this theme in the University's history. Many Mexicans, in conversations with me, have seen the establishment of the new Metropolitan University in Mexico City as an attempt to decrease the influence of UNAM. The first rector was Pedro Ramírez Vázquez, the younger brother of Mariano and Manuel Ramírez Vázquez, two prominent members of the Alemán regime. Pedro resigned to become the Secretary of Press and Publicity of the National Executive Committee of PRI during López Portillo's presidential campaign, and was later appointed Secretary of Public Works.
[40]Jeremy Boissevain, *Friends of Friends: Networks, Manipulators, and Coalitions* (Oxford: Basil Blackwell, 1974), p. 27.

[41]Keith R. Legg, "Interpersonal Relationships and Comparative Politics: Political Clientelism in Industrial Society," *Politics* **7** (May 1972): 10; and Lester G. Seligman, *Recruiting Political Elites* (New York: General Learning Press, 1971), p. 3.

[42]Robert Scott, "The Established Revolution," p. 380.

[43]Octavio Paz, *The Other Mexico: Critique of the Pyramid* (New York: Grove Press, 1972).

[44]For some insight into this generational relationship, see Enrique Krauze, *Caudillos culturales en la revolución mexicana* (Mexico: Siglo XXI, 1976).

[45]Personal interview with Miguel Alemán, Mexico City, October 27, 1976.

[46]Aurora Loyo Brambila and Ricardo Pozas Horcasitas, "Notes on the Mechanisms of Control Exercised by the Mexican State Over the Organized Sector of the Working Class, A Case Study: The Political Crisis of 1958," paper presented to the Center for Inter-American Relations, April, 1975, p. 63; John H. Coatsworth, "Los orígenes del autoritarismo moderno en México," *Foro Internacional* **16** (October–December 1975): 205–32; and Robert Monson, "Political Stability in Mexico: The Changing Role of Traditional Rightists," *Journal of Politics* **35** (August 1973): 611.

Appendix A:
Positions and Size of Sample in the Mexican Political Biography Project (MPBP)

The Mexican Political Biography Project is a data set that provides detailed biographical data on 59 variables for those individuals who have held certain political and educational positions in Mexico from June 17, 1935 to November 30, 1976. It contains data on three overlapping groups of individuals: a general political elite, a government political elite, and an educational elite.

Government Political Elite. These individuals have served in the highest appointive and elective positions in Mexico controlled by the official political system. The MPBP includes data on 824 cases (or 76 percent of all officeholders) in this category. To be included in this group, individuals must have held one or more of the following positions:

Size of Sample[a]		Positions	
%	Number of Positions Held	Available	Title of Position Held
100	7	7	President of Mexico
88	414	470	Secretary and subsecretary of the cabinet-level agencies of Government, Presidency, Treasury, National Properties, Tourism, Industry and Commerce, Public Works, Labor, Health and Public Welfare, Agrarian Reform, Agriculture and Livestock, Defense, Navy, Hydraulic Resources, Foreign Relations, Federal District; attorney general, attorney general of the Federal District and Federal Territories, Public Education, Communications and Transportation; and Private Secretary to the President of Mexico.

%	Size of Sample[a] Number of Positions Held	Positions Available	Title of Position Held
82	71	87	Directors of CONASUPO, Mexican Social Security Institute, PEMEX, National Steel Industry, National Coffee Company, National Sugar Finance Company, National Railroads of Mexico, Institute of Insurance and Social Services for Federal Employees, INFONAVIT, Mexican Institute of Foreign Trade, Federal Electric Commission, and the Federal Highways and Bridges and Adjacent Entrances.
74	32	42	Directors and subdirectors of the Foreign Trade Bank, Bank of Mexico, Agricultural Credit Bank, and the National Finance Bank.
71	74	105	Presidents and justices of the Supreme Court and presidents of the Superior Court of the Federal District, 1935–1974.
100	30	30	Ambassadors to the United States, France, and Great Britain.
55	229	414	Senators.
86	299	349	State Governors.
79	136	172	Presidents, secretaries general, and secretaries of the National Executive Committee of PRI and its antecedents.[b]
64	37	58	National sector leaders and union leaders of the National Confederation of Popular Organizations (CNOP), the National Farmers Confederation (CNC), the Confederation of Mexican Workers (CTM), the Federal Bureaucrats Union (FSTSE), and the National Teachers Union.
62	81	130	*Official Mayor* of the Department of the Federal District, Treasury, Government, Industry and Commerce, Labor, Navy, Defense, National Properties, Public Education, Foreign Relations, and Health and Welfare.
76	1410	1864	Totals

[a]These figures total more than the actual number of cases, since a large number of them have held two or more of these positions, and in some cases, the same position in different administrations. The 824 individuals in our sample accounted for 1410 of the 1864 positions available in the Mexican Political System from 1935 to 1976.
[b]Congressional leaders have all held party secretariat positions and are included in that category.

General Political Elite. This group includes all of the above officeholders, as well as opposition party (PAN, PPS, PARM) presidents, secretaries general, and secretaries. It also includes federal deputies from opposition parties since that is the highest position held by an active member of the opposition party from 1935 to 1976. To give greater representation to female political leaders in Mexico, most of whom have served in the Chamber of Deputies, one-time federal deputies who were women have been included in this category. Lastly, to increase the representation of national and state labor and agrarian leaders, most of whom have confined their careers to the Chamber of Deputies, federal deputies who have served two or more times have been included. This group contains 937 cases, or 113 additional individuals not included in the *Government Political Elite.*

Educational Elite. This group contains individuals who served in prominent leadership positions in public education. The majority of prominent educators, particularly at the National University, have held offices included in the *Government Political Elite.* However, an additional 62 persons are included who did not have careers in government. These individuals have held one or more of the following positions:

Size of Sample[a]			
%	Number of Positions Held	Positions Available	Title of Position Held
100	17	17	Rectors of the National University, 1929–1976.
89	8	9	Rectors of the National Polytechnic Institute, 1937–1976.
85	17	20	Secretaries general of the National University, 1929–1976.
86	6	7	Directors of the National Preparatory School, 1929–1944.
75	15	20	Deans of the National School of Law, 1929–1976.
91	10	11	Deans of the National School of Economics, 1929–1976.
83	10	12	Deans of the National School of Engineering, 1929–1970.
86	83	96	Totals

A Note About the Tables. Any reference in the titles of tables to first through fifth-time officeholders refers only to those cases in the *Government Political Elite.* Where it may not be obvious, a note at the bottom of the table indicates whether or not the table is based on the *General Political Elite* or the *Government Political Elite.* The total numbers for each table will vary slightly according to the group and variable examined since those cases with no information for both variables have been excluded from the figures. Biographical data for individual cases were not included in the data set unless complete information was available on 55 or more of the 59 variables. This has been done to increase the accuracy of the sample as a whole and of the data contained in each individual table.

Appendix B:
Mexicans Who Were Interviewed and/or Corresponded With the Author

Name	Highest Public or Academic Position
Salvador Aceves	Secretary of Public Health
Sealtiel Alatriste	Director General of IMSS
Miguel Alemán	President of Mexico
Roberto Arias y Soria	Lawyer and Historian
Antonio Armendáriz	Sub-Secretary of the Treasury
Salvador Azuela	Secretary General of UNAM
Mariano Azuela	Justice of the Supreme Court
Praxedis Balboa	Governor of Tamaulipas
Alfonso Barnetche	Sub-Director of Production of Pemex
Juan Barragán	President of PARM
Enrique Beltrán	Sub-Secretary of Agriculture
Armando Beltrán Beltrán	President of the Federal Arbitration Board
María Beneítez García	Department Head, Secretariat of Industry & Commerce
Salvador Benítez	Lawyer
Carlos Bermúdez Limón	Director General of PIPSA
Clemente Bolio	Historian
Efraín Brito Rosado	Senator from Yucatán
Eduardo Bustamante	Secretary of National Properties
Miguel E. Bustamante	Sub-Secretary of Public Health
Ezequiel Burguete F.	Justice of the Supreme Court
Raúl Cardiel Reyes	Private Secretary to the Secretary of Public Education
Ricardo Carrillo Durán	Sub-Director of Pemex
Ángel Carvajal	Secretary of Government
Antonio Carrillo Flores	Secretary of the Treasury
Fernando Castaños Patoni	*Oficial Mayor* of Hydraulic Resources
Rafael Cástol García	Department Head, Secretariat of the Treasury
José Castro Estrada	Sub-Secretary of Agriculture
Ignacio Chávez Sánchez	Rector of UNAM
Mario Colín Sánchez	Federal Deputy from México
José Angel Conchello	President of the CEN of PAN

Name	Highest Public or Academic Position
Víctor Correa Racho	Mayor of Mérida
Roberto A. Cortés	Federal Senator from Nuevo León
Daniel Cosío Villegas	Secretary General of UNAM
Irina del Castillo N.	Department Head, *Nacional Financiera*
Rafael de la Colina	Ambassador to the United States
Miguel de la Madrid Hurtado[c]	Sub-Secretary of the Treasury
Luis de la Peña Porth	Sub-Secretary of National Properties
Jorge de la Vega Domínguez[c]	Director General of Conasupo
José Juan de Olloqui[c]	Ambassador to the United States
José Andrés de Oteyza[c]	Director General National Sugar Bank
Antonio Dovalí Jaime	Director General of Pemex
Ernesto Enríquez Coyro	Sub-Secretary of Public Education
Arturo Espinosa[b]	
Jorge Espinosa de los Reyes[c]	Sub-Director of Pemex
Julio Faesler	Director General of IMCE
Antonio Fernández del Castillo	Lawyer and Historian
Horacio Flores de la Peña[a]	Secretary of National Patrimony
Manuel Franco López	Secretary of National Patrimony
Rafael P. Gamboa	President of the CEN of PRI
Trinidad García	Dean of the Law School
Luis Garrido Díaz	Rector of UNAM
Julián Garza Tijerina	Senator from Nuevo León
F. Javier Gaxiola	Secretary of Industry & Commerce
Rubén Gleason Galicia	Department Head, Secretariat of Industry & Commerce
Alejandro Gómez Arias	Vice-President of the PPS
Marte R. Gómez S.	Secretary of Agriculture
Hugo Pedro González	Governor of Tamaulipas
Francisco González de la Vega	Attorney General of Mexico
Alfonso González Gallardo	Sub-Secretary of Agriculture
Manuel González Ramírez	Secretary General of Quintana Roo
Gonzalo Guajardo Hernández	PAN Candidate for Senator
Martín Luis Guzmán	Senator from the Federal District
Leopoldo Hernández Partida	Secretary of the CEN of PRI
José Hernández Terán	Secretary of Hydraulic Resources
Manuel Hinojosa Ortiz	Sub-Secretary of Agriculture
Luciano Huerta Sánchez	Governor of Tlaxcala
Guillermo Ibarra Ibarra	*Oficial Mayor* of Hydraulic Resources
Sylvia Klee González	Private Secretary to the *Oficial Mayor* of Foreign Relations
Agustín López Munguía[c]	Sub-Director General of Treasury Statistics
Gilberto Loyo	Secretary of Industry & Commerce
Mauricio Magdaleno	Sub-Secretary of Public Education
Roberto Mantilla Molina	Secretary General of UNAM
Hugo B. Margáin[c]	Secretary of the Treasury
Pedro Daniel Martínez	Sub-Secretary of Public Health

Name	Highest Public or Academic Position
Antonio Martínez Báez	Secretary of Industry & Commerce
Manuel Martínez Báez	Sub-Secretary of Public Health
Lucio Mendieta y Núñez	*Oficial Mayor* of Agrarian Affairs
Alfonso Noriega C.	Secretary General of UNAM
Salvador Novo	Official Historian of Mexico City
Carlos Novoa	Director General of the Bank of Mexico
Nazario Ortiz Garza	Secretary of Agriculture
Manuel R. Palacios	Director General of the National Railroads
Emilio Portes Gil	President of Mexico
Alfonso Pulido Islas	Secretary General of IMSS
Carlos Tomás Peñaloza	Attaché Mexican Embassy in the United States
Pablo Quiroga Treviño	Governor of Nuevo León
Alfonso Francisco Ramírez	Justice of the Supreme Court
Raúl Rángel Frias	Governor of Nuevo León
Pedro Ramírez Vázquez[c]	Secretary of Press and Publicity of the CEN of PRI
Jesus Reyes Heroles[c]	President of the CEN of PRI
Ricardo Rivera P.	Director of the National Preparatory School
Carlos Roman Celís	Senator from Guerrero
Manuel Ruiz Castañeda	Senator from México
Gonzalo Robles	Director General of the Bank of Mexico
Roberto Robles Martínez	General Manager of the Public Works Bank
Agustín Salvat	Treasurer of the CEN of PRI
César Sepulveda	Dean of the Law School
Andrés Serra Rojas	Secretary of Labor
Santiago X. Sierra	Secretary General of Government of Durango
Jorge Tamayo[c]	Sub-Director of Mexican Light & Power
Ramiro Támez	Senator from Nuevo León
Manlio Favio Tapia Camacho	Senator from Veracruz
Antonio Taracena	Senator from Tabasco
María Emilia Téllez[c]	*Oficial Mayor* of Foreign Relations
Jaime Torres Bodet	Secretary of Foreign Relations
Carlos Torres Manzo[a]	Secretary of Industry & Commerce
Oscar Treviño Ríos	Assistant Attorney General of Mexico
Manuel Ulloa Ortiz	Secretary of the CEN of PAN
Alberto Vázquez del Mercado	Justice of the Supreme Court
Eduardo Villaseñor	Director of the Bank of Mexico
Víctor Manuel Villaseñor	Director General of National Railroads
Agustín Yáñez	Secretary of Public Education
Adolfo Zamora	Director General of the Urban Mortgage Bank
Ricardo José Zevada	Director of the National Foreign Trade Bank
Fernando Zertuche Muñoz[c]	*Oficial Mayor* of Labor
Pedro Zorrilla Martínez	Governor of Nuevo León
Salvador Zubirán	Sub-Secretary of Public Health

[a] These persons answered written questions through their private secretaries.
[b] Arturo Espinosa is the son of the late Fernando Espinosa Gutiérrez, Sub-Secretary of Public Works.
[c] These persons were appointed to positions at the sub-cabinet level or higher in the administration of José López Portillo.

Bibliography

Readers interested in the numerous biographical sources for any individual political leader should see my *Mexican Political Biographies, 1935–1975* (Tucson: University of Arizona Press, 1976). The libraries where difficult-to-locate sources may be found are abbreviated as follows: A = University of Arizona; CM = Colegio de México; DS = United States Department of State; H = Harvard University; HN = Hermoteca Nacional; I = University of Iowa; IADB = Inter-American Development Bank; LC = Library of Congress; PAU = Pan American Union (Columbus Memorial Library); T = University of Texas (Austin); UC = University of California at Berkeley; UCI = University of California at Irvine; UCLA = University of California at Los Angeles; UNAM = National Autonomous University of Mexico; and W = University of Wisconsin at Madison.

AGOR, WESTON H. "The Decisional Role of the Senate in the Chilean Political System," in Weston H. Agor, ed., *Latin American Legislatures: Their Role and Influence*. New York: Praeger, 1971, pp. 3–52.

——— . *Latin American Legislatures: Their Role and Influence*. New York: Praeger, 1971.

AGRAZ GARCÍA DE ALBA, G. *Ofrenda a México*. Guadalajara, 1958. W

AGUILAR, GILBERTO F. *El barrio estudiantil de México*. Mexico: Editorial Latina, 1951. LC,T

AGUIRRE BERNAL, CELSO. *Compendio Histórico-Biográfico de Mexicali, 1539–1966*. Mexicali, 1966. UCI

AGUIRRE SANTOSCOY, RAMIRO. *Historia sociológica de la educación*. Mexico: Secretaria de Educación Pública, 1963. LC

ALATRISTE DE LA FUENTE, MIGUEL. *Un liberal de la reforma, ensayo biográfico del General Miguel C. de Alatriste*. Mexico: Secretaría del Patrimonio Nacional, 1962.

ALBA, VÍCTOR. *Las ideas sociales contemporáneas en México*. Mexico: Fondo de Cultura Económica, 1960.

ALEMÁN, MIGUEL. *Miguel Alemán Contesta*. Austin: Institute of Latin American Studies, University of Texas, 1975.

————— . *Program of government*. San Antonio, 1946.

ALISKY, MARVIN. *The Governors of Mexico*. El Paso: Texas Western College, 1965.

————— . *Guide to the Government of the Mexican State of Nuevo Leon*. Tempe: Arizona State University, 1971.

————— . *Guide to the Government of the Mexican State of Sonora*. Tempe: Arizona State University, 1971.

————— . "Mexico's Population Pressures." *Current History* (March 1977): 106–10, 131.

————— . "U.S.-Mexican Governments in Transition." *Latin American Digest* **11** (Fall 1976): pp. 1–4.

————— . *Who's Who in Mexican Government*. Tempe: Arizona State University, 1969.

ALMADA, FRANCISCO R. *Diccionario de historia, geografía y biografía de Colima*. Colima, 1939.

————— . *Diccionario de historia, geografía y biografía sonoreneses*. Chihuahua: Impresora Ruiz Sandoval, 1952.

ALMOND, GABRIEL A. and SIDNEY, VERBA. *The Civic Culture: Political Attitudes and Democracy in Five Nations*. Princeton: Princeton University Press, 1963.

ALVAREZ, CONCHA. *Así paso mi vida*. Mexico: Editorial Porrúa, 1962.

AMES, BARRY. "Bases of Support for Mexico's Dominant Party." *American Political Science Review* **64** (March 1970): 153–67.

ANDERSON, CHARLES W. "Bankers as Revolutionaries." In William P. Glade, Jr, and Charles W. Anderson, eds., *The Political Economy of Mexico*. Madison: University of Wisconsin, 1963.

ANDERSON, ROGER C. "The Functional Role of the Governors and their States in the Political Development of Mexico, 1940–1964." Unpublished Ph.D. Dissertation, University of Wisconsin, 1971.

La Antorcha. Vols 1–4. (Paris, 1931). LC

APONTE, BARBARA B. *Alfonso Reyes and Spain*. Austin: University of Texas Press, 1972.

ARMENDÁRIZ, ANTONIO. "Evocación al Maestro Caso." *Universidad de México* **3** (May 1949): 9.

————— . *El método de la doctrina del estado*. Mexico, 1930.

————— . *Semblanzas*. Mexico, 1968.

ARONSON, SIDNEY H. *Status and Kinship in the Higher Civil Service*. Cambridge: Harvard University Press, 1964.

ARRIAGA RIVERA, AGUSTÍN. "El movimiento juvenil." In *Mexico, Cincuenta años de revolución*. Vol. 2: *La vida social*. Mexico: Fondo de Cultura Económica, 1963, 353–80.

ARRIOLA, CARLOS. "El Partido Acción Nacional (origen y circunstancia)." *Foro Internacional* **16** (October–December 1975): 233–51.

AUSTIN, RUBEN VARGAS. "The Development of Economic Policy in Mexico With Special Reference to Economic Doctrines." Unpublished Ph.D. dissertation, Iowa State University, 1958.

AZUELA, MARIANO. *Two Novels of Mexico*. Berkeley: University of California Press, 1965.

————— . *The Underdogs*. New York: New American Library, 1963.

BAGHOORN, FREDERICK C. "Trends in Top Political Leadership in the USSR." In Barry Farrell, ed., *Political Leadership in Eastern Europe and the Soviet Union*. Chicago: Aldine, 1970.

BAILEY, DAVID C. *Viva Cristo Rey!* Austin: University of Texas Press, 1974.

BALÁN, JORGE, HARLEY BROWNING, and ELIZABETH JELIN. *Men in a Developing Society: Geographic and Social Mobility in Monterrey, Mexico*. Austin: University of Texas Press, 1973.

BALBOA, PRAXEDIS. *Apuntes de mi vida*. Mexico, 1975.

BANCO DE MÉXICO. *Programa de becas y datos de los becarios*. Mexico, 1961. PAU

BAROCIO, ALBERTO. *México y la cultura*. Mexico: Secretaría de Educación Pública, 1946.

BARROS SIERRA, JAVIER. *1968*. Mexico: Siglo XXI, 1972.

BARTON, ALLEN H., BOGDAN DENITCH, and CHARLES KADUSHIN, eds. *Opinion-Making Elites in Yugoslavia*. New York: Praeger, 1973.

BARTRA, ROGER, et al. *Caciquismo y poder político en el México rural*. Mexico: Siglo veintiuno, 1975.

BASSOLS, NARCISO. *Obras*. Mexico: Fondo de Cultura Económica, 1964. LC

BASSOLS BATALLA, NARCISO. *Obregón*. Mexico: Editorial Nuestro Tiempo, 1967.

BECK, CARL. "Leadership Attributes in Eastern Europe: The Effects of Country and Time." In Carl Beck, et al. *Comparative Political Leadership*. New York: David McKay, 1973, pp. 86–153.

BELTRÁN, ENRIQUE. "Alfonso L. Herrera (1868–1968) primera figura de la biología mexicana." *Revista de la Sociedad de Historia Natural* **29** (December 1968): 37–91.

——— . "Veinticinco años de ciencias biológicas en México." *Revista de la Sociedad Mexicana de Historia Natural* **10** (December 1949): 17–26.

BENVENISTE, GUY. *Bureaucracy and National Planning, A Sociological Case Study in Mexico*. New York: Praeger, 1970.

BERMÚDEZ, ANTONIO J. and OCTAVIO VÉJAR VÁZQUEZ. *No dejes crecer la hierba*. Mexico: Costa Amic, 1969.

BERNAL SAHAGÚN, VÍCTOR M. *Anatomía de la publicidad en México*. Mexico: Editorial Nuestro Tiempo, 1974.

BETETA, RAMÓN. *Entrevistas y pláticas*. Mexico: Editorial Renovación, 1961. A

——— . *Jarano*. Austin: University of Texas Press, 1970.

——— . *The Mexican Revolution, a Defense*. Mexico: DAPP, 1937. A

BEZDEK, ROBERT R. "Electoral Oppositions in Mexico: Emergence, Suppression, and Impact on Political Processes." Unpublished Ph.D. dissertation, Ohio State University, 1973.

Bibliografía Histórica Mexicana. Mexico: El Colegio de México, 1967–1976.

BIELASIAK, JACK. "Modernization and Elite Cooptation in Eastern Europe." Paper presented at the 1977 Annual Meeting of the Midwest Political Science Association, Chicago, Illinois, April 21–23, 1977.

Biographical Encyclopedia of the World. 3rd edition. New York: Institute for Research in Biography, 1946.

BIZZARRO, SALVATORE. "Mexico's Government in Crisis." *Current History* (March 1977): 102–5, 130.

BLACK, GORDON S. "A Theory of Political Ambition: Career Choices and the Role of Structure Incentive." *American Political Science Review* **66** (March 1972): 144–59.

224   *Bibliography*

BLAIR, CALVIN P. "Nacional Financiera: Entrepreneurship in a Mixed Economy." In Raymond Vernon, ed., *Public Policy and Private Enterprise in Mexico*. Cambridge: Harvard University Press, 1964, pp. 191–240.

BLANCAS, ARTURO R. and TOMÁS L. VIDRIO. *Indice biográfico de la XLIII legislatura federal*. Mexico, 1956. CM

BOISSEVAIN, JEREMY. *Friends of Friends: Networks, Manipulators, and Coalitions*. Oxford: Basil Blackwell, 1974.

BOLIO ONTIVEROS, EDUARDO. *Diccionario histórico, geográfico y biográfico de Yucatán*. Mexico, 1945.

BONAVIT, JULIÁN. *Fragmentos de la historia del Colegio Primitivo y Nacional de San Nicolás de Hidalgo*. México, 1940. PAU

BONILLA, FRANK. *The Failure of Elites*. Cambridge: MIT Press, 1970.

BOWMAN, LEWIS and G. R. BOYNTON. "Recruitment Patterns Among Local Party Officials." *American Political Science Review* 60 (September 1966): pp. 667–76.

BRANDENBURG, FRANK. *Making of Modern Mexico*. Englewood Cliffs: Prentice-Hall, 1964.

———— . "Mexico, An Experiment in One-Party Democracy." Unpublished Ph.D. dissertation, University of Pennsylvania, 1956.

BRAVO IZQUIERDO, DONATO. *Un soldado del pueblo*. Puebla, 1964. LC

BRAVO UGARTE, JOSÉ. *La educación en México*. Mexico: Jus, 1966.

———— . *Efraín González Luna, abogado, humanista, político, católico*. Mexico: Ediciones de Acción Nacional, 1968.

———— . *Historia sucinta de Michoacán*. Mexico: Editorial Jus, 1964.

BREMAUNTZ, ALBERTO. *Autonomía universitaria y planeación educativa en México*. Mexico: Ediciones Jurídicas Sociales, 1969.

———— . *Setenta años de mi vida*. Mexico: Ediciones Jurídicas Sociales, 1968.

BRITTON, JOHN A. "The Mexican Ministry of Education, 1931–1940; Institutional Development and Radicalism." Unpublished Ph.D. dissertation, Tulane University, 1971.

———— . "Urban Education and Social Change in the Mexican Revolution, 1931–40." *Journal of Latin American Studies* 5 (November 1973): 233–45.

BROWN, ESTHER L. *Lawyers, Law Schools and the Public Service*. New York: Russell Sage Foundation, 1948.

BROWN, LYLE C. "General Lázaro Cárdenas and Mexican Presidential Politics, 1933–40." Unpublished Ph.D. dissertation, University of Texas, 1964.

BRUSH, DAVID ALLEN. "The De la Huerta Rebellion in Mexico, 1923–24." Unpublished Ph.D. dissertation, Syracuse University, 1975.

BRZEZINSKI, ZBIGNIEW and SAMUEL P. HUNTINGTON. *Political Power: USA/USSR*. New York: Viking Press, 1964.

BUENO, MIGUEL. *Estudio sobre la universidad*. Mexico: UNAM, 1962.

BUSTILLO ORO, JUAN. *Vientos de los veintes*. Mexico: SepSetentas, 1973.

BYARS, ROBERT S. and JOSEPH L. LOVE. *Quantitative Social Science Research on Latin America*. Urbana: University of Illinios Press, 1973.

CADENA Z., DANIEL. *El candidato presidencial, 1976*. Mexico, 1975.

CALDERÓN VEGA, LUIS. *Los 7 sabios de México*. Mexico, 1961. LC

CALL, TOMME CLARK. *The Mexican Venture*. New York: Oxford University Press, 1953.

CALVERT, PETER. "Regional Development in Mexico." *Bolsa Review* 6 (June 1972): 304–10.

CAMACHO, MANUEL. "El poder: estado o 'feudos' políticos." *Foro Internacional* **14** no. 3 (1974): 331–51.

CÁMARA DE SENADORES. *Directorio*. 26th to 48th legislatures. Mexico: Cámara de Senadores, various years.

CAMP, RODERIC A. "Autobiography and Decision-Making in Mexico: A Review Essay." *Journal of Inter-American Studies and World Affairs* **19** (May 1977): 275–83.

―――――. "The Cabinet and the Tecnico in Mexico and the United States." *Journal of Comparative Administration* **3** (August 1971): 188–213.

―――――. "Education and Political Recruitment in Mexico: the Alemán Generation." *Journal of Inter-American Studies and World Affairs* **18** (August 1976): 295–321.

―――――. "La campaña presidencial de 1929 y el liderazgo político en México." *Historia Mexicana*, **27**, no. 2 (1977): 231–59.

―――――. "Losers in Mexican Politics: A Comparative Study of Official Party Precandidates for Gubernatorial Elections, 1970–75." In James W. Wilkie and Kenneth Ruddle, eds., *Quantitative Latin American Studies: Methods and Findings* **6**, Statistical Abstract of Latin America Supplement Series. Los Angeles: UCLA Latin American Center, 1977, pp. 23–34.

―――――. "Mexican Governors Since Cárdenas, Education and Career Contacts." *Journal of Inter-American Studies & World Affairs* **16** (November 1974): 454–81.

―――――. *Mexican Political Biographies, 1935–1975*. Tucson: University of Arizona Press, 1976.

―――――. "The Middle-level Technocrat in Mexico." *Journal of Developing Areas* **6** (July 1972): 571–82.

―――――. "Military and Political Military Officers in Mexico: A Comparative Study." Paper presented before the North Central Council of Latin Americanists, Eau Claire, Wisconsin, 1977.

―――――. "The National School of Economics and Public Life in Mexico." *Latin American Research Review* **10** (Fall 1975): 137–51.

―――――. "A Reexamination of the Political Leadership and Allocation of Federal Revenues in Mexico, 1934–1973." *Journal of Developing Areas* **10** (January 1976): 193–213.

―――――. *The Role of Economists in Policy-making: A Comparative Study of Mexico and the United States*. Tucson: University of Arizona Press, 1977.

―――――. "El sistema mexicano y las decisiones sobre el personal político." *Foro Internacional* **17** (July–September 1976): 51–82.

―――――. "Women and Political Leadership in Mexico: A Comparative Study of Female and Male Political Elites." Paper presented before the Western Illinois University League of Latin Americanists, MacComb, Illinois, 1977.

CÁRDENAS, LÁZARO. *Obras-Apuntes 1913/1940*. Mexico: UNAM, 1972.

CÁRDENAS, JR, LEONARD. *The Municipality in Northern Mexico*. El Paso: Texas Western College, 1963.

CAREAGA, GABRIEL. *Los intelectuales y la política*. Mexico: Editorial Extemporáneos, 1971.

CARLOS, MANUEL L. *Politics and Development in Rural Mexico*. New York: Praeger, 1974.

CARRASCO PUENTE, RAFAEL. *La Caricatura en México*. Mexico: Imprenta Universitaria, 1953.

CARRILLO FLORES, ANTONIO. *La defensa de los derechos del hombre en la coyuntura del México de hoy.* Mexico, 1971.

————. *La defensa jurídica de los particulares frente a la administración en México.* Mexico: Porrúa, 1939. H

CASO, ANTONIO. *Sociología.* Mexico: Porrúa, 1946. UCLA

————. *Sociología genética y sistemática.* Mexico: Talleres Gráficos de la Nación, 1927.

CASTRO, EUSEBIO. *Centenario de la Escuela Nacional Preparatoria.* Mexico, 1968. UCLA

CAVAZOS GARZA, ISRAEL. *El Colegio Civil de Nuevo León.* Monterrey: Universidad de Nuevo León, 1957. T

CEBALLOS, MIGUEL. *La Escuela Nacional Preparatoria.* Mexico: Imprenta Mundial, 1933. UCLA

CECEÑA, JOSÉ LUIS. *México en la orbita imperial.* Mexico: Ediciones "El Caballito," 1975.

CENTRO DE ESTUDIOS INTERNACIONALES. *La vida política en México 1970–1973.* Mexico: El Colegio de México, 1974.

CHAVARÍ, JUAN N. *El Heroico Colegio Militar en la historia de México.* Mexico: Librería México, 1960. LC

CHÁVEZ, EZEQUIEL A. *Los últimos sesenta años de la historia de México y sus enseñanzas relativas a México, Francia y el mundo latino.* Paris: Lahure, 1926. UCLA

CHÁVEZ, IGNACIO. "Discurso pronunciado en la ceremonia conmemorativa del XXV aniversario de la fundación de El Colegio Nacional." *Memorial de El Colegio Nacional* **6,** nos 2–3 (1967–68): 249–56.

————. "Dos discursos." San Luis Potosí: Universidad Autónoma de San Luis Potosí, 1970.

————. *México en la cultura médica.* Mexico: El Colegio Nacional, 1947.

————. Unpublished speech to the University of Michoacán, Morelia, November 11, 1972.

CHÁVEZ, LETICIA. *Recordando a mi padre.* 10 vols. Mexico: Asociación Civil E. A. Chávez, 1967. UCLA

CHENG, PETER. "The Japanese Cabinets, 1885–1973: An Elite Analysis." *Asian Survey* **14** (December 1974): 1055–71.

CLARK, MARY J. "A Biography of Miguel Alemán, President of Mexico." Unpublished MA Thesis, Texas College of Arts and Industries, 1951.

CLINE, HOWARD F. *Mexico Revolution to Evolution: 1940–1960.* New York: Oxford University Press, 1963.

————. *The United States and Mexico.* New York: Atheneum, 1965.

CLUBOK, ALFRED B., NORMAN M. WILENSKY and FORREST J. BERGHORN. "Family Relationships, Congressional Recruitment, and Political Modernization." *Journal of Politics* **31** (November 1969): 1035–62.

COATSWORTH, JOHN H. "Los orígenes del autoritarismo moderno en México." *Foro Internacional* **16** (October–December 1975): 205–32.

COCHRANE, JAMES D. "Mexico's *'New Científicos':* The Díaz Ordaz Cabinet." *Inter-American Economic Affairs* **21** (Summer 1967): 61–72.

COCKCROFT, JOHN D. "Coercion and Ideology in Mexican Politics." In John D. Cockcroft, et al., eds., *Dependence and Underdevelopment: Latin America's Political Economy.* Garden City: Doubleday, 1972, pp. 245–68.

COHEN, LEONARD. "The Social Background and Recruitment of Yugoslav Political Elites, 1918–48." In Allen H. Barton, et al., eds., *Opinion-Making Elites in Yugoslavia*. New York: Praeger, 1973, pp. 25–68.

COLEGIO DE ECONOMISTAS DEL DISTRITO FEDERAL. *Directorio nacional de economistas*. Mexico: Rivero, 1960 LC

COLEMAN, KENNETH M. "Diffuse Support in Mexico: The Potential for Crisis." *Sage Professional Papers in Comparative Politics* 5. Beverly Hills: Sage Publications, 1976.

COLÍN SÁNCHEZ, MARIO. "Salvador Azuela, Maestro Emérito de la Preparatoria." In *Testimonios de Atlacomulco*. Atlacomulco, 1968.

————. *Una semblanza de Luis Echeverría*. Mexico: Testimonios de Atlacomulco, 1969.

————. *Semblanzas de personajes del estado de México*. Mexico, 1972.

COLMENERO, SERGIO. "Problemas universitarios y política nacional." *Revista Mexicana de Ciencia Política* 19, no. 73 (1973): 5–16.

Comparative Education Review 10 (June, 1966).

CONKLIN, JOHN G. "Elite Studies: The Case of the Mexican Presidency," *Journal of Latin American Studies* 5, no. 2 (1973): 247–69.

CORBETT, JOHN G. "The Context of Politics in a Mexican Community: A Study in Constraints on System Capacity." Unpublished Ph.D. dissertation, Stanford University, 1974.

CORDERO Y TORRES, ENRIQUE. *Diccionario biográfico de Puebla*. 2 vols. Mexico, 1972.

————. *Diccionario general de Puebla*. 4 vols. Puebla, 1958. HN

CÓRDOVA, ARNALDO. *La formación del poder político en México*. Mexico: Ediciones Era, 1972.

————. *La ideología de la revolución mexicana: formación del nuevo régimen*. Mexico: Ediciones Era, 1973.

CORNELIUS, JR, WAYNE A. "Contemporary Mexico: A Structural Analysis of Urban Caciquismo." In Robert Kern, ed., *The Caciques*. Albuquerque: University of New Mexico Press, 1973, pp. 135–50.

————. "Nation-building, Participation and Distribution: the Politics of Social Reform under Lazaro Cardenas." In Gabriel Almond, et al., eds., *Crisis, Choice and Change: Historical Studies of Political Development*. Boston: Little Brown, 1973, pp. 392–498.

————. *Politics of the Migrant Poor in Mexico City*. Stanford: Stanford University Press, 1975.

CORONA DEL ROSAL, ALFONSO. "Las Fuerzas Armadas de la Revolución." In *Mexico, cincuenta años de revolución* 3. Mexico: Fondo de Cultura Económica, 1960, pp. 317–38.

CORREA, EDUARDO J. *El Balance de Avila Camacho*. Mexico, 1946.

————. *El Balance de Cardenismo*. Mexico, 1941.

COSÍO VILLEGAS, DANIEL. *Ensayos y notas*. 2 vols. Mexico: Editorial Hermes, 1966.

————. *El estilo personal de gobernar*. Mexico: Joaquín Mortiz, 1974.

————. ed., *Historia moderna de México, El Porfiriato, La vida social*. Mexico: El Colegio de México, 1957.

————. *Labor periodística, real e imaginaria*. Mexico: Ediciones Era, 1972.

————. *Memorias*. Mexico: Joaquín Mortiz, 1976.

————. "Mexico's Crisis." In Daniel Cosío Villegas, *American Extremes*. Austin: University of Texas Press, 1964.

EL COLEGIO DE MÉXICO, 1957. *Continued*
————— . *El sistema político mexicano.* Mexico: Joaquín Mortiz, 1973.
————— . *La sucesión: desenlace y perspectivas.* Mexico: Joaquín Mortiz, 1976.
————— . *La sucesión presidencial.* Mexico: Joaquín Mortiz, 1975.
COVARRUBIAS, RICARDO. *Los 67 gobernantes del México independiente.* Mexico: PRI, 1968.
CREAGAN, JAMES F. "Minority Political Parties in Mexico, Their Role in a One-Party Dominant System." Unpublished Ph.D. dissertation, University of Virginia, 1965.
CRONON, E. DAVID. *Josephus Daniels in Mexico.* Madison: University of Wisconsin Press, 1960.
CROWSON, BENJAMIN F. *Biographical Sketches of the Governors of Mexico.* Washington: Crowson International Publications, 1951. LC
CUMBERLAND, CHARLES C. *Mexico, the Struggle for Modernity.* London: Oxford University Press, 1968.
DANIELS, JOSEPH. *Shirt-Sleeve Diplomat.* Chapel Hill: University of North Carolina Press, 1947.
D'ANTONIO, WILLIAM V. and WILLIAM H. FORM. *Influentials in Two Border Cities: A Study in Community Decision-Making.* Notre Dame: University of Notre Dame Press, 1965.
DAVIS, CHARLES L. "The Mobilization of Public Support for an Authoritarian Regime: The Case of the Lower Class in Mexico City." *American Journal of Political Science* **20** (November 1976): 653–70.
————— . "The Regime Legitimating Function of External Political Efficacy in an Authoritarian Regime: The Case of Mexico." Paper presented at the Annual Meeting of the American Political Science Association, New Orleans, 1974.
————— . "Social Mistrust as a Determinant of Political Cynicism in a Transitional Society: An Empirical Examination." *Journal of Developing Areas* **11** (October 1976): 91–102.
————— . "Toward an Explanation of Mass Support for Authoritarian Regimes: A Case Study of Political Attitudes in Mexico City." Unpublished Ph.D. dissertation, University of Kentucky, 1974.
DAVIS, JEROME. "A Study of One Hundred and Sixty-three Outstanding Communist Leaders." In Glenn Paige, ed., *Political Leadership.* New York: Free Press, 1972, pp. 262–72.
DAVIS, THOMAS B. *Aspects of Freemasonry in Modern Mexico.* New York: Vantage Press, 1976.
D'CHUMACERO, ROSALIA. *Perfil y pensamiento de la mujer mexicana.* Mexico: Edición de la autora, 1961.
DE BEER, GABRIELLA. *José Vasconcelos and his World.* New York: Las Americas Publishing Co., 1966.
DE FLORES, LOUIS J. "The Evolution of the Role of Government in the Economic Development of Mexico." Unpublished Ph.D. dissertation, University of Southern California, 1968.
DE IMAZ, JOSÉ. *Los Que Mandan.* Albany: State University Press of New York, 1970.
DE LA GARZA, RUDOLPH O. "La función reclutadora de la cámara de diputados." *Revista Mexicana de Ciencia Política* **21** (April–June 1975): 65–74.
————— . "The Mexican Chamber of Deputies and the Mexican Political System." Unpublished Ph.D. dissertation, University of Arizona, 1972.

DE LA RIVA RODRÍGUEZ, XAVIER. "Salubridad y asistencia médico-social." In *México, cincuenta años de revolución* 2. Mexico: Fondo de Cultura Económica, 1960, pp. 383–442.

DELHUMEAU, ANTONIO. "Elites culturales y educación de masas en México." *Revista Mexicana de Ciencia Política* **19**, no. 73 (1973): 21–6.

Diario del Sureste (Mérida, Yucatán). 1934 to 1974.

DÍAZ GUERRERO, ROGELIO. *Psychology of the Mexican*. Austin: University of Texas Press, 1975.

DÍAZ Y DE OVANDO, CLEMENTINA. *La Escuela Nacional Preparatoria, los afanes y los días, 1867–1910*. 2 vols. Mexico: UNAM, 1972.

Diccionario biográfico de México. 3 vols. Monterrey: Editorial Revesa, 1968, 1970. CM

Diccionario Enciclopedia UTEHA. Mexico: UTEHA, 1950.

Diccionario Jalisco Ilustrado. Mexico: Editores Fernández, 1965.

Diccionario Porrúa. 2 vols. Mexico: Editorial Porrúa, 1964.

Diccionario Porrúa. 2 vols. Mexico: Editorial Porrúa, 1970.

Diccionario Porrúa. 2 vols. Mexico: Editorial Porrúa, 1977.

Diccionario Puebla Ilustrado. Mexico: Editores Fernández, 1965.

Diccionario Tamaulipas Ilustrado. Mexico: Editores Fernández, 1965.

Diccionario y enciclopedia de Coahuila. Mexico: Editores Fernández, 1966.

Directorio de la Asociación Nacional de Abogados de México. Mexico, 1939. HN

Directorio de la Cámara de Diputados. 37th through 49th legislatures. Mexico: Imprenta de la Cámara de Diputados, various years.

"Directorio general de presuntos diputados al XLVIII congreso de la unión, 1970–73." Unpublished.

Directorio jurídico biográfico mexicano, 1972. Mexico: Sociedad Mexicana de Información Biográfica Profesional, 1972.

Directorio Nacional de Abogados. Mexico, 1934. LC

"Discursos pronunciados durante los festejos del 50th aniversario de la recepción profesional del Maestro Ignacio Chávez." *Archivos del Instituto de Cardiología de México* **40** (July–August 1970): 491–586.

DOGAN, MATTEL. "Political Ascent in a Class Society: French Deputies 1870–1958." In Dwaine Marvick, ed., *Political Decision-makers*. New York: Free Press, 1961, pp. 57–90.

DOMÍNGUEZ, VIRGILIO. "La enseñanza del derecho y la Biblioteca Antonio Caso." *Revista de la Escuela Nacional de Jurisprudencia* **37** (January–March 1948).

DRAKE, PAUL W. "Mexican Regionalism Reconsidered." *Journal of Inter-American Studies & World Affairs* **12** (July 1970): 401–15.

DROMUNDO, BALTASAR. *La Escuela Nacional Preparatoria Nocturna y José María de los Reyes*. Mexico: Porrúa, 1973.

——— . *Mi barrio de San Miguel*. Mexico: Antigua Librería, 1951. PAU

——— . *Mi calle de San Ildefonso*. Mexico: Editorial Guaranía, 1956.

——— . *Los oradores del 29*. Mexico: Ediciones "Una Generación," 1949.

——— . *Rojo Gómez*. Mexico, 1946.

DULLES, JOHN W. F. *Yesterday in Mexico*. Austin: University of Texas Press, 1961.

DYE, THOMAS R. *Who's Running America? Institutional Leadership in the United States*. Englewood Cliffs: Prentice-Hall, 1976.

ECHEVERRÍA, AMILCAR. *Enrique Martínez Sobral*. Guatemala, 1964. UCLA

EDINGER, LEWIS J., ed., *Political Leadership in Industrialized Societies*. New York: John Wiley & Sons, 1967.

EDINGER, LEWIS J. *Continued*
————. "Post-Totalitarian Leadership: Elites in the German Federal Republic." *American Political Science Review* **54** (March 1960): 58–82.

EDINGER, LEWIS J. and DONALD D. SEARING. "Social Background in Elite Analysis: A Methodological Inquiry." *American Political Science Review* **61** (June 1967): 428–45.

EMMERSON, DONALD K., ed., *Students and Politics in Developing Nations.* New York: Praeger, 1968.

Enciclopedia de México. 12 vols. Mexico: Enciclopedia de México, S.A., 1966–1977.

ENCINAS JOHNSON, LUIS. *La alternativa de México.* Mexico: Ediciones Sonot, 1969.

ESCÁRCEGA, ALFONSO. *Gómez Morín (anecdotario Chihuahuense).* Mexico: Editorial Jus, 1973.

ESTRADA, GERARDO R. "Universidad y cambios sociales y políticos en México, los antecedentes de la 'apertura' 1958–1968?" Paper presented at the 7th National Latin American Studies Meeting, Houston, November 2–6, 1977.

Excélsior, 1934–1978.

EVERETT, MICHAEL D. "The Role of the Mexican Trade Unions, 1950–1963." Unpublished Ph.D. dissertation, Washington University, 1967.

Ex Alumnos, 1943–45.

EZCURDIA, MARIO. *Análisis teórico del partido revolucionario institucional.* Mexico: Costa-Amic, 1968.

FAGEN, PATRICIA W. *Exiles and Citizens: Spanish Republicans in Mexico.* Austin: University of Texas Press, 1973.

FAGEN, RICHARD and WILLIAM TUOHY. *Politics and Privilege in a Mexican City.* Stanford: Stanford University Press, 1972.

FALKWOWSKI, DANIEL C. "Nacional Financiera, S.A. de México: A Study of a Development Bank." Unpublished Ph.D. dissertation, New York University, 1972.

FARRELL, R. BARRY. *Political Leadership in Eastern Europe and the Soviet Union.* Chicago: Aldine, 1970.

FELIX, DAVID. "Income Inequality in Mexico." *Current History* (March 1977): 111–14.

FERNÁNDEZ, JULIO A. *Political Administration in Mexico.* Boulder: University of Colorado, 1969.

FERNÁNDEZ DEL CASTILLO, ANTONIO. "Palabras del Señor Lic. Antonio Fernández del Castillo." Mexico: Academia Nacional de Historia y Geografía, 1968.

FIERRO VILLALOBOS, ROBERTO. *Esta es mi vida.* Mexico, 1964.

FLORES ZAVALA, ERNESTO. *El estudiante inquieto.* Mexico, 1972.

FLOWER, EDITH. "The Mexican Revolt Against Positivism." *Journal of the History of Ideas* **10** (January 1949): 115–29.

FORSTER, MERLIN H. "The 'Contemporáneos,' 1915–1932: A Study in Twentieth-Century Mexican Letters." Unpublished Ph.D. dissertation, University of Illinois, 1960.

FREITAG, PETER J. "The Cabinet and Big Business: A Study of Interlocks." *Social Problems* **23** (December 1975): 137–52.

FREY, FREDERICK. *The Turkish Political Elite.* Cambridge: MIT Press, 1965.

FUENTES, CARLOS. *The Death of Artemio Cruz.* New York: Noonday Press, 1964.

————. *The Good Conscience.* New York: Noonday Press, 1970.

————. *Tiempo mexicano*. Mexico: Joaquín Mortiz, 1972.

————. *Where the Air is Clear*. New York: Ivan Obolensky, 1960.

FUENTES DÍAZ, VICENTE. *Los partidos políticos en México*. Mexico: Editorial Altiplano, 1969.

GABBERT, JACK BENTON. "The Evolution of the Mexican Presidency." Unpublished Ph.D. dissertation, University of Texas, 1963.

GALINDO, SERGIO. *The Precipice*. Austin: University of Texas Press, 1969.

GARCÍA CANTÚ, GASTÓN. *Política mexicana*. Mexico: UNAM, 1974.

GARCÍA PURÓN, MANUEL. *México y sus gobernantes, biografías*. Mexico: Porrúa, 1964.

GARCÍA RIVAS, HERIBERTO. *Breve historia de la revolución mexicana*. Mexico: Editorial Diana, 1964.

GARCÍA TÉLLEZ, IGNACIO. *Socialización de la cultura*. Mexico: La Impresora, 1936. LC

GARRIDO DÍAZ, LUIS. *Antonio Caso, una vida profunda*. Mexico: UNAM, 1961. PAU

————. *Palabras universitarias, 1951–53*. Mexico: Ediciones Botas, 1954.

————. *El tiempo de mi vida, memorias*. Mexico: Porrúa, 1974.

GAXIOLA, FRANCISCO JAVIER. *Memorias*. Mexico: Porrúa, 1975.

GILL, CLARK. *Education in a Changing Mexico*. Washington, D.C.: U.S. Government Printing Office, 1969.

GLADE, WILLIAM P., JR. "The Role of Government Enterprise in the Economic Development of Underdeveloped Regions: Mexico, a Case Study." Unpublished Ph.D. dissertation, University of Texas, 1955.

GLADE, WILLIAM P., JR. and CHARLES W. ANDERSON. *The Political Economy of Mexico*. Madison: University of Wisconsin, 1963.

GLADE, WILLIAM P. and STANLEY R. ROSS, eds., *Críticas constructivas del sistema político mexicano*. Austin: Institute of Latin American Studies, 1973.

GLAZER, MYRON. "Chile." In Donald K. Emmerson, ed., *Students and Politics in Developing Nations*. New York: Praeger, 1968, pp. 286–314.

GLEASON GALICIA, RUBÉN. *Las estadísticas y censos de México*. Mexico: UNAM, 1968.

GLICK, HENRY R. "Political Recruitment in Sarawak: A Case Study of Leadership in a New State." *Journal of Politics* **28** (February 1966): 88–99.

GOLDRICH, DANIEL. *Sons of the Establishment: Elite Youth in Panama and Costa Rica*. Chicago: Rand-McNally, 1966.

GOLDTHORPE, J. E. *An African Elite: Makerere College Students, 1922–1960*. Nairobi: Oxford University Press, 1965.

GÓMEZ CASTRO, ARTURO. *¿Quién será el futuro presidente de Mexico?* Mexico, 1963. A

GÓMEZ MAGANDA, ALEJANDRO. *Bocetos presidenciales*. Mexico: Editorial Joma, 1970. I

GÓMEZ MORÍN, MANUEL. *1915 y otros ensayos*. Mexico: Editorial Jus, 1973.

GONZÁLEZ, HÉCTOR. *Historia del Colegio Civil*. Monterrey: SPI, 1945. PAU

GONZÁLEZ, LUIS. *San José de Gracia, Mexican Village in Transition*. Austin: University of Texas Press, 1975.

GONZÁLEZ CÁRDENAS, OCTAVIO. *Los cien años de la Escuela Nacional Preparatoria*. Mexico: Editorial Porrúa, 1972.

GONZÁLEZ CASANOVA, HENRIQUE. "La comunicación gubernamental." *Revista Mexicana de Ciencia Política* **16** (1970): 353–66.

GONZÁLEZ CASANOVA, PABLO. *La democracia en México*. Mexico: ERA, 1965.

GONZÁLEZ COSÍO, ARTURO. *Historia estadística de la universidad, 1910–1967*. Mexico: UNAM, 1968.

GONZÁLEZ DÁVILA, AMADO. *Diccionario geográfico, histórico, biográfico y estadístico del estado de Sinaloa*. Culiacán: Talleres de Imprenta, 1959. HN

GONZÁLEZ DE LA VELA, FRANCISCO. "El Aula 'Manuel Borja Soriano.'" *La Universidad* 3 (September 1949): 5.

GONZÁLEZ GRAF, JAIME. *La perspectiva política en México*. Mexico: Instituto de Estudios Políticos, 1974.

GONZÁLEZ LLACA, EDMUNDO. "El presidencialismo o la personalización del poder." *Revista Mexicana de Ciencia Política* 21 (April–June 1975): 35–42.

GONZÁLEZ NAVARRO, MOISÉS. *La Confederación Nacional Campesina*. Mexico: Costa-Amic, 1968.

GONZÁLEZ RAMÍREZ, MANUEL. *Antología de la Escuela Nacional Preparatoria*. Mexico: Secretaria de Educación Pública, 1967.

————. *México, litografía de la ciudad que se fue*. Mexico, 1962.

GONZÁLEZ ROA, FERNANDO. *Las cuestiones fundamentales de actualidad en México*. Mexico: Secretaría de Relaciones Exteriores, 1927.

GONZÁLEZ TORRES, JOSÉ. *Campaña electoral*. Mexico: Editorial Jus, 1976.

GOODSPEED, STEPHEN S. "El papel del jefe del ejecutivo en México." *Problemas Agrícolas e Industriales en México* 7 (January–March 1955): 13–208.

GOTARI, ELI DE. *La ciencia en la historia de México*. Mexico: Fondo de Cultura Económica, 1963.

GRAHAM, LAWRENCE S. *Mexican State Government: A Prefectural System in Action*. Austin: Bureau of Government Research, University of Texas, 1971.

————. *Politics in a Mexican Community*. Gainesville: University of Florida Press, 1968.

GRAHAM, RICHARD and PETER H. SMITH. *New Approaches to Latin American History*. Austin: University of Texas Press, 1974.

GRAYSON, GEORGE W. "The Making of a Mexican President, 1976." *Current History* 70 (February 1976): 49–52, 83–84.

GREENBERG, MARTIN H. *Bureaucracy and Development: A Mexican Case Study*. Lexington: D.C. Heath, 1970.

GREENE, GRAHAM. *The Lawless Roads*. London: William Heinemann, 1955.

————. *The Power and the Glory*. New York: Time Incorporated, 1962.

GREENLEAF, RICHARD E. and MICHAEL C. MEYER. *Research in Mexican History*. Lincoln: University of Nebraska Press, 1973.

GRIMES, C. E. and CHARLES E. P. SIMMONS. "Bureaucracy and Political Control in Mexico: Towards an Assessment." *Public Administration Review* 29 (January–February 1969): 72–9.

GRINDLE, MERILEE S. *Bureaucrats, Politicians, and Peasants in Mexico: A Case Study in Public Policy*. Berkeley: University of California Press, 1977.

————. "Patrons and Clients in the Bureaucracy: Career Networks in Mexico." *Latin American Research Review* 12, no. 1 (1977): 37–66.

————. "Policy Change in an Authoritarian Regime, Mexico Under Echeverría." *Journal of Inter-American Studies & World Affairs* 19 (November 1977): 523–55.

————. "Power, Expertise and the "Tecnico": Suggestions from a Mexican Case Study." *Journal of Politics* 39 (May 1977): 399–426.

GROMPONE, ANTONIO M. *Universidad oficial y universidad viva*. Mexico: UNAM, 1953. UNAM

GRUBER, WILFRIED. "Career Patterns of Mexico's Political Elite." *Western Political Quarterly* **24** (September 1971): 467–82.

GRUENING, ERNEST. *Mexico and Its Heritage*. New York: D. Appleton-Century, 1928.

GUEVARA OROPESA, MANUEL. "El Estudiante." In *Doctor Salvador Zubirán, 50 Años de Vida Profesional*. Mexico: Asociación de Médicos del Instituto Nacional de Nutrición, 1973, pp. 15–33.

GUILLÉN, FEDRO. *Jesús Silva Herzog*. Mexico: Empresas Editoriales, 1969. UCLA

GUZMÁN, MARTÍN LUIS. *Apunte sobre una personalidad*. Mexico, 1955.

HADDOX, JOHN H. *Antonio Caso, Philosopher of Mexico*. Austin: University of Texas Press, 1971.

————. *Vasconcelos of Mexico*. Austin: University of Texas Press, 1967.

HALPERIN, ERNST. *Communism in Mexico*. Cambridge: MIT Press, 1963.

HAMILTON, NORA. "The State and Class Formation in Post-Revolutionary Mexico." Paper presented at the 7th National Latin American Studies Association Meeting, Houston, November 2–5, 1977.

HANSEN, ROGER D. *The Politics of Mexican Development*. Baltimore: Johns Hopkins University Press, 1971.

————. "PRI Politics in the 1970's: Crisis or Continuity?" In James W. Wilkie, et al., eds., *Contemporary Mexico*. Los Angeles: UCLA Latin America Center, 1976.

HARRISON, JOHN P. "The Role of the Intellectual in Fomenting Change: The University." In J. J. Te Paske and S. Nettleton, eds., *Explosive Forces in Latin America*. Columbus: Ohio State University Press, 1964, pp. 27–42.

HART, JEFFREY. "Geopolitics and Dependency: Cognitive Maps of Latin American Foreign Policy Elites." Paper presented at the 1976 Annual Meeting of the American Political Science Association, Chicago, September 25, 1976.

HENRÍQUEZ UREÑA, PEDRO. "The Revolution in Intellectual Life." *Survey Grafic* (May 1924): 165–6.

————. *Universidad y educación*. Mexico: UNAM, 1969.

HERMAN, DONALD L. "The Comintern and the Development of Communism in Mexico." Unpublished Ph.D. dissertation, University of Michigan, 1964.

HERNÁNDEZ LUNA, JUAN. *Conferencias del Ateneo de la Juventud por Antonio Caso, et al*. Mexico: UNAM, 1962.

————. "Polémica de Caso contra Lombardo sobre la Universidad." *Historia Mexicana* **19** (July–September 1969): 87–104.

HEWES, GORDON W. "Mexicans in Search of the 'Mexican': Note on Mexican National Character Studies." *American Journal of Economic Sociology* **13** (January 1954): 209–23.

HILTON, RONALD, ed. *Who's Who in Latin America: Mexico*. Stanford: Stanford University Press, 1946.

HILTON, STANLEY E. "The Church-State Dispute over Education in Mexico from Carranza to Cárdenas." *The Americas* **21** (October 1964): 163–83.

Hispano Americano, 1944–1978.

HOLT, ROBERT T. "Age as a Factor in the Recruitment of Communist Leadership." *American Political Science Review* **48** (June 1954): 486–99.

HOLTZMAN, WAYNE H., ROGELIO DIAZ-GUERRERO, and JON D. SWARTZ. *Personality Development in Two Cultures*. Austin: University of Texas Press, 1975.

HOPKINS, JOHN W. *The Government Executive of Modern Peru*. Gainesville: University of Florida Press, 1967.

HUTINI, HUGO G., PEDRO CARRASCO, and JAMES M. TAGGART, eds. *Essays on Mexican Kinship*. Pittsburgh: University of Pittsburgh Press, 1976.

IDUARTE, ANDRÉS. *Niño, Child of the Mexican Revolution*. New York: Praeger, 1971.

IGUÍNIZ, JUAN B. *Bibliografía Biográfica Mexicana*. Mexico: UNAM, 1969.

INNES, JOHN S. "The Universidad Popular Mexicana." *The Americas* 30 (July 1973): 110–12.

INTER-AMERICAN DEVELOPMENT BANK. *Economic and Social Progress in Latin America, 1976 Report*. Washington, D.C.: IADB, 1976.

INTERNATIONAL STUDIES OF VALUES IN POLITICS. *Values and the Active Community*. New York: Free Press, 1971.

International Who's Who. London: Europa Publications, various years.

International Yearbook and Statesmen's Who's Who, 1952–1971.

Investigaciones contemporáneas sobre historia de México. Mexico: UNAM, 1971.

JACOB, HERBERT. "Initial Recruitment of Elected Officials in the United States: A Model." *Journal of Politics* 24 (November 1962): 703–16.

——— . *German Administration since Bismarck*. New Haven: Yale University Press, 1963.

JACOBSON, PETER. "Opposition and Political Reform in Mexico, An Assessment of the Partido Acción Nacional and the "Apertura Democrática'." *New Scholar* 5, no. 1 (1975): 19–30.

JALISCO, Departamento de Relaciones Públicas del Gobierno del Estado. *Directorio Oficial*. Jalisco, 1966.

JOHNSON, CHARLES W. *México en el siglo xx*. Mexico: UNAM, 1969.

JOHNSON, JOHN J. *Political Change in Latin America*. Stanford: Stanford University Press, 1958.

JOHNSON, KENNETH F. "Ideological Correlates of Right-Wing Political Alienation in Mexico." *American Political Science Review* 59 (September 1965): 656–64.

——— . *Mexican Democracy: A Critical View*. Boston: Allyn and Bacon, 1971.

——— . "Political Alienation in Mexico: A Preliminary Examination of UNS and PAN." *Rocky Mountain Social Science Journal* 2 (May 1965): 155–63.

JOHNSTON, MARJORIE C. *Education in Mexico*. Washington, D.C.: U.S. Government Printing Office, 1956.

JUNCO MEYER, VICTORIA. "Women in Mexican Society." *Current History* (March 1977): 120–3, 130.

La Justicia, 1962–1976.

KAHL, JOSEPH A. *The Measurement of Modernism, A Study of Values in Brazil and Mexico*. Austin: University of Texas Press, 1974.

KARSEN, SONJA. *Jaime Torres Bodet*. New York: Twayne Publishers, 1971.

KAUFMAN, ROBERT R. "Mexico and Latin American Authoritarianism." In José Luis Reyna and Richard S. Weinert, eds., *Authoritarianism in Mexico*. Philadelphia: Institute for the Study of Human Issues, 1977, pp. 193–232.

KAUTSKY, JOHN H. *Patterns of Modernizing Revolutions: Mexico and the Soviet Union*. Beverly Hills: Sage Publications, 1975.

KESSELMAN, MARK. "Recruitment of Rival Party Activists in France: Party Cleavages and Cultural Differentiation." *Journal of Politics* 35 (February 1973): 2–44.

KING, RICHARD G. *The Provincial Universities of Mexico: An Analysis of Growth and Development*. New York: Praeger, 1971.

KIRK, BETTY. *Covering the Mexican Front*. Norman: University of Oklahoma Press, 1942.

KIRSHNER, ALAN M. "Tomás Garrido Canabal and the Mexican Red Shirt Movement." Unpublished Ph.D. dissertation, New York University, 1970.

KLING, MERLE. *A Mexican Interest Group in Action*. Englewood Cliffs: Prentice-Hall, 1961.

KORNBERG, ALLAN and HAL H. WINSBOROUGH. "Recruitment of Candidates for the Canadian House of Commons." *American Political Science Review* **62** (December 1968): 1242–57.

KRAUZE, ENRIQUE. *Caudillos culturales en la revolución mexicana*. Mexico: Siglo XXI, 1976.

LABASTIDA, HORACIO, and ANTONIO PÉREZ ELÍAS, eds. *Congreso de crítica de la revolución mexicana, 1910–1945–1970*. Mexico: Editorial Libros de México, 1972.

LABASTIDA MARTÍN DEL CAMPO, JULIO. "Algunas hipótesis sobre el modelo político mexicano y sus perspectivas." *Revista Mexicana de Sociología* **36** (July–September 1974): 629–42.

————. "El régimen de Echeverría." *Revista Mexicana de Sociología* **34** (July–December 1972): 881–907.

LADD, EVERETT C. and SEYMOUR M. LIPSET. *The Divided Academy, Professors and Politics*. New York: W. W. Norton, 1976.

LAJOIE, LUCIEN F. *Who's Notable in Mexico*. Mexico, 1972. DS

LAMARTINE YATES, PAUL. *El desarrollo regional de México*. Mexico: Banco de México, 1961.

LARROYO, FRANCISCO. *Historia comparada de la educación en México*. Mexico: Porrúa, 1967.

LASSWELL, HAROLD D. and M. S. MCDOUGAL. "Legal Education and Public Policy." In Harold Lasswell, ed., *The Analysis of Political Behavior*. London: Routledge, Kegan Paul, Ltd, 1948, pp. 21–119.

LASSWELL, HAROLD D. and DANIEL LERNER. *World Revolutionary Elites*. Cambridge: MIT Press, 1966.

Latin America Political Report, 1967–1977.

LAZARSFELD, PAUL F. and WAGNER THIELENS, JR. *The Academic Mind*. Glencoe: Free Press, 1958.

LEAL, JUAN FELIPE. *La burguesía y el estado mexicano*. Mexico: Ediciones "El Caballito," 1972.

————. "The Mexican State: 1915–1973, A Historical Interpretation." *Latin American Perspectives* **2** (Summer 1975): 48–63.

LEGG, KEITH R. "Interpersonal Relationships and Comparative Politics: Political Clientelism in Industrial Society." *Politics* **7** (May 1972): 1–11.

LEMUS, GEORGE. "Partido Acción Nacional: A Mexican Opposition Party." Unpublished MA Thesis, University of Texas, 1956.

LEVINE, DANIEL H. "Thinking about Students and Politics: Venezuela in the 1960s." Paper presented at the 7th National Latin American Studies Meeting, Houston, November 2–6, 1977.

LEWIS, GEORGE K. "An Analysis of the Institutional Status and Role of the Petroleum Industry in Mexico's Evolving System of Political Economy." Unpublished Ph.D. dissertation, University of Texas, 1959.

LEWIS, OSCAR. *The Children of Sánchez, Autobiography of a Mexican Family*. New York: Vintage, 1961.

————. *A Death in the Sánchez Family*. New York: Random House, 1969.

————. *Five Families*. New York: Basic Books, 1959.

————. *Pedro Martínez*. New York: Vintage, 1964.

LEWIS, PAUL H. "The Spanish Ministerial Elite, 1938–1969." *Comparative Politics* 5 (October 1972): 83–106.

Libro de Oro de México, 1934–1972. LC

LIEBMAN, ARTHUR, KENNETH WALKER, and MYRON GLAZER. *Latin American University Students: A Six Nation Study.* Cambridge: Harvard University Press, 1972.

LIEUWEN, EDWIN. *Mexican Militarism.* Albuquerque: University of New Mexico Press, 1968.

LOAEZA, SOLEDAD. "El Partido Acción Nacional." *Foro Internacional* 14, no. 3 (1974): 351–73.

LOMBARDO TOLEDANO, VICENTE. "The Labor Movement." *Annals of the American Academy of Political and Social Science* 208 (March 1940): 48–54.

LOMELÍ GARDUÑO, ANTONIO. *Anecdotario político mexicano.* Mexico: Costa-Amic, 1974.

LOMNITZ, LARISSA. "Conflict and Mediation in a Latin American University." *Journal of Inter-American Studies and World Affairs* 19 (August 1977): 315–38.

————. "Universidad tecnológica y mediación en la UNAM." *Plural* 5 (March 1976).

LÓPEZ, HÉCTOR F. *Diccionario geográfico, histórico, biográfico y linguístico del estado de Guerrero.* Mexico: Editorial Pluma y Lápiz, 1942.

LÓPEZ BARROSO, EPIGMENIO. *Diccionario geográfico, histórico y estadístico del distrito de Abasolo, del Estado de Guerrero.* Mexico: Ediciones Botas, 1967. CM

LÓPEZ CARRASCO, FIDEL. *Historia de la educación en el estado de Oaxaca.* Mexico: Museo Pedagógico Nacional, 1950.

LÓPEZ ESCALERA, JOSÉ. *Diccionario biográfico y de historia de México.* Mexico: Editorial del Magistrado, 1964.

LÓPEZ GALLO, MANUEL. *Economía y política en la historia de México.* Mexico: Ediciones Solidaridad, 1965. LC

LÓPEZ REYES, AMALIA and GUADALUPE PÉREZ SAN VICENTE. *Joaquín Ramírez Cabañas, el maestro y su obra.* Mexico, 1948. PAU

LOYO BRAMBILA, AURORA and RICARDO POZAS HORCASITAS. "Notes on the Mechanisms of Control Exercised by the Mexican State Over the Organized Sector of the Working Class, a Case Study: the Political Crisis of 1958." Paper presented to the Center for Inter-American Relations, April, 1975.

LOZOYA, JORGE ALBERTO. *El Ejército Mexicano (1911–1965).* Mexico: El Colegio de México, 1970.

MABRY, DONALD J. "Changing Models of Mexican Politics, A Review Essay." *The New Scholar* 5, no. 1 (1975): 31–7.

————. *Mexico's Acción Nacional: A Catholic Alternative to Revolution.* Syracuse: Syracuse University Press, 1973.

MABRY, DONALD and RODERIC A. CAMP. "Mexican Political Elites 1935–1973: A Comparative Study." *The Americas: A Quarterly Journal of Inter-American Cultural History* 31 (April 1975): 452–69.

McALISTER, LYLE N. *The Military in Latin American Socio-Political Evolution: Four Case Studies.* Washington, D.C.: Center for Research in Social Systems, 1970.

McDONOUGH, PETER. "Cohesion and Mobility in a Technocratic-Authoritarian System: Kinship, Friendship and Class Ties Among Brazilian Elites." Paper presented at the 7th National Latin American Studies Association Meeting, Houston, November 2–5, 1977.

McFARLAND, FLOYD B. "An Analysis of Relationships between Foreign Economic Policy and Economic Development in Mexico." Unpublished Ph.D. dissertation, University of Texas, 1964.

McQUAIL, D. L. O'SULLIVAN and W. G. QUINE. "Elite Education and Political Values." *Political Studies* **16** (1968): 257–66.

McGREGOR, JR, EUGENE. "Politics and the Career Mobility of Bureaucrats." *American Political Science Review* **68** (March 1974): 18–26.

MAGDALENO, MAURICIO. *Las palabras perdidas*. Mexico: Fondo de Cultura Económica, 1956.

MALAGÓN BARCELO, JAVIER. "Breve reseña histórica de la Escuela Nacional de Jurisprudencia." *Revista de la Facultad de Derecho de México* **1** (January–June 1951): 163–88. LC

————. "Four Centuries of the Faculty of Law in Mexico." *Hispanic American Historical Review* **32** (August 1952): 442–51.

MALDONADO, BRAULIO. *Baja California: comentarios políticos*. Mexico: Costa Amic, 1960. T

MANNHEIM, KARL. "The Problem of Generations." In Karl Mannheim, ed., *Essays on the Sociology of Knowledge*. London: Routledge and Kegan, 1952, pp. 276–322.

MAPLES ARCE, MANUEL. *Soberana juventud*. Madrid: Editorial Plenitud, 1967.

MARGIOTTA, FRANKLIN D. "Changing Patterns of Political Influence: The Mexican Military and Politics." Paper presented at the Annual Meeting of the American Political Science Association, New Orleans, 1973.

————. "The Mexican Military: A Case Study in Non-intervention." Unpublished MA thesis, Georgetown University, 1968.

MARÍA Y CAMPOS, ARMANDO. *Múgica crónica biográfica*. Mexico: Compañía de Ediciones Populares, 1939.

MARIAS, JULIAN. *Generations, A Historical Method*. University: University of Alabama Press, 1970.

MARTIN, PERCY A., ed. *Who's Who in Latin America*. Stanford: Stanford University Press, 1935 and 1940.

MARVICK, DWAINE, ed. *Political Decision-makers*. New York: Free Press, 1961.

————. "Political Recruitment and Careers." *International Encyclopedia of the Social Sciences* **12**. New York: Crowell, Collier and Macmillan, 1968, pp. 273–82.

MASSIALAS, BYRON G. *Education and the Political System*. Reading: Addison-Wesley, 1969.

————. ed. *Political Youth, Traditional Schools*. Englewood Cliffs: Prentice-Hall 1972.

MASSIEU-HELGUERA, GUILLERMO. "Centros de enseñanza tecnológica." *Anales de la Sociedad Mexicana de Historia de la Ciencia y de la Tecnología*, no. 3 (1972): 93–132.

MATTHEWS, DONALD R. *The Social Background of Political Decision-Makers*. New York: Garden City, 1954.

————. *U.S. Senators and Their World*. Chapel Hill: University of North Carolina Press, 1960.

MAYO, SEBASTIÁN. *La educación socialista en México: el asalto a la Universidad Nacional*. Rosario: Editorial Bear, 1964. LC

MEANS, INGUNN NORDERVAL. "Political Recruitment of Women in Norway." *Western Political Quarterly* **25** (September 1972): 491–521.

MEDÍN, TZVI. *Ideología y práxis política de Lázaro Cárdenas*. Mexico: Siglo veintuno, 1975.

MEDINA, LUIS. "Origen y circunstancia de la idea de unidad nacional." In Centro de Estudios Internacionales, *La vida política en México, 1970–1973*. Mexico: El Colegio de México, 1974, pp. 7–32.

MEISTER, MARGARET. "Mérida: Community Power Structure in a Mexican Town in Transition." Unpublished Ph.D. dissertation, Columbia University, 1966.

MENDIETA Y NÚÑEZ, LUCIO. "Apuntes para la historia de derecho de la Facultad de Derecho." *Revista de la Escuela Nacional de Jurisprudencia* 1 (September–December 1939): 385–419.

——— . "Un balance objectivo de la revolución mexicana." In Lucio Mendieta y Núñez, *Tres ensayos de sociología política nacional*. Mexico: UNAM, 1961, pp. 129–66.

——— . *Historia de la Facultad de Derecho*. Mexico: UNAM, 1956.

MENDIETA Y NÚÑEZ, LUCIO and JOSÉ GÓMEZ ROBLEDO. *Problemas de la Universidad*. Mexico: UNAM, 1948.

MENDIVIL, JOSÉ ABRAHAM. *Directorio político de Mexico*. Hermosillo: Editorial Esquer, 1965. UC

MENDOZA, VICENTE T. *El corrido mexicano*. Mexico: Fondo de Cultura Económica, 1976.

MENÉNDEZ, MIGUEL ANGEL. *Nayar*. New York: Farrar & Rinehart, 1942.

México, cincuenta años de revolución. 4 vols. Mexico: Fondo de Cultura Económica, 1960.

MEXICO, DIRECCIÓN TÉCNICA DE ORGANIZACIÓN. *Directorio del gobierno federal, 1947*. Mexico, 1947.

——— . *Directorio del gobierno federal, 1948*. Mexico, 1949.

——— . *Directorio de gobierno federal, 1951*. 2 vols. Mexico, 1951.

——— . *Directorio de gobierno federal, 1956*. Mexico, 1956.

Mexico 1946–73. New York: Facts on File, 1974.

México: realidad política de sus partidos. Mexico: Instituto Mexicano de Estudios Políticos, 1970.

México, realización y esperanza. Mexico: Editorial Superación, 1952. UCLA

MEXICO, SECRETARÍA DE EDUCACIÓN PÚBLICA. *México y la cultura*. Mexico, 1961.

——— . *Biografías*. 2 vols. Mexico: Secretaría de Educación Pública, 1961. LC

MEXICO, SECRETARÍA DE LA PRESIDENCIA. *Directorio del poder ejecutivo, 1971*. Mexico, 1971.

——— . *Directorio del poder ejecutivo, suplemento, 1972–73*. Mexico, 1973.

——— . *Manual de organización del gobierno federal, 1969–70*. Mexico, 1970.

——— . *Manual de organización del gobierno federal, 1973*. Mexico, 1973.

MEXICO, SECRETARÍA DEL PATRIMONIO NACIONAL. *Directorio del poder ejecutivo, 1961*. Mexico, 1961. DS

——— . *Directorio del poder ejecutivo, 1965*. Mexico, 1965.

——— . *Directorio del poder ejecutivo, 1968*. Mexico, 1968. LC

MEXICO CITY, ESCUELA LIBRE DE DERECHO. *Décimo aniversario de su fundación, 1912–22*. Mexico, 1922. LC

——— . *La Escuela Libre de Derecho XL aniversario*. Mexico, 1952. LC

MEXICO CITY, UNIVERSIDAD NACIONAL. *Catálogo de la Universidad Nacional de México, 1926–27*. Mexico: Talleres Gráficos de la Nación, 1926. PAU

——— . *Plan de estudios, 1924*. Mexico: Universidad Nacional, 1924. HN

MEXICO CITY, UNIVERSIDAD NACIONAL, ESCUELA NACIONAL PREPARATORIA. *Memoria del primer congreso de escuela preparatorias de la República.* Mexico: Editorial Cultura, 1922. PAU

—————. *Plan de estudios de la ENP.* Mexico: Universidad Nacional, 1920. PAU

—————. *Plan de estudios de la ENP.* Mexico: Universidad Nacional, 1924. PAU

MEXICO CITY, UNIVERSIDAD NACIONAL AUTÓNOMA DE MÉXICO. *Anuario de la Escuela Nacional de Jurisprudencia, 1940.* Mexico, 1940. HN

—————. *Anuario de la Escuela Nacional Preparatoria, 1940.* Mexico, 1940. HN, LC

—————. *Anuario General, 1931–32.* Mexico: UNAM, 1931. UNAM

—————. *Anuario General, 1954.* Mexico: UNAM, 1954. PAU

MEXICO CITY, UNIVERSIDAD NACIONAL AUTÓNOMA DE MÉXICO, ESCUELA NACIONAL DE ECONOMÍA. *Anuario, 1959.* Mexico: UNAM, 1959.

—————. *2 conferencias sobre el problema petróleo.* Mexico: Imprenta Universitaria, 1938. H

MÉXICO CITY, UNIVERSIDAD NACIONAL AUTÓNOMA DE MÉXICO, ESCUELA NACIONAL PREPARATORIA. *Anuario de la Escuela Nacional Preparatoria, 1950.* Mexico: Sociedad de Alumnos, 1950. HN

MEXICO CITY, UNIVERSIDAD NACIONAL AUTÓNOMA DE MÉXICO, FACULTAD DE DERECHO Y CIENCIAS SOCIALES. *Plan de estudios, programas y reglamentos de reconocimientos.* Mexico: Talleres Gráficos de la Nación, 1929. PAU

MEYER, JEAN A. *The Cristero Rebellion: The Mexican People Between Church and State (1926–1929).* Cambridge: Cambridge University Press, 1976.

MEYER, LORENZO. "Continuidades e innovaciones en la vida política mexicana del siglo XX, el antiguo y el nuevo régimen." *Foro Internacional* 16 (July–September 1975): 37–63.

—————. "The Origins of Mexico's Authoritarian State, Political Control in the Old and New Regimes." Paper presented at the Center for Inter-American Relations, New York, June 6–7, 1975.

MICHAELS, ALBERT L. "The Mexican Election of 1940." *Special Studies No. 5,* Council on International Studies. Buffalo: State University of New York, 1971.

—————. "Mexican Politics and Nationalism from Calles to Cárdenas." Unpublished Ph.D. dissertation, University of Pennsylvania, 1966.

MILLER, RICHARD U. "The Role of Labor Organizations in a Developing Country: The Case of Mexico." Unpublished Ph.D. dissertation, Cornell University, 1964.

MILLON, ROBERT P. *Mexican Marxist—Vicente Lombardo Toledano.* Chapel Hill: University of North Carolina Press, 1966.

—————. "Vicente Lombardo Toledano: Critic of the Mexican Revolution." Unpublished Ph.D. dissertation, University of North Carolina, 1963.

MIRANDA, JOSÉ P. *Marx in Mexico.* Mexico: Siglo XXI, 1972.

MIRÓ QUESADA, FRANCISCO. "The University South and North: the University and Society." *Américas* 12 (December 1960): 2–5.

MONCADA, CARLOS. *Años de violencia en Sonora, 1955–1976.* Mexico: Editorial V Siglos, 1977.

MONSON, ROBERT. "Political Stability in Mexico: The Changing Role of Traditional Rightists." *Journal of Politics* 35 (August 1973): 594–614.

—————. "Right-Wing Politics in Mexican Education: the Textbook Conflict." Unpublished Ph.D. dissertation, Georgetown University, 1966.

MORALES DÍAZ, CARLOS. *Quién es quién en la nomenclatura de la ciudad de México.* Mexico, 1962.

————. *Quién es quién en la nomenclatura de la ciudad de México.* Mexico, 1971.

MORENO, DANIEL. *Los partidos políticos del México contemporáneo.* Mexico: Costa-Amic, 1970.

————. *Colima y sus gobernadores.* Mexico, 1953.

MORENO, PABLO. *Galería de coahuilenses distinguidos.* Torreón: Imprenta Mayagoitia, 1966.

MORENO SÁNCHEZ, MANUEL. *Crisis política de México.* Mexico: Editorial Extemporáneos, 1970.

————. *Mexico: 1968–72.* Austin: Institute for Latin American Studies, University of Texas, 1973.

MORTON, WARD. *Women Suffrage in Mexico.* Gainesville: University of Florida Press, 1962.

MULLEN, EDWARD J. *"Contemporáneos* in Mexican Intellectual History, 1928–1931." *Journal of Inter-American Studies* **13** (January 1971): 121–30.

MUÑOZ LEDO, PORFIRIO. "La Educación Superior." In *México, 50 años de revolución* **4.** Mexico: Fondo de Cultura Económica, 1960.

MYERS, CHARLES N. *Education and National Development in Mexico.* Princeton: Princeton University Press, 1965.

La Nación, 1946–1970.

Narciso Bassols en memoria. Mexico, 1960.

NASH, MANNING. "Economic Nationalism in Mexico." In Harry G. Johnson, ed., *Economic Nationalism in Old and New States.* Chicago: University of Chicago Press, 1967, pp. 71–84.

NEEDLEMAN, CAROLYN and MARTIN NEEDLEMAN. "Who Rules Mexico? A Critique of Some Current Views on the Mexican Political Process." *Journal of Politics* **31** (November 1969): 1011–34.

NEEDLER, MARTIN C. "A Critical Time for Mexico." *Current History* (February 1972): pp. 81–5.

————. "Daniel Cosío Villegas and the Interpretation of Mexico's Political System." *Journal of Inter-American Studies & World Affairs* **18** (April 1976): 245–52.

————. "The Political Development of Mexico." *American Political Science Review* **55** (June 1961): pp. 308–12.

————. *Politics and Society in Mexico.* Albuquerque: University of New Mexico Press, 1971.

————. "Problems in the Evaluation of the Mexican Political System." In James W. Wilkie, et al., eds. *Contemporary Mexico.* Los Angeles: Latin American Center, UCLA, 1976, pp. 339–47.

NELSON, CYNTHIA. *The Waiting Village.* Boston: Little, Brown, 1971.

The New York Times, 1934–1976.

NICHOLSON, NORMAN K. "Integrative Strategies of a National Elite: Career Patterns in the Indian Council of Ministers." *Comparative Politics* **7** (July 1975): 533–57.

NIEMEYER, E. V., JR. *Revolution at Querétaro.* Austin: University of Texas Press, 1974.

NIGGLI, JOSEPHINE. *Step Down, Elder Brother.* New York: Rinehart, 1947.

NORTH, ROBERT C. and ITHIEL DE SOLA POOL. "Kuomintang and Chinese Communist Elites." In Harold D. Lasswell and Daniel Lerner, eds., *World Revolutionary Elites.* Cambridge: MIT Press, 1966, pp. 319–455.

Novo, Salvador. *La vida en México en el período presidencial de Lázaro Cárdenas.* Mexico: Empresas Editoriales, 1964.

————. *La vida en México en el período presidencial de Manuel Avila Camacho.* Mexico: Empresas Editoriales, 1965.

————. *La vida en México en el período presidencial de Miguel Alemán.* Mexico: Empresas Editoriales, 1967.

Ocampo, Aurora M. *Diccionario de escritores mexicanos.* Mexico: UNAM, 1967.

Oleszek, Walter. "Age and Political Careers." *Public Opinion Quarterly* **33** (Spring 1969): 100–3.

Ortega Molina, Gregorio. *El sindicalismo contemporáneo en México.* Mexico: Fondo de Cultura Económica, 1975.

Ortiz Rubio, Pascual. *Memorias, 1895–1928.* Mexico: Editorial Periodística e Impresora de Mexico, 1963.

Osborn, Thomas N. *Higher Education in Mexico.* El Paso: Texas Western Press, 1976.

Othón de Mendizábal, Miguel, et al. *Ensayos sobre las clases sociales en México.* Mexico: Editorial Nuestro Tiempo, 1968.

Pacheco Calvo, Ciriaco. *La organización estudiantil en México.* Mexico: Confederación Nacional de Estudiantes, 1934. LC

Padgett, Leon. *The Mexican Political System.* Boston: Houghton, Mifflin, 1966.

————. *The Mexican Political System.* 2nd edition. Boston: Houghton, Mifflin, 1976.

Pallares Ramírez, Manuel. *La Escuela Nacional de Economía, Esbozo Histórico 1929–1952.* Mexico, 1952. UCLA, LC

Pastro y Carreto, L. G. *Los presidentes poblanos.* Mexico: Costa-Amic, 1965. LC

Patterson, Samuel C. "Characteristics of Party Leaders." *Western Political Quarterly* **16** (June 1963): 332–52.

Paz, Octavio. *The Labyrinth of Solitude, Life and Thought in Mexico.* New York: Grove Press, 1961.

————. "Mexico: Freedom as Fiction." *Atlas World Press Review* **20** (October 1976): 44.

————. *The Other Mexico: Critique of the Pyramid.* New York: Grove Press, 1972.

Peral, Miguel A. *Diccionario biográfico mexicano.* Mexico, 1944. A

————. *Diccionario biográfico mexicano, suplemento.* Mexico: Editorial PAC, 1947. A

————. *Diccionario histórico, biográfico, geográfico e industrial de la república.* 2 vols. Mexico: Editorial PAC, 1960. LC

Pérez Correa, Fernando. "La universidad: contradicciones y perspectiva." In Centro de Estudios Internacionales, *La vida política en México (1970–1973).* Mexico: El Colegio de México, 1974, pp. 129–55.

Pérez Galaz, Juan de Dios. *Diccionario geográfico e histórico de Campeche.* Campeche, 1944.

Pérez Rubio, Rafael, et al. *El desarrollo económico de México.* Mexico: Centro Nacional de Productividad, 1968.

Personalidades de Monterrey. Nuevo León: Vega y Asociados, 1967 and 1977.

Peterson, John H. "Recent Research on Latin American Students." *Latin American Research Review* **5** (Spring 1970): 37–58.

Phelan, John Leddy. "Mexico y lo mexicano." *Hispanic American Historical Review* **36** (August 1956): 309–18.

PINEDA, HUGO. "José Vasconcelos, Político Mexicano." Unpublished Ph.D. dissertation, George Washington University, 1971.

————. *José Vasconcelos, político mexicano, 1928–1929.* Mexico: Edutex, 1975.

PINEDA, SALVADOR, et al. *Problemas universiatrios y agonía de la ENP.* Mexico: Stylo, 1950. UCLA

POITRAS, GUY E. "Welfare Bureaucracy and Clientele Politics in Mexico." *Administrative Science Quarterly* 18 (March 1973): 18–26.

POLEMAN, THOMAS T. *The Papaloapan Project.* Stanford: Stanford University Press, 1964.

PORRAS Y LÓPEZ, ARMANDO. *Luis Cabrera, revolucionario e intelectual.* Mexico: Biblioteca Mexicana, 1968.

PORTER, THOMAS A. "Subversion, Opposition, and Legitimacy in Mexican Politics." Unpublished Ph.D. dissertation, Harvard University, 1967.

PORTES GIL, EMILIO. *Quince años de política mexicana.* Mexico: Ediciones Botas, 1954.

————. *El quincuagésimo aniversario de la fundación del Partido Socialista Fronterizo.* Mexico, 1974.

————. *Raigambre de la revolución en Tamaulipas, autobiografía en acción.* Mexico, 1972.

————. "Sentido y destino de la Revolución Mexicana," in *México, cincuenta años de revolución* 3. Mexico: Fondo de Cultura Económica, 1960, pp. 479–585.

PORTUONDO, ALONSO. "The Universidad Nacional Autonoma de Mexico in the Post-Independence Period: A Political and Structural Review." Unpublished MA Thesis, University of Miami, 1972.

PREWITT, KENNETH. *The Recruitment of Political Leaders: A Study of Citizen-Politicians.* Indianapolis: Bobbs-Merrill Co., 1970.

PREWITT, KENNETH and HEINZ EULAU. "Social Bias in Leadership Selection, Political Recruitment and Electoral Context." *Journal of Politics* 33 (May 1971): 293–315.

PRICE, JOHN A. *Tijuana: Urbanization in a Border Culture.* Notre Dame: University of Notre Dame Press, 1973.

PRICE, JOHN W. "Education and the Civil Service in Europe." *Western Political Quarterly* 10 (December 1957): 817–32.

PRIETO LAURENS, JORGE. *Cincuenta años de política mexicana, memorias políticas.* Mexico, 1968.

PURCELL, JOHN F. and SUSAN K. PURCELL. "Mexican Business and Public Policy." In James Malloy, ed., *Authoritarianism and Corporatism in Latin America.* Pittsburgh: Pittsburgh University Press, 1977, pp. 191–226.

————. "The State and Economic Enterprise in Mexico: The Limits of Reform." *Nueva Política* 1 (April–June 1976): 229–50.

PURCELL, SUSAN K. "Decision-Making in an Authoritarian Regime: Theoretical Implications from a Mexican Case Study." *World Politics* 26 (October 1973): 28–54.

————. "The Future of the Mexican Political System." In Jose Luis Reyna and Richard S. Weinert, eds., *Authoritarianism in Mexico.* New York: ISHI Press, 1977, pp. 173–91.

————. *The Mexican Profit-Sharing Decision, Politics in an Authoritarian Regime.* Berkeley: University of California Press, 1975.

PUTNAM, ROBERT D. *The Beliefs of Politicians: Ideology, Conflict, and Democracy in Britain and Italy.* New Haven: Yale University Press, 1973.

————— . *The Comparative Study of Political Elites.* Englewood Cliffs: Prentice-Hall, 1976.

————— . "Studying Elite Political Culture: The Case of Ideology." *American Political Science Review* **65** (September 1971): 652–83.

QUANDT, WILLIAM B. "The Comparative Study of Political Elites." *Comparative Politics Series* **1.** Beverly Hills: Sage, 1970.

————— . *Revolution and Political Leadership: Algeria, 1954–1968.* Cambridge: MIT Press, 1969.

¿Quién es quién: diccionario biográfico peninsular. Mérida: Editorial Marina, 1971.

QUIRK, ROBERT E. *An Affair of Honor, Woodrow Wilson and the Occupation of Veracruz.* New York: Norton, 1967.

————— . *The Mexican Revolution and the Catholic Church: 1910–1929.* Bloomington: Indiana University Press, 1973.

QUIROZ, ALBERTO. *Biografías de educadores mexicanos.* Mexico: Secretaría de Educación Pública, 1962. PAU

RAAT, WILLIAM DIRK. "The Antipositivist Movement in Prerevolutionary Mexico, 1892–1911." *Journal of Inter-American Studies & World Affairs* **19** (February 1977): 83–98.

RABY, DAVID L. *Educación y revolución social en Mexico.* Mexico: Secretaría de Educación Pública, 1974.

————— . "Rural Teachers and Political and Social Conflict in Mexico, 1921–40." Unpublished Ph.D. dissertation, University of Warwick, 1970.

RAMÍREZ, ALFONSO FRANCISCO. *Historia de la revolución mexicana en Oaxaca.* Mexico, 1970.

RAMÍREZ VÁZQUEZ, MANUEL. *En torno de una generación; glosa de 1929.* Mexico: Ediciones "Una Generación," 1949. LC

RAMOS, SAMUEL. *Profile of Man and Culture in Mexico.* Austin: University of Texas Press, 1962.

————— . *Veinte años de educación en México.* Mexico, 1941. LC

RANGEL FRÍAS, RAÚL. *Cosas nuestras.* Monterrey: Fondo Editorial Nuevo León, 1971.

————— . *El reyno.* Monterrey, 1972.

RANNEY, AUSTIN. *Pathways to Parliament: Candidate Selection in Britain.* Madison: University of Wisconsin Press, 1965.

"El Rector Garrido habla sobre la generación de 1929." *Universidad de México* **3** (June 1949): 12–13.

REJAI, MOSTAFA. "Toward the Comparative Study of Political Decision-Makers." *Comparative Political Studies* **2** (October 1969): 349–60.

REQUEÑA, JOSÉ LUIS. "Recuerdos de la Escuela Nacional de Jurisprudencia." *Revista de la Escuela Nacional de Jurisprudencia* **1** (March–May 1939): 127–34.

REYES, ALFONSO. *Mexico in a Nutshell.* Berkeley: University of California Press, 1964.

————— . "Pasado inmediato." *Obras completas* **12** (Mexico, 1941): 182–216.

REYES ROSALES, JOSÉ JERÓNIMO. *Historia de la educación en Veracruz.* Jalapa: Biblioteca del Maestro Veracruzano, 1959.

REYNA, JOSÉ LUIS. "An Empirical Analysis of Political Mobilization: The Case of Mexico." Unpublished Ph.D. dissertation, Cornell University, 1971.

————— . "Redefining the Established Authoritarian Regime: Perspectives of the Mexican Polity." Paper presented at the Center for Inter-American Relations, New York, February, 1975.

REYNA, JOSÉ LUIS and RICHARD S. WEINERT, eds. *Authoritarianism in Mexico*. New York: ISHI Press, 1977.

REYNOLDS, CLARK W. *The Mexican Economy: Twentieth Century Structure and Growth*. New Haven: Yale University Press, 1970.

RICHMOND, PATRICIA M. "Mexico: A Case Study of One-Party Politics." Unpublished Ph.D. dissertation, University of California at Berkeley, 1965.

RIVERA SILVA, MANUEL. *Perspectivas de una vida, biografía de una generación*. Mexico: Porrúa, 1974.

ROD, GILBERTO. *Diccionario biográfico mexicano, 1941*. Mexico: Editorial Paraguay, 1941. HN

RODMAN, SELDEN. *Mexican Journal*. Carbondale: Southern Illinois University Press, 1958.

RODRÍGUEZ, VALDEMAR. "National University of Mexico: Rebirth and Role of the Universitarios, 1910–1957." Unpublished Ph.D. dissertation, University of Texas, 1958.

RODRÍGUEZ FRAUSTRO, JESÚS. *Gobernantes de Guanajuato*. Guanajuato: Universidad de Guanajuato, 1965.

ROJAS GARCIDUEÑAS, JOSÉ. *El Antiguo Colegio de San Ildefonso*. Mexico: UNAM, 1951. LC

ROMANELL, PATRICK. *Making of the Mexican Mind*. Notre Dame: University of Notre Dame Press, 1967.

ROMERO, JOSÉ RUBÉN. *The Futile Life of Pito Pérez*. New York: Prentice-Hall, 1966.

ROMERO FLORES, JESÚS. *Diccionario michoacano de historia y geografía*. Morelia, 1960.

————. *Historia de la educación en Michoacán*. Mexico: Talleres Gráficos de la Nación, 1948. LC

————. *Maestros y amigos*. Mexico: Costa-Amic, 1971.

RONFELDT, DAVID. *Atencingo, The Politics of Agrarian Struggle in a Mexican Ejido*. Stanford: Stanford University Press, 1973.

————. *The Mexican Army and Political Order Since 1940*. Santa Monica: RAND, 1973.

ROSE, RICHARD. *Politics in England*. Boston: Little, Brown, 1974.

ROSS, STANLEY R., ed. *Is the Mexican Revolution Dead?* New York: Knopf, 1966.

ROUAIX, PASTOR. *Diccionario geográfico, histórico y biográfico del estado de Durango*. Mexico: Instituto Pan Americana de Geografía y Historia, 1946. HN

RUIZ, RAMÓN E. *Mexico. The Challenge of Poverty and Illiteracy*. San Marino: Huntington Library, 1963.

RUIZ SANDOVAL, H. *Directorio social, 1935–36*. Mexico, 1936.

RULFO, JUAN. *The Burning Plain and Other Stories*. Austin: University of Texas Press, 1971.

SÁNCHEZ, GEORGE I. *The Development of Higher Education in Mexico*. Westport: Greenwood Press, 1944.

SANDERS, THOMAS G. *Mexico in the '70's*. Hanover: American Universities Field Staff, 1976.

SANSORES PREN, ROSARIO. *Libro azul de la sociedad mexicana*. Mexico: Carbac, 1946. LC

SCHERS, DAVID. "The Popular Sector of the Mexican PRI." Unpublished Ph.D. dissertation, University of New Mexico, 1972.

SCHLESINGER, JOSEPH A. *Ambition and Politics: Political Careers in the United States*. Chicago: Rand McNally, 1966.

————— . "Lawyers and American Politics: A Clarified View." *The Midwest Journal of Political Science* **1** (May 1957): 26–39.

————— . "Political Careers and Party Leadership." In Lewis D. Edinger, ed., *Political Leadership in Industrialized Societies*. New York: John Wiley & Sons, 1967, pp. 266–93.

SCHMIDT, HENRY C. "Antecedents to Samuel Ramos, Mexicanist Thought in the 1920's." *Journal of Inter-American Studies and World Affairs* **18** (May 1976): 179–202.

SCHMITT, KARL M. "Congressional Campaigning in Mexico: A View From the Provinces." *Journal of Inter-American Studies & World Affairs* **11** (January 1969): 93–110.

————— . "Communism in Mexico Today." *Western Political Quarterly* **15** (March 1962): 111–24.

————— . *Communism in Mexico Today: A Study in Political Frustration*. Austin: University of Texas Press, 1965.

————— . *Mexico and the United States, 1821–1973*. New York: Wiley and Sons, 1974.

SCHUELLER, GEORGE K. "The Politburo." In Harold Lasswell and Daniel Lerner, eds., *World Revolutionary Elites*. Cambridge: MIT Press, 1966.

SCHWARTZ, DAVID C. "Toward a Theory of Political Recruitment." *Western Political Quarterly* **22** (September 1969): 552–71.

SCOTT, ROBERT C., ed. *Latin American Modernization Problems*. Urbana: University of Illinois Press, 1973.

————— . "The Government Bureaucrats and Political Change in Latin America," *Journal of International Affairs* **20** (1966): 289–308.

————— . *Mexican Government in Transition*. 2nd edition. Urbana: University of Illinois Press, 1964.

————— . "Mexico." In Gabriel Almond, ed., *Comparative Politics Today*. Boston: Little, Brown, 1974, pp. 366–403.

————— . "Mexico: the Established Revolution." In Lucian Pye and Sidney Verba, eds., *Political Culture and Political Development*. Princeton: Princeton University Press, 1965, pp. 330–95.

SEGOVIA, RAFAEL. *La politización del niño mexicano*. Mexico: El Colegio de México, 1975.

————— . "La reforma política: el ejecutivo federal, el PRI y las elecciones de 1973." *Foro Internacional* **14,** no. 3 (1974): 305–30.

————— . "Las tendencias políticas en México de los próximos diez años." Paper presented at the American University, School of International Service, March 18, 1976.

SELIGMAN, LESTER G. "Elite Recruitment and Political Development." *Journal of Politics* **26** (August 1964): 612–26.

————— . "Political Parties and the Recruitment of Political Leaders." In Lewis J. Edinger, ed., *Totalitarian Leadership in Industrialized Societies*. New York: John Wiley & Sons, 1967, pp. 294–315.

————— . "Political Recruitment and Party Structure: A Case Study." *American Political Science Review* **55** (March 1961): 77–86.

————— . *Recruiting Political Elites*. New York: General Learning Press, 1971.

SERRA DOMÍNGUEZ, SERGIO and ROBERTO MARTÍNEZ BARREDA. *México y sus funcionarios*. Mexico: Litográfico Cárdenas, 1959. T

SHAFER, ROBERT J. *Mexican Business Organizations*. Syracuse: Syracuse University Press, 1973.

SHAPIRA, YORAM. "Mexico, The Impact of the 1968 Student Protest on Echeverria's Reformism." *Journal of Inter-American Studies and World Affairs* **19** (November 1977): 557–80.

SHEED, MARGARET. "Thunder on the Right in Mexico—The Sinarquista in Action." *Harper's Magazine* (April 1945): 414–25.

SIEGRIST CLAMONT, JORGE. *En defensa de la autonomía universitaria; trayectoria histórico-jurídica de la universidad mexicana*. 2 vols. Mexico: Universidad Nacional, 1955. UCLA

SIERRA, CARLOS J. *Luis Echeverría*. Mexico: Testimonios de Atlacomulco, 1969.

————— . *Historia de la administración hacendaria en México*. Mexico: Secretaría de Hacienda y Crédito Público, 1970.

SIERRA, JUSTO. *The Political Evolution of the Mexican People*. Austin: University of Texas Press, 1969.

SILLER RODRÍGUEZ, RODOLFO. *La crisis del Partido Revolucionario Institucional*. Mexico: Costa-Amic, 1976.

SILVA HERZOG, JESÚS. "El desarrollo de la enseñanza de las ciencias económicas en México, 1929–1953." *El Trimestre Económico* **21** (January–March 1954): 1–5.

————— . *Una historia de la Universidad de México y sus problemas*. Mexico: Siglo veintiuno, 1974.

————— . *Mis últimas andanzas, 1947–1972*. Mexico: Siglo veintiuno, 1973.

————— . *El pensamiento económico en México*. Mexico: Fondo de Cultura Económica, 1947.

————— . *Una vida en la vida de México*. Mexico: Siglo veintiuno, 1972.

SIMMONS, MERLE E. *The Mexican Corrido as a Source for Interpretative Study of Modern Mexico, 1870–1950*. Bloomington: Indiana University Press, 1957.

SKIDMORE, THOMAS E. and PETER H. SMITH. "Notes on Quantitative History: Federal Expenditure and Social Change in Mexico since 1910." *Latin American Research Review* **5** (Spring 1970): 71–85.

SMITH, DAVID H. *Latin American Student Activism*. Lexington: D. C. Heath, 1973.

SMITH, DONALD L. "Pre-PRI: The Mexican Government Party, 1929–46." Unpublished Ph.D. dissertation, Texas Christian University, 1974.

SMITH, NORMAN M. "The Role of the Armed Forces in Contemporary Mexican Politics." Unpublished MA thesis, University of Florida, 1966.

SMITH, PETER H. "Continuity and Turnover Within the Mexican Political Elite." In James Wilkie, et al., eds. *Contemporary Mexico: Papers of the IV International Congress of Mexican History*. Berkeley: University of California Press, 1976, pp. 167–86.

————— . *Labyrinths of Power: Political Recruitment in Twentieth-Century Mexico*. Princeton: Princeton University Press, 1979.

————— . "Making it in Mexico: Aspects of Political Mobility Since 1946." Paper presented at the Annual Meeting of the American Political Science Association, August 28–September 2, 1974.

————— . "La movilidad política en el México contemporáneo." *Foro Internacional* **15,** no. 3 (1975): 379–413.

————— . "La política dentro de la revolución: el congreso constituyente de 1916–1917." *Historia Mexicana* **22,** no. 3 (1973): 363–95.

SMYTHE, HUGH H. "Nigerian Elite: Role of Education." *Sociology and Social Research* **45** (October 1960): 71–3.

SOLARI, ALDO. "Secondary Education and the Development of Elites." In Seymour Martin Lipset and Aldo Solari, eds., *Elites in Latin America*. New York: Oxford University Press, 1967, pp. 457–83.

SOMOLINOS D'ARDOIS, GERMÁN. "Ignacio Chávez," in *Forjadores del mundo moderno*. Mexico: Editorial Grijalba, n.d., pp. 266–80.

STANSFIELD, DAVID E. "The Mexican Cabinet, An Indicator of Change." Unpublished paper, 1974.

STEVENS, EVELYN P. "Information and Decision Making in Mexico." Unpublished Ph.D. dissertation, University of California at Berkeley, 1968.

———— . "Legality and Extra-legality in Mexico." *Journal of Inter-American Studies and World Affairs* 12 (January 1970): 62–75.

———— . "Mexican Machismo: Politics and Value Orientations." *Western Political Quarterly* 18 (December 1965): 848–57.

———— . "Mexico's PRI: The Institutionalization of Corporatism?" In James Malloy, ed., *Authoritarianism and Corporatism in Latin America*. Pittsburgh: University of Pittsburgh Press, 1977, pp. 227–58.

———— . *Protest and Response in Mexico*. Cambridge: MIT Press, 1974.

SUÁREZ VALLES, MANUEL. *Lázaro Cárdenas*. Mexico: Costa-Amic, 1971.

SUPREMA CORTE DE JUSTICIA DE LA NACIÓN. *Discursos pronunciados por los Ministros Mariano Azuela y José Castro Estrada*. Mexico, 1967.

SUTTON, DELIA L. M. *Antonio Caso y su impacto cultural en el intelecto mexicano*. Mexico: Secretaría de Hacienda y Crédito Público, 1971.

SZYLIOWICZ, JOSEPH S. "Elite Recruitment in Turkey: The Role of the Mulkiye." *World Politics* 23 (April 1971): 371–98.

TAMAYO, JORGE. *Breve reseña sobre la Escuela Nacional de Ingeniería*. Mexico: UNAM, 1958. LC

TAPLIN, G. W. *Middle American Governors*. Metuchen: Scarecrow, 1972.

TAPPER, TED. *Political Education and Stability, Elite Responses to Political Conflict*. New York: John Wiley, 1976.

TARACENA, ALFONSO. *Cartas políticas de José Vasconcelos*. Mexico: Editorial Librera, 1959.

TARACENA, ANTONIO. "Mexico—Sus Problemas." Unpublished paper, 1976.

Testimonio en la muerte de Manuel Gómez Morín. Mexico: Editorial Jus, 1973.

THURBER, CLARENCE and LAWRENCE S. GRAHAM, eds. *Development Administration in Latin America*. Durham: Duke University Press, 1973.

TORREA, JUAN MANUEL. *Diccionario geográfico, histórico, biográfico y estadístico de la republica mexicana*. Mexico: Sociedad Mexicana de Geografía y Estadística, 1940.

TORRES BODET, JAIME. *Años contra el tiempo*. Mexico: Porrúa, 1969.

———— . *Equinoccio*. Mexico: Porrúa, 1974.

———— . "Tiempo de arena." In *Obras escogidas*. Mexico: Fondo de Cultura Económica, 1961, pp. 191–386.

———— . *La tierra prometida*. Mexico: Porrúa, 1972.

———— . *La victoria sin alas*. Mexico: Porrúa, 1970.

TREVIÑO, JACINTO B. *Memorias*. Mexico: Editorial Orión, 1961.

TRIBUKAIT, ALBRECHT. "El presidencialismo en México." *Revista Mexicana de Ciencia Política* 18, no. 70 (1972): 39–60.

TRUEBLOOD, FELICITY M. "The Contemporary Political Novel in Mexico." Unpublished MA thesis, University of Florida, 1962.

TUCKER, WILLIAM P. *The Mexican Government Today.* Minneapolis: University of Minnesota Press, 1957.

TUOHY, WILLIAM S. "Centralism and Political Elite Behavior in Mexico," in Clarence E. Thurber and Lawrence S. Graham, eds., *Development Administration in Latin America.* Durham: Duke University Press, 1973, pp. 260–280.

————. "Psychology in Political Analysis: The Case of Mexico." *Western Political Quarterly* **27** (June 1974): 289–307.

TUOHY, WILLIAM S. and BARRY AMES. *Mexican University Students in Politics: Rebels Without Allies?* Denver: University of Colorado Monograph Series in World Affairs, 1970.

TUOHY, WILLIAM S. and DAVID RONFELDT. "Political Control and the Recruitment of Middle-Level Elites in Mexico: An Example from Agrarian Politics." *Western Political Quarterly* **22** (June 1969): 365–74.

TURNER, FREDERICK C. "Compatibility of Church and State in Mexico." *Journal of Inter-American Studies and World Affairs* **9** (October 1967): 591–602.

————. *The Dynamic of Mexican Nationalism.* Chapel Hill: University of North Carolina Press, 1968.

————. *Responsible Parenthood, the Politics of Mexico's New Population Policies.* Washington, D.C.: American Enterprise Institute for Public Policy Research, 1974.

TURNER, RALPH H. "Sponsored and Contest Mobility and the School System." *American Sociological Review* **25** (December 1960): 855–67.

UGALDE, ANTONIO. "Contemporary Mexico: From Hacienda to PRI, Political Leadership in a Zapotec Village." In Robert Kern, ed., *The Caciques.* Albuquerque: University of New Mexico Press, 1973, pp. 119–34.

————. *Power and Conflict in a Mexican Community: A Study of Political Integration.* Albuquerque: University of New Mexico Press, 1970.

El Universal, 1934–1974.

Universidad de México. HN

Universidad, Mensual de Cultura Popular, 1936–1955. HN

Universidad Michoacana, 1937–40, 1942–44, 1947, 1951–54. HN

URÍA-SANTOS, MARÍA ROSA. "El Ateneo de la Juventud: su influencia en la vida intelectual de México." Unpublished Ph.D. dissertation, University of Florida, 1965.

URIÓSTEGUI MIRANDA, PÍNDARO. *Testimonios del proceso revolucionario de México.* Mexico: Argrin, 1970.

UROZ, ANTONIO. *Hombres y mujeres de México.* Mexico, 1972.

URQUIDÍ, VÍCTOR L. and ADRIÁN LAJOUS VARGAS. *La educación superior en México, 1966.* Mexico: ANUIES, 1966.

VALADÉS, JOSÉ C. *El presidente de México en 1970.* Mexico: Editores Mexicanos Unidos, 1969.

VALLEJO Y ARIZMENDI, JORGE. *Testimonio 1930–34.* Mexico: Editorial Stylo, 1947. LC

VASCONCELOS, JOSÉ. *En el ocaso de mi vida.* Mexico: Populibros la prensa, 1957.

————. *A Mexican Ulysses.* Translated by William Rex Crawford. Bloomington: Indiana University Press, 1963.

VAUGHAN, MARY K. "Education and Class Struggle in the Mexican Revolution." *Latin American Perspectives* **2** (Summer 1975): 17–33.

VÁZQUEZ DE KNAUTH, JOSEFINA. "La educación socialista de los años treinta." *Historia Mexicana* **18** (January–March 1969): 408–23.

————. *Nacionalismo y educación en México*. Mexico: El Colegio de México, 1970.

VÁZQUEZ GALINDO, RAÚL. *Quién es quién en Durango, 1966–67*. Durango, 1967.

VEJAR LACAVE, CARLOS and AMPARO ESPINOSA DE SERRANO. *El pensamiento contemporáneo en México*. Mexico: Porrúa, 1974.

VELASCO, GUSTAVO R. *Al servicio de la Escuela Libre de Derecho*. Mexico: Editorial Humanidades, 1967. UCLA

VELEZ, CARLOS G. "An Evening in Ciudad Reyes: A Processual Approach to Mexican Politics." *The New Scholar* **5**, no. 1 (1975): 5–18.

VERNER, JOEL G. "Characteristics of Administrative Personnel: The Case of Guatemala." *Journal of Developing Areas* **5** (October 1970): 73–86.

————. "Educational Backgrounds of Latin American Legislators: A Three-Country Analysis." *Comparative Politics* **6** (July 1974): 617–34.

————. "The Guatemalan National Congress: An Elite Analysis." In Weston H. Agor, ed., *Latin American Legislatures: Their Role and Influence*. New York: Praeger, 1971.

————. "The Recruitment of Cabinet Ministers in the Former British Caribbean: A Five-Country Study." *Journal of Developing Areas* **7** (July 1973): 635–52.

VERNON, RAYMOND. *The Dilemma of Mexico's Development*. Cambridge: Harvard University Press, 1963.

VILLASEÑOR, EDUARDO. *Memorias-testimonio*. Mexico: Fondo de Cultura Económica, 1974.

VILLASEÑOR, VÍCTOR MANUEL. *Memorias de un hombre de izquierda*. 2 vols. Mexico: Editorial Grijalba, 1976.

VON SAURER, FRANZ A. *The Alienated "Loyal" Opposition, Mexico's Partido Accion Nacional*. Albuquerque: University of New Mexico Press, 1974.

WALTON, JOHN and JOYCE A. SWEEN. "Urbanization, Industrialization and Voting in Mexico: A Longitudinal Analysis of Official and Opposition Party Support." *Social Science Quarterly* **52** (December 1971): 721–45.

WASSERSPRING, LOIS. "Politics and Authority in Corporatist Society: A Study of Mexico." Unpublished Ph.D. dissertation, Princeton University, 1974.

WELLHOFER, E. SPENCER. "Background Characteristics and Dissident Behavior: Test with Argentine Party Elites." *Journal of Developing Areas* **9** (January 1975): 237–52.

WELSH, WILLIAM A. "Methodological Problems in the Study of Political Leadership in Latin America." *Latin American Research Review* **5** (Fall 1970): 3–33.

————. "Toward Effective Typology Construction in the Study of Latin American Political Leadership." *Comparative Politics* **3** (January 1971): 271–80.

WENCES REZA, ROSALIO. *El movimiento estudiantil y los problemas nacionales*. Mexico: Editorial Nuestro Tiempo, 1971.

WIGHT BAKKE, E. "Students on the March: The Cases of Mexico and Colombia." *Sociology of Education* **37** (Spring 1964): 200–28.

WILGUS, A. CURTIS. *The Caribbean: Contemporary Education*. Gainesville: University of Florida Press, 1960.

WILKIE, JAMES W. *Elitelore*. Los Angeles: UCLA Latin American Center, 1973.

————. *The Mexican Revolution: Federal Expenditure and Social Change Since 1910*. Berkeley: University of California Press, 1970.

WILKIE, JAMES W., MICHAEL C. MEYER and EDNA MONZÓN DE WILKIE, eds. *Contemporary Mexico*. Los Angeles: UCLA Latin American Center, 1976.

WILKIE, JAMES W. and EDNA MONZÓN DE WILKIE. *México visto en el siglo xx.* Mexico: Instituto Mexicano de Investigaciones Económicas, 1969.

WILKINSON, RUPERT. *Gentlemanly Power: British Leadership and the Public School Tradition: A Comparative Study in the Making of Rulers.* New York: Oxford University Press, 1964.

————. "Political Leadership and the Late Victorian Public School." *British Journal of Sociology* 13 (1962): 320–30.

WILLIAMS, EDWARD J. "Mutation in the Mexican Revolution: Industrialism, Nationalism and Centralism." *SECOLAS Annals* (March 1976): 34–43.

WING, GEORGE GORDON. "Octavio Paz: Poetry, Politics, and the Myth of the Mexican." Unpublished Ph.D. dissertation, University of California at Berkeley, 1961.

WISE, GEORGE S. *El México de Alemán.* Mexico: Editorial Atlante, 1952.

WOMACK, JOHN. "The Spoils of the Mexican Revolution." *Foreign Affairs* 48 (July 1970): 677–87.

World Biography, New York: Institute for Research in Biography, 1948 and 1954.

ZARAGOZA-CARBAJAL, MAXIMINO. "Vicente Lombardo-Toledano: His Role in the Socio-Political Evolution of Mexico Since the 1920s." Unpublished Ph.D. dissertation, St Louis University, 1971.

ZEA, LEOPOLDO. *Latin America and the World.* Norman: University of Oklahoma Press, 1969.

ZEVADA, RICARDO J. *Calles el presidente.* Mexico: Editorial Nuestro Tiempo, 1971.

ZILLI BERNARDI, JUAN. *Reseña histórica de la educación pública en el estado de Veracruz.* Jalapa, 1961.

Index

Adams, John, administration and family ties, 29, 31
Administrative-elective careers, 62
Administrators: at the National Preparatory School, 185–86; at the National University, 184ff; dominance of public men at the National University, 169, 191; importance to public life of, 185ff, 191; preparatory schools and public careers of, 98
Age, as a variable for study of political elites, 49
Agraz, Juan Salvador, 182
Aguilar y Maya, José: as a recruiter, 129; his *camarilla*, 60, 102
Ahumada, Herminio, 133
Alatriste, Sealtiel Jr., 31
Alatriste, Sealtiel L., 31
Alemán, Miguel: and his generation, 77, 107ff, 128 ff; as student of Alfonso Caso, 177; as student supporter of Arnulfo R. Gómez, 136; childhood friendships of, 41; collaborators from the North, 55; educational contacts of, 21, 104; praises private sector, 64; presidential *camarilla* of, 19–27
Almazán, Juan Andreu, 33–34
Almond, Gabriel, on role specialization, 89

Alvarado, Salvador, 127
American Revolution, administrations following, 29
Armendáriz, Antonio, 145
Army, and involvement in politics, 5, 57
Ateneo, The, 187
Ávila Camacho, Manuel: and appointment of brother, 32; *camarilla* of, 20–21; career of, 60; gentleman President, 34; formal education of, 69; presidential campaign of, 34
Azuela Rivera, Salvador: education of, 76; as student leader, 133, 136

Bassols, Narciso: and career of Víctor Manuel Villaseñor, 138; as dean of the National Law School, 136; as mentor, 177; as recruiter, 102–3, 123; as student leader, 126; as student of Antonio Caso; relationship to President Calles, 180
Baz, Gustavo, 154, 201
Beltrán, Enrique, 154
Benveniste, Guy, on rural school attendance in Mexico, 46
Beteta, Ignacio, 31
Beteta, Mario Ramón, 31
Beteta, Ramón, 129, 131
Biographical data bank, 1–4

Mexican Political Biographies, 1935–1975

by Roderic A. Camp

"There is good news for Mexicanist scholars in this collection of biographies of Mexican political figures. To say that it fills a long-felt need is a trite understatement, given the paucity of reliable and up-to-date information heretofore available to researchers. It is a good antidote to the many incomplete and inaccurate biographies offered, often as part of image-building publicity campaigns aimed more at promoting an individual's candidacy for political office than at presenting verifiable data...Professor Camp deserves praise and gratitude for his painstaking work of scholarship."

(The Americas)

"...virtually a government organization manual for Mexico since 1935."

(Latin American Research Review)

"Everyone interested in the political life of twentieth-century Mexico needs a personal copy of this book."

(Hispanic American Historical Review)

468 pages, 1976.